TIME OF TROUBLES

Dmitrii Mikhailovich Pozharskii. Portrait

RUSLAN G. SKRYNNIKOV

The
TIME OF TROUBLES

RUSSIA IN CRISIS   1604–1618

Edited and Translated
by
Hugh F. Graham

Academic International Press

1988

THE RUSSIAN SERIES/Volume 36

Ruslan G. Skrynnikov, *The Time of Troubles.*
Russia in Crisis, 1604–1618.

Original manuscript prepared by the author for first publication
by Academic International Press

English translation and special contents of this book
Copyright © 1988 by Academic International Press.

ISBN: 0-87569-097-1

Composition by Donna Harrell and Mary Virginia McDaris

Plan of Moscow by Sandra L. Carlson

Printed in the United States of America

A list of Academic International Press publications
is found at the end of this volume.

ACADEMIC INTERNATIONAL PRESS
Box 1111 Gulf Breeze FL 32561

CONTENTS

	Editor's Introduction	vi
	Author's Introduction	viii
1	Rule by a Monk	1
2	Boyar Opposition	14
3	The Fall of Grigorii Otrepev	23
4	Rebellion	41
5	The Tushino Cabal	59
6	Intervention	73
7	Military Defeat	80
8	The Council of Seven	90
9	Mercenaries in the Capital	105
10	Moscow Burns	121
11	At the Brink	136
12	Dual Power	153
13	Conflict	169
14	False Dmitrii III	176
15	The Second National Militia	183
16	The Yaroslavl Government	199
17	Gosiewski's Flight	218
18	A Split in the National Government	223
19	Chodkiewicz's Rout	232
20	The Liberation of Moscow	245
21	National Electoral Assembly	258
22	The End of the War	283
	Notes to the Editor's Introduction	306
	Notes to the Author's Introduction	306
	Notes	308
	Index	315
	Illustrations	326
	Maps	330
	The Author	336

Professor Ruslan G. Skrynnikov has become widely known for his extensive work on the *oprichnina* or personal fiefdom phase of Ivan the Terrible's reign. Now research professor of history at Leningrad State University, he has transferred the center of his scholarly attention to the Time of Troubles. Besides the present, original manuscript he has investigated other aspects of this period in two books,[1] and in journal articles.

Professor Skrynnikov takes a more positive view of Boris Godunov's achievements as regent and ruler than many other historians, but he holds that Boris' willingness to tie peasants to the land in order to secure gentry support rendered civil war inevitable. Furthermore, in the pedigree-conscious society Russia was at that time Boris' humble origins were bound to provoke opposition from the great noble families. Professor Skrynnikov has discussed the ramifications of this in detail in the last part of his recent book on Boris Godunov.[2] The information he presents there forms a necessary prolog to the events with which the present volume is concerned.

Ivan the Terrible had a son, Dmitrii Ivanovich, born in 1582, by his seventh wife, Mariia Nagaia. Upon the accession of Fedor Ivanovich, Ivan's second son, in 1584 Dmitrii was relegated to an appanage estate in Uglich, where he died under mysterious circumstances in 1591. He had been almost forgotten until Boris won the throne on Fedor's death in 1598. Soon after that rumors began to circulate to the effect that Dmitrii was still alive. In 1602 an individual appeared in Lithuania and claimed he was indeed Dmitrii, who miraculously had survived the attempt Godunov had made to assassinate him. After carefully sifting the available evidence, Professor Skrynnikov has come to the firm conclusion that the pretender was a defrocked monk, Grigorii, or Grishka, Otrepev. He was a man of considerable attainment, who had served the Romanov and Cherkasskii boyars, worked at the Miracles monastery in the Kremlin, and assisted in the patriarch's court. After numerous adventures this resourceful, cunning, and ambitious young man was taken up by a few Polish magnates who, discerning a splendid opportunity for an intrigue against Russia, commended him to Sigismund III, the Polish king.

Otrepev's chief patron was Jerzy Mniszech, palatine of Sambor. With the king's covert support, he collected a small mercenary army to use in overturning Godunov. This motley force failed to accomplish its purpose, but when False Dmitrii I and Mniszech entered Russia in 1604 cossacks from the southern frontiers, peasants resisting the imposition of serfdom, and simple folk who believed Otrepev was the genuine Dmitrii flocked to the pretender's standard. It was popular disaffection, not the rabble of foreign mercenaries, that rendered him formidable. Few knew that while in Poland the opportunist secretly had become a Catholic and been affianced to Mniszech's daughter, Marina.

Godunov's commanders inflicted a severe defeat on Otrepev's force in January, 1605, but they failed to follow up their victory and expel or capture the pretender because the hostile populace hindered them from doing so. Boris no longer displayed his customary vigor, but as long as he held the throne it was difficult for the pretender, even with cossack support, to prevail. Everything changed when Boris suddenly died of apoplexy in April, 1605. His young son Fedor succeeded him.

At this juncture the tsar's armies were besieging a cossack host in the town of Kromy, south of Moscow. Petr Basmanov, the new commander Boris had sent there, grew disaffected, as did a number of gentry, including the men of Riazan led by Prokofii Liapunov. They secretly negotiated with the cossacks and changed sides. The tsar's army collapsed. Rebels in Moscow showed their strength. The Godunov family shut themselves up in the Kremlin, which the people, egged on by the noblility, often raided. False Dmitrii in the meantime was proceeding leisurely towards Moscow, garnering support wherever he went. His representatives moved freely about the capital. His emissary, Prince Vasilii Golitsyn, had Boris' wife and son murdered. At this the way was clear for Otrepev to enter the Kremlin and become tsar. It is at this point *The Time of Troubles* takes up the tale.

The Time of Troubles is a painful episode in Russian history; it is understandable why Russian historians on the whole have not been anxious to explore it in depth. The sole exception has been Platonov, who devoted much of his scholarly career to this era.[3] Western work in the field only recently has begun to expand. Professor Skrynnikov is correct when he states that a full-length study covering the epoch in its entirety heretofore has not been available.

As the historiographical commentary reveals, scholars have tended to be influenced by prevailing trends; this has proved particularly true of the Soviet period. As an example, Bolotnikov's movement has received a great amount of attention because it can be interpreted as a seventeenth-century manifestation of the class struggle.

Professor Skrynnikov avoids extremes in painting his broad panorama. He makes but little reference to the class struggle; he regards the entire sequence of incidents that occurred during the Time of Troubles as interconnected, as parts of a single whole, and as manifestations of civil strife that turned into a war for national independence. He reveals a partiality for Minin and Pozharskii, but only as embodiments of the indomitable spirit of the Russian people, who are the true heroes of his book.

AUTHOR'S INTRODUCTION

Early in the seventeenth century Russia endured a civil war and suffered severe damage. Foreign foes took advantage of the country's enfeebled condition. Russia was on the verge of dissolving and losing its independence. Contemporaries who lived through that tragic time were accurate when they designated it a "Time of Troubles."

The historiography pertaining to events in the early seventeenth century is ample. The chronicle tradition influenced the views formulated by early court historians. V.N. Tatishchev considered the Time of Troubles "a senseless struggle among noble gentry clans." At the same time he was the first to hazard a guess that the great misfortune that occurred at the beginning of the seventeenth century was the result of laws promulgated by Boris Godunov that deprived peasants and slaves of their freedom.[1] Tatishchev's notion was a fundamental contribution to achieving a scientific understanding of the Time of Troubles.

M.M. Shcherbatov also made extensive use of chronicles in his description of the Time of Troubles. Seeking reasons for popular rioting, like Tatishchev he drew attention to Godunov's policies that robbed the lower orders of their freedom, which aroused disaffection in both peasants and boyars.[2]

The official court historiographer N.M. Karamzin [1766-1826] was unable to detect formal laws governing popular revolts; he called Bolotnikov's rebellion "Shakhovskoi's rising" and declared that at the time all layers of society from commons to the nobility were corrupt.[3] Interference on the part of Russia's foreign enemies was the main cause of the Troubles. The sovereign and the leading elements in society were the forces that assumed the initiative in the war of national liberation.

The mighty bourgeois historian S.M. Soloviev [1820-1879] sharply disagreed with those who declared Godunov's prohibition of the right of peasant movement was the reason for the Time of Troubles. As the chief causes he listed what he termed a low level of morality, dynastic crisis and, above all, the growth of the cossack movement. He wrote: "we are right to consider the Time of Troubles a struggle between society and the forces arrayed against it, a struggle waged by the nation's propertied elements, whose interest it was to maintain peace and public order...against so-called cossacks, landless people, wanderers, people whose concerns were foreign to the interests of society..."[4] Soloviev's view that the cossacks sparked the revolt in the early seventeenth century led him to a paradoxical conclusion: Bolotnikov's rebellion, which often harmed service-tenure landholders, actually was directed against the peasants. Soloviev identified the rise of pretenders as a manifestation of domestic, not external, forces and regarded the liberation movement primarily as the reestablishment of government power.

In a critique of Soloviev, N.I. Kostomarov [1817-1885] stressed that cossacks had been a positive force, defending the frontiers. But the violent cossack risings which shook Russia from top to bottom and aimed to destroy the entire structure of society produced highly unfortunate results "because whenever the cossacks tried to break away from the state they behaved foolishly and prevented Russian society from developing successfully."[5] Kostomarov considered the pretender phenomenon primarily an internal one.

The work of V.O.Kliuchevskii constitutes the peak of bourgeois historiography. He devised an entire synthesis to explain the Time of Troubles. He took the position that the Time of Troubles began when the dynasty of Kalita died out. The unequal distribution of government offices indigenous in the [Muscovite] state was the root cause of it. This engendered social conflict.[6] Kliuchevskii wrote: "when the lower orders rose up, the Troubles were converted into a contest in which they tried to eliminate the upper."[7] Next, the internecine war turned into a national struggle: "by late 1611 politics was played out; emotions of religion and patriotism surfaced and proceeded to deliver the prostrate realm."[8] Only intervention by outside elements in the fratricidal contest could bring the Troubles, which had fed on the clash of classes in Russian society, to an end.[9]

In a lucid and capacious study S.F. Platonov [1860-1933] closely analyzed the complex internal crisis in the second half of the sixteenth century that subsequently became the Time of Troubles. Platonov discerned three stages in the development of the Troubles in Muscovy. He termed them dynastic, social, and national.

When the dynasty came to an end at the close of the sixteenth century a political crisis ensued. It was rooted in the ancient hostility the Muscovite monarchy entertained for the native princely aristocracy. Platonov considered the *oprichnina* a manifestation of this phenomenon. Decay of state order and the decline of Moscow's political independence caused by the civil war characterized the second period of troubles. Platonov believed Bolotnikov's revolt, intended both to acquire a new tsar and to bring about a social revolution that would destroy the system of serfdom, was the most important factor during the social phase of the conflict.

During the struggle for liberation, national independence and the social order, which the Troubles and foreign aggression had destroyed, were reconstituted.[10] Platonov thought False Dmitrii II was a tool of Polish lords and the king; he associated the start of the national liberation movement with the years 1608-1610, which witnessed rebellion against the Thief [as a pretender was regularly called–ed.]. The church and the conservative nucleus of Muscovite society, which included servingmen and urban dwellers, emerged as the driving force during the final stage of the contest. This was why the second militia took a strong stand against anything that was strange to the traditional Muscovite system. The militia led by Minin and Pozharskii inspired dread in Poles, traitorous Moscow boyars, and cossack Thieves identified with the original militia. In the final analysis, the Time of Troubles destroyed old boyar families and defeated the cossacks. The upper and lower levels in Muscovite society lost out; victory went to the middle ranks.[11]

Platonov adopted and developed Kliuchevskii's celebrated thesis, according to which one class after another were caught up in the Troubles "in the same order in which they found themselves in Russian society as it then existed." Boyars started the Troubles; then it was the gentry's turn, and eventually the lower orders rose up.

After the Revolution, Soviet historians were critical of the theory concerning the Time of Troubles Kliuchevskii and Platonov had devised and sought to dispel it. Their work laid great emphasis on the class struggle. M.N. Pokrovskii [1868-1932] elaborated a view that the Troubles started from below, not on high.[12] Regarding events occurring in the early seventeenth century as manifestations of "merchant capitalism," some historians came to the conclusion that a massive explosion of class struggle, called "peasant revolution" or "peasant war," broke out in Russia at that time.[13] The issue of pretenders also was handled differently. Now their appearance was connected with domestic issues, not foreign intervention. S.M. Dubrovskii thought False Dmitrii I was a cossack tsar who presided over a cossack revolution.[14]

The work of B.D. Grekov [1862-1953] and I.I. Smirnov [1909-1965] inaugurated a new era in the study of events of the early seventeenth century. Grekov thoroughly investigated the enserfment of the peasantry at the end of the sixteenth century to prove that the establishment of serfdom led to the revolts of the early seventeenth century.[15] Rejecting the notion that pretenders were a manifestation of cossack and peasant revolution, Smirnov was the first to scrutinize Bolotnikov's rising closely. In his monumental study Smirnov demonstrated that Bolotnikov's rising in 1606-1607 was actually Russia's initial peasant war.[16]

By disposing of the contention that the early seventeenth-century revolution was an ongoing process fueled by the risings led by Bolotnikov and the pretenders, early Soviet historiography also had broken definitely with the concept that the Time of Troubles constituted a single complex of events internally related to one another.[17]

Next, research on the Time of Troubles diverged in several separate directions. In addition to Bolotnikov's peasant war, numerous studies appeared focusing on the struggle against Polish-Lithuanian intervention in the early seventeenth century.[18] Here the term "intervention" originally meant foreign military involvement in Russia's affairs. The pretenders, False Dmitrii I and the others, were regarded solely as tools of the foreign aggressors. This ignored the fact that the lower orders supported the pretenders, which was a demonstration of class struggle. Political conflict, intervention, and the class struggle each were studied in isolation. These disparate tendencies were not overcome until I.S. Shepelev published *Liberation and Class Struggle in Russia,1608-1610*[19] and, more significantly, until discussions of the problems posed by the initial peasant war took place during 1958-1961, in which A.A. Zimin, Smirnov, V.I. Koretskii, and others participated.[20] Opposing

Smirnov, Zimin contended that peasant war raged unceasingly throughout the whole period from 1603 to 1614, serving as a kind of fulcrum around which all other events of the time were clustered. Although terming False Dmitrii I a plaything in the hands of the Polish magnates, Zimin attributed an element in his success to intensification of peasant warfare on the country's southern frontiers and the revolt of the commons in Moscow.[21] Zimin's periodization of the first peasant war has found reflection in subsequent literature on the topic.

In a monograph D.P. Makovskii was the first to attempt to marshal facts in support of the new periodization. He regarded all the events of the Time of Troubles as successive stages in the peasant war. While holding that False Dmitrii I was the chief of the revolutionary cossacks, he identified the occurrences at the start of the seventeenth century as an early form of bourgeois revolution.[22] However, historians have refused to accept Makovskii's attempt to revive the conception Pokrovskii's school had devised to explain the Time of Troubles.

The appearance of V.I. Koretskii's book *The Establishment of Serfdom and the First Peasant War in Russia*, based on a huge amount of archival material, was an event of considerable importance in recent historiography. Koretskii carefully analyzed the social policies adopted by the government at various stages during the Time of Troubles. He paid particular attention to Khlopko's revolt [an indigenous peasant rising over numerous areas of Muscovy in 1603—ed.] and False Dmitrii I's efforts to reestablish St. George's Day[23] [November 26, around which time peasants traditionally had enjoyed the right to change masters–ed.].

Investigating the motive forces of the peasant war, V.D. Nazarov came up with an intriguing proposition describing the features that made the first peasant war unusual. He noted: "Russia's singularity lay in the fact that objectively the cossacks assumed the task of actively fomenting, ideologically formulating, and to a considerable degree actually organizing an open class struggle." However, as events unfolded, they became divided into a host of rival factions and "proved incapable of holding together a greater or lesser union of oppressed elements in town and country for any length of time."[24]

Observations made by L.V. Cherepnin and V.I. Kutanov are important for understanding the Time of Troubles. They dealt with the time when class struggle fused with the national liberation movement:[25] the fight with the interventionists acquired a markedly antifeudal character because the lower orders saw the aggressors not only as national but also as class enemies.[26] Substantial interest attaches to

studies of Russia's foreign policy during the Time of Troubles and to
the foreign-policy views held by the rebel forces at the time of Bolotnikov's rising.[27] Cherepnin has devoted a monograph to land assemblies in the early seventeenth century.[28]

However, no complete study of the history of the political struggle
Russia waged during the Time of Troubles has yet been written. The
problems involving interrelationships between the social and national
liberation movements have still not been concretely elucidated. Only
after the interaction and interdependence among all the political, social
and economic factors have been evaluated properly can the complex
period known as the Time of Troubles be understood. This approach
alone will make it possible to recreate a comprehensive concept.

Russia unquestionably had reached a major turning point in the
second half of the sixteenth century that would determine the nation's
subsequent development. This period gave birth to the institution of
serfdom, which, together with changes in the composition and structure of the feudal estates, transformed society and determined the
future political course the country was to follow.

Feudal fragmentation in Russia had come to an end by the beginning
of the sixteenth century and unification had exerted substantial influence on domestic political development. Once Moscow had absorbed
the land that formerly had belonged to regional appanage nobles, these
men took service with the Muscovite sovereigns; but the monarchy had
subdued the aristocracy only to fall under its domination. The feudal
structure altered significantly during the course of the sixteenth century. Members of the petty and middle gentry substantially increased
their influence. The ruler had grown so powerful that he might contem-
plate claiming that he asserted unrestricted authority. The gentry
supported his autocratic pretensions. This rendered inevitable a clash
with the aristocracy, which turned on what form the future structure
of the country should take.

Reforms undertaken in the mid-sixteenth century somewhat re-
stricted the nobility's power, fostered a strong chancellery apparatus
which opened the way for gentry serving in the bureaucracy to enter
the aristocratic boyar council, and devised machinery to represent the
estates and develop local self-government. National assemblies were
the first to emerge. These changes reinforced the gentry's influence
and furthered the process of centralization.

The oprichnina [Ivan's personal bailiwick or lands, as distinct from
the *zemshchina*, the remainder of the country, which continued to be
ruled in the traditional way—ed.], established during the second half

of the sixteenth century, complicated Russia's development. Hundreds of the most aristocratic princely families were banished to the eastern frontiers and the treasury confiscated many princes' patrimonial estates. Ivan the Terrible had hoped he might employ this device to clip the wings of the aristocracy constraining his authority, but the resources at his disposal were insufficient to achieve his purpose. The only way the monarchy could contain the aristocracy was to rely on the gentry, but shortly before instituting the oprichnina the ruler broke with his gentry reformers and refused to countenance further changes. He was charting a dangerous course.

Rather than rely upon the whole gentry mass in order to buttress his personal authority, Ivan decided to form a special police unit containing comparatively few gentry. Members of this new corps enjoyed exceptional privileges, to the detriment of other serving men. However, the traditional army structure, precedence [assigning high civilian and military offices on the basis of pedigree rather than capacity— ed.], and other institutions that had guaranteed the predominance of the boyar aristocracy remained intact. Such a move was bound to lead to serious political conflict. The monarchy lacked the strength to crush the nobility's foundations of power and form a new entity comprised exclusively of gentry. The privileges [Ivan's personal] guard corps received provoked intense dissatisfaction among serving men. This meant the oprichnina actually diminished the amount of support the crown enjoyed. As the situation progressed, this inevitably led to the application of terror.

Ivan the Terrible had overestimated his strength grievously. The monarchy still lacked an effective administrative apparatus and a regular army. The crown was in no position to carry out policies opposed by the leaders of the dominant class for any length of time. The oprichnina had aroused their opposition. Relations between the monarch and the ruling group had soured. The sovereign's authority drastically declined.

Faced with universal disaffection, Ivan was compelled to recognize his policy of repression had failed. A little more than a year after he had disgraced and banished his nobles he reversed course sharply and announced he had forgiven the princes. Exiles were allowed to return to Moscow and were given the opportunity to recover their lands.

Contrary to accepted opinion, the oprichnina frequently altered and changed course. Originally directing its blows at the princely nobility, it subsequently struck at the gentry, chancellery personnel, and urban dwellers; eventually it aimlessly and unjustifiably persecuted the very forces that had supported the ruler's policy of centralization. The terror shocked contemporaries, who declared that thousands upon thousands were slaughtered and major towns were devastated. It was long believed that their claims that Russia lay in ruins in the wake of the oprichnina were accurate, but a reconstruction of the vanished oprichnina archives[29] provides more precise information. It appears that the terror coincided with a time of unprecedented natural disaster; famine and pestilence caused the deaths of hundreds of thousands of people. No more than 4,000 may be laid at the door of the oprichnina.

Ivan's reforms and the terror shaped Russia's political development for a long time. The oprichnina separated leading feudal courtiers who had served in what had been called the Sovereign's Court into two opposing halves. The old, traditional court now had a double, the Special Court, which intially was known as the Oprichnina or Appanage Court, later simply as the Court.

For years Ivan had tried stubbornly to curb the boyar aristocracy by using the Oprichnina Court as his device to achieve an autocratic mode of governance. His death revealed that his system of centralization, which had pitted the court against the rest of the country, was unstable. Boris Godunov was confronted with the task of effacing Ivan's political legacy. He restored a single Sovereign's Court and ended the twenty-year rift with the leading feudatories. Abolition of the Special Court temporarily weakened the monarchy and conflict with the aristocracy intensified. Boris' harassment of the nobility vividly reminded contemporaries of the oprichnina, but Boris had no intention of reverting to Ivan's methods. His repressions were mild; he devoted his energies to winning support for his policies from broader elements in society. During the oprichnina years Ivan had relied on his privileged gentry bodyguard and had ignored the rest of the feudatories. As regent, Godunov curried favor with the gentry at large. By freeing service-tenure landholders from taxation and suspending the right of peasants to depart on St. George's Day he satisfied the serf-owning gentry. It was their support that enabled Boris Godunov to win the throne.

Chapter One

RULE BY A MONK

The boyars had not gotten rid of the lowborn Godunov family merely to hand the crown over meekly to an unknown rogue. The highborn Shuiskii princes had never forgotten that their ancestral pedigree was more illustrious than that of Ivan IV himself. Otrepev had no reason to expect the senior Shuiskii would defer to him. Prince Vasilii sprang to action immediately. The brief interregnum afforded him a splendid opportunity to acquire the crown but in order to do so he had to prevent Dmitrii from entering the Kremlin.

Otrepev's supporters overheard Shuiskii talking to a man in Moscow. Said the boyar: "He's no son of a tsar, devil take him. You yourself know the tsar's real son is dead. This one's no such thing; he's a defrocked monk and a traitor!"[1] Although the Shuiskii faction had many partisans in the boyar council they were well aware that in times of stress the man who won over the population of Moscow would come out on top. Vasilii Shuiskii thus naturally tried to attract popular leaders in the town sector to his side. He communicated his plans to Fedor Kon, the eminent builder, Fedor Kalachnik, a merchant, and Kostia, a medic, as well as to other citizens, fusiliers, parish priests, and monks.[2] Shuiskii's endeavors met with some success.

The pretender hoped that once the Godunov family was gone from Moscow the inhabitants would submit to him, but in fact, far from dying down, agitation against the Thief grew unexpectedly more widespread. He remained in Kolomenskoe awaiting word that Fedor Godunov had been removed. On June 10 he received the long-awaited news. It appeared that nothing now could prevent him from entering Moscow. However, his supporters soon informed Otrepev about fresh dangers. Their alarming reports led the Thief to delay his departure for ten days.

Then on June 20 Dmitrii's partisans began earnestly entreating him to come quickly to his ancestral abode. Fearing ambush, Otrepev took elaborate precautions. His men diligently examined the entire route between Kolomenskoe and the Kremlin. Noble boyars rode beside the pretender and the tsar accomplished the entire journey tightly encircled by detachments of cossacks and mercenaries. An armed company of boyars and courtiers brought up the rear of the column. The pretender insisted that a group of Moscow gentry and soldiers be dismissed once the cortege started to draw near the Kremlin.

The narrow city streets were jammed with residents. People clambered up on fences, roofs, and even into belfries the better to behold the procession. Otrepev rode on horseback through a sea of faces. Mobs uttered shouts of welcome and bells rang out in his wake. His triumph was momentarily marred when the procession had almost reached the Kremlin. A strong gust of wind whirled up a great cloud of dust that blinded people and blotted out the sun. Witnesses asserted the city grew dark at noon. This baleful portent caused a moment of confusion among the people but the dust storm ceased as quickly as it had begun.

The royal procession halted at the shrine of Vasilii the Blessed. Three years earlier Otrepev had left that place to seek his fortune in Lithuania. Now he had returned to it as tsar. Stopping his horse, Dmitrii removed his tall hat and bowed in the direction of the golden cupolas of the Kremlin cathedrals. At that instant the Kremlin gate swung open and a procession with crosses and icons slowly issued forth, led by bishops wearing mitres and mantles sparkling with gold and precious stones. Otrepev moved quickly to anticipate the metropolitan, received his blessing, and bent down before the cross. The Orthodox clergy began intoning prayers. In the end the pretender's entourage spoiled the triumph. Polish hussars, formed in a semicircle, assumed this was a fine time to blow trumpets and bang drums. The loud, discordant noise they made drowned out the chanting clergy.

Closely attended by his mercenary guard Otrepev proceeded immediately from the square to the Kremlin. After spending a brief time in the Cathedral of the Dormition Dmitrii went to the Cathedral of the Assumption. In the domestic shrine of the Muscovite tsars he had to listen to a lengthy address by Archpriest Terentii. Indulging in a fulsome comparison between the newfound tsar and the lamp of Christianity shining down upon all under Heaven more brightly than the sun, Terentii asked Dmitrii to pay no attention to counsellors who slandered loyal subjects and sowed enmity between him, the lamp of Russia, and his people. The loquacious priest tried to allay suspicion of the new ruler: "God has strengthened and confirmed you," he trumpeted beneath the stone cathedral vaults. "Who can topple you? Repair to your abode in peace."[3]

The Russian church categorically forbade people of other faiths and heretics to cross the threshold of Orthodox shrines but Otrepev scorned what were deemed holy laws. His gang of foreigners swarmed into the cathedral. The pretender was afraid to be without his bodyguard even in church.

After listening to Archpriest Terentii's peroration Dmitrii entered the palace. The Polish units with their banners remained formally drawn up next to the porch until the pretender disappeared inside. The main hall was filled with boyars. Everyone noticed that Ivan the Terrible's throne was too high to accommodate the new sovereign. The dwarfish Otrepev solemnly took his seat upon it but his legs waved in the air and did not touch the floor. Dmitrii addressed the nobility from his ancestral throne. Weeping freely he told the assemblage the tale of his miraculous escape. The boyars knew how much it was worth but their countenances assumed a respectful expression. Everyone bowed low before the autocrat.

Skilled actor though he was, Dmitrii felt the tension and had difficulty controlling his nerves. A considerable number of those residing in the Kremlin had known Grisha personally when he was a monk in the Miracles monastery. The trick with a False Otrepev that had worked for the pretender in remote Putivl had no chance of success in Moscow [Otrepev had tried to pass off an Elder Leontii as himself—ed.]. Several people from the capital already had recognized the fugitive defrocked monk during an audience he had given in Tula. In the Kremlin he might expect scandal and exposure at any moment. Informers warned Otrepev that the agitation against him had increased sharply and a disturbance might soon break out. Fearing for his safety, Ivan the Terrible's self-proclaimed son changed the entire Kremlin guard almost as soon as he entered the fortress. All gates were closed at once. Cossacks and mercenaries guarded the exits from the fortress with pistols at the ready.

A vast throng of citizens jammed Red Square and stood before the closed gates, refusing to disperse. The alarmed Dmitrii had to send Bogdan Belskii and some princes and crown secretaries out to the people. While the crowd looked on, Belskii removed a cross from his neck and bowing to it swore the sovereign was the genuine son of Tsar Ivan whom he, Belskii, himself had concealed from assassins. This was the reason Boris had persecuted him. Belskii, Maliuta's nephew, for many years had been Ivan IV's avenging sword. Those assembled fully grasped the purport of his words. His speech was designed as a warning to dissidents. Otrepev knew the power the Orthodox church exercised over men's minds and lost no time forging relations with the ecclesiastical council. The princes of the church recently had been cursing him as a renegade and heretic and had condemned him to death *in absente*. Now they obediently trooped to the palace the minute he summoned them. Iov, the first Russian patriarch, who had received his office from the leader of the church ecumenical [the patriarch of Constantinople— ed.], was exiled without benefit of formal inquiry. The pretender was prepared to approve this arbitrary action taken against Most Holy Iov. After convening the church hierarchs, Otrepev told them Iov was no longer fit to occupy the patriarchal chair because he was old and short-sighted. Without a trace of embarrassment the patriarch told Dmitrii he was very old and blind.[4] This did not sound particularly convincing but no one dared say a word.

The churchmen awkwardly tried to save their prestige and create the impression they enjoyed full freedom of expression. Retiring to confer in the Cathedral of the Dormition they adopted one resolution that Iov should be restored to the patriarchate and then another stating he had been removed from office because of his age and poor sight. Bowing to the will of the fugitive Defrocked One, the church fathers elected a Greek, Ignatii, as patriarch. Among the Muscovite clergy Ignatii had a bad reputation as a "coarse, besotted, and troublesome man." Coming from Cyprus in Boris Godunov's time he had been assigned the bishopric of Riazan, which he had administered for three years, and where he had managed to compromise himself thoroughly. When the Riazan gentry defected in a bloc to the pretender, Ignatii followed their example. He was the first churchman to go to Otrepev's camp and he had accompanied him when he entered Moscow. The new patriarch pledged to serve Dmitrii loyally and honorably.

It was more difficult to come to terms with the boyars. For almost two months after the revolt at Kromy, Dmitrii's counsellors in Putivl had been working to reach agreement with the boyar leaders in Moscow. At last they came to terms on the distribution of ranks and offices. Otrepev approved the agreement and instructed his secretary to draw up a list of members in what was now termed the tsar's senate. The reform of the highest state body changed nothing but its name. Although calling the ancient council a senate in the Polish style, Dmitrii allowed it to retain all its old functions. He kept the promise he had made to the boyar conspirators. None of Otrepev's Polish counsellors attained the rank of senator.

The Moscow nobles tried to convince the pretender to confirm as senators all those to whom Boris had awarded boyar rank. Members of the deposed dynasty were expelled from the council along with their immediate relatives in the Saburov and Veliaminov families. The boyar council was glad to admit nobles and officials who had been subjected to persecution in Boris' day. Boyar rank was bestowed on Ivan Vorotynskii and Ivan Romanov; Vasilii Shchelkalov [the foreign secretary—ed.] became an associate boyar. To satisfy the Shuiskii faction Otrepev created a new conciliar rank of swordbearer, hitherto unknown in the ascending order of Muscovite officialdom. Young Skopin [a member of the Shuiskii family, soon to become a distinguished military leader—ed.], not yet twenty years old, became the first swordbearer.[5]

Dmitrii generously rewarded those who had taken part in the conspiracy at Kromy. Ivan Golitsyn, Fedor Sheremetev, and Prince Boris Tatev were made boyars and Prince Boris Lykov a royal steward. The Moscow nobles did not approve of the assignments the Thief had made while still in Putivl but they had to make the best of it and sanction them. The humble courtiers Vasilii Mosalskii and Petr Shakhovskoi were elevated to the high rank of conciliar boyar.

In reactivating the shade of Ivan the Terrible the pretender was involuntarily reinvigorating the shadow of the almost-forgotten *oprichnina*. His closest confederates were Petr Basmanov, grandson of a leader in the oprichnina, and Maliuta's nephew, Bogdan Belskii, hero of the Moscow rising. Belskii had earned his distinction and Otrepev made him a boyar. As guardian of Ivan IV's fictive son, Belskii was not loathe once more to serve as regent. When Belskii entrenched himself in the Kremlin after the disturbance the great boyars grew concerned that with the support of Basmanov and other former members of the oprichnina he would try, if he could, to bring back oprichnina forms of governance. Belskii possessed enormous political experience and knew how to head off boyar disaffection in a timely manner.

At the outset of his administration Otrepev had to face formidable boyar opposition, which was preparing to strike him a mortal blow. However, the Shuiskii interests acted too soon and Dmitrii's partisans soon succeeded in unraveling a conspiracy they had organized. Three days after his triumphant entry into Moscow, Otrepev issued an order to arrest the rebels. If the Shuiskii family's complicity had been demonstrated earlier they would have met the same fate as Fedor Godunov, but now the pretender was constrained by his understanding with the boyars and had to refer the question to his senators, who insisted the Shuiskii brothers must be tried in council.

Dmitrii assigned Petr Basmanov and Mikhail Saltykov to guard those arrested. Together with Belskii they soon concluded their investigation, during which it was revealed that Shuiskii had assembled trusted men in his house and sworn that Dmitrii was none other than the fugitive monk Otrepev, a covert foe of Orthodoxy and a tool of the Jesuits. The conspirators had recruited numerous supporters and worked out plans for an uprising. They proposed to set fire to the Foreign Affairs chancellery, which had been occupied by Polish forces, and murder Dmitrii in the palace.[6] Prince Vasilii Shuiskii was tortured and made a full confession, implicating his co-conspirators.

The trial before the council did not last long. The pretender set the tone by functioning as prosecutor. He called the Shuiskii princes long-standing traitors and enemies of Ivan IV and his successors. Otrepev declared his father, pious Tsar Ivan, had executed seven members and his brother Fedor one member of this disloyal clan. "Prince Vasilii," he cried, "simply has been waiting for the right moment to take us unawares and murder us in our chamber. We have irrefutable proof!"[7]

Shuiskii made no attempt to defend himself. At the trial he merely fell on his knees, admitted his folly, and called himself a stupid peasant who in insulting the tsar had offended God Almighty. The Greek, Igna-tii, named patriarch the day before the trial, displayed the greatest of righteous anger. Many boyars had been privy to the conspiracy and sympathized with the Shuiskii position but fear constrained them to revile the accused more fiercely than the rest. Witnesses declared that the common people too angrily condemned the rebels.

The assembly sentenced Vasilii Shuiskii, ringleader of the conspiracy, to death and his brothers to life imprisonment. But after sentence was imposed the boyars and clergy did everything in their power to save the senior Shuiskii. The quarrels over the fate of the conspirator revealed the situation that had developed among the leaders in Moscow. If Belskii and Basmanov had insisted on Shuiskii's execution they would have been able to consolidate their position in the government. The Golitsyn princes, Lykov, and Tatev were alarmed. They had not brought the pretender to Moscow merely to yield primacy in council to former members of the oprichnina. All the nobles and princes of the church supported the Golitsyn position. Otrepev did not dare quarrel with his senators.

Three days after the trial a large army occupied a broad area near the Kremlin wall. Polish spearmen and cossacks with drawn swords stood in the foreground. Fusiliers in battle array were present in the square and all over the Kremlin. They were stationed at gates, on walls, and in towers, their weapons cocked. Forgetting their recent exaltation, the crowds grew quiet. The silence seemed menacing. Mounted on horseback, Basmanov read out the sentence. An executioner strode up and down by a block into which a great axe had been driven. At Basmanov's signal he began to remove Shuiskii's clothing. Prince Vasilii was still hoping for clemency and at the block continued to pray for mercy. Weeping, he kept affirming that only folly had led him to rebel against the Trueborn Sovereign; the autocrat was mighty and clement, and he, Shuiskii, deserved life imprisonment for his stupid remarks. Basmanov was clearly impatient, but acting on prior instructions the executioner dawdled. At the last moment a mounted man rode out of the Kremlin bearing a screed. It was a royal edict sparing Shuiskii.

The authorities were merciful only to the nobles who had taken part in the conspiracy. Their less august confederates met with a dreadful fate. The courtier Petr Turgenev and the merchant Fedor Kalachnik were beheaded in the square, and monks who had joined the conspirators were stealthily murdered in prison.[8]

None of Otrepev's royal predecessors had decided anything without the boyar council. The pretender, now seated on his ancestral throne, did the same. He met almost daily with his senate about pressing problems confronting his administration. The council's initial success was to prevent Shuiskii's execution. The ignorant interloper had been taught his first lesson.

The counsellors who had urged harsh punishment for the boyar conspirators had sustained a defeat. The results soon became apparent. Bogdan Belskii was not allowed to resume his post as regent and guardian. The boyar council heaved a sigh of relief when Dmitrii transferred Belskii out of Moscow to take command in Novgorod. The die was cast. Once domiciled in the capital, the false tsar rapidly was becoming a prisoner of the Moscow nobility.

The council considered the cossacks its chief irritant. Boyars could not rest easy as long as free Don cossack atamans [chieftains or commanders of cossack companies or units—ed.] guarded the tsar's person. The cossacks and fusiliers who had come to Moscow with Otrepev had been keenly interested in Shuiskii's trial, often bringing to Dmitrii untrustworthy boyars and commanders they had apprehended. They were puzzled each time one of these men was not executed; they felt their leader was drawing closer to those who wished them ill. Things had changed in Moscow. The noblest of the boyars should have lost his head. Yesterday's mutineers thirsted to finish off the seditious boyars but their time had passed. Otrepev had won the throne because a mighty revolutionary movement existed in the country but after he came to terms with the boyars he decisively rejected his allies among the people.

Fugitive slaves, peasants, townsmen, and petty serving men comprised the cossack ranks. All had fought for the Good Sovereign, believing they would be treated fairly. Otrepev had brought them to the Kremlin but then had tried to get rid of them. Mutineers were not at all the sort of people who should attend a freshly-minted tsar. The boyar council managed to get the rebellious cossack units out of the Kremlin and subsequently from the capital. The pretender kept Karela alone [the doughtiest and most fearless of the cossack commanders—ed.]. If events had gone differently Karela might have become leader of a peasant uprising but life at Dmitrii's court proved too much for him. He was accustomed to the dangers and alarums of life in the open steppe; he could find no place among the royal courtiers. He cared nothing for rank, wealth, or honors. He spent money like water. He felt an outcast among the haughty nobles. The ataman preferred taverns where he could be himself to the court. In the end this remarkable man simply went to sleep.

While still in Tula the pretender had recalled his supposed mother Marfa (the nun Mariia) Nagaia and tried to use her name to win over the towns. Imitating Godunov, he had people take an oath both to himself and the widowed nun-queen. The name of Ivan IV's widow, Marfa Nagaia, always came first. The body of the oath began with the words: "I kiss the cross to my sovereign queen and grand princess, the nun Marfa Fedorovna of all Russia, and to my trueborn sovereign, Tsar and Grand Prince Dmitrii Ivanovich of all Russia."[9]

Once settled in the Kremlin the pretender secretly sent his chamberlain, Semen Shapkin, to Marfa. Later it was assumed the nun agreed to acknowledge the pretender as her son because the chamberlain had threatened to kill her. This is highly unlikely. Shapkin approached Marfa on grounds of kinship and tried to arrange matters on that basis with promises and gifts. The widow had no reason to refuse. As queen she had resided in the Kremlin approximately three years. No subsequent humiliation could efface that unforgettable period. The tsar's widow had been forcibly tonsured. Her best years had been spent in exile in a miserable northern cloister on the Vysksa river, where abbots and elders kept close watch on her. Marfa was naturally ready to pay any price to win freedom from her prison of a nunnery and be restored to long-forgotten luxury and honor. Contemporaries were merely guessing when they said the humiliated queen accepted Grisha as her son of her own volition.[10]

If the meeting between son and fictive mother went off badly it might lead to Dmitrii's exposure as a scoundrel. Otrepev thus had good reason to do everything he could to put on a good show. After the chamberlain, he sent Vasilii Mosalskii, who had carried out a number of intimate commissions for him, to meet with Marfa.

In the middle of July, Dmitrii and a throng of boyars guarded by Polish mercenaries set out for the village of Taininskoe. There in a field Ivan IV's widow, alighting from a carriage, got her first glimpse of an individual who bore no resemblance to her son. Otrepev overcame momentary embarrassment and artfully played his part. Jumping down from the saddle he threw himself at his mother's feet. She had no choice but to carry out her role in the charade. The next day widow and son entered Moscow. Crowds escorted their cortege from the outer gate to the palace. Displaying dignified humility, Otrepev dismounted, took off his hat, and walked beside the queen's vehicle. Dmitrii distributed generous alms to the people at the Cathedral of the Dormition. The encounter between Ivan IV's widow and her newfound son made a strong impression on those present. Tears came into many eyes.

Dmitrii had a residence built for Marfa in the Resurrection nunnery near the Frolov gate leading into the Kremlin. Her fine new palace was a cell in name only. Himself defrocked, Otrepev restored his fictive mother to secular life as well. The nun received food from the royal kitchens and was attended by a large corps of servants. Dmitrii visited her almost daily.

Otrepev was crowned three days after Queen Marfa arrived. The route between the palace and the Cathedral of the Dormition was strewn with purple cloth, on top of which Persian brocade sewn with gold had been laid. Violating firmly-established ceremonial, Dmitrii made a speech about his miraculous deliverance at the cathedral altar. At first his voice sounded hoarse but he soon mastered his emotions. After a prayer Ignatii the Greek set the crown on his head and handed him the sceptre, the highest token of sovereignty. One dignitary after another came forward to congratulate him and kiss his hand. On leaving the Cathedral of the Dormition the boyars followed the custom of throwing small gold coins, expressly minted for the occasion, on the road at the tsar's feet.

Dmitrii desired to invest his coronation with the authority of Ivan IV and introduced several changes into the ceremony to achieve his purpose. On visiting the Cathedral of the Archangel he prostrated himself before the stone tombs of the tsars, invoking Ivan's shade. A Greek, Arsenios of Elassoniki, who had long served as archbishop in the royal bedchamber, waited nearby, holding the Cap of Monomakh [the crown which Muscovite rulers traditionally wore—ed.]. The pretender wanted it placed on his head above the tomb of his presumed father. In Poland Otrepev had vowed to the Jesuits he would confess to them before he was crowned tsar. The papal nuncio had inquired of the Vatican concerning the doubts that had overtaken the covert Catholic but the papal curia was slow to respond. In Moscow the renegade overcame his doubts at the coronation and took communion in the Orthodox way.

It was enough that the pretender had invited the Jesuits he had brought into the Kremlin for his coronation. Indignation felt by Orthodox Christians reached its height when a Jesuit father in a sutane pressed up to the throne and made a speech in Polish honoring the tsar at a solemn reception in the Kremlin directly after the coronation. Such obvious lack of tact with respect to the Lamp of Orthodoxy caused embarrassment and confusion. In an effort to retrieve the situation the pretender hastily translated several sentences from the speech of this man, who was considered a God-hated Latin.

In earlier times everyone could count on a festival in the palace or on the square at a coronation. Boris piously had observed this custom and had entertained the people at every street intersection. Dmitrii's coronation was celebrated in the palace only. Long tables were set out in a hall. Guards carefully scrutinized guests and the doors were thrown open to Poles and cossacks, the veterans of the Moscow campaign. The Moscow nobility never would previously have associated with such people.

The gentry always had received generous supplements from the treasury at coronation time. When he was elected Boris had enacted that serving men should be given two years' salary. Dmitrii followed his example. Boyars receiving 1,000 rubles a year were given 2,000 immediately. Members of the gentry paid ten rubles got twenty. Such lavishness made the new sovereign popular among the gentry.

Otrepev was far less generous to the people. He felt his only obligation lay to the population of the Seversk region, which had supported him during times of failure and defeat. Furthermore, his soldiers had plundered and devastated the Seversk towns and districts. They were in ruins. Influenced by such considerations Dmitrii persuaded the council to exempt the Seversk region from taxes for ten years.[11]

The future of the mercenary army the pretender had brought to Moscow became a source of lengthy argument in council. The capital distrusted the motley crew surrounding the pretender. The mercenaries often had quarreled with Otrepev and had left him to his fate at critical junctures. But when they came to Moscow they tried to live this down and proclaimed on every street corner that only their bravery had enabled the tsar to win the crown. These statements were utterly false. Dmitrii had entered the capital with no more than seven Polish contingents numbering at most 1,000 men, all of whom were accommodated in the Foreign Affairs chancellery.

The condottieri serving under Otrepev's banner were interested in nothing but gain. Dmitrii generously rewarded them but it was never enough. Considering Moscow an occupied city, the knights were enjoying themselves. Inhabitants hid in their homes when drunken soldiers appeared on the streets. Quarreling and violence were epidemic. Very few managed to settle accounts with their persecutors. Soon after the coronation a boyar court convicted a spearman of criminal behavior. The law of the land mandated a public thrashing. Fusiliers drove the guilty man along the streets, striking him with staves. Mercenaries rushed in to rescue their comrade while people came from everywhere to support the fusiliers. Beaten back, the spearmen retreated to the Foreign Affairs chancellery, where they opened fire. Many were left to die on the street and even more were wounded. The encounter threatened to turn into a general uprising. The tocsin sounded. Boyars issuing from the Kremlin had difficulty calming the crowds even though they proclaimed those responsible for the attack on the fusiliers would be punished. The knights refused to surrender the guilty parties and the boyars threatened to bring up cannon to destroy the Foreign Affairs chancellery and those defending it. The mercenaries replied by letting the palace know they would immediately attack the thousands who were besieging them. Dmitrii did not want his mercenary guard destroyed and begged it to hand over a few men in order to calm his subjects. The tsar secretly promised they would come to no harm. Three spearmen were locked up in a bathhouse and released a day later.[12]

The boyar council used this incident to disperse the guard. During the campaign the pretender solemnly had promised to give the soldiers thousands of gold pieces as soon as he entered the capital, but the treasury's resources were insufficient. Otrepev had to compensate the mercenaries with Russian money and furs. The veterans were fed from palace supplies. In the final reckoning they each received forty gold pieces. Some hussars thereupon left Moscow and others did so at the end of the year. After squandering and drinking up their money the knights went off home, loudly complaining that the tsar had betrayed them. Otrepev was forced to get rid of his cossacks and mercenaries in order to secure his throne and stabilize the political situation.

Now in power, Otrepev had to contend with a host of unresolved problems. The secret agreement he had made with King Sigismund seriously constrained him. Attempting to fulfill his obligations, the tsar tried abruptly to change the direction of Russia's foreign policy. He issued orders to prepare a move against Narva. Sweden assumed war was imminent and began concentrating troops in Finland. Russia's ruling groups strongly disapproved of the tsar's plan. The three-year famine, the uprising by the commons, and the war with the Thief's army had led to internal exhaustion. The country needed peace, not war. The boyar council decisively rejected breaking the perpetual peace with Sweden and the boyars forced the tsar to give up his plans to conquer Narva. When a Polish negotiator arrived in Moscow in October, 1605 to concert a common front against Sweden the pretender made only the vaguest promises.

During secret audiences the king's envoys told the tsar he must fulfill the terms of the clandestine agreements and cede the Seversk land to the *Rzeczpospolita* [the term Professor Skrynnikov uses to denote the combined kingdom of Poland and Lithuania—ed.] including the ancient Russian towns of Chernigov and Novgorod-Seversk. Fearing exposure, the pretender hesitated openly to deny his obligations and offered money instead of the towns. The boyars followed the tsar's secret discussions with Sigismund's emissaries with growing concern. Otrepev contrived a ruse to allay their suspicions. He announced he would adopt the title of emperor, and he engaged in a noisy quarrel with the Polish king.

Communications to Sigismund now began: "We, all-victorious monarch, Dmitrii Ivanovich, by God's grace emperor and grand prince of all Russia, and of many lands sovereign and tsar...."[13] Otrepev's pretensions were not empty boasting. He had contrived this loud argument involving titles to serve as a smokescreen. The pretender revealed the motives that lay behind his actions to a Vatican emissary: "There is a rumor I have promised to cede territory to the Polish king. This must be categorically refuted. That is why I insist on my titles."[14]

The title of king stood far lower on the hierarchical scale than that of emperor and Sigismund was seriously annoyed at his protege's impudence. The farsighted statesman Jan Zamojski repeatedly had warned the king not to get involved in Russian affairs. Now that his puppet had gotten out of hand the king was forced to reap the fruits of the adventuristic policy he had initiated. Otrepev was in no position either to surrender Russian lands to the king or to refuse to honor his secret undertakings. All Sigismund needed to do was to publish the secret agreements and brand the tsar a covert Catholic in order to compromise or actually overturn his insecure throne. An impatient man, the king refused to tolerate delay and deception on the part of his protege. He vowed Otrepev would pay with his life for betraying Poland's national interest. The pretender was driven into a corner.

He had, however, one faint hope. A situation had developed in the Rzeczpospolita that might at any moment cost Sigismund his throne. The king's thoughtless and rash actions had decreased his popularity drastically. Tolerance long had been a traditional hallmark of the Rzeczpospolita; Sigismund was a fanatical proponent of Catholicism, which arrayed Protestants and Orthodox gentry against him. The opposition was preparing to depose the king, and its leaders hoped the Muscovite tsar might help them.

The opposition leader, Mikolaj Zebrzydowski, had been a patron of the pretender while he was a sojourner in Poland. Zebrzydowski's confederate, Stanislaw Stadnicki, was related to the Mniszech family and a friend of Otrepev. Sigismund's fall would be manna from heaven for Dmitrii. The secret agreement threatening to destroy him no longer would be enforceable. The Polish throne would be vacant, which would open up fresh opportunities. The opposition understood Otrepev's soaring ambition and that this lure would entice him. Sigismund's confessor confidently told friends that Tsar Dmitrii was inclined to delude himself into thinking he had been promised the Polish crown. The king was beside himself when he learned about this. Information arriving in Cracow indicated the ruler of Muscovy secretly had promised the opposition 100,000 florins and military support. In March, 1606 the government of the Rzeczpospolita published all it knew. The chancellor of Lithuania told members of the parliament in Warsaw that the king's enemies had offered the Polish crown to Tsar Dmitrii and were in clandestine contact with him.

Before finishing one adventure the pretender heedlessly embarked upon another. His Polish advisors dangled marvellous opportunities before him. The invincible emperor would unite Muscovy with the Rzeczpospolita. They were already dreaming about returning in triumph to Cracow, but they swiftly came to regret their incautious recommendations. Dmitrii sent Jan Buczynski, his chief secretary, to Poland in December, 1605. A month later Buczynski informed his lord that King Sigismund was aware of his intentions. The trustworthy secretary wrote that the court knew that "I have said your tsarist eminence will be king of Poland."[15] Upon receiving Buczynski's letter Otrepev realized that his closest boyars had betrayed him. Only a handful of high crown officials had been privy to his secret plans. One of them had forewarned Sigismund.

The boyars formerly had distrusted Dmitrii because he was a protege of the king, but now roles had changed. The tsar wanted to help the opposition overthrow Sigismund whereas the boyars had emerged as his supporters. It is easy to explain the abrupt alteration in their attitude. No matter what it cost, the nobility was determined to drive the detested defrocked monk from the ancient throne of Muscovy.

Chapter Two

BOYAR OPPOSITION

While still in Putivl Otrepev had promised the boyar conspirators the rights magnates enjoyed in Poland. Muscovite nobles subsequently received many proofs that the new autocrat intended to honor their privileges. In discussions with his closest councillors he condemned the harsh mode of governance his presumed father, Ivan IV, had employed. "I have two ways to retain power," he said. "One is to be a tyrant; the other is to spare no expense, to reward everybody. It is better to reward; not to be a tyrant."[1]

Tsar Ivan had been born to the purple but even he could not bridle the aristocracy without resorting to the fearsome oprichnina. The pretender consoled himself with hopes that the nobility would appreciate his generosity. The boyars enthusiastically supported his naive illusions. The pretender found it hard to resist the exaggerated praise that greeted him at every turn. Flattery lulled Otrepev's suspicions and he did everything the boyar council asked of him. The conspirators, the Shuiskii princes, spent little time in exile. Dmitrii granted them full pardon and permitted them to take up their former prominent positions in council. He was digging his own grave.

His Polish advisors in Moscow vainly represented with him as to how dangerous such amnesties were, but Jerzy Mniszech, regarding events in Russia from afar, supported the course his protege was following. He wrote to the boyars and knights, promising to support enhancement of their privileges. In Moscow this was widely interpreted to mean the sovereign had promised that boyars might enjoy privileges the Polish nobility possessed, which were much greater than the rights the ancient Muscovite aristocracy had known.

Otrepev zealously tried to play the part of a gentle and merciful sovereign. Amnesties were ordered to erase memories of the murder of Boris Godunov's family and the savage persecution of his relatives. Mikhail Saburov had defended Astrakhan bravely against the Thief. The ruler pardoned him and made him a boyar. Members of the Saburov and Veliaminov families who had been sent into exile were brought back and allowed to serve again. The sovereign graciously pardoned other members of the Godunov family and appointed them commanders in Tiumen, Ustiug, and Sviiazhsk. One devoted supporter of Boris after another had his conciliar rank and service position restored. Boyar A.A. Teliatevskii was released from prison and sent to command Chernigov. Boyar M. Katyrev took over the administration of Great Novgorod.

Fedor Mstislavskii had once routed the pretender but Dmitrii forgave him and retained him as chairman of his senate. Tsar Boris had forbidden Mstislavskii to marry so that on the prince's death his vast appanage would escheat to the treasury but Dmitrii spared no effort to win the chief boyar's friendship. He bestowed upon him Boris Godunov's old palace in the Kremlin, married him to his supposed aunt on the Nagoi side, and celebrated the wedding for two days. Otrepev married Vasilii Shuiskii to another Nagoi relative and arranged for the wedding to take place a month after his own.

Otrepev calculated the Nagoi family would be bound to help him attach the nobility to his new dynasty. However, the sovereign went much too far in his efforts to establish a connection with its members. He assigned them higher places in council than representatives of the Golitsyn, Sheremetev, Kurakin, Tatev, and Lykov families. Mikhail Nagoi, a worthless drunkard, was a case in point. He received the rank of senior conciliar boyar and master of horse.

This excessive exaltation of the Nagoi family did not sit well with princes in whose veins flowed the blood of Rurik and Gedimin [founders of the royal houses of the grand duchies of Muscovy and Lithuania respectively—ed.]. The native nobility never forgot that Tsar Ivan had contracted his seventh marriage within the oprichnina and that his oprichnina favorite, Afanasii Nagoi, had supplied the bride. The Nagoi family was not a distinguished noble line and the name of Afanasii Nagoi was as hateful to the boyars as that of Maliuta Skuratov [chief "enforcer" in the last and most violent phase of the oprichnina—ed.].

No matter how hard Otrepev tried to draw close to princes of the blood he always felt a stranger among them. His intimate associates were very different. Almost all the tsar's favorites, like Petr Basmanov, the new steward, Prince Ivan Khvorostinin, and Mikhail Molchanov came from families prominent during the oprichnina. The nobility despised these new men who all too sharply reminded them of the oprichnina era, but their chief animus was reserved for the pretender himself.

Otrepev was not one of those mysterious adventurers who carry the secret of their origins to the grave. His true name was mentioned almost as soon as he assumed that of Dmitrii. His fantastic successes had caused the authorities momentarily to hesitate but this dissipated the minute the court in Moscow had a chance to observe Otrepev at close quarters. A comedy involving a change of clothes would not work in the capital. Elder Leonid, the False Otrepev, was brought to Moscow but was quickly disposed of. He was held for a time in Yaroslavl but then disappeared for good.

Otrepev's rise to the throne brought great misfortune to his real relatives and close associates. Thought to be clement, he made his fictive uncle Nagoi master of horse but his real uncle Smirnoi was banished to Siberia. The tsar showered favors on his supposed mother while his actual mother lived in penury in Galich. Soon after the coronation a monk incautiously told acquaintances he was the man who had taught Otrepev to read and write in the Miracles monastery and now he saw his pupil on the throne. When the monk was interrogated he stuck to his story and was drowned one night in the Moscow river. Several other monks from the Miracles monastery also disappeared without trace. Otrepev sacrificed his grandfather, who had once looked after him in his cell. Without regard for his age and debility Zamiatin Otrepev was exiled to Siberia. The pretender vainly tried to sever threads linking him to his past. Too many people in Moscow knew what he looked like and powerful forces were anxious to expose him. Otrepev was forced to contrive innumerable stratagems to keep proving he was descended from the true tsars. One of these finally ruined him.

When Queen Marfa, his assumed mother, gave him her blessing she helped Dmitrii convince others, but agreement in the so-called family did not last long. After the rumors he was a pretender surfaced again, the tsar contrived a new scenario that would ostensibly prove it was a priest's son, not the heir, who had perished in Uglich. Otrepev ordered the grave in Uglich containing Heir Dmitrii to be desecrated and the child's corpse removed from the church. The Defrocked One was a poor psychologist; his plan mortally offended Marfa Nagaia. She had no wish to see her only son's remains defiled. Otrepev insisted, and Marfa asked the boyars for help.[2] They at once urged Dmitrii to abandon his design but the service they rendered Marfa was not motivated by altruism. The boyars stripped the mask of loving mother from her face and made her an accomplice in their intrigues. Ivan's widow helped the conspirators make contact with the Polish king.

In his memoirs the Polish hetman [commander-in-chief of the army in Poland and Lithuania—ed.], Zolkiewski, stated that Marfa Nagaia employed a certain Swede to inform the king about the self-proclaimed tsar. The name of the Swede who executed the commission for Marfa and her sympathizers can be determined. It was Peter Petreius. The boyars chose him because Petreius was both personally known to Sigismund III and in the tsar's service in Moscow. At a meeting with Sigismund Petreius said "Dmitrii is not who he pretends to be," and gave facts to prove the tsar was an impostor. He told the king that Queen Marfa had admitted it and went on to cite the opinion of Gosiewski, an envoy just returned from Moscow, who had "the same correct, reliable information about Grisha as I have myself."[3]

Petreius met with the king in December, 1605 while the latter was celebrating his marriage to Constanza of Austria. Sigismund himself confirmed it was at the time of his wedding that Muscovite boyars began negotiating with him to overthrow Otrepev. A courier from the tsar, Ivan Bezobrazov, arrived in Cracow soon after Petreius. He had been charged to give Sigismund letters from the Muscovite tsar but besides delivering official communications he was to execute a secret commission from the boyars, Dmitrii's clandestine foes. The least publicity could bring the courier and his patrons to the block. Bezobrazov was received at the king's court and in his sovereign's name requested Sigismund to grant safe-conducts for Muscovite ambassadors to enter Poland. A rescript quickly was drawn up but the courier, following instructions, refused to accept it because it had omitted Dmitrii's imperial title. Before he left, Bezobrazov seized an oppor-

tunity to inform the king that the Shuiskii and Golitsyn boyars had sent
him a special message. Sigismund entrusted the matter to Lord Gosiewski, who met with Bezobrazov in deepest secrecy. Sigismund's closest
advisors, however, were kept informed and Hetman Stanislaw Zolkiewski has made the substance of the parleys available in his memoirs.
The Muscovite nobles used Bezobrazov to tell the king they intended
to get rid of the Deceiver and offer the throne to Sigismund's son
Wladyslaw. The way in which the courier referred to the tsar astounded
Gosiewski. He reproached the king for imposing on Moscow a tsar who
was lowborn and trivial-minded and complained that Dmitrii was
brutal, dissolute, and prone to extravagance. His final conclusion was
that the Deceiver was unworthy to occupy the Muscovite throne.[4]

Ivan Osechka Bezobrazov did not need to take refuge in circum-
locution and diplomatic language. The boyar conspirators already had
established direct contact with the king and had rendered him a
valuable service by warning him the tsar had his eye on the Polish
throne. The conspiracy against Otrepev included individuals in whom
the pretender placed implicit trust—Vasilii Golitsyn, Marfa Nagaia,
the Shuiskii brothers, who had returned from exile, Mikhail Tatishchev, and other men of conciliar rank. The conspirators quietly conducted agitation against Dmitrii among those who still held firm and
spread tales about the ruler designed to harm him as much as possible.
They also organized attacks on his person. Early in September, 1605
some monks were arrested and under torture one admitted he had been
bribed to poison the tsar.

Early in January, 1606 the conspirators made another attempt to
eliminate the pretender. In the dead of night unknown persons succeeded in eluding the fusilier guards and penetrated the royal bedchamber. The palace was aroused. Not taking time to dress the pretender
snatched up a weapon and rushed with two fusilier captains, Fedor
Briantsev and Ratmin Durov, to hunt for the assassins. He managed
to apprehend three men, but they refused to talk and were hastily
executed.[5] These attacks posed no problems for the boyars because
the pretender entrusted the investigations to none other than the conspirators themselves, who at once covered up any leads to those more
prominent.

Alarmed by these attempts on his life, Otrepev acquired a new
palace guard composed of foreign mercenaries. Captain Domoracki,
who had accompanied the pretender on his original campaign against
Moscow, assembled 100 men to form a cavalry detachment and a

Frenchman, Jacques Margeret, commanded 100 spearmen. Two additional units were comprised of Germans living in the Foreign Suburb of Moscow. The tsar commandeered a number of houses in the Arbat and Chertole regions close to the Kremlin walls to provide quarters for his mercenary guards. He now could summon them at any time, day or night. The foreigners watched over the interior palace rooms and escorted the ruler wherever he went. Otrepev had no chance to build up a real mercenary force in Moscow because just when events were taking a serious turn he was forcibly reminded of Jerzy Mniszech, his original commander-in-chief, and Marina, his bride-to-be.

Meanwhile, Dmitrii had built a spacious new palace that rose above the threefold Kremlin wall. He was fond of hunting foxes, wolves, and above all, bears. A pack of the best hunting dogs would be released to attack a bear in an enclosure, or a skillful hunter with a spear would overcome the ferocious animal in single combat.

In preparation for war with the Tatars Otrepev had a mobile fortress built, a device the Russians had long used in their conflicts with the Crimea. It consisted of wagons which had wooden walls and contained cannon. When an alarm sounded the wagons were joined together in a circle. Dmitrii adorned the wooden walls of the mobile fortress with pictures of devils and the nether world. The small cannon poking through the apertures emitted what seemed to be the fires of hell. Early in winter Dmitrii positioned Hell near the palace windows on the ice of the Moscow river and indulged in war games before the people. His guards stormed a small fort containing boyars. The pretender enjoyed his mock war with the boyars, for he liked to display bravado and embarrass his courtiers. Snowballs served as weapons and the warriors left the battlefield covered with welts and bruises.

At night the tsar enjoyed other diversions. The former monk seemed to be trying to make up for lost time. Together with Basmanov and Molchanov, he gave himself over to unrestrained debauchery with any who took his fancy—married women, pretty girls, and nuns. His boon companions were generous, but when money would not avail they used threats and violence. The palace contained many secret doors. Women were brought there under cover of darkness and disappeared into unknown labyrinths. The Dutchman Isaac Massa, who knew of the secret life that went on in the palace, wrote that Dmitrii must have left behind him several dozen illegitimate children. Most were born after his death.

A scandalous report linked Otrepev with Kseniia Godunova. Deprived of her father and mother, Kseniia was staying in the women's wing of Prince Mosalskii's house. The princess became another of the pretender's trophies. Tsar Boris had much loved his daughter and took pains with her education. Kseniia learned how to read and write. She received musical training and loved to sing. Concerned for her future, Boris tried to find her a husband everywhere; envoys negotiated in London, Vienna, and remote Georgia. Gustav, a Swedish prince, and Johann, a Danish count, were invited to Moscow.

While Godunov was still alive a lament filled with sorrow for the orphan was composed in Moscow .

> "A tiny bird laments, a little white dove;
> Alas, alack, the young princess
> bewails her woe in Moscow.
> Alas, alack, youth grieves.
> A traitor advances on Moscow;
> 'Tis he, Grisha Otrepev, the defrocked one.
> He wishes to ensnare me.
> Ensnaring, me he wants to tonsure;
> Put a dark habit on me;
> He wishes to breach the *terem*;*
> He wants to seize me, a princess,
> And pack me off to iron Ustiug.
> He wishes to tonsure me, a princess,
> To immure me in a barred hell.
> Oh woe is me!
> Must I enter a dark cell?"[6]

*[the women's quarters—ed.].

In those far off times girls were affianced at twelve or thirteen. Over twenty, Kseniia was considered an old maid although the princess was an enviable catch. Contemporaries praised her modesty and decorous speech. They described a genuine Russian beauty, well-proportioned, with white skin and a ruddy complexion. Thick hair fell to her shoulders and her great black eyes sparkled.

Compared with the well-formed Kseniia, Otrepev looked like a misshapen dwarf. Squat and much less than medium height, he was disproportionately broad in the shoulders, had almost no waist, and his neck was short like a bull's. His arms were exceptionally strong and unusually long. His face was a blend of coarseness and strength. The pretender bore not the slightest semblance to a tsar. In the sixteenth century people esteemed a beard as a sign of manliness. Dmitrii looked like a eunuch; his round wrinkled face sported neither beard nor moustache. He was portrayed wearing large beards, the biggest of which was hung below his thick nose and resembled a boot. The harsh, morose gaze of his little eyes completed the dismal impression. Once in Otrepev's power Kseniia was debauched. It is easy to imagine the feelings she entertained for the man who had murdered her mother and brother.

In spite of his diversions the tsar had not given up his plans to marry Marina Mniszech. It looked as though the bridegroom had forgotten his betrothed while his fortunes ran high (he had not thought to invite her to his coronation) but he remembered the Mniszech family when his throne began to totter. By autumn couriers were overtaking one another on their way to Sambor bearing impatient missives from Otrepev. It was the pretender's fear of his uncertain future, not love, that prompted the haste.

Marina Mniszech was neither beautiful nor striking. Artists, whom the palatine of Sambor generously recompensed, tried hard to improve her looks but even in her official portrait the future queen's countenance did not appear especially attractive. Thick lips, denoting pride and vengefulness, a stretched-out visage widening at the bottom, too long a nose, thin black hair, a frail body and a diminutive stature— this was very far from what was then considered beauty. Like her father, Marina was inclined to adventurism and her passion for luxury and prodigality actually surpassed his. No one could divine what her real thoughts were. She knew how to write but not once during her long separation from her fiance did she take up a pen and pour out her heart to him. Marina's feelings towards Otrepev were a combination of vanity and calculation.

The boyar council and Orthodox clergy would not hear of a marriage between their tsar and a Catholic. Marina was an unexceptionable choice in every respect. Her family was not of noble blood; it was steeped in debt, and had long been on the verge of ruin. Otrepev kept the boyars and princes of the church out of the marriage negotiations entirely. He used a crown secretary, Afanasii Vlasev, as his go-between. His humble origins contrasted sharply with the nature of his mission. A Muscovite embassy estimated at 300 men brought genuinely regal gifts to Poland. The ambassador gave Jerzy Mniszech the tsar's own fur coat, a raven horse with gold trappings, a jeweled rifle, carpets, and furs. The gifts for the bride, on display at the king's residence, provoked universal wonder. There was a boat made of precious stones sailing on silver waves, valued at 60,000 rubles, a casket shaped like a golden bull, filled with emeralds, rings, bejeweled crosses and huge precious stones, a gold elephant-clock equipped to play tunes, mobile figurines, and piles of brocade and filigree.

In November, 1605 the Polish nobility solemnly celebrated Dmitrii's wedding with Marina at the king's castle in Cracow. Secretary Afanasii Vlasev stood in as proxy for the tsar. In spite of the outward pomp the ceremony did not go off smoothly. Finding himself before a Catholic altar surrounded by wicked heretics, Vlasev delivered the groom's greeting to the bride with noticeable lack of enthusiasm. When a cardinal asked him whether the tsar was pledged to another the secretary shot back: "How should I know? Nobody gave me instructions about that."[7] This answer, which provoked laughter in the hall, was not an example of Muscovite barbarism. Vlasev deservedly was considered a skilled diplomat; his prank showed that the secretary disapproved of his own sovereign's actions.

Jerzy Mniszech sent letters to his future son-in-law imploring him for money to discharge his enormous debts. In December, 1605 he found out about the tsar's liaison with Kseniia Godunova and immediately rebuked him: "Insofar as the notorious princess, Boris' daughter, is close to you, be so good as to take the advice of those who mean you well and get rid of her."[8] In no position to go against his father-in-law, the pretender had to sacrifice fair Kseniia. She was tonsured and hidden away in a remote nunnery in Beloozero.

Dmitrii's envoys brought 200,000 gold pieces and a further 6,000 gold doubloons to Sambor. It was not only because he was anxious to cover his debts that Otrepev sent his future father-in-law such colossal amounts. The Sambor proprietor had been instructed to raise another mercenary army for Dmitrii and bring it quickly to Moscow. The mercenaries were demanding large sums and Mniszech was at his wits' end. In Sambor they were hurriedly making new dresses and getting together a dowry worthy of a tsar's bride. At the same time Mniszech's agents were buying large quantities of weapons and recruiting soldiers everywhere. The funds proved inadequate; his representatives obtained 14,000 gold pieces from the tsar's envoys and acquired furs and cloth valued at 12,000 gold pieces from Muscovite merchants.

The intrigues were steadily becoming more complex. Finding himself in an impossible position, the pretender was beguiled by the hope that a revolt in Poland would hand him the crown and his troubles

would be over. Opposition was rife in the Rzeczpospolita and Sigismund was expecting an attack any day. The Mniszech family had been
behaving with extreme duplicity and the king did all he could to
facilitate its departure for Moscow. He issued a moratorium on Jerzy's
debts and let him gather his army without interference. Many gentry
and unemployed mercenaries, who might well have supported the bur-
geoning rebellion, left Poland with him.

The tsar's bride and her suite reached Moscow on May 2, 1606. The
inhabitants derived a strong impression that an army, not a marriage
train, had entered their city. Infantry with rifles marched ahead,
followed by knights completely encased in iron plate and carrying
spears and swords. The same hussars who had accompanied the
pretender at the start of his campaign proudly pranced along the streets
of Moscow. Uniformed gentry followed Marina's carriage, which was
escorted by throngs of armed retainers. The guests obligingly were
shown to the residences where they were intended to lodge. Scores of
baggage carts disappeared down side streets and behind the gates of
houses. The Muscovites' astonishment was complete when servants
started unloading household goods. Dragoons removed trunks and
bundles from carts and carried armfuls of weapons upstairs.

Feeling the ground slipping away under his feet, Dmitrii instinctively expected he would be saved by those who earlier had helped him
spread his wings and soar. Jerzy Mniszech, his original commander-
in-chief, and the knights stood once more at his side. But reports of
treason were coming in from every quarter and Otrepev had run out
of options. He was trying to play a risky game all over again and now
his power and his very life were at stake.

Chapter Three

THE FALL OF GRIGORII OTREPEV

Dmitrii's administration had not improved the people's lot. The
inhabitants of Moscow's town sector again grew restless; the boyars'
agitation merely compounded the situation. The pretender had to take
the people into consideration whether he wanted to or not. He made
an example of a few chancellery officials accused of wrongdoing. At

bazaars, heralds proclaimed the Good Tsar would receive petitions from the people twice a week on the Red Porch,[1] but Muscovites had no opportunity to take advantage of their sovereign's graciousness. Dmitrii ordained that the laws of the Muscovite realm should be collected and codified but the crown secretaries failed to obey even this royal edict. Taxes remained as burdensome as they had been before. The new administration had to cope with open disobedience on the part of the rural population when it tried to squeeze out extra revenue and supplementary imposts. Contemporaries noted that the tsar's taxation policies had begun to weigh heavily upon his subjects.

Popular movements declined after the Godunov dynasty was overthrown but pockets of peasant resistance continued to smoulder in remote outposts of the realm. Ataman Smaga Chertenskii and his comrades returned from Moscow to Razdory [the cossack capital—ed.] on the Don river. Munificent rewards had reconciled them to the autocrat. For the moment the Quiet Don was genuinely peaceful but the distant Terek region was in ferment. Large numbers of free cossacks, fugitive serfs, and runaway slaves deceived in their expectations had gathered there. In faraway Moscow the sovereign once more was surrounded by evil councillors, the wicked boyars; cossacks must look to their own interests. On the Terek 300 cossacks decided to march on Moscow and set on the throne another heir, Petr, one of their number, who proclaimed himself son of Tsar Fedor Ivanovich. The cossacks got the idea of having a tsar of their own from their comrades, runaway slaves who had been in the boyars' service. The choice lay between two young cossacks, Ileika from the town of Murom and Mitka, son of an Astrakhan fusilier. Mitka begged off on the grounds he had never been to Moscow. Ileika had spent a few months there in the service of an undersecretary. Since he had once resided in the capital he was called upon to assume the role of heir. Leaving the mouth of the Terek river the cossacks pushed past Astrakhan into the Volga region.[2] The uprising soon spread. Heir Petr had no worry about increasing the size of his force. Mobs of the commons flocked to him from all over; the mutiny was threatening to turn into a peasant war at any moment. The rebels occupied three Volga forts and seized cannon they found in them. They stubbornly pressed north along the Volga, plundering merchant caravans as they went. Petr soon had some 4,000 men in his service. Cossack atamans guiding the Heir sent menacing letters to Moscow, demanding the throne should pass to the son of Fedor Ivanovich, the last legitimate tsar.

The alarmed authorities watched the signs of popular discontent multiplying. This unwelcome turn of events stimulated the boyar council to reform the laws affecting slaves and indentured peasants. Circumstances had rendered it imperative to offer concessions to the commons but the council members, possessing as they did many slaves and peasants, refused to make sacrifices. It was only after lengthy debate that the council approved a decree on slaves on January 7 and one on peasants on February 1, 1606. After the death of the Defrocked One chancellery officials struck Tsar Dmitrii's name from the laws but it is virtually certain Otrepev had had something to do with framing them. Witnesses asserted he met daily with his senate, listened attentively to the boyars' views, and then dictated a decision to scribes. A fine speaker, Dmitrii loved to orate and act like a teacher instructing pupils. Ivan's putative son had been a boyar slave; his experiences had prepared him to discuss these new laws.

Boris Godunov once had forbidden masters to bequeath indentured slaves; a master's death sundered the ties of dependency. This system worked hardship for the gentry and its members found ways to circumvent it. A master would designate his son or brothers as joint owners of an indentured slave. Such abuses as this provoked discontent on the part of the indentured, who refused to consider themselves slaves for life and harbored genuine aspirations to become free again. The new law categorically forbade two proprietors to list indentured individuals in both names and stipulated that victims of such abuse must be freed. Any attempt to transfer an indentured man through inheritance by amending an existing contract now automatically entailed granting a slave his freedom. This law was not applicable to boyars, Moscow nobles, or clergy. Only petty slaveowners like lesser boyars, chancellery people, merchants, and prominent traders had to pay a penalty if they perpetrated such abuses.[3]

Dmitrii and the council dealt with the peasantry even more conservatively than Boris Godunov had done. There was no longer the slightest question of reinstituting the provisions of St. George's Day even temporarily (say for a year). During the famine, masses of enserfed peasants, receiving no aid from their landlords, sought salvation on the fertile steppe frontier, where they could survive lean years more easily. The new law forbade original owners to bring back peasants whom dire want and poverty had forced to flee during the famine to remote frontier areas (150 to 200 miles or more), or from the frontier to the center, or from one town to another. Peasants whom poverty had forced into indenture during those years likewise were not to be returned. However, if a peasant had been dragooned into indenture he was to be restored to his former condition. The law did not envision freedom for fugitives; it merely confirmed their status as serfs or slaves to new masters.[4] There was no question of making concessions to indentured peasants; they were made to the ranks of the gentry who had managed to attract peasants from elsewhere trying to save themselves from dying of hunger to till their farms or lands. The decree especially favored landlords in the black-earth region stretching from Chernigov and Novgorod-Seversk to Riazan. Servingmen in this area had been the first to favor the pretender and he had not forgotten them.

Although the law made an exception for peasants ruined during the famine, it reaffirmed the inviolability of Godunov's statute providing that peasants could be tracked down and returned to their original masters during a period of up to five years.

Otrepev consciously was orienting his policy to favor the Russian gentry. Even those condemning the man they called a vile heretic were surprised at his strong regard for the military. In the palace Dmitrii often loudly proclaimed he was happy to follow his father in rewarding the military because "all monarchs glory in their soldiers and knights (gentry) who uphold them; they enhance the state and menace its enemies."[5]

Those of Dmitrii's councillors whose task it was to estimate treasury outlays calculated that during his first six months the ruler spent seven and a half million gold pieces, or more than two million Russian rubles. The lion's share went to the nobility and gentry. Silver rained down on their heads during the coronation. A few months later Dmitrii decided to conduct a general review of the gentry all over the country in order to make sure they had adequate allotments and salaries. Contemporaries averred this was a means whereby he sought to curry favor with everybody, reward all members of the gentry, and, as he thought, to become beloved.

His increasing differences with the nobility caused Otrepev to solicit support directly from the gentry at large. In order to do so he was prepared to broaden the gentry's elective, representative institutions. Boris Godunov had invited as delegates with voting powers those whom provincial gentry chose to attend national assemblies. Otrepev tried to establish direct contact with elected representatives from the districts. In order to take their interests fully into consideration he ordered them to elect and send to Moscow representatives "with

petitions about equality in land allotments and salaries."[6] These elected representatives had the right to submit petitions directly to Tsar
Dmitrii Ivanovich. The impoverished petty gentry had not managed
to recover from the great famine. To satisfy their needs would require
thousands upon thousands of acres of land and the treasury did not have
any such amounts available. These pressing problems affected the
pretender's military plans. Peresvetov [a sixteenth-century publicist
who favored strong monarchical power—ed.] once suggested to Ivan
IV that it was improper to leave the fertile steppe lands—"a heaven
on earth"—in Muslim hands. Otrepev shared this view. The Crimean
khan had refused to help him; as soon as he was ensconced in Moscow
the tsar prepared for war.

Preoccupied with a series of campaigns against Hungary, the Crimean Tatars had refrained from attacking Russia for a whole decade,
but the Azov Tatars continued to break the peace, frequently raiding
the area around the town of Riazhsk and causing much damage to Don
Cossack enclaves. The southern frontiers were in a state of undeclared
war. Late in 1605 the cossacks achieved a spectacular success; they
captured Dosmagmet, commandant of Azov, and brought him to
Moscow.

The Don cossacks' triumph elated Dmitrii, who long had been
intrigued by the prospect of a decisive assault on the Turks and Tatars.
As a secret Catholic, the Orthodox tsar often and impatiently had urged
the Vatican to form a coalition against the Turks comprised of the
Catholic states, the Habsburg empire, Spain, and the Rzeczpospolita—
and Orthodox Russia. His timing was not particularly auspicious. The
pope cautiously advised him: "Let the tsar take the field first; let him
draw Europe in, and cover himself with eternal glory."[7]

The Habsburgs were preparing for peace negotiations with the Ottoman empire and had no intention of joining an anti-Turkish league.
Sigismund III was trying to get Dmitrii involved in a war with the Turks
but he had no wish to ally himself with the tsar in the enterprise. In
1606 Moscow learned the king had declined the pope's call to adhere
to an anti-Turkish coalition. Although he had no allies in Europe,
Dmitrii did not abandon his war plans because the Russian gentry
enthusiastically supported them. A thrust to the south would free the
holdings of southern landholders from ceaseless nomad raids and give
proprietors a chance to acquire new lands. With the aid of the allied
armies of the Don Otrepev calculated he would soon take Azov. Its
fall would clear the Turks from the Don region and drive a broad wedge

between the territory the Tatars held in the Crimea and in the northern Caucasus.

The fortress of Elets became the staging area for the Azov campaign. Moscow sent siege engines and field artillery to the place and built warehouses to hold the huge amounts of military equipment and supplies. By spring 1606 preparations for the campaign were well advanced. Contingents of soldiers kept arriving in Elets from all over the country. But the pretender's plans were not destined to be fulfilled.

Orthodox priests remembered how they had pronounced anathema on the wicked defrocked monk and heretic. Seeing the pretender at close quarters rekindled their suspicions. Dmitrii had decided his Catholic friends should not stand at his side but his closest aides were Protestants, the brothers Buczynski. The tsar assigned the Jesuits a large building in which to worship, and on occasion he would secretly invite them to meet with him in the Kremlin.

Payment of gentry salaries and preparations for war had depleted the treasury. Faced with financial difficulties, Otrepev decided to improve his position at the expense of the church. He extracted 3,000 rubles from the Joseph of Volokolamsk monastery, 5,000 rubles from the Kirillo-Belozersk monastery, and 30,000 from the Trinity-St. Sergius cloister. That was merely a beginning. Impoverished gentry were casting greedy eyes on the inexhaustible wealth the monasteries enjoyed. Otrepev eagerly discussed with his Protestant advisors plans for partially secularizing church revenues to benefit the treasury and gentry. Up to now churchmen had forgiven the pretender for maintaining suspicious ties with Catholics and Protestants but to encroach on their purses was the last straw.

The tsar's engagement to Marina Mniszech poured oil on the fire. Fanatics considered the tsar's bride a pagan and heretic. Hermogen, archbishop of Kazan, demanded she be baptized a second time but Patriarch Ignatii refused to support him. To help the tsar, the pliant Greek agreed to do no more than perform the ceremony of annointing, which was supposed to take place after a person had renounced Catholicism. Dmitrii managed to shatter the clergy's opposition. On January 10, 1606 the Jesuits close to him reported that opponents of the tsar's marriage had been punished but none was executed. Dmitrii also mentioned this to Buczynski on his return from Poland: "I have gotten rid of any archbishop who has contumaciously tried to talk me out of my marriage and refuses to bless the match. Now no one dares utter a word; they meekly perform my bidding."[8] The contentious Hermogen, the first to be punished, was packed off to his diocese in Kazan and shut up in a monastery. Dmitrii's clerical opponents fell silent. But not for long.

Agitation against the pretender fueled by the boyar conspirators and abetted by princes of the church and monks was intensifying and growing stronger. It became so serious that Elder Elena, a holy fool, started predicting the tsar would die at his wedding feast. Dmitrii was at once informed of her prophecy but he merely laughed.

His exposure could not be long delayed. Friends and enemies alike declared the tsar was a pretender. Otrepev could not even count on the veterans with whom he had initially concerted his intrigue. Early traitors, the Khripunov brothers who had fled to Lithuania, had been the first to acknowledge the fugitive monk as Dmitrii. After Otrepev became tsar one brother returned to Russia. At the frontier he met an old acquaintance, Captain Borsza, who had accompanied the tsar from Putivl to Moscow. Swearing him to secrecy, Khripunov told Borsza that Moscow already knew the tsar was not the true Dmitrii and would soon be disposed of, for he was nothing but an impostor.

Similar discussions took place not only in roadside taverns and on streets but in the rooms of the tsar's closest confederates in the palace. Once, after a friendly wassail, the mercenary Konrad Bussow stayed behind in Petr Basmanov's house after the other guests had left. When they were alone the German asked his host whether the sovereign was genuine. Basmanov replied: "Pray for him. He is not the son of Tsar Ivan Vasilevich but he is still our sovereign."[9]

The pretender had ample detractors. Ivan Bezobrazov told the Poles that when he was a child his family had been neighbors of the Otrepev family; their homes had adjoined one another in Moscow. Yushka Otrepev used to play with the Bezobrazov boys. After mounting the throne the pretender could not rely even on friends from his youth. Bezobrazov helped the boyars organize the conspiracy against the tsar.

The nobles opposed to the tsar already were quarreling over who should succeed him while he was still on the throne. Diplomatic considerations impelled the boyars to offer the Cap of Monomakh to Wladyslaw [son of the Polish king, Sigismund III—ed.]. The prince's candidacy was raised in order to prevent a split that would doom the conspiracy to failure. A Catholic prince on the throne found little favor with most Muscovites. Wladyslaw's opponents bethought themselves of Tsar Simeon Bekbulatovich, who once had been placed on the Muscovite throne by Ivan IV himself. Rumors concerning Simeon reached the court and Otrepev decided it would be a good idea to end the secular career of the baptized khan. On March 25, 1606 Simeon was tonsured and taken under guard to the Kirillov monastery in Beloozero.

The Moscow garrison contained 5,000 fusiliers, commanded by Petr Basmanov and loyal to the tsar, who guarded the Kremlin. As long as they stayed faithful to the ruler the conspirators were not likely to succeed, but by early March the guard began to vacillate. Many said openly the tsar was not the true Dmitrii. When their words came to Basmanov's attention he conducted a discreet but thorough investigation and arrested seven fusiliers. The authorities usually disposed of traitors without undue publicity, but this time the tsar decided to hold a show trial. The fusiliers were told to assemble without their weapons in the Kremlin on a certain day. The sovereign appeared before them surrounded by his German guards. Once again he repeated the oft-told tale of his miraculous deliverance and inquired whether they had any proof he was not the true tsar. His speech, which had been so often repeated, failed to produce its previous effect but everyone was alerted when the pretender called on those present openly to state reasons why they did not believe in him.

To punish all who had been engaged in covert agitation would have led to massive slaughter among the fusiliers. The pretender shrank from taking such a step for fear of losing military support. He did no more than hand the seven troublemakers over to their fellows to deal with. A conciliar courtier, Grigorii Miliutin, made a sign to the loyal fusiliers, who tore the condemned men to pieces on the spot. The bodies of the slain were carried through the city in an open cart in an effort to frighten conspirators. This savage execution temporarily checked loose talk. Some were afraid to say another word, but others were outraged and showed their impatience.

The situation in the Kremlin was getting out of hand, as an event that took place in the palace in early April well illustrated. Otrepev invited the boyars to a banquet and offered them choice viands, including roast veal. Vasilii Shuiskii started quietly scolding the tsar for his violation of church rules. The sovereign interrupted him but Mikhail Tatishchev, who was considered a favorite of the tsar, intervened in the quarrel. His father had done Ivan IV many a good turn, for which he had been appointed a conciliar courtier in the oprichnina. Mikhail had not done anything outstanding for Dmitrii, but although he was of humble origin the ruler had made him an associate boyar. Tatishchev sternly took the sovereign to task for eating unclean food. To punish such presumption Otrepev ordered Tatishchev banished to Viatka and confined in a prison well "so as to efface all memory of him." He confiscated Tatishchev's estate and gave it to a member of the Polish gentry who had recently arrived.

The Tatishchev affair alarmed the conspirators, who did everything in their power to free their confederate. Vasilii Golitsyn had initiated Petr Basmanov into the plans for a rising against Godunov in the camp at Kromy. In Moscow he was more cautious. Basmanov invariably obeyed his relative and entrusted him with his secrets. The conspirators could not imagine a more powerful intercessor. The commander of the fusilier garrison, to whom the pretender had entrusted his safety, became like putty in their hands. Basmanov earnestly entreated the sovereign to forgive Tatishchev and the entire boyar council intervened on behalf of this champion of piety. Dmitrii had to rescind his order and have the seditious associate boyar quickly brought back to Moscow. The incident showed how completely dependent Otrepev had become on the senate he had formed.

As the ground slipped from under his feet the pretender found consolation in conversations with his secret friends, the Jesuits. He introduced them into the palace mostly at night. Amid the illusory trappings of power the tsar complained bitterly of loneliness. He said the time would come when he could surround himself with educated foreigners and assign the chief duties in the realm to them. The ceremonials of court life required the autocrat to spend much time during the day in the company of his boyars. Dmitrii's Polish advisors were surprised at this and planned to put an end to the tsar's close association with the nobility. They even thought of transferring the capital from Moscow to some other place.

The pretender was stronger in the provinces than the capital but even there unrest was growing. Rebellious units once again were operating in the lower Volga region, although their leaders' purposes were as yet unclear. The name of Good Dmitrii still continued to be as popular as before in remote hamlets and many cossack villages. The southern provinces occupied a special place in Dmitrii's political calculations. On mounting the throne Otrepev had tried to reward the inhabitants of the Seversk towns who had supported him at the crucial moment. As he coped with opposition among the capital leaders the pretender thought more and more often about the Seversk and southern steppe towns, on the loyalty of whose inhabitants he could apparently rely.

Domestic political considerations indirectly influenced Otrepev's conduct of foreign affairs. Preparing for war now with the Tatars, now with King Sigismund, the pretender considered the southern provinces his main base of operations. The fortress of Elets was designated the place where the gentry levy and the country's whole military force should muster. The tsar emptied the treasury and extorted loans from monasteries in order to maintain the gentry and gain its sympathy. The pretender proposed to depart for the army on the southern frontier immediately after his marriage. Surrounded by the gentry levy in Elets Dmitrii might feel safe from boyar conspirators; he would be inaccessible to them and far more formidable.

Otrepev assumed the arrival of the Mniszech family and a mercenary army would shore up his crumbling position in Moscow, but the Mniszech family brought enemies as well as friends to the pretender. Sigismund had sent Alexander Gosiewski as his envoy to Moscow and at a Kremlin reception he cruelly humiliated Otrepev by calling him no more than "grand prince." Sigismund refused to allow his former protege to be addressed even as tsar, to say nothing of emperor. The pretender was forced to swallow the affront. A few days later he invited one of his Jesuit friends to a private audience and told him that 100,000 men were massed in Elets under his banners. All that force needed to attack an enemy was a sign from him, but he had not yet decided whether he would send it against the Turks or someone else. Dmitrii then straightway launched into a tirade about the insults the Polish king had inflicted upon him. He had no doubt his words would soon reach the person they were intended for.

Otrepev knew that disaffected Polish gentry secretly were preparing a rising against Sigismund. The king's position would indeed be unenviable if the rebels received military aid from the Muscovite tsar. Aware of the danger threatening him, Sigismund was ready to make a pre-emptive strike against his former protege. He had named Gosiewski his envoy deliberately; he was in close contact with the boyar conspirators. Mniszech's arrival with the army cheered Dmitrii but the success had been purchased at a high political cost that far outweighed any military advantage. Otrepev's marriage to Marina, concluded against the wishes of the boyar council and the clergy, had confounded the situation utterly.

The royal wedding was to be celebrated on Sunday, May 4, 1606, but it did not take place at the appointed time. The clergy and boyars needed a few more days to complete procedures for marrying Marina to the tsar and her coronation. The bridegroom secretly asked the pope for permission to annoint and administer Marina communion in the Orthodox style, for unless this was done she could not become the

Muscovite queen. The Vatican refused categorically. Fearing a church scandal, Otrepev decided to hold the wedding and the coronation simultaneously. The Orthodox clergy and council agreed to honor his wishes only after serious objections and quarrels.

The wedding took place on May 8 in the palace. In the morning the young couple were escorted to the banquet house, where Fedor, a court archpriest, solemnly united them. Prince Shuiskii greeted the bride briefly in the Palace of Facets and the newlyweds were conducted to the Cathedral of the Dormition, where the patriarch solemnly crowned Marina with a royal crown, annointing her only. To Russians' great dismay the queen did not take communion as the formula worked out by the council had stipulated.

This was a dark moment for Otrepev. Many of those present could not conceal their embarrassment and indignation. Murmurs were heard in the cathedral and the crowd's agitation communicated itself to the young couple. Right up to the moment of the ceremony the pretender was prey to nagging doubts. He confided his fears to Buczynski: "At the very moment I was being married I was greatly afraid because Orthodox law provides that the bride must first be baptized and only after that be conducted into church, but an unbaptized person of another faith may not enter a church. I was particularly afraid the hierarchs might prove stubborn, withhold their blessing, and refuse to annoint."[10] Otrepev had been obliged to endure many humiliations during his short life. He never forgot them and they seared his soul even at times of greatest triumph. The mask might fall from his face at any moment; he endured instances of inexpressible terror over and over again.

To crown Marina in the Cathedral of the Dormition was an unprecedented innovation. Pious zealots termed the ceremony absolutely illegal. In Godunov's time people had begun chanting *Long Life* to Orthodox queens but contemporaries had considered even this harmless innovation as monstrously shameful. Marina's refusal to take communion angered the Orthodox but pleased the envoys and Polish guests. The coronation was no sooner over than deacons invented various excuses to get the envoys and foreigners out of the cathedral and locked the doors behind them. Once the unwelcome visitors were gone the patriarch crowned Marina and the tsar in the Orthodox manner.

The Polish ladies who had remained with the bride laughed when they described to their husbands how the young couple received a small piece of bread and a sip of wine when the patriarch gave them his blessing. The spectators hailed the queen's conversion to Orthodoxy and that day Marina showed herself an apt pupil of the Jesuits. Ignoring the Vatican's prohibition, she took Orthodox communion without the slightest confusion or hesitation. Apostasy did not bother her much; her vanity was more engaged: did she look well in the Russian attire in which the boyars had insisted she be arrayed?

Although the nobles long had understood their sovereign's nature, they still assiduously acted out their parts. Grishka had merely to nod and Vasilii Shuiskii would bend slavishly over the throne and arrange the ruler's feet, which did not reach the floor, more comfortably on a stool. The Invincible Monarch's power was, however, no more than a shadow and monumental drama was beginning to look like farce. Boyars gazed down impassively on the short-statured pair without the slightest legal title to the throne, as they tried to appear imposing. Although the icons were hung low, the young couple could not reach them; servants had to place stools to enable them to do so.

The boyars had their own reasons for scheduling the wedding on the Thursday instead of the Sunday. Friday was St. Nicholas' Day, a highly revered Orthodox holiday. The pretender knew no restraint; scorning convention he arranged that the marriage feast should take place at an unsuitable time. In the palace Otrepev showered attentions upon the Mniszech family and the mercenaries they had brought from Poland. To the great indignation of Moscow nobles, he seated soldiers and lords' retainers at the festal board.

Everything about the tsar's wedding seemed strange to Russians. Boyars and clergy were shocked at the queen's costume. In Russia a woman was not considered fully dressed unless she wore at least three chemises—the inside one invariably of flannel and the outer of silk. The long sleeves of the blouse came together in large folds at the wrist. It was thought improper to be without a belt that fastened the blouse. One outer garment was a sarafan, or long sleeveless gown, over which another garment of velvet or brocade would be worn with artificial collars adorned with jewels. Women wore velvet shoes with high insteps. Unmarried boyar girls wore their hair in a plait and might go about bareheaded. Married women appeared in public in a headdress that concealed their hair, foreheads, and cheeks.

The palace tailors did their best to fit Queen Marina out properly but the Russian dress they made for her was not to her liking. She got rid of it right after the wedding and put on her usual costume. She was not particularly concerned over what Muscovites might say about her.

The crowd stared with intense curiosity at Marina during the brief times she left the palace. The tiny, vain Polish woman was utterly unlike former queens and noble Moscow boyar ladies.

Foreigners who visited Russia contemptuously described the passion Moscow women of fashion displayed for cosmetics, claiming they darkened their eyes and sometimes their teeth too, plucked their eyebrows, thickly whitened their faces, and heavily rouged their cheeks. Visitors were describing what struck them the most. They were beholding at close hand these prisoners of the women's quarter. Their makeup might well have been an indication of what people thought constituted beauty in that epoch. A Russian beauty was invariably sturdy and stately, with ruddy cheeks. In the last analysis, Marina's appearance furnishes no real clues to her character.

Monks muttered spitefully, but the people welcomed the new queen in a rather friendly way. On the wedding day a large crowd of Muscovites gathered at the palace windows and began applauding Marina, inviting her to come out on the porch. The new bride had no time for Muscovites. She had no intention of allowing them to interrupt her pleasures, even for a short time. At her insistence Dmitrii sent courtiers to tell the people not to shout any longer.

Dmitrii was anxious to entertain his hussars. Near the end of the festivities he actually announced he would bestow 100 rubles cash upon each of them. The boyars sitting at a distance found it hard to conceal their annoyance. They knew the tsar's treasury had long been empty.

Otrepev had quartered Mniszech's army in homes belonging to rich merchants, bishops, and courtiers. This turbulent lot showed no consideration for their hosts. Relying on the protection of the tsar they had made, they cleaned out storerooms without permission and locked Muscovites out of their own houses. Feeling affronted, the latter raised a hue and cry. The lords' retainers robbed those they came across on the street, insulted women, and looked for a chance to use their swords on anyone who resisted their violent ways. One evening some drunken dragoons stopped an elegant carriage on a street and dragged out a boyar's daughter. The retainers went after the girl and people from the town sector rushed to her aid. Somebody rang a bell and the dragoons fled. Those who had endured the affront tried to obtain redress at the palace against the perpetrators. Dmitrii pretended he would have the mercenary who had been apprehended at the scene of the crime tortured, but let him go unpunished.

The incessant lawless violence by the newcomers provoked a strong reaction among the people. Boyar agitation against the pretender acquired fresh forrader. After May 12 people started openly saying the tsar was a pagan and an unbaptized foreigner who did not keep St. Nicholas' Day, was remiss in attending church, and ate unclean food. Orthodox people assailed Dmitrii chiefly for flouting Muscovite religious customs. Heretics had never been allowed in the Cathedral of the Dormition but there they were in full force at the coronation. During service these godless ones (as they were called) laughed aloud, did not remove their hats, and sat wherever they pleased. Monks inclined to fanaticism quietly fueled the fires of hatred for those they termed accursed Latins. In a market the palace guard arrested several agitators bitterly assailing the tsar for apostasy. Dmitrii was alarmed and ordered those captured be tortured. Trying to allay his fears, the boyars assured Dmitrii these men were merely chatterers who were drunk and did not know what they were saying.

The arrival of the mercenary force did not so much stabilize as aggravate the situation in Moscow. The large population of the town sector, which the year before had overthrown Godunov in favor of Dmitrii, was now menacing the tsar it had created. A week after the royal wedding serious popular disturbances broke out in Moscow. A dragoon in the service of Prince Wisniowiecki murdered a man of the town and hid in the prince's house. The people besieged it, demanding Wisniowiecki surrender the guilty party. By nightfall some 4,000 people had gathered around the residence, threatening to smash it to pieces, and remained there until morning. The popular discontent took Dmitrii by surprise. He doubled patrols at the Kremlin and placed several thousand fusiliers on alert. Polish units kept vigil all night with their weapons at the ready. Now and then they fired into the air in hopes of deterring the Muscovites.

Next day Moscow was ominously quiet. Traders refused to sell foreigners powder and shot. The pretender received numerous warnings. Several times German mercenaries secretly tossed anonymous notes into his chambers and finally Jerzy Mniszech appeared in the palace with a host of denunciations. The tsar replied that none of his people had cause to assail the sovereign but if he, the tsar, noticed anything, all those in his power "would lose their lives in a single day."[11]

The confident attitude the pretender displayed could not conceal his real feelings from his entourage. During the wedding festivities he had been gloomy and withdrawn, at times extremely irritable. Otrepev knew a conspiracy existed but he had no idea that his favorites, who shamelessly fell at his feet to allay his suspicions, were the ones guilty of treason. Dmitrii was like a cornered animal. He turned this way and that but could find no refuge. In a moment of utter despair he bethought himself of the mutinous cossacks and secretly sent Tretiak Yurlov, a trusted courtier, to the Volga region. The courier was to establish contact with Heir Petr and order him to march on Moscow as soon as possible. Otrepev had forgotten that the days of Godunov were over. The Volga cossacks had not taken up arms against Boris but against his officials. Heir Petr was coming to Moscow to seize the throne. The boyars knew of Dmitrii's appeal; it spurred them to mature their plans.

The conspirators dogged the pretender and used his decrees against him. On May 12-13 Dmitrii requested cannon be moved outside the fortress gate and a fort made ready to entertain guests with fusillades and war games. The conspirators immediately disseminated a rumor that foreigners would slaughter boyars at the games. Their agitation was successful. Disturbances broke out again in the city on the evening of May 14. The conspirators summoned their supporters to arms, but Dmitrii's forces reached their posts in the nick of time. The Shuiskii and Golitsyn faction reconsidered and canceled the order for a rising at the last minute. Next day the tsar, acting on Basmanov's and Mniszech's advice, ordered several individuals arrested. The Kremlin guard was instructed to deal arbitrarily with suspicious persons. The night of May 16 three unknown men who had sneaked into the Kremlin were killed unceremoniously and three others were tortured.

After the disturbance was over, everyone in Moscow was saying that Crown Secretary Timofei Osipov, who had resolved to become a martyr for Orthodoxy, had come to the palace and openly charged that the tsar was a heretic and pretender. It was the conspirators who had concocted such a story in order to clothe the rebellion in the mantle of a man of blameless life. Margeret states that Osipov was arrested after revealing the conspirators' secret plans and tortured in Basmanov's presence. Osipov realized he would never come out alive and displayed rare fortitude. Lashed to a rack, he never stopped saying it was Grishka Otrepev, an accursed heretic, who sat on the throne. However, a man privy to the secrets of the conspiracy had fallen into the hands of the authorities. There was not a moment to lose.

Otrepev arose at dawn, as was his custom, on May 17. Basmanov, who had spent the night in the interior chamber, informed him that all had been quiet. Secretary Vlasev was waiting for the sovereign on the

Red Porch. After conferring with him Dmitrii went to his rooms. He noticed nothing amiss.

Meantime the conspirators, including as many as 200 armed gentry, already were on their way to the Kremlin. The boyars had arranged to make their move at the time when the palace guard was changing. Margeret, commander of the lead unit of spearbearers, was ill and absent from the palace. Rumor had it that he favored the conspiracy and personally had ordered the interior guard to withdraw from the tsar's chambers, so that no more than thirty men were left. The fusiliers stationed at Frolov gate knew Vasilii Shuiskii and Golitsyn by sight and showed no concern when the two boyars approached. The conspirators' assault took them by surprise and they fled without offering resistance. In control of the gate, Shuiskii and Golitsyn sounded the tocsin to rouse the people of the town sector. Not relying on his confederates alone, Shuiskii raced through Red Square to the trading stalls. The citizenry had been coming in to buy since the crack of dawn and thus considerable numbers of people were already there. Shuiskii told them to ring the bells in Ilin church. On hearing the sound Dmitrii sent Basmanov to find out what it meant. Dmitrii Shuiskii and other boyars, who had been watching the pretender like a hawk since morning, told him a fire probably had broken out.

The noise intensified and spread throughout the city. Shouts were heard: "The Kremlin's on fire! Let's go there! Let's go there!" Citizens everywhere rushed to Red Square. The noise aroused the pretender's supporters as well. Seizing their weapons, the foreigners hastened to the palace. Units near the Kremlin marched in battle formation with banners unfurled. A spirited attack might still have saved the pretender but the boyars managed to avert the danger. They called on the people to smite the "pagan Latins" and stand up for Orthodoxy. Heralds fanned out from the square in every direction, crying at the top of their lungs: "Brothers, the Poles are trying to murder the tsar and his boyars; don't let them in the Kremlin!"[12] The boyars' appeals fell upon fertile soil. A mob charged the Polish gentry and their retainers. Streets leading to the Kremlin were barricaded with beams and other obstacles. The wild riot prevented the foreigners from coming to hapless Dmitrii's aid. The mercenaries furled their flags and withdrew to barracks.

Events were reaching a climax on the square in front of the palace. Frightened by the noise, Dmitrii sent Basmanov from his chambers a second time and he reported on his return the mob was demanding the tsar should come out to them. The pretender would not risk an appearance on the Porch but leaned out of a window with an axe in his hands. Brandishing the weapon, he cried: "You'll learn I'm no Boris!" Several shots were fired at the window from the square and he hastily pulled back.

Basmanov sought to retrieve the situation. Appearing on the Red Porch, where all the boyars were assembled, he invoked the tsar's name in an attempt to persuade the people to calm down and disperse. A critical moment had arrived. Many were running to the palace to save the tsar from the Poles and there were more than a few fusiliers ready to obey their commander. The conspirators noticed the crowd was irresolute and moved quickly to put an end to the game they had begun. Coming up on Basmanov from behind, Tatishchev struck him with a dagger. Other conspirators hurled the twitching body from the Porch into the square.

This deed served as a signal to storm the palace. The mob charged into the forecourt and disarmed the spearmen. Otrepev and fifteen Germans barricaded themselves in the interior chambers. The noise grew louder. The door was shattered by attackers' blows. The pretender tore his hair. At last he threw away his weapon and took to his heels. At Marina's rooms Otrepev managed to cry out: "Treason, my love!" The craven tsar did not even try to save his wife. He used a secret passage to sneak from the palace to the stone chamber adjacent to it. A remote yard below the chamber windows was deserted and Otrepev quickly jumped out of one of them. Usually deft, this time he fell to the ground in a heap and sprained his leg. Fusiliers were standing guard at a gate to the stone chamber. Hearing Otrepev's cries they ran to his aid. Lifting the helpless tsar carefully they carried him from the yard into the building.

Failing to find Dmitrii in the palace, the rebels started looking all over the Kremlin for him and soon managed to discover where he had taken refuge. The pretender promised the fusiliers huge sums of gold if they would save him. The conspirators tried to seize the tsar. The fusiliers opened fire and wounded them but the forces were too unequal. A mob invested the entire chamber and burst in. The fusiliers threw down their arms.

Fallen into enemy hands, Otrepev knew the game was up but he still clung desperately to life. Lying there looking up at familiar faces the pretender humbly begged them to let him see his mother or convey him to the Place of Execution, where he might repent before the whole people. His enemies were implacable. One of the Golitsyn brothers deprived Grishka of his last hope of deliverance. He told the crowd that Marfa Nagaia had long since disowned the false tsar and did not consider him her son. Golitsyn's words ended all vacillation. Gentry tore the garment that was the sign of the autocrat off the fallen man. Driving away the fusiliers, the conspirators surrounded the writhing figure on the ground in a tight circle. Those close to Grishka beat him with their fists. Those who could not get nearer reviled him, interrupting each other: "Such tsars I have enough of in my stable at home! Who are you, you son of a bitch?" On horseback Vasilii Shuiskii cut through the crowd and invited the people to come closer and regale themselves with a sight of the Thief.

Afraid to let Otrepev out of their sight the conspirators rushed in for the kill before they left the chamber. Grigorii Valuev, a lesser boyar, moved up and fired a pistol at him. Ivan Voeikov, a courtier, hit him on the head with his sword. Then the conspirators cut and hacked the corpse lying on the ground until all signs of life were gone. The affair was over by approximately one in the afternoon. Otrepev's body was carried to Marfa Nagaia's residence. The people confronted Ivan's widow and she tremorously denied her putative son, calling him the Thief.

The mercenaries had not lived up to expectations. They had once abandoned Dmitrii on the frontier at a crucial juncture and now in Moscow they showed no more disposition to die for the man who paid their salaries, although some did try to force their way into the palace. They took a drubbing. At the same time the crowd fiercely was assailing foreigners who chanced to be out of doors, egged on by the conspirators and abetted by monks and priests. Under siege in their houses the Poles observed the turbulent monks from their windows. Elders were darting in and out of the mob, crying: "Smite the pagans!"

It was rumored abroad that as many as two thousand perished during the Moscow rising. Poles who witnessed the riot wrote down the names of those slain in their diaries. Comparison of these lists reveals that the victims of the uprising amounted to no more than twenty members of the gentry close to the pretender and some 400 servants and retainers.[13]

Envoy Gosiewski and his suite almost came to grief. By urging the conspirators to take resolute action he was responsible for the results of the disturbance. The king had not spared the pretender's supporters who had launched an armed uprising against him in Poland; his envoy saw no reason to spare the pretender's partisans in Moscow. When some Poles who had come with the Mniszech family knocked on the gate of Gosiewski's abode and asked for asylum, the envoy refused. The Poles had to seek refuge elsewhere. Vasilii Shuiskii and the other conspirators were anxious to shield the envoy and his retinue from the popular wrath. Directly after the rising they sent forces to protect his residence. In fostering the pretender's intrigue the Mniszech interests had dreamed of acquiring the fabled wealth of the Muscovite tsars. They had sewn the wind and reaped a whirlwind. The Mniszech family and their entire line were utterly despoiled.

The minute the pretender was dead the boyars hastened to end the bloodshed and restore order on the streets of the capital.

Chapter Four

REBELLION

After the pretender was murdered the boyars ordered his body thrown outside the gate into the square, shut themselves up in the Kremlin away from the people, and deliberated all night. The following morning they announced Patriarch Ignatii, head of the church, had been removed. Shortly before the coup Orthodox magnates in the Ukraine had sent a burgher from Lwow with a message for the patriarch. This courier informed him the tsar was a secret Catholic. After Dmitrii fell, this message came into boyar hands and the council used it to overthrow the patriarch. Its members knew Otrepev was an apostate as well as the head of the church did, but Ignatii was used as the scapegoat: the boyars held him solely responsible for crowning Dmitrii and Marina. The Greek was expelled ignominiously from the patriarchal palace and immured in the Miracles monastery.

Fearing popular disturbances might break out all over the country, the boyars completed the task of choosing a new tsar within a day or two. While Dmitrii was still alive the conspirators had promised the crown to Wladyslaw, heir to the Polish throne. The behavior of the mercenary army Mniszech had brought had been so disgraceful and the subsequent popular ferment had given rise to such outbursts of emotion that the issue of handing the throne over to a prince of another faith became moot. A remarkable change had taken place. It was not difficult for the boyars to renounce their pledge to King Sigismund. The struggle with his own domestic opposition consumed all his energies; Moscow had no reason to anticipate interference from that quarter.

The decision to choose a tsar from the ranks of the Muscovite nobility brought to an end the unanimity the council had achieved during the coup. All too many longed for the crown. The boyars fell to wrangling and quarreling incessantly among themselves. Shuiskii, Mstislavskii, and the Romanov and Golitsyn brothers vigorously courted support in council and among the people. The gentry favored their patrons and those who rewarded them.[1]

Ivan Nikitich Romanov, one of the conspirators, was unpopular in the capital and seriously ill. The ambitious Filaret Romanov was a monk and his son Mikhail was too young. The Romanov circle thus could not put forward a candidate for the throne.

Fedor Mstislavskii was a prime contender. His family had been first among the boyars since Ivan IV's time. He had not been involved in the conspiracy, which made his candidacy more attractive to boyars who owed their careers to Dmitrii. Mstislavskii's colorless nature constituted another advantage. Queen Marfa, who was related to him, Boyar Mikhail Nagoi, the master of horse, and his brothers, and Petr Sheremetev were his most ardent supporters. The Nagoi family understood that its power would cease unless one of their relatives occupied the throne.

Vasilii Shuiskii, the leader of the conspiracy, advanced his own candidacy. A scion of Aleksandr Nevskii's elder brother, he had as good a claim to the Muscovite throne as Ivan Kalita's line. A cunning, resourceful politician, Shuiskii possessed a far different reputation from that of Mstislavskii.

The boyar council was prepared to summon an assembly and to invite representatives from the provinces to elect the tsar. But the situation in Moscow was still critical and the boyars had to abandon their intention. The people would not lay down arms. No matter whom the council elected, its appointee would not retain power unless he enjoyed popular support. An appeal to the people appeared unavoidable.

Council members had just assembled in the Kremlin two days after the coup when bells rang all over the city. Soon a crowd filled Red Square. An impromptu assembly convened in the palace, including council, clergy, and many Moscow gentry, merchants, and traders. The assembly endorsed the two senior and most noble council members, Princes Fedor Mstislavskii and Vasilii Shuiskii, as candidates for the throne. The conciliar ranks left the final decision to the "whole Orthodox people." Appearing at the Place of Execution, leaders publicly presented the candidates the assembly had selected.

Mstislavskii was not popular. A featureless, weak-willed man, he failed to spark enthusiasm. The crowd was silent when a secretary announced his name. The people greeted Shuiskii's candidacy with shouts of approval. This decided the outcome. Watching the ceremony, Konrad Bussow observed that Shuiskii became tsar because only a handful of boyars and princes but all the merchants, shoemakers, and the rest of Moscow's inhabitants wished it.[2]

Muscovites had long known the senior courtier. In Dmitrii's time he had almost lost his head for championing Orthodoxy and with a cross in his hands he had urged on the mob against the heretic. As the head of the rebellious population Shuiskii had become the most popular man in the capital. Boyars and men from the town quarter escorted Prince Vasilii from the Place of Execution to the Cathedral of the Dormition, where the metropolitan of Krutitsa proclaimed him tsar and offered prayers for the occasion.

Vasilii Shuiskii's relations with the council were complicated. Almost a year earlier the boyars had condemned him to death and many feared his vengeance. The council's chief candidate was apparently Mstislavskii, not Shuiskii. Margeret, in the palace at the time, claimed that most of the nobles refused to vote for Shuiskii and the sceptre would unquestionably have passed to Mstislavskii if all had closed ranks at the electoral assembly.

In order to win a majority in council the tsar-designate had to sign a special covenant. When he was sworn in, the autocrat pledged not to execute courtiers or deprive them of their wives and children, patrimonial estates or other possessions, without a formal trial in which boyars would participate. The tsar could condemn the lower ranks, merchants and traders, to death on his own initiative but even then he was not to appropriate the property of the criminal's family. Shuiskii promised to refuse to listen to calumny, sternly to punish bearers of false witness and informers, and to judge everyone fairly and impartially.[3]

In the aftermath of the coup the capital remained tense and the situation fluid. Even after Shuiskii's elevation the boyars disposed of more actual power than did the tsar himself. The nobility lost no time advancing plans to limit the autocratic mode of government. An informed contemporary wrote that the conciliar lords still could not agree after the election: each great noble wanted to rule and the last thing any of them wanted to do was to share his revenues with the tsar. This was why they supported an idea that the realm should be divided into principalities.[4]

Mistrusting his brother princes, Shuiskii was not afraid to attach humble folk to his cause. Artemii Izmailov, a crown secretary, Vasilii Yanov, and a peasant, Mikhalko Smyvalov, were among his chief favorites. The same differences prevailed among churchmen as among the boyars but their situation was further complicated by the fact that the church had no head. Pafnutii, Otrepev's former mentor, had abandoned his cell in the Miracles monastery to become metropolitan of Krutitsa. He had played a prominent role in exposing the pretender and in the conpiracy against him. Now he expected to share the fruits of Shuiskii's success. It was he who had proclaimed Prince Vasilii tsar although only senior hierarchs, the metropolitans of Novgorod and Rostov, had the right to preside over such a ceremony.

After the tsar's election the boyar and ecclesiastical councils began to confer about naming a patriarch. Shuiskii's supporters were in a difficult position; they had failed to elevate Pafnutii to the patriarchal chair. The candidacy of Hermogen, Dmitrii's most violent opponent, had not prospered either. Most council votes unexpectedly went to Filaret, who had been Boyar Fedor Nikitich Romanov in secular life.

Elder Filaret had become a monk involuntarily. Tsar Boris had forcibly confined him to the Antoniev-Siiskii monastery in the far north. Filaret was overjoyed at the news of the pretender's success. Dmitrii brought Romanov back from exile, but he was in no hurry to restore him to court. Shortly before the coup Kirill, metropolitan of Rostov, had incurred the tsar's suspicion and was deposed. His empty seat went to Filaret Romanov, who enjoyed Otrepev's complete trust.

Why did the council and the princes of the church prefer figures like Mstislavskii and Romanov, who had demonstrated unquestioned loyalty to Dmitrii? The answer is obvious. The council still contained a variety of individuals who owed their careers to Otrepev. He had bestowed upon them ranks that were out of all proportion to their birth or service; they naturally feared for their positions and sought to avoid far-reaching changes.

After seizing Otrepev the coup leaders could have tried and convicted him of being a pretender but they preferred to kill him. For three days his mutilated corpse lay in the marketplace on Red Square. Hordes of people crowded around it morning and night. The pretender's enemies did not leave him alone even in death. His naked body was dragged hither and thither, kicked and abused, and spat upon. After this shameful interlude Otrepev was removed from the city, thrown into a pit, and pinned to the ground with a stake to prevent a man believed to be a sorcerer ever rising from the dead.

The murder of two sovereign autocrats in the space of a year was an unprecedented event in Russian history and was bound to astonish the subjects of the realm. Confused minds immediately detected a mass of ominous portents that foretold fresh disasters. One story went that flames burst forth from the grave of the fallen Dmitrii at night, strange singing was heard, and other weird things happened. The night after Otrepev's death an unexpected frost set in that lasted a whole week. Grain froze in the fields; grass and leaves withered on the trees. The frightened people attributed the misfortune to interference by supernatural powers. The werewolf, reaching out from the other world, magically had caused the cold wave.

Of course Dmitrii had friends as well as enemies. They spread rumors about the city that were damaging to Shuiskii. At dawn on the first Sunday after his elevation unknown persons affixed broadsheets to many homes claiming Dmitrii was alive; God Almighty had saved him a second time from traitors. These proclamations worried the people. Anxious crowds of Muscovites once more filled Red Square, demanding explanations from the boyars. They appeared at the Place of Execution and swore that God Almighty had punished the false tsar, the defrocked Otrepev, and the people would soon behold the remains of the true Dmitrii with their own eyes.

A master of petty intrigue, Shuiskii already had arranged to send the newly-elected patriarch to Uglich to obtain the body of Heir Dmitrii. The Uglich commission also included Petr Sheremetev and a few others who had opposed Shuiskii's election. By offering the office of head of the church to Metropolitan Filaret, Tsar Vasilii calculated he would win over the Romanov family and their influential line. Dmitrii's favorite, Ivan Khvorostinin, was sent off to repent in a monastery. Shuiskii deprived him of his rank of steward and straightway handed the office over to Filaret's nephew, Ivan Cherkasskii. However, the new tsar gained nothing by lavishing favors on boyars in the Romanov circle.

The coup had awakened earlier ambitions in the heart of Fedor Romanov. The former boyar had no intention of forsaking the church and returning to secular life (defrocked monks had a very bad name in Old Russia) but he had a nine-year old son, Mikhail, who had a claim to the throne because he was a nephew of Fedor, the last lawful tsar. The boyar council had rejected young Romanov's candidacy, but people throughout the country were speculating about the possibility he might be elected. In late May Germans in Narva quoted Russians as saying that a member of the Romanov family would someday be ruler of Russia.

Fedor Nikitich was an impatient man. As soon as he became patriarch he plunged headlong into intrigues. When the authorities investigated the source of the anonymous broadsheets the track led back to the Romanov faction. It appeared that Filaret Romanov himself had supplied the malcontents with these letters.

Men who had belonged to the slain pretender's closest circle were working hard to bring about the second coming of Dmitrii's shade. They included his chamberlain, Khvalibog, who refused to recognize that his sovereign was dead; his secretary, Stanislaw Buczynski, who told tales about a tsaric double; a cook, Mnishkov, and other persons of Polish origin. Almost all were closely watched and would have been powerless if influential Russian nobles had not protected them. The Romanov faction had no plans to create another pretender. Their aim was more modest. They were determined to do whatever they could to defer Shuiskii's coronation.

The authorities tried to put an end once and for all to the baneful rumor that True Dmitrii had been miraculously saved. They decided to expose Otrepev's corpse again. The body was taken from its grave and publicly conveyed in an open cart all over Moscow. The village of Kotly became Grishka's final resting-place on earth. In preparation for his last pleasures the pretender had transferred his movable fortress there. Muscovites called the engine, with its decorations, a monster from hell. Its wooden sides were knocked down. The pieces made a pyre, on top of which Otrepev's body was burned. Wind scattered his ashes.

The day the sorcerer's body was cremated the Kremlin circulated a report that the patriarch and boyars had found the remains of True Tsar Dmitrii in Uglich. Marfa Nagaia had granted permission for the authorities to transfer his dust to the Cathedral of the Archangel.

Shuiskii was anxious to convey an impression that the conspirators had been forced to act. The day after the tsar was murdered Secretary Jan Buczynski was coerced into making a false statement to the effect that Dmitrii had been planning to use his mercenaries to slay the boyars. His assertions were immediately given the widest publicity. The government published the secret treaties Otrepev had made with Mniszech, his correspondence with the Vatican, and other documents seized in a hiding-place in the royal chamber. Secretaries read out the papers incriminating the pretender to a huge throng and explained why he had been killed. The accusers at this trial after the fact claimed that before he died the murdered man had admitted he was Grishka Otrepev, a fugitive monk; the Nagoi family promptly affirmed this. It was charged that Otrepev had dabbled in black arts, was a heretic, had been planning to destroy the Orthodox faith, had emptied the treasury, was prone to vice, had extorted money from the holy monasteries, and had protected the self-proclaimed Heir Petr.[5] These offical pronouncements failed to achieve their objective. Belief in a Good Tsar remained as strong as hatred for the wicked boyars.

Fearing boyar intrigue and popular disturbance, Shuiskii decided to be crowned as quickly as possible. Tsar Vasilii's predecessors waited a month after their elevation before assuming the Cap of Monomakh. Even the pretender had not dared to violate this tradition, but Shuiskii waited less than two weeks. The patriarch alone was empowered to place the crown on his head but Tsar Vasilii had become convinced Filaret was covertly intriguing against him with the rest of his enemies. Not waiting for Romanov to return from Uglich, he was crowned on June 1 with Isidor, metropolitan of Novgorod, officiating in the patriarch's place at the cathedral. Once more bells rang all over Moscow, but the ceremony was glum and somber.

The large numbers of gentry who had managed to gather in Moscow were bitterly disappointed. Both Boris and Dmitrii on their accession had given them two years' salary. Shuiskii found the treasury bare and thus he was taken for an exceptionally frugal monarch. He received many gifts from boyars and bishops at his coronation but was unable to reciprocate properly. The popularity Shuiskii had acquired during the uprising vanished.

People had assumed ceremonies attendant upon the discovery of Heir Dmitrii's remains would precede the coronation. Shuiskii's precipitate action had nullified their expectations. The patriarch brought the body from Uglich two days too late. Tsar and boyars, accompanied by priests and a large crowd of citizens, proceeded on foot to a field in order to greet the relics outside the city. Marfa Nagaia had her last chance to see her son, or rather what was left of him. Shaken by the gruesome sight, Marfa was unable to utter the words expected of her. To retrieve the situation, Tsar Vasilii himself proclaimed that the corpse the commission had brought was indeed the remains of Dmitrii. Neither the queen's silence nor Shuiskii's statements moved the crowd. Everyone vividly recalled Marfa's meeting with her supposed son while he was alive. Shuiskii and Marfa both had told too many lies and played too many tricks for anyone to believe them now.

No sooner had Shuiskii said what he had to say than bearers quickly sealed the casket. After a moment of confusion the procession resumed and wended its way through the city streets to the Kremlin and the gate of the Cathedral of the Archangel, into which only the highest boyars and bishops had been admitted. Filaret Romanov had sent a deposition describing a miracle that had occurred in Uglich when the tomb was opened.

The cathedral was surrounded by a huge crowd of holy fools, the sick, and the halt, all yearning to approach the holy martyr's grave. Guards thrust back the most importunate. The group allowed into the cathedral was chosen so adroitly that a blind man regained his sight the minute he touched the men bearing Dmitrii's bier. The miracle had been carefully planned. As soon as the man who had regained his sight appeared on the battlements bells began to ring throughout the Kremlin. Churchmen recently had been extolling the miracles performed by the newly-created saint. Shuiskii's enemies wanted to stop this vulgar show. They carried a man at death's door into the cathedral; he died beside the remains. The mob swarming around the entry fell back as the dead man was removed from the cathedral.

The Uglich commission wrote that when True Dmitrii's grave was opened the shrine was filled with a glorious scent. Monks, who immediately set themselves to compose lives of the new martyr, repeated this tale. In Moscow the falsehood spread like wildfire. Priests burned incense in the cathedral day and night. The fumes made it hard to breathe but the stench of the decomposed corpse was more powerful than the odor of incense. To avoid scandal, the holy relics had to be consigned to the earth and the cathedral temporarily closed.

This contrived display of Dmitrii's body had not produced the desired results. It had convinced no one and instead provoked further doubts. One story ran that disaffected persons intended to throw stones at Shuiskii on the street. The capital braced for fresh popular turbulence. One night unknown individuals drew crosses on residences inhabited by Poles and belonging to boyars considered traitors. A rumor went around that the sovereign personally had ordered the houses so designated to be robbed and plundered. It was false: Shuiskii immediately doubled the guard around the residence of the Polish envoys to keep them safe from the people. These precautionary measures were well taken. Mobs buzzing like bees clustered around the marked homes and were dispersed only with great difficulty.

The disturbances culminated on Sunday, June 15. Many thousands, carrying various weapons, gathered at the Place of Execution facing the Kremlin gate to demand explanations from the tsar. Shuiskii was on his way to church when he was informed of the danger. People who somehow had gotten into the Kremlin were converging on the palace from all sides. Completely surrounded, Tsar Vasilii collapsed and wept, threw down his sceptre, and told the boyars he would abdicate if he did not suit them: "If you don't want me," he cried, "choose whom you wish." Pressing close, courtiers expressed their devotion to the tsar and encouraged him to punish the guilty. Shuiskii needed no urging; with obvious haste he seized an iron rod which subservient hands had placed before him.

Margeret, head of the palace guard, who was at the sovereign's side during the entire day, experienced many unpleasant moments. He later wrote that if Shuiskii had gone to the square he would have suffered the same fate as Dmitrii. Several times boyars went out to the mob and begged the men of the town quarter in Christ's name to disperse. As time passed the crowd began to thin out. By nightfall no one was left on Red Square. The guard kept an eye on some noisy persons, who soon fell into a trap and were apprehended. A few days later the leaders of the unruly town quarter were beaten up and sent into exile.[6]

Tsar Vasilii took advantage of the incident to distance himself from his opponents in the boyar council. He charged his principal rival, Fedor Mstislavskii, and the Nagoi boyars, who had only just come over to him, with inciting to riot, but Mstislavskii and Marfa Nagaia experienced only brief alarm. The people might misinterpret harassment of Ivan's widow and so she was left in peace. The charge against Mstislavskii stated he was suspected of harboring evil designs, but he made a good case for himself, and the blame was lodged upon Petr Sheremetev.

Shuiskii used the struggle against the disorders that had broken out as an excuse to remove from Moscow many persons who had opposed his election. Petr Sheremetev was packed off to be commander of Pskov. Ivan Cherkasskii, a relative of the Romanov family, was deprived of the rank of steward and expelled from council. Patriarch-elect Filaret was driven out of his palace. Many of Dmitrii's recent favorites were stripped of their titles and banished to border fortresses and the steppes of Bashkiria. The lesser clergy, whose position much resembled that of townmen, had been drawn into the mass movement. A church author reports that at the time many priests and monks had gone crazy, renounced holy office, and shed much Christian blood. Only a shepherd possessing a firm, decisive character could repress the disorder among them. This led the tsar and the boyars opposed to Filaret to name as patriarch Hermogen, metropolitan of Kazan, although even those who admired the prelate thought he was too blunt in word and deed. Hermogen relentlessly combated dissension in clerical ranks. He called down curses and prohibitions upon the unruly,[7] but they proved of little avail. A new wave of unrest was inexorably rising.

The members of the boyar council had no wish to give up lands they had received from the pretender and declared all his bequests were legal. The decree did not apply to persons under sentence of official displeasure or petty taxpayers. Mikhail Molchanov, a boon companion of the pretender, was charged with theft and dabbling in black arts. He was lifted up on a block and thrashed so severely that he nearly died, but he had supporters at court. They stole fast horses from the tsar's stable and helped him escape. Along the way he was joined by Prince Grigorii Shakhovskoi, who had been told off to become commander of Putivl. At first Molchanov was afraid of pursuit but later he took heart, left his inn, and informed his hosts he was escorting a certain prominent personage. On reaching the frontier Molchanov publicly stated he had helped to save Tsar Dmitrii but, unwilling to risk another drubbing, he fled to Lithuania. Grigorii Shakhovskoi, who remained in Putivl, soon grew convinced that the population of the Seversk region was thoroughly roused and ready to revolt against the boyar tsar. Desiring to settle accounts with Shuiskii, he told the people of Putivl that True Dmitrii was still alive and Shuiskii was preparing to take reprisals against them for their devotion to the lawful tsar. Putivl was ripe for a new uprising. Shuiskii promised he would "hold them in his tsarist favor higher than before,"[8] but met with no success when he invited them to send three or four leading citizens to Moscow to petition for their needs. Putivl cossacks and serving men had not farmed land belonging to the crown for two years; townsmen and peasants in the parts of the Komaritskii district belonging to the True Tsar had been enjoying reduced taxes. No one expected anything good from the new ruler.

The clouds of civil war gathering over the country steadily were growing thicker. The feudal gentry had reaped great benefits from the system of serfdom, which had increased enormously their power over the downtrodden peasantry. The gentry repressed the peasants more than ever but the latter refused to accept the outrageous new conditions. Justice, tradition, and custom were on their side. A right of peasant departure had existed for centuries. In abolishing St. George's Day the feudatories had transgressed law and equity. Appeals and entreaties had proved unavailing; now only force could contain feudal arbitrariness. A social explosion had been on the way for a long time.

Dmitrii had promised much and delivered little, but illusions about the monarch died hard in the countryside. Peasants reasoned that if the

True Tsar had failed to grant them the freedom they desired it was because the wicked boyars had prevented him. They had murdered the tsar; that was proof enough. The ruler had fallen victim to the same evil forces that were making the people suffer. The lordly nobles on high had turned out to be traitors. The struggle against social injustice mysteriously and unexpectedly had become an effort to extirpate boyar sedition.

When Dmitrii's partisans organized a revolt against Shuiskii they could not have foreseen the social consequences of their action. During the pretender's march on Moscow rebels had seized commanders and dragged them before the Lawful Tsar, but he had rewarded them and taken them into his service. A year and a half later the populace was far more determined and relentless. The seeds of rage planted by the lords' violent and arbitrary actions produced a crop of blood. In Putivl rebels slew the commander, Prince Bakhteiarov, and several gentry; Commander Buturlin in Oskol, and Commander Saburov in Borisovgorod. In Livny Associate Boyar Shein took to his heels; the people seized whatever he and his gentry left behind. Astrakhan and some Volga towns fell to the rebels.

In July, 1606 Moscow looked like an armed camp. Soldiers took weapons up to towers and were readying the fortress for a siege. Detachments were arriving daily. The authorities tried to conceal from the people that a rising had engulfed south Russia. Tsar Vasilii issued a proclamation that the Crimean khan was threatening to attack the capital, but the population soon learned the real state of affairs. The Moscow garrison was preparing to fight the rebellious people, not the Tatars. On July 20 new broadsheets, supposedly from Dmitrii,[9] appeared on the streets. The tsar's armies received orders to use force to suppress revolts in the southern towns. The small steppe fortress of Elets soon became the focal point in the conflict.

While preparing to campaign against Azov, Dmitrii had sent many cannon, ammunition, and supplies to Elets. Shuiskii tried to win over the town's mutinous garrison. Marfa Nagaia sent her brother to the fortress to prove the dead tsar had been a pretender but persuasion had no effect. Shuiskii then sent Commander Vorotynskii and an army to Elets. The movement backing Good Dmitrii was again headed by the inhabitants of Putivl. Remembering how important Elets was, the men of Putivl mustered every available man and dispatched the group to relieve the beleaguered fortress. Istoma Pashkov, a lieutenant from Venev, led the attack.

Putivl dispatched couriers everywhere. The summons to revolt did not fall upon deaf ears. Ataman Ivan Isaevich Bolotnikov came from the Ukraine to Putivl. Like Istoma Pashkov, Bolotnikov came from pettry lesser-boyar agriculturalists. His fate had been a hard one. Need had compelled him to indenture himself to a boyar's household but he had refused to live the life of a slave and had fled to the free cossacks in the steppe expanse. There his luck finally ran out. The Tatars took him prisoner and sold him into slavery in Turkey. For a number of years Bolotnikov was chained to a bench, a rower in Turkish galleys. Sailors from western Europe who had seized his galley in a battle ransomed the slaves. After further adventures Bolotnikov fell in with Ukrainian cossacks and fought under Polish auspices against the Turks in Hungary. The cossacks esteemed the former slave's bravery and resoluteness and elected him their ataman. After peace was concluded with the Turks Bolotnikov's unit returned to the Ukraine. On the way the ataman called in at Sambor, where he met a man represented to him as Tsar Dmitrii, who had survived. The inhabitants of the Sambor fortress were quite ready to revive the intrigue involving the pretender. They provided Mikhail Molchanov with a refuge and helped him dupe Bolotnikov. The fictitious Dmitrii gave the ataman letters in Shakhovskoi's name, sealed with a seal stolen from the Kremlin palace.

Bolotnikov reached Putivl in the summer of 1606 and at once took charge of the rebels' assault on Kromy. His first campaign ended as badly as Pashkov's against Elets. Commander Vorotynskii beat Pashkov back from before Elets and Commander Nagoi pushed Bolotnikov back from Kromy. However, Bolotnikov collected new forces and Yurii Bezzubtsev and he forced their way inside the Kromy fortress.

Government armies had been fruitlessly besieging Elets and Kromy for almost three months. They had sustained losses in manpower and as autumn approached they began to experience a lack of provisions. Rebellious towns surrounded the tsar's commanders on every side. This led Commander Vorotynskii to retire through Tula in the direction of Moscow while Trubetskoi made for Kaluga through Orel. Their armies had for all intents and purposes disintegrated. Crowds of gentry were leaving for their estates.

Istoma Pashkov followed on the heels of Vorotynskii's fleeing army. He occupied Tula, where a revolt broke out, and then proceeded through Serpukhov; by mid-September he was swiftly bearing down on Moscow. However, Commander Skopin-Shuiskii encountered Pashkov's detachments on the Pakhra river and beat them back from

Moscow in the direction of Serpukhov. Bolotnikov took Orel and came out on the Ugra river before Kaluga. On September 23 Commander Ivan Ivanovich Shuiskii defeated him but failed to hold Kaluga because the people there had risen in revolt. After his defeat at the hands of Skopin-Shuiskii, Istoma Pashkov went off to before Kolomna, where he linked up with the rebellious Riazan gentry led by Prokofii Liapunov. The garrison and people of Kolomna rose in revolt and came over to Pashkov's and Liapunov's side.

Bolotnikov's army still lacked combat experience and was often defeated in encounters with the tsar's commanders. The Kromy garrison acknowledged Dmitrii's authority; whereupon crown troops moved up to the town walls. Bolotnikov tried to force his way through to aid the rebel garrison. Both armies fought fiercely amid much bloodshed, but the result was a draw.

Disorders broke out in the royal army. Gentry from Novgorod and Pskov departed for home. Vorotynskii's defeat at Elets discouraged the commanders. Fearful of becoming bogged down all autumn at Kromy the boyars withdrew to Orel, but disturbances broke out there too. A revolt in the Orel garrison caused the army finally to disintegrate. Encountering no further opposition, Bolotnikov attacked Kaluga. Tsar Vasilii sent his brother, Ivan Shuiskii, against him with Poles and artillery. On September 23, 1606 Ivan Shuiskii gave battle to the rebels and prevented them from crossing the Ugra river. Bolotnikov's forces sustained heavy casualties, but the victory proved hollow and did not bring success to the tsar's commanders. The rebels came to an understanding with the people of Kaluga. Disturbances broke out in towns along the Oka river and Ivan Shuiskii had to withdraw to Moscow. Bolotnikov made for Serpukhov.

His victory at Elets gave Istoma Pashkov a chance to proceed directly to Moscow but he did not as yet have a large enough army. He decided to make for the capital indirectly, via Riazan. Riazan landholders had helped Otrepev overthrow Godunov and Pashkov had every reason to assume they would aid him. The rebels stayed in Riazan approximately a month, transferring from Elets essential supplies of ammunition, which allowed them to forge a large army. Units from Putivl and Elets still constituted the core of the army and so Istoma Pashkov was named its chieftain. Prokofii Liapunov was the leader of the Riazan landholders but the gentry levy he collected was insignificant; Liapunov had to be content with the office of adjutant to the lieutenant from Venev.

After occupying Kolomna Pashkov set out for Moscow. Tsar Vasilii sent Mstislavskii, Vorotynskii, and the Golitsyn brothers, the cream of the Moscow boyars, against him. Abandoning pursuit of Bolotnikov, Skopin-Shuiskii sped to Mstislavskii's aid. The boyars were not united. Mstislavskii and the Golitsyn brothers were still unable to forgive Shuiskii for winning the throne. The gentry also fought for Shuiskii without any particular enthusiasm. Many still sympathized with the Good Dmitrii. Servingmen had not forgiven the tsar for his stinginess. Shuiskii had proved a master of intrigue but had not yet displayed his capacities as head of state. This quintessential nobleman appeared neither attractive nor regal. His small round figure created a comic impression; his nearsighted eyes peered out cunningly, and he was almost bald. This unpopular tsar might have been able to rule in tranquil times, but the rampant difficulties rendered his throne extremely shaky. Mstislavskii's force was larger but it could not withstand the rebel army. Pashkov attacked the tsar's commanders in the village of Troitskoe on the Kolomna road and routed them. Dmitrii's partisans captured several thousands of the tsar's gentry and soldiers. They were beaten with knouts and sent home.

On October 28, 1606 Pashkov occupied the village of Kolomenskoe below the walls of the capital, where Bolotnikov joined him after November 1. The rebel army was now 20,000 strong. A dispute at once broke out in the camp. Pashkov had achieved a considerable military success and thus expected to remain commander of the army, but Bolotnikov displayed his appointment as great commander, which the presumed Dmitrii personally had given him. A document alone could not decide the issue; only the man enjoying the support of the armed masses could become leader of the rebel forces. Bolotnikov splendidly articulated the aspirations and expectations of the lower orders; regular cossacks, slaves, peasants and townsmen were drawn to him. Pashkov had to yield the office of commander-in-chief to Bolotnikov.

Shuiskii had lost his army and his fall was momentarily anticipated. The mutiny in the south had cut the capital off from cheap bread. The people were seething. They reasoned: "the sovereign is unpopular with the boyars and the entire population. Great hostility exists between the boyars and the realm. The tsar has no money or servingmen."[10] The boyars secretly were plotting to remove Shuiskii. Pashkov was not averse to coming to an agreement with them; he merely insisted that the Shuiskii brothers be handed over to him because they were the ones responsible for the rising against the Lawful Tsar. When Bolotnikov took charge he advanced more resolute demands. He wrote to Moscow, calling upon the lower orders to bring the boyars' power to an end and seize their property. The rebels were trying to bring about a social revolution. They could count upon the support of the humble people in the capital and Moscow recently had been rent by popular uprisings. However, during those critical November days the powerful propertied elements managed to restrain the commons from rising. Displaying his customary dexterity, Shuiskii found a solution to what had seemed an impossible situation. He rounded up townsmen loyal to him and sent them to the rebel camp as Moscow's representatives. These so-called representatives of the town quarter promised to surrender the city without a struggle if the rebels would show them Dmitrii alive and well. The credulous Bolotnikov believed them. Instead of acting determinedly he kept dispatching couriers to Putivl, stubbornly insisting that Dmitrii should return quickly. There was no sign of him; Bolotnikov's appeal was like a voice crying in a wilderness.

The boyars had outwitted the people. They were playing for time, waiting for reinforcements. A deputation to the mutineers' camp took advantage of the situation in order to divide the forces under Bolotnikov's command. They initiated secret parleys with gentry who felt out of place among the rebels.

The massive reprisals the rebels had carried out against landholders helped the feudal estates finally to compose the divisions that existed in their ranks. Despite his detestation of Shuiskii, Prokofii Liapunov, the chief gentry leader, began thinking about rapprochement with the ruler in order to preserve the existing order. Circumstances strongly impelled him to adopt such a course. Churchmen had been helping Shuiskii bring erring gentry back into the fold. Patriarch Hermogen frightened gentry and propertied townsmen by declaring that the rabble would divide up their holdings and their wives and children. Liapunov decided to break with Bolotnikov after Shuiskii promised he would be made a conciliar courtier and receive new grants of land. Liapunov revealed the rebels' military plans to the tsar.

In mid-November Bolotnikov tried to storm Moscow from the south. The boyars knew where the attack would fall and prepared to resist. At the height of the battle Liapunov and 500 Riazan gentry cavalry and fusiliers switched sides and the insurgents had to retire. A week and a half later, Bolotnikov sent a force to the village of Krasnoe to close the line encircling Moscow. Traitors forewarned Shuiskii, who took advantage of the divisions in the rebel army. Bolotnikov fought the commanders but was pushed back to Kolomenskoe.

At the end of the month a gentry detachment arrived in Moscow from Smolensk. The crown now had sufficient forces to risk a major engagement. Unwilling to entrust his fate to Mstislavskii a second time, the tsar put all his available forces under the command of his nephew Skopin, twenty years old, whom he trusted fully. On December 2 Skopin did battle with the rebels at the village of Kotly. At the height of the conflict Istoma Pashkov and his servingmen turned their weapons against their own soldiers. Profiting from the confusion, Skopin emerged victorious. Bolotnikov fled to Kolomenskoe and from there to Kaluga via Serpukhov. The defeat of the core of his army before Kolomenskoe sealed the fate of the cossacks entrenched in their camp at Zabore. They defended themselves furiously for three days from all attacks of the tsar's army but finally were forced to lay down their arms. Tsar Vasilii treated any who refused to surrender with barbarous cruelty. Every night hundreds of the defeated were hauled off to the Moscow river, struck over the head with clubs, and thrust under the ice.

The defeat before Moscow did not destroy the insurgents. Fresh forces rallied around Bolotnikov in Kaluga, which he had managed to fortify. His men put up palings along the length of the walls and cleaned out the moats beneath them. Dmitrii Shuiskii failed to storm Kaluga and was defeated decisively in a conflict lasting from December 11 to December 12. A few days later Ivan Shuiskii came up to Kaluga and renewed the siege. Heavy artillery brought from Moscow blasted the wooden fort day and night. The tsar's soldiers breached the moat and moved an observation platform of brambles and wood up to a wall. Burrowing a tunnel underground, Bolotnikov's men hurled the platform and the soldiers on it up into the air. A great panic arose in the Shuiskii brothers' camp. This daring sortie from the fortress crowned the rebels' triumph. Bolotnikov acquired the enemy's siege engines and a good deal of artillery.

Even during Dmitrii's lifetime the lower Volga region had been a major center of peasant warfare. Heir Petr, hastening to Moscow, had veered sharply south and vanished into the steppe among the Don cossacks as soon as he heard his fictive uncle had been murdered. When Bolotnikov found himself in difficulties at Moscow, the authorities in Putivl summoned Petr to the Seversk area. When the two previously separate entities were linked together the peasant war acquired a new lease of life. Petr brought some 4,000 free cossacks, runaway peasants, and slaves with him to Putivl. Prince Grigorii Shakhovskoi was relegated to the sidelines; leadership passed to the cossacks who had groomed and put forward the new pretender. Putivl became the gentry's nemesis. They had been held under guard in anticipation that True Dmitrii would judge them. Now they were executed in the name of True Petr.

The insurgents had often sent couriers to Lithuania, ostensibly to find the saved Dmitrii, actually to recruit men in Belorussia and the Ukraine. These efforts met with some success. Detachments of Zaporozhian cossacks kept arriving at the camp in Putivl. Captains Botvinia and Furs busied themselves abroad forming Polish units to aid the Russian rebels. Zaporozhian cossacks, Poles, Lithuanians, Kasimov Tatars, and Germans from Livonia fought side by side with Russian peasants and Don cossacks in Bolotnikov's army.

Tsar Vasilii Shuiskii did everything he could to win over the capital's population. First he had disturbed the remains of Dmitrii of Uglich; now it was the Godunov family's turn. A resolution of council and clergy authorized their bodies to be disinterred from a pit in the yard of the modest Barsanophius monastery and moved for solemn burial in the Trinity-St. Sergius monastery. Twenty Trinity monks escorted the remains through the streets of Moscow and boyars joined the mournful procession, paying their last respects to the fallen dynasty. Kseniia Godunova, attired in a nun's black habit, walked behind her father's bier, sobbing and loudly bemoaning her sad fate. The ceremony had definite political overtones. Convicting Dmitrii of evildoing would strengthen the new tsar.

The popular disturbances left the ruling groups no choice but to rally around the throne. The boyars summoned the deposed Iov from Staritsa and on February 16, 1607 allowed the two patriarchs and the ecclesiastical council to scrutinize the charter electing Vasilii Shuiskii to the throne. Its compilers had tried to prove Shuiskii had been a lawfully elected tsar like Boris and Fedor Godunov, whereas Dmitrii had been an usurper and pretender when he seized the throne.[11]

On February 20 the boyars summoned the people of Moscow to Red Square, "every last man from the neighborhoods, town precincts, and shops." After that, merchants and traders were invited to the Cathedral of the Dormition. After service the town representatives begged Patriarch Iov's pardon because "everyone" had once deposed him. Iov absolved the townsmen of their sin in rising against the Godunov family and adjured them to remain loyal to the new autocrat.

While Bolotnikov was under siege in Kaluga, Tsar Vasilii promulgated a rescript extending the time to search for runaway serfs to fifteen years. Feudal landlords enthusiastically hailed the measure, which threw down the gauntlet to the militant peasantry. Shuiskii, realizing how strong the rebels were, was trying to split their ranks. His rescript, dated March 7, promised freedom to "involuntary" slaves whose masters had indentured them forcibly.

As long as the insurgents merely referred to a Good Tsar, their hands were free. When Heir Petr appeared on the scene the situation began to change. Titled adventurers made their way to the false tsar's court. By a quirk of fate Boyar Prince Andrei Teliatevskii, whose slave Bolotnikov once had been, became Petr's chief boyar. The revolt overtook Teliatevskii while he was serving as commander of Chernigov; he had no alternative.

Petr left Putivl for Tula. Vorotynskii was sent to apprehend him but Boyar Teliatevskii crossed his path and the noble commander barely escaped. At the head of a force of Don and Zaporozhian cossacks, Teliatevskii marched to relieve beleaguered Kaluga. Istoma Pashkov tried to stop him. In all his fighting on the insurgent side the Venev lieutenant had never known defeat, but at Kaluga he was overwhelmed, and he shamefully fled from the battlefield. Bolotnikov followed up Teliatevskii's victory by making a sortie from Kaluga and compelling the tsar's brothers to retire. Teliatevskii avoided going to Kaluga to link up with his former slave and hastily returned to Tula. Bolotnikov with his thinning army also made for Tula to defend the stone fortress.

In May Shuiskii mustered and took personal command of a huge force to march on Tula. The insurgents held out for four months, made valiant sorties, and harried the gentry. Unable to take Tula by storm, the besiegers constructed a dam on the Upa river and inundated the beleaguered town. Dissension broke out among Heir Petr's boyars. The mutineers thrust Grigorii Shakhovskoi into prison. Bolotnikov persuaded the people to hold out in the fortress until all hope was gone. "If you have nothing to eat," he told them, "I'll let you consume my corpse."[12] But the position was becoming progressively worse. Food supplies that had survived the flood were gone. Soldiers and civilians were dying. In order to save the soldiers who were left, Bolotnikov decided to capitulate. Shuiskii solemnly swore he would not harm anyone in Tula who surrendered.

On October 10 the town opened its gates to the tsar's commanders. Shuiskii assigned the prisoners to various homes, but many were detained in his camp and then sent in custody to other towns. Heir Petr was taken to Moscow, where he was executed; Bolotnikov was

banished to Kargopol. On his way there the gentry threatened to load
the captive with chains and bring him to book. The people's leader
proudly replied: "I shall soon bring you down and sew you up in
bearskins."[13] His spirit was undaunted, but his attitude towards Good
Tsar Dmitrii had undergone a change. For months Bolotnikov had been
appealing earnestly for help to the man who had entrusted him with
the command of the rebel forces. In Tula Bolotnikov at last had realized
the false Dmitrii was utterly indifferent to him. The rebel leader was
courageous and unaccustomed to concealing the truth, no matter how
unpleasant it might be. He publicly admitted he could not say whether
the man to whom he had sworn fealty in Sambor was the genuine or
a false tsar. Bolotnikov continued to terrify the gentry even when a
prisoner. As a result, Tsar Vasilii had him blinded and a little later
drowned. Thus ended the life of the most eminent figure in the first
peasant war. Bolotnikov's rising was a major event of the Time of
Troubles.

The social struggle in this feudal society had reached a culmination.
The rising by the downtrodden populace had fully exposed the tragedy
the people were enduring. In destroying the gentry the rebels hoped
they were eradicating the system of serf exploitation and violence they
loathed. It seemed as though they might indeed reach their cherished
goal. The Kremlin cupolas gleamed before their eyes. But still they
could not take Moscow. The authorities had managed to prevent the
capital's townsmen from rising and Great Novgorod, Kazan,
Smolensk, Nizhnii Novgorod and other major towns had held aloof
from the fray.

Chapter Five

THE TUSHINO CABAL

The mutinous population in the Seversk region had been waiting a year
for the Good Tsar to arrive from Poland. Putivl, Starodub and other
towns often had sent men abroad to hunt for Dmitrii. A tsar there had
to be. He duly appeared.

In May, 1607 the inhabitants of Starodub came across three strang-
ers on the street. One, more elegantly dressed, called himself Andrei
Nagoi, a relative of the Muscovite sovereign. He was attended by two

Russians, Grigorii Kashinets, and Aleshka Rukin, a Muscovite under-secretary. The new arrivals told the people of Starodub exciting news: they had been sent from abroad by Dmitrii and the sovereign himself might be expected any day. Time passed, but the promised tsar failed to appear. Bolotnikov sent Ivan Zarutskii, an efficient cossack ataman, from beleaguered Tula to Starodub. The insurgent people soon grew annoyed at waiting and put Aleshka Rukin to torture. The undersec-retary admitted they had been deceived. He stated the True Tsar had been in Starodub a long time, but fearing his enemies would track him down, he had been calling himself Nagoi. The play was well rehearsed and doubters were drowned out in the flood of enthusiasm. In June the people of Starodub swore fealty to Dmitrii II.

Fusiliers, cossacks, and townsmen from everywhere began to mus-ter under the new pretender's standard. The rebels asked for help from abroad and Belorussians and Ukrainians responded to their appeal. In Belorussia an impovished member of the Polish gentry, Miechowiecki, managed to contribute several thousand men to the tsar's army. A large contingent of Zaporozhian cossacks joined False Dmitrii II near Karachev soon after he had set out on campaign. Whenever his army approached, towns hailed the long-awaited ruler. The pretender pro-claimed everywhere he was on his way to deliver Bolotnikov from besieged Tula, a short distance away. False Dmitrii's army occupied Bolkhov, but the Tula garrison was in a hopeless position and could not endure until the reinforcements arrived.

Once he had taken Tula, Tsar Vasilii stopped campaigning and sent his weary army home. He underestimated the rebels' tenacity. His commanders could not take Kaluga, which was protected by a strong detachment of Bolotnikov's partisans. Shuiskii decided to employ one group of rebels to defeat another. He ordered cossacks captured at Mos-cow released from prison and supplied with arms, and named Ataman Yurii Bezzubtsev, one of Bolotnikov's chief lieutenants, to be their commander. Bezzubtsev was to proceed to Kaluga immediately and persuade the fortress garrison to surrender. Shuiskii could not rest easy as long as Bolotnikov's supporters held Kaluga, but he had grievously miscalculated. The minute escorts brought the cossacks, 4,000 strong, to Kaluga, a dispute broke out in the besiegers' camp. The boyars could not make these recent rebels obey them and armed clashes between cossacks and gentry occurred. Losing their heads, the commanders fled back to Moscow, abandoning their artillery and supplies of powder and shot. The cossacks appropriated the ammunition, handed it over to Kaluga's defenders, and headed west to join Dmitrii.

In the stark light of failure the pretender stood revealed as a mean coward. The fall of Tula convinced him the game was up and he should leave Russia as quickly as possible. He fled from Bolkhov to Putivl, and after he left his army rapidly disintegrated. The Zaporozhian cossacks went abroad. In panic-stricken flight False Dmitrii II reached the Komaritskii district, where he was detained by allied armies recruited in his name that had arrived from abroad.

On the highway through Komaritskii False Dmitrii II encountered Tiszkiewicz, and Lord Valiazhskii, who had brought 1800 cavalry and infantry to serve the pretender. Soon the cossacks on the point of departure returned. This encouraged the pretender to attack Briansk a second time, but he suffered a reverse and withdrew to winter quarters in Orel. Shuiskii had been unable to find sufficient forces to humble the Starodub Thief. Moscow had failed to appreciate how dangerous a new pretender might become.

False Dmitrii II's forces increased substantially during the winter. Remnants of Bolotnikov's shattered armies made their way to him from all over the country in groups and individually. Masses of peasant soldiers fleeing the center again swamped the southwest borderlands. Local service landholders who originally had favored the Thief had second thoughts, hastily arranged their affairs, and secretly made their way to Tsar Vasilii. More than 1,000 gentry from northern towns soon mustered in Moscow. To stem gentry defection the pretender took steps which Bolotnikov's supporters suggested. He proclaimed estates of gentry who fled to Moscow were confiscate and issued a special appeal to serfs and slaves belonging to these traitors, calling on them to come to True Dmitrii's camp, take an oath of loyalty to him, and serve him with arms in their hands. The pretender confidently declared that if they did so he would give them their masters' holdings and they could marry any landlord's wife or daughter left on an estate. These appeals produced an effect. Slaves in villages began attacking the hated gentry, beating their bailiffs and driving them out, and dividing up their property. The pretender's scribes issued peasants patents of proprietorship to confiscated landholdings in Rylsk and Kursk.[1]

The slogans and aims of the peasant war had struck a responsive chord among the lower orders in Russia, the Ukraine, and Belorussia. Many Belorussian peasants and townsmen had come to Starodub with

Miechowiecki's army. The gentry showed utter contempt for them.
Zaporozhian cossacks from the Ukraine were as enthusiastic as the
Belorussians, and for a time it looked as though a new peasant war was
in the offing. Nothing of the sort occurred. A decline set in as soon
as the new pretender became leader of the movement and contingents
of Polish and Russian gentry appeared in his camp.

No one knew the new pretender's identity. Shuiskii's government
called him the Thief of Starodub. Members of his entourage thought
he was a Muscovite who had lived a long time in Belorussia.[2] He could
read and write Russian and Polish. Contemporaries were surprised how
familiar he was with Dmitrii I's activities. The Jesuits offered an explanation: he had been one of the first pretender's scribes and had fled
to Lithuania after his fall. They claimed this scribe's name was Bogdan
and he was a Jew.[3] Eventually the Russian authorities officially came
round to this point of view. The Thief's advisors reported curious
details about him. When tortured, Prince Dmitrii Mosalskii averred:
"the Thief is called Tsar Dmitrii; he is actually from Moscow, from
the Arbat, from Prechiste Znamenie, from the stables; a priest's son,
Mitka. Prince Vasilii Mosalskii dismissed him from Moscow five
years before the Defrocked One was murdered." The Mosalskii family
was very close to the new pretender, but even they knew nothing about
his early career. However this may be, they suspected that, like Otrepev, the new pretender came from a priestly background. Muscovite
chroniclers shared this opinion. They called the Thief a priest's son
because he "knew all about church matters."

The most comprehensive investigation was undertaken by an
unknown Belorussian priest, who lived in the suburbs of Mogilev and
had observed the pretender's first moves. The essence of his narrative
is the following: Dmitrii originally had taught children their letters in
the house of a priest in Shklova; then he moved to the home of Priest
Fedor in a village in the Mogilev area. The teacher wore a sheepskin
hat and a wretched, tattered jacket all year long. To make ends meet,
he went into the service of the priest of the Nikolskii church in Mogilev
and to earn a few pennies chopped wood and drew water for him. The
Shklova scholar was not a moral man. Priest Fedor once found him
with his wife. In a rage, the priest thrashed the teacher and drove him
out of the house.[4]

The pedagogue was reduced to desperate straits. He had to sleep
under fences on the streets of Mogilev. There he attracted the attention
of enterprising gentry members who formerly had been in Dmitrii I's

service. Lord Zortynski came up with the idea that the diminutive vagrant might pass for the slain Muscovite tsar. Miechowiecki encouraged the notion and made the scheme practicable. The teacher's nature was a mixture of cowardice and obsequiousness. The fate of the first pretender frightened him and he fled from Mogilev to Propoisk, where he was soon discovered and placed under arrest. His Mogilev patrons got him out of prison and this time the tramp showed himself more compliant. Retainers in the service of the commandant of Propoisk conducted the newly-minted tsar to Popov hill, a stone's throw from the Muscovite border. Before sending the pretender out into the world his patrons sought to bind him with commitments. "In my holy tsaric name" Dmitrii gave Lord Zertynski and his comrades a wide-ranging rescript.[5]

Petty gentry eagerly supported the intrigue involving a pretender. Sigismund III had managed to put down the revolt in Poland and disperse the mercenary units. Many mercenaries, who had been paid no salaries, were living on the king's estates. In eastern Belorussia these fine warriors were devouring the local populations like locusts. Unemployed, these impoverished members of the gentry were looking for somebody to whom they might sell their services. Miechowiecki was anxious to enroll them in the tsar's army. Once False Dmitrii II had been acknowledged by numerous Russian towns his cause became viable. The Polish-Lithuanian nobility began to display a growing interest in the pretender's intrigue. Magnates and gentry who had fostered Otrepev began to stir again.

An impoverished Ukrainian magnate, Prince Roman Ruzynski, borrowed money to hire a large contingent of hussars. Dmitrii II and his patron Miechowiecki knew a few unpleasant moments when they learned Ruzynski had appeared in the suburbs of Orel. The pretender had no wish to take him into his service, but Ruzynski did not allow this to deter him. In April, 1608 he reached Dmitrii's camp and carried out a coup of his own. An army assembly demoted Miechowiecki, proclaimed him an outlaw, and the soldiers called for Ruzynski to be their new ataman. The assembly summoned the pretender and told him in no uncertain terms to hand over the new ataman's enemies. When Dmitrii II tried to temporize there was a tremendous furor. People yelled right in his face: "Seize the scoundrel!" Others demanded he be put to death on the spot.

The unruly mercenary army set armed guards around Dmitrii's court. The Shklova vagrant tried to drown his fears in vodka and stayed drunk all night. His master of horse, Adam Wisniowiecki, sought rapprochement with Ruzynski. The pretender had to drain the cup of humiliation to the dregs. No sooner had he sobered up than he was brought before the Poles and forced to beg the mercenaries' pardon. The change of leaders in the camp at Orel had important consequences. Bolotnikov's men, who previously had enjoyed great influence, were shunted aside. Following the example of the Polish magnates and gentry, Russian boyars began turning up in Dmitrii's entourage. The movement was losing its social character.

When spring was coming to an end the pretender's army renewed its attack on Moscow. Tsar Vasilii sent his brother Dmitrii with 30,000 men to oppose the Thief. They clashed at Bolkhov and after two days of fighting Shuiskii was defeated. Prince Dmitrii's cowardice was the cause. At the height of the battle he ordered the cannon removed to the rear; this led to a general retreat, which became a panic-stricken route. Dmitrii's units seized a host of cannon and a large wagon train of supplies. After the battle the pretender made a new agreement with the Polish contingents in order to keep them on his side. He pledged to share with them the treasure he would acquire when he mounted the tsar's throne. The people, who were hailing the new True Dmitrii, had no idea he had concluded such an understanding behind their backs.

Tsar Vasilii recalled his brother Dmitrii and replaced him with his nephew, Prince Mikhail Skopin. He was sure he could destroy the Thief when he came close to Moscow, but he was unable to accomplish his design. Treachery broke out in the ranks of his army. Some noble princes organized a conspiracy in favor of Dmitrii. Skopin withdrew to Moscow and arrested the conspirators.

In June, 1608 the pretender's army pitched camp at Tushino; Skopin took up a position facing it at Khodynka, while Tsar Vasilii and his court disposed themselves at Presna. The presence of Polish contingents in the pretender's army alarmed the Kremlin. The Russian authorities were making feverish efforts to avoid an armed conflict with the Rzeczpospolita. Tsar Vasilii lost no time holding peace talks with the Polish envoys and promised immediately to send home the Mniszech family and other Poles held in Moscow since Otrepev was murdered. The envoys agreed in principle straightway to recall from Russia their forces fighting on behalf of the pretender. Shuiskii joyfully informed Ruzynski peace was at hand and he promised that as soon as they quitted the camp at Tushino he would pay the ataman's mercenaries the salaries they had earned while serving the pretender.

As a diplomat Tsar Vasilii proved myopic. His commanders were immobilized and idle for two weeks; his men grew convinced the war was over. Taking advantage of the commanders' slackness, on June 25 Ataman Ruzynski suddenly fell upon Skopin's army. The tsar's forces retreated in disarray, but when the men of Tushino tried to follow on their heels into Moscow fusiliers beat them back. Ruzynski was on the point of sounding a general retreat, but the tsar's commanders decided not to pursue his units as they withdrew. Three days later they routed an army with which Lord Lisowski [a noble Lithuanian soldier of fortune, destined to be a thorn in the side of the Russian authorities for some time—ed.] was trying to force his way into the capital from the south.

The Polish government had had nothing to do with the intrigue involving the pretender of Mogilev. Dmitrii had met with no luck in concluding an alliance with the king, although he had expressed willingness to make major concessions. Poland's most discerning politicians sharply criticized interference in Russia's internal affairs. Sigismund III took their advice; he had not forgotten his failure with Otrepev nor had he completely stamped out domestic opposition. But the ease with which Dmitrii scored victories turned his head. The king ordered his armies to prepare immediately to occupy the Russian fortresses of Chernigov and Novgorod-Seversk. His aggressive designs found no support in Polish ruling groups. Hetman Stanislaw Zolkiewski pointed out that the royal army was unprepared to wage a major war. Sigismund was obliged to defer his intention, but he kept looking for pretexts to intervene in Russian affairs. With his blessing a mighty Lithuanian magnate, Jan Sapieha, collected a few thousand men and made for the Russian frontier.

In Moscow Tsar Vasilii dictated peace terms to the Polish envoys. Weary after two years in Russia, they signed in order to obtain permission to return home. The document was not worth the paper it was written on; Sapieha's invasion had rendered it null and void, but inspired by what he believed was a diplomatic triumph Shuiskii released the Mniszech family in accordance with the terms of the treaty. When they returned to Moscow from their place of exile in Yaroslavl Jerzy swore to Shuiskii that he would never recognize the new pretender as his son-in-law and promised to cooperate fully in ending the war. He was lying in his teeth. The inveterate intriguer secretly had informed the king that True Tsar Dmitrii had survived and begged Sigismund to offer him armed assistance. Mniszech was doing everything he could to start another war.

Many who had been well acquainted with the first Dmitrii made haste to warn Marina that the Tushino pretender bore no resemblance to her husband. The queen of Muscovy was impervious. Trustworthy individuals informed the Thief she was ready to become his lawful wife. The Mniszech family swore they would leave Muscovy. The authorities provided a force to escort them to the border. Marina traveled almost a month through remote settlements until her carriage attained the frontier. The Mniszech family was in constant covert contact with the pretender. Right at the border, in accordance with a prearranged signal, Lord Jerzy and his daughter moved away; at that instant a detachment from Tushino fell upon the convoy and put its men to flight. Early in September, escorted by Polish units, the queen reached the outskirts of Tushino. On the way chivalric convictions led a young Polish courtier to try to warn Marina for the last time what a deception awaited her. He was at once handed over to Dmitrii, who ordered him impaled alive in the camp.

The impending meeting with his wife made Dmitrii nervous. He feigned illness. Ruzynski performed the honors in his stead. The ataman conveyed Jerzy to the camp as quickly as possible in order to negotiate the conditions under which the Mniszech family would recognize the new pretender. The hardened intriguer did not bat an eye when he beheld the deceiver, who was not the least bit like Otrepev. Jerzy was quite ready to become the new tsar's ataman and handle his affairs and revenues. Ruzynski abruptly brought an end to his ambitious scheming and put the tsar's father-in-law in his place. The atamans and the pretender haggled for three days but finally came to an understanding. Jerzy agreed to consign his daughter to the anonymous newcomer for a good round sum. The compact was drawn up in the form of an enabling document. Dmitrii vowed to pay Mniszech a million Polish zloty; Jerzy did his best to protect his daughter's honor and his purse. Dmitrii would not become Marina's husband until he was actually sitting on the throne and, naturally, not until he had paid over the money. The day after these complicated negotiations were concluded the pretender secretly conveyed Marina to Jan Sapieha's camp. She was not impressed with the pretender's uncouth appearance but she was ready to make any sacrifice in order to win the crown. Less than a week later Marina solemnly entered Tushino and brilliantly carried out her role as a loving wife who has learned her husband is miraculously alive. Her glances expressed tenderness and admiration; she wept copiously and bowed down at Dmitrii's feet.

Mniszech had insisted that the agreement he had executed be punctiliously observed, but Marina disobeyed her father. Dmitrii's tent lay in full view of the entire camp; the consort realized that to live apart from her husband would immediately spark unwelcome rumors and expose the tsar as a fake. To her father's and brothers' great indignation Marina became Dmitrii's mistress. Deceived in his expectations, Jerzy quitted the camp. Six months later Marina had to make an explanation to one of her brothers, whom she met by chance. Young Mniszech reproached his sister, alleging lewd conduct. To allay his anger the queen stated without batting an eye that a Polish priest secretly had married them. Marina might have been able to conceal the union from outsiders but it is incredible that the ceremony would have remained a secret to her father and brothers in camp with her. Her personal attendant, Marcin Stadnicki, testified that his mistress was not married to the pretender. Her lust for power was stronger than shame or honor. The comedy Dmitrii and Marina performed could not deceive the gentry and mercenaries who had known the first pretender well, but it made an impression on simple people. Word that the duly crowned queen had met with True Dmitrii went out all over the country.

The defeat of Shuiskii's army and the siege of Moscow caused the flickering flame of civil war to burst out again with new fury. In Pskov the town poor drove out the tsar's administrators and recognized Dmitrii's authority. His successes were greeted enthusiastically in Astrakhan, which had become a center of opposition to Shuiskii the minute Otrepev died. The non-Russian peoples in the Volga area again took up arms. Units from Tushino encountered no opposition in the towns around Moscow: Dmitrii's authority was acknowledged in Pereiaslavl-Zaleskii, Yaroslavl, Kostroma, Balakhna, and Vologda. Supported by the lower orders, detachments from Tushino occupied Rostov, Vladimir, Suzdal, and Arzamas. Contingents of townsmen, peasants, and cossacks rushed to Tushino from all over the country. These waves of people would inevitably have overwhelmed the camp before Moscow if the mercenary army had not remained firmly in charge.

Rumors about the pretender's amazing success reached Lithuania and Poland. Bands of adventurers and swashbucklers hastened to the camp to fill the ranks of the newly-arisen Muscovite tsar's mercenary army. Relying on the mercenaries, Ruzynski finally took control of the pretender's camp. The triumph of the foreign, alien elements became total after Jan Sapieha and his picked band arrived to enter the pretender's service. Ruzynski straightway made amicable overtures to him. The two soldiers of fortune, who detested one another, met at a party and over a cup of wine pledged to keep out of each other's way. As a token of friendship they exchanged swords and on the spot carved up the Muscovite realm into spheres of influence. Ruzynski would remain the power in Tushino and the southern towns. Sapieha undertook to subdue the Trinity-St. Sergius monastery and conquer the territory north of Moscow.

Although the mercenary army openly scorned the pretender, considering him a worthless scoundrel, it could not do without him. The fictitious rights to the kingdom the pretender claimed constituted the sole justification for the invasion the army had already undertaken. While committing acts of violence and rapine, the knights incessantly proclaimed their sole purpose was to restore the lawful sovereign the Moscow boyars had overthrown. Dmitrii may have been utterly insignificant, but no matter how worthless and vile the Thief of Tushino might seem, he was important, not in himself but for who he was supposed to be. To simple people he was still Good Tsar Dmitrii. In his name Bolotnikov and his men had fought against the boyar tsar.

Rebel units that had joined the pretender in Starodub and Orel followed him to Tushino. They had their own leaders. Bolotnikov's famous atamans like Yurii Bezzubtsev could be seen on Tushino streets. Bezzubtsev had rendered exceptional service to the insurgent cause, but he occupied a position in the camp at Tushino different from the one he had held with Bolotnikov. Like other leaders of the peasant war, Bezzubtsev had to be content with a modest role under the Tushino tsar. Ivan Martynovich Zarutskii had emerged as a key figure in Tushino. Aspects of his life recalled Bolotnikov's. Both had drunk from the cup of constraint and slavery. Son of a Tarnopol townsman, Zarutskii had been taken prisoner as a child by the Crimean Tatars. Through summer heat and winter snow Russian captives toiled without interruption on their masters' estates. Among the Tatars Zarutskii was exposed to cruelty and injustice. Maturing in adversity, the prisoner risked his life to flee to the free Don cossacks. Among them he grew extraordinarily proficient in the use of swords and pistols and acquired a reputation for exceptional bravery among his comrades. Zarutskii

served with the men of the Don in the first pretender's army and then
joined Bolotnikov in the siege of Moscow.

Bolotnikov had noticed and appreciated the Don ataman's remarkable capacities. When beleaguered Tula was in deadly danger and
prompt dispatch of reinforcements from outside was the only thing that
might have saved the insurgent army, Bolotnikov entrusted Zarutskii
with a responsible mission. He was to charge through the encircling
forces, make his way to Lithuania, somehow find Dmitrii, and bring
a new army to relieve Tula. Zarutskii unexpectedly witnessed Dmitrii's
appearance in Starodub. Bolotnikov's emissary rendered the pretender
a great service by recognizing him as the True Tsar. Zarutskii was
already known in the Seversk towns; Dmitrii did him the honor of
asking him to join in a mock jousting tournament.

Cossacks and other rebels were suspicious when Lord Ruzynski and
his hussars arrived at their camp. At the time Zarutskii was in command
of thousands of Don and Zaporozhian cossacks. He enjoyed the advantage and could have ensured that the pretender would remain a free
agent, but instead he chose to come to terms with the new ataman. The
undisputed leader of the cossack host in Tushino, Zarutskii suppressed
all signs of disaffection in the cossack army and actually became an
agent of the foreign elements that had assumed control in the pretender's camp. The ataman dealt skilfully with Ruzynski's officers;
boyars now clustered around Dmitrii.

A covert struggle accompanied the shift at the top. Ordinary rebels
gazed mistrustfully at the hated nobles arriving in Tushino. The pretender had renounced his old social slogans in order to attract gentry.
Tushino had a dampening effect on rebels who had come there from
areas aflame with peasant war. It was as though a bucket of cold water
had been thrown over a heated organism.

The Astrakhan region continued to be a leading center of insurrection. After Heir Petr, other heirs-apparent, whom cossacks, taxpaying
peasants, and slaves had produced from their midst, made appearances
there. The most influential was Heir Ivan-Avgust, who gave himself
out to be a son of Tsar Ivan the Terrible. He had enjoyed at least a year
of real power in Astrakhan. Insurgent towns sent their commanders
for him to dispose of; foreign envoys asked him for safe-conducts.
Ivan-Avgust had intended to help Bolotnikov while he was besieged
in Tula; now he and his forces made their way to Dmitrii.

The Starodub Thief at first welcomed leaders of the mutinous cossacks with honor but later abruptly changed his attitude. Crowds of

gentry dissatisfied with Shuiskii were going over to Tushino, but there they came in contact with peasants claiming to be sons of tsars. They ran back in fright to Moscow to seek shelter under the wing of the lawful autocrat.

Ivan-Avgust was particularly dangerous because he enjoyed the sympathy of many disaffected cossacks. Dmitrii had been careful not to provoke this self-proclaimed tsar as long as the latter received support from the cossack atamans, but the alliance between Zarutskii and Ruzynski drastically altered the position. Zarutskii helped the pretender suppress discontent among the men who had served with Bolotnikov. Ivan-Avgust, leader of the Astrakhan insurgents, was hanged at Tushino, as were other cossack and peasant pretenders and leaders of popular groups. These repressions meant that the forces which had joined Bolotnikov to struggle against the yoke of feudal injustice had been completely defeated.

The Tushino headquarters bore a strange appearance. It was set on a hill near a place where a brook, the Skhodnia, fell into the Moscow river. It struck contemporaries as untidy. The top of the hill was covered with hussars' tents, among which towered the hut serving as the pretender's residence. Abodes of Russian nobles stood nearby. Lords and those trying to look like lords lived on the hill. The common people swelled the broad suburbs that lay at the foot. Huts hastily thrown up and roofed with straw were jammed together and packed with cossacks, fusiliers, slaves, and the rest of the commons. When it rained the camp was a sea of mud. The stench was unbearable.

The Tushino boyars felt entirely secure in the Polish encampment. The mercenary army successfully protected them from popular wrath. The Romanov and Saltykov families predominated at Dmitrii's court. Filaret Romanov, metropolitan of Rostov, had been captured by men from Tushino but he soon became a force in their camp. Dmitrii restored to him the rank of patriarch of which he had been deprived. His relatives, members of the Troekurov, Sitskii, and Cherkasskii families, who had gone over to Tushino, clustered around Filaret. Presided over by the highborn boyar Mikhail Saltykov and Prince Dmitrii Trubetskoi, the Tushino council welcomed Otrepev's favorite, Mikhail Molchanov, under the new pretender's auspices. Bogdan Sutupov and the boyar servitor Prince Grigorii Shakhovskoi likewise found refuge there.

Zarutskii occupied a prominent place on the Tushino council. Dmitrii had rewarded him generously for changing sides. In defiance of tradition he had raised the former free cossack to boyar rank and assigned him patrimonial estates and service-tenure lands. The Tushino nobility had accepted him with great reluctance but Hetman Zolkiewski, who was excellently informed about the pretender's affairs, considered him one of the real leaders in Tushino. Ruzynski, head of the mercenary army, was usually drunk and seldom interfered; it was Zarutskii who disposed of and checked the guard, sent out patrols, undertook to correlate information, and employed scouts to keep abreast of what the enemy was doing.

When the first snows signaled the coming of winter, mercenary bands fanned out into adjacent villages. They would espy a hut that was better than average, drive its inhabitants out into the cold, smash it up, and remove the rubble to camp. Soldiers took whatever they wanted from the population and brought so much booty back to Tushino that they did not know what to do with it.

The pretender issued charters full of lavish promises to the people, offering them exemption from royal imposts and other concessions. The people believed in Tsar Dmitrii. The inhabitants of Yaroslavl sent a rich treasure and a supply train to Tushino and promised to equip 1,000 cavalrymen. They were cruelly deceived: the Tushino authorities laid supplementary exactions upon them and confiscated merchandise from their traders. Sapieha's representatives requisitioned whatever Ruzynski's men had left.

After acquiring control of Yaroslavl the men of Tushino strove diligently to seize Nizhnii Novgorod and open a route to the lower Volga region. Dmitrii's emissaries established themselves in Balakhna, next door to Nizhnii Novgorod. They still hoped they could provoke the townsmen there to rise against Shuiskii. Rebellious non-Russian peoples came over to the Good Tsar; the town was invested on all sides, and relations with Moscow were severed, but although they were bereft of support, the people of Nizhnii Novgorod did not fall prey to fear or dejection. Power in the city passed to a council that included all ranks, headed by the local commandant, Aleksandr Repnin, gentry, town elders, and the people. The influential town league supported the council's actions. Nizhnii Novgorod quickly became a center of opposition to Tushino aggression. The people cut down a detachment advancing from Balakhna and cleared the bandits from the area. Alarmed at their success, Dmitrii dispatched Prince Semen Viazemskii to Nizhnii Novgorod with orders to punish the disobedient town. Undismayed by threats, the people of Nizhnii

Novgorod defeated the approaching forces, apprehended unlucky Commander Viazemskii, and hanged him in the town square.

Ataman Ruzynski blocked the roads linking Moscow with the southern and western regions. Jan Sapieha laid siege to the Trinity-St. Sergius monastery and took control of the road leading north out of Moscow. The route to Kolomna was the only one left open; it carried grain convoys from Riazan and contingents of soldiers to Moscow. In the fall of 1608 the men of Tushino tried to take Kolomna in an effort to close the road to Riazan. Ivan Pushkin, the local commander, asked Moscow for help. Tsar Vasilii sent Prince Dmitrii Pozharskii and a small contingent of soldiers to relieve him. This was the first command for Pozharskii, then aged thirty, the future hero of the liberation movement. The commander of Kolomna was hostile to him and refused to sully his family's honor by submitting to a lowborn prince who had held no previous command. Prince Dmitrii had to rely solely on his own forces. He did not await the enemy under the protection of the fortress walls; he marched out to meet him. Encountering a group of foreigners in the village of Vysotskii, twenty miles from Kolomna, Pozharskii attacked at dawn and routed them. He took many prisoners, baggage, treasure, and supplies.

The engagement at Kolomna first revealed Pozharskii's military skills. His victory was not fraught with decisive consequences, but in the chain of defeats and failures it stood out like a flash of fire in the dark. The people of Moscow did not realize how important it had been until later, when they were deprived of Riazan grain.

Chapter Six

INTERVENTION

Dmitrii did all he could to win over the Moscow nobility. Tushino boyars conducted a secret correspondence with relatives in Moscow. Tushino was not far away and many Russian gentry fled there, seeking riches and rank. Dmitrii rewarded those who changed sides and issued charters entitling them to land. Although he was prodigal with rescripts, the pretender had no money to pay the Moscow gentry good salaries. Deceived in their expectations, the runaways returned to Moscow. There were instances when a man would shift his allegiance from Shuiskii to the pretender and back again. Shuiskii eagerly listened to informers but he tried not to provoke the powerful. He did not execute such people when they changed sides and used their tales of repentance in an effort to expose the pretender. When defectors were of lesser stature the tsar did not stand on ceremony. He pushed them through holes cut in the ice and drowned them. This was done at night to avoid unneccessary rumors.

On February 25, 1609 Shuiskii's enemies attempted a palace coup. The ringleaders of the conspiracy were Moscow courtiers—Prince Roman Gagarin and Timofei Griaznoi, Grigorii Sumbulov of Riazan, Mikhail Molchanov, who had returned clandestinely to Moscow, and others. They broke into the Kremlin with a band of armed confederates and charged into the room where the boyar council was in session. The conspirators shouted at the boyars, demanding that the stupid, indecent, and obscene tsar be overthrown. Fearing violence, the council members offered little resistance. After the rioters left the palace for the square the councillors took advantage of the turmoil to disperse to their homes. Vasilii Golitsyn was the sole exception; he repaired to the square.

Along the way the group seized Patriarch Hermogen and dragged him to the Place of Execution. The patriarch tried to resist but the rebels prodded him in the back, spattered him with mud, and loudly upbraided him. At the Place of Execution the conspirators called upon the people to rise against Shuiskii. "He was elected without popular consent," cried some. "The tsar has killed 2,000 gentry and their wives and children," shouted others. The conspirators summoned the mob to protect gentry,"our brothers," whom the tsar's guards had been taking out since morning to drown in the river.[1] The mob grew more impassioned and emissaries from Tushino, Mikhail Molchanov and Prince Fedor Meshcherskii, began yelling at the top of their lungs, reading an appeal Tsar Dmitrii and the Tushino boyars had sent to the people of Moscow.

Despite their best efforts the conspirators failed to arouse the people in Moscow's town quarter to revolt. While the rioters were yelling in the square the tsar succeeded in summoning loyal units from the camp at Khodynka. The conspirators charged into the royal residence to arrest Shuiskii, but the moment was lost. Vasilii shut himself up in the palace and declared he would never be forced to vacate his office. The crowd began to break up and participants in the unsuccessful coup had to leave Moscow in a hurry.

Vasilii Golitsyn and Mikhail Tatishchev had helped Shuiskii overthrow the previous pretender, but now the tsar's former confederates were deserting him. Golitsyn behaved in a most duplicitous manner. He did not lift a finger to aid the Shuiskii family and was quite ready to support the insurgents if they prevailed. Tatishchev had been sent to Novgorod in the nick of time; it was rumored he was planning to take a detachment of soldiers to Moscow and overthrow Tsar Vasilii. As soon as Skopin came to Novgorod he arrested Tatishchev and handed him over for a street crowd to deal with.

The spring of 1609 brought fresh trials for the people of Moscow. The men of Tushino besieged Kolomna and blockaded the capital. The city poor starved to death; every day hundreds of corpses were removed from the streets. Famished people often gathered by the palace windows to demand the tsar give them an explantion. Malcontents tried to utilize the crisis in order to organize another conspiracy against Shuiskii. The conspirators planned to murder the tsar at Easter, during a solemn procession when he rode on an ass. They were counting on the support of many Moscow gentry and traders, but Vasilii Buturlin, one of their number, betrayed their plans to Tsar Vasilii.

The tsar was devastated because one member of this conspiracy turned out to be Ivan Fedorovich Kriuk-Kolychev, his longtime champion and personal friend. In Boris Godunov's time Kriuk had suffered banishment for the devotion he had shown to the Shuiskii family. Tsar Vasilii had made him a boyar and entrusted him as a courtier with the management of the estates belonging to the royal family. Kriuk had many partisans in the boyar council, and so Shuiskii chose not to investigate the affair too closely. He merely ordered Kriuk to be seized and questioned. After brutal torture he was taken to the square and beheaded.[2] Cowed by this savage execution, the tsar's enemies in council temporarily lowered their sights.

The pretender had been remarkably successful but his fortunes inevitably began to decline. The Thief of Tushino controlled vast territories but his regime was steadily becoming more harsh and less attractive to the people. Ataman Ruzynski and his officers abandoned all pretense and behaved in the pretender's possessions as though they were occupying enemy territory. They were not interested in conciliar rank or patrimonial estates. What they wanted was real power, and as always the mercenaries thought only about cold cash. Since the pretender could not pay the monies he owed them, he issued charters authorizing them to live off the land and collect taxes from the people. The pretender's debts increased; so did his expenses. Alarmed at this, the Polish gentry elected a commission of ten men, who established strict control over Dmitrii's finances. Neither Dmitrii nor Marina might make further expenditures without their authorization. The decisions of the ataman and the council of ten were binding on everyone, including Tushino boyars.

If the lower orders had not supported the pretender he would never have succeeded, but their attitude began to change when they realized that aggressors lurked behind him. Their belief in Good Dmitrii was shaken. Experience had convinced the people that the foreigners and the Tushino commanders were harsher in their exactions than the old authorities. Ruzynski and Sapieha billeted their armies throughout the greater Moscow region. Soldiers took horses from peasants and stripped villages of their grain and forage. Opposition to their plundering was punished savagely.

The violence provoked the people to resist. The populace rose up and struggled against the aggressors. Tushino dominion lasted only a few weeks in Vologda. Its inhabitants received support from Galich and Kostroma, the Dvina land, and the north coast region. Jan Sapieha defeated regiments led by Prince Ivan Shuiskii but he was held up for a long time at the walls of the Trinity-St. Sergius monastery. Preoccupied with what was happening in the north, Sapieha instructed Lisowski to pacify rebel areas. The interventionists took Kostroma and Galich but their success was brief. With help from the tsar's commanders, local units cleaned up the Volga region. During April and May, 1609 Lisowski's forces were driven out of Yaroslavl.

Shut up in Moscow, Tsar Shuiskii was unable to profit from the wave of popular discontent. His government was seriously compromised because it had fought the insurgent people so fiercely. Passive and inactive, the crown had failed to inspire either fear or respect. Distrusting his own people and lacking support among his closest associates, Tsar Vasilii hoped more and more that foreigners would come to his aid.

For three years Karl IX, king of Sweden, had been sending couriers to Moscow with offers of military aid. This was actually a pretext to interfere in Russia's internal affairs. The Swedish government's efforts finally achieved success. Shuiskii sent his nephew, Mikhail Skopin, to Novgorod, charged to conclude an alliance with Sweden. On February 28, 1609 Skopin initialed an agreement. The king pledged to provide Russia with a mercenary army in return for territorial concessions. Skopin yielded, promising to cede Sweden the fortress and district of Korela. The understanding compromised Russia's territorial integrity and national honor and stirred up resentment among the inhabitants of the Karelian peninsula. It was an unequal treaty: Tsar Vasilii expected a experienced, battle-hardened Swedish army would come to his aid but Karl IX had no intention of committing his own troops. His plan was to defeat the Poles cheaply. Recruiters scoured Europe, hiring Germans, Frenchmen, Englishmen, and Scotchmen, and transferred them as quickly as possible to Russia, where the tsar's treasury would have to maintain them. Shuiskii paid the mercenaries huge sums.

Skopin left Novgorod on May 10, 1609 with 3,000 Russians and 15,000 Swedes. At Tver he routed men of Tushino who had come out against him. The mercenaries immediately insisted on their pay. The result was a foregone conclusion. The commander long since had expended the resources allocated to him and was unable to satisfy their demands. The mercenaries mutinied and retired to the frontier, robbing and pillaging as they went. There were only 300 Swedes left in Skopin's army, although their numbers later increased to 1,000 men. It was a popular rising, not the Swedes, that allowed Skopin to prevail. Armed men joined him from everywhere: 3,000 soldiers from Smolensk were waiting for the commander at Torzhok, and detachments from Yaroslavl, Kostroma, and the north coast towns flocked to his standard. Skopin now had as many as 15,000 men.

North of Moscow the Trinity-St. Sergius monastery remained the chief center of opposition to the interventionists. For sixteen months Ataman Jan Sapieha had been vainly besieging the large place with its high towers and strong walls. Fusiliers, monks, and peasants courageously beat back enemy attacks. The adjacent population regularly supplied the defenders of the fortress with men and provisions. The approach of Skopin's army alarmed the camp before the monastery. Sapieha tried to destroy it at Kaliazin but was defeated in a two-day battle, August 18-19, 1609. But Skopin's achievements failed to improve the military position because Russia's international situation had deteriorated drastically. The country was exposed to attack from the Crimean Tatars and Polish interventionists simultaneously.

After the death of the first Dmitrii, Shuiskii had dispatched an envoy to the Crimea to renew the peace treaty with the khan, but he was seized and executed by insurgents in Putivl. The mutiny in the southern towns long since had closed off diplomatic contacts between Russia and the Crimea. In spring, 1609 the Crimean horde took the initiative. In July Janibeg, the new khan, invaded Russia with a large army. In the past Tatars on plundering raids swiftly retired into the steppe, but this time they advanced on Moscow leisurely, burning villages and enslaving the population on the way. The Crimeans crossed the Oka after destroying Tarusa; their units appeared at Serpukhov, Kolomna, and Borovsk.

The situation in Moscow was fluid. The crafty Shuiskii tried to conceal the Crimean invasion from the people. In a rescript to the towns he asserted that the Tatars had come as allies to help Russia against the Polish king. His prevarications failed to produce the desired result. The people of Kolomna and other shattered areas bitterly assailed the tsar for having called in the pagans to ruin the country.

Ruzynski was firmly in control at Tushino, close to the capital's walls; Jan Sapieha was maintaining his position before the Trinity-St. Sergius monastery, and the Crimean Tatars were approaching Moscow from the south. Russia's position was unenviable. Sigismund III and his advisors decided to intervene openly. It was not hard to find a pretext for war. The king based it on Russia's rapprochement with Sweden. Tsar Vasilii had hoped the Swedes would help him defeat the men of Tushino and expel the foreigners, but the Russo-Swedish alliance simply had played into the king's hands.

Sigismund was heir to the Swedish crown when he mounted the Polish throne. He had inherited the title after the death of his father, the Swedish king John III, but the personal union between the Rzeczpospolita and Sweden did not last long. Karl IX staged a coup and war broke out between Sweden and Poland over Livonia. Sigismund considered his uncle an usurper and hoped to win back the Swedish throne. The alliance Karl made with the Muscovite tsar threatened Sigismund's dynastic ambitions. He did not hesitate to sacrifice Poland's interests in pursuit of his goal. Mired in the war with Russia, Poland had been unable to prevent Swedish intrusion into Livonia and Sweden's control of the Baltic sea deleteriously affected both Russia and Poland. Such were the long-range consequences of Sigismund's policies.

Swedish by birth and background, Sigismund poorly understood the temperament of the Polish people, or their country. A fanatical Catholic, he determinedly persecuted the Orthodox in the Ukraine and Belorussia and was pondering how to submit Russia to the Roman church. But his aggressive plans and efforts to achieve unlimited power aroused opposition in Poland. In order to convince popular opinion that war with Moscow was necessary the king was forced to hire publicists. A certain Pawel Palchowski brought out a pamphlet calling for the immediate conquest of Russia. He claimed the gentry would acquire fertile Russian lands as easily as Spanish conquistadores had won the New World. Military colonies like those that had existed in Rome would be created in the subject country. Gentry anxious for land would obtain vast holdings in Russia; Russian gentry would be permitted only small allotments. The Russian were Christians in name only; a crusade should be proclaimed against them.

The king and his circle dreamed of grandiose conquests but clearly lacked the means to accomplish them. The gentry showed no enthusiasm for a crusade. Sigismund decided not to submit the question of war with Russia to the Polish assembly [Sejm] for discussion and conducted his military preparations in secret. Crown Hetman Zolkiewski expressed strong doubts and fears concerning the adventure. He warned the king that many people and even senators would refuse to approve such a war and would think the king was anxious to benefit himself, not the republic.[3] Zolkiewski refused to have anything to do with these extravagant schemes for colonizing Russia; he came out in favor of reaching an understanding with the Russian nobility and forming a union of the two countries. But the Polish envoys returning from Moscow assured the king that the boyar nobles were ready to hand the tsar's throne over to him and conclude a dynastic union. Similar assertions were coming in from the most disparate quarters.[4]

Lew Sapieha, chancellor of Lithuania, advised the king to begin by taking Smolensk. He was sure the fortress would open its gates voluntarily; the king had merely to knock on them. In September, 1609 Sapieha's units converged on the city and Sigismund joined them a few days later. The royal force before Smolensk amounted to little more than 12,000 men and contained more cavalry than infantry. Available artillery amounted to no more than a dozen pieces. Sigismund was planning an outing, not the siege of a first-class fortress.

Smolensk, one of Russia's most ancient cities, had been ruled for a century by grand princes of Lithuania. Smolensk and Riazan were the last Great Russian enclaves to enter the unified Russian principality in the early seventeenth century. A major trading and artisan center, the city was a focal point for Russian trade with the west. Merchants came there from Lithuania, Poland, Czechoslovakia, Germany, and other European countries. Among Russian cities only Moscow and Pskov paid the treasury more taxes. Contemporaries affirmed that its town quarter contained as many as 6,000 residences. The total population may have exceeded 20,000 people.

Smolensk was the key to the entire Russian defense system in the west. Under Boris Godunov the city was girt with strong stone walls, built under the supervision of the distinguished Russian architect Fedor Kon. Godunov compared the new fortress to a precious necklace worn to protect the Russian land. The walls of Smolensk were almost four miles long and more than sixteen feet thick. No less than 1,500 fusiliers made up the garrison and on outbreak of hostilities the commander could summon the town dwellers. About 1,800 citizens armed with muskets and swords constantly patrolled the fortress walls and almost 1,200 gentry soldiers were in the city. This meant the garrison was substantial. After the struggle with the first pretender the Moscow high command had stored immense amounts of provisions and powder in Smolensk.

Embarking on his Smolensk campaign, Sigismund widely disseminated a proclamation in which he stated he had taken pity on ruined Russia. This was his sole reason for action; he intended to protect the Russian people. The king ordered Smolensk to open the fortress gates and welcome him with bread and salt. The people replied they would rather die than submit. They defended their city for an unprecedented twenty months.

On October 12 the king's army tried to take Smolensk by storm. Soldiers charged into breaches on two sides. They managed to knock down the Abraham gate but every effort to force their way into the fortress was beaten back. The enemy had to undertake a protracted siege. Mercenaries placed mines beneath the fortress walls but the people of Smolensk replied in kind and eliminated the danger. The besieged made frequent sorties, which alarmed the enemy camp. A daring band once left Smolensk at noon, crossed the Dneiper, seized an enemy standard, and returned safely.

Meanwhile Skopin and his army continued their slow progress towards Moscow, cleaning out men of Tushino and Poles from the areas and towns north of the capital. Realizing the danger, the rival chiefs Ruzynski and Jan Sapieha decided to join forces to stop Skopin. They attacked Aleksandrovskaia Sloboda, which the commander had occupied, but suffered a defeat.

With one blow King Sigismund had hoped to breach the Russian defense system and bring the war quickly to an end but his plan failed. Though weakened by civil war, Russia found the strength to repel the first onset of the foreign foe.

Chapter Seven

MILITARY DEFEAT

Dmitrii's power declined rapidly. His men surrendered one town after another. Failure provoked dissension in the camp at Tushino. The Thief's boyar council was falling apart. Some of its members entered into secret negotiations with Shuiskii while others sought safety with the interventionists at Smolensk.

His mercenaries were not averse to reentering the king's service but their greed stood in the way. They calculated Dmitrii owed them the impossible sum of four to seven million rubles and they had no intention of forfeiting these millions they claimed they had earned. Late in 1609 the pretender and Marina dejectedly watched through an aperture in their quarters as the knights triumphantly greeted Sigismund's envoys, who did not bother to pay them a courtesy call. The Polish officers and men in Tushino asserted that to serve Dmitrii was the same thing as serving Sigismund because all of them were advancing the king's interests in his war with Russia. They accordingly demanded that the king's treasury should reward them for their efforts; then they would repair immediately to the camp at Smolensk.[1] Sigismund had no millions to spare and the negotiations were abortive. Dmitrii was saved by his debts.

He was at a loss. Treason was rife. Dmitrii bethought himself of Miechowiecki, his former patron. He was summoned secretly to the palace and had a long intimate conversation with the pretender. Ruzynski was furious when he learned of it. Bursting into the royal chambers he killed Miechowiecki before the terrified sovereign's eyes. The next day Dmitrii planned to complain to the army about what the hetman had done but Ruzynski threatened he would behead him. Dmitrii next called in Adam Wisniowiecki, his other benefactor. Closeted in the royal quarters the two men started drinking hard. Ruzynski soon put an end to their protracted bout. Smashing down the door he belabored tipsy Lord Adam with a cane until it broke. The pretender sobered up in a flash and hid in a chicken coop near the residence.

The situation in Tushino had gone out of control. Ruzynski was too weak to make the army obey him. Sensing his end was nigh he got drunk almost every day. The ataman had never paid much attention to Dmitrii and now he ignored him entirely. Dmitrii was given no more horses and forbidden to ride, but he managed to outwit his watchful guards. People living just outside Tushino continued to believe Dmitrii's cause was righteous and would hide him whenever he managed to leave his quarters. The mercenaries augmented patrols at the camp's gates. One evening cossacks and a wagon loaded with boards came to the south gate. Detecting nothing amiss, the soldiers passed them through, unaware that the self-styled autocrat lay cramped on the bottom of the vehicle, underneath wood on top of which a rough cossack was seated.

As soon as word spread throughout the camp that Dmitrii had disappeared, mercenaries ran to plunder his quarters and steal his goods and regalia. The king's envoys kept their soldiers on the alert. Their train was searched; it was suspected Dmitrii's body was concealed in one of their carriages. Lord Tiszkiewicz charged that Ruzynski had captured or murdered the pretender. His unit fired at Ruzynski's tents and tried to seize army wagons. The ataman's men shot back as they retreated. Tushino soon learned that Dmitrii was alive and in Kaluga. Couriers brought the army an appeal he had issued. He told the mercenaries that Ruzynski and Boyar Saltykov had made an attempt on his life and demanded the ataman be removed.

When danger struck, Dmitrii treated Marina in the same way as Otrepev had. Left to her fate by her husband, Marina strove diligently to save her tottering throne. The haughty queen went round the tents, trying to move some soldiers with tears and others with feminine charms. She "wantonly spent nights with soldiers in their barracks, oblivious to shame and virtue,"[2] is what her chamberlain wrote in his diary. These efforts proving unproductive, Marina fled to Kaluga.

Various groups in the camp, which already had found it difficult to get along with one another, clashed openly after Dmitrii disappeared. The lower orders instinctively felt the agreement with the aggressors besieging Smolensk had placed the country in jeopardy. The foreign mercenaries were preparing to go over to Sigismund. The cossacks, having no wish to emulate them, intended to follow the Good Sovereign to Kaluga. In vain Zarutskii urged the rank and file to proceed to the king's camp. They refused to obey. The ataman had long ago reached an understanding with Ataman Ruzynski and the Tushino boyars and he continued to serve them loyally. He tried to deal with cossack disobedience by holding the men in camp by force. The encounter ended badly for Zarutskii. More than 2,000 Don cossacks made their way past the gates of Tushino, unfurled their banners, and marched off to Kaluga. Zarutskii was accustomed to having his own way, no matter what it cost. He rushed to Ruzynski's tent. The latter called out the cavalry and treacherously fell upon the cossacks, who were proceeding on foot. These men paid dearly for their error. The road from Tushino to Kaluga was littered with corpses.[3] But the mercenaries too soon had to pay for the slaughter they had perpetrated. This bloodbath hastened the demarcation of forces in Tushino. Patriots broke decisively with those who had gone over to the interventionists. Ataman Yurii Bezzubtsev, Bolotnikov's closest collaborator, headed the opposition. Lord Mlotski, stationed in Serpukhov, was the first to suffer. The inhabitants of that city rose in revolt, supported by Bezzubtsev's cossacks, who had refused to enter the king's service. Mlotski's detachment was wiped out.[4] Popular risings occurred in several other towns loyal to the pretender.

The civil war had confounded established norms and procedures. Champions of social justice that fate had thrust into Tushino were truly in a tragic position. They did not belong with those who had brutally suppressed Bolotnikov's revolt. They had no choice but to follow the Good Tsar to Kaluga, but no one less resembled a popular leader than the Thief. He had learned nothing from his encounter with Ruzynski. He was mortally afraid his foreign soldiers would abandon him. German mercenaries surrounded his quarters in Kaluga. After the break with Ruzynski, Dmitrii turned for help to Jan Sapieha and tried to win his support.

The cossacks were annoyed to see the Good Sovereign was bent on restoring the old Tushino cabal. Wearied with war, many Don cossacks stopped believing the revolt would succeed. Crowds of them left Kaluga to return to their enclaves.

Events in Tushino followed their own course. The king's envoys tried to obtain support from the Tushino nobles and to convince Patriarch Filaret and the boyars that the king had come to Russia for the sole purpose of taking the Russians under his protection.

The hypocrisy the envoys displayed fooled none of the Russians in Tushino. The pretender was finished and the charade was coming to an inglorious close, but the Thief's boyars were ready to do anything in their power to save the lost cause. Patriarch Filaret and Saltykov wept when they kissed the king's rescripts. They declared they were ready to consign the Russian throne to Sigismund's heir, Wladyslaw.[5] Once, while trying to get rid of the first pretender, Vasilii Shuiskii had offered the Muscovite throne to the king's son. The men of Tushino resurrected this project, but now with the view of getting rid of Shuiskii. The idea of unifying Russia and the Rzeczpospolita, which had had a number of advantages in peacetime, acquired sinister import during the intervention. Thousands of enemy soldiers were besieging Smolensk and armed bands were seizing Russian towns and villages. To expect that electing the Polish heir to the Muscovite throne would end foreign invasion was nonsense.

Although the Tushino camp was visibly breaking up, the patriarch and boyars continued trying to form a government. For two weeks envoys from Tushino (Boyar Saltykov, Mikhail Molchanov, and others) negotiated with the king in his camp before Smolensk. This resulted in an agreement to transfer the throne to the Polish pretender. The Russian articles, hammered out by February 4, 1610, stipulated that "Vladislav Sigismundovich" would adopt the Greek faith and be crowned by the Muscovite patriarch in accordance with Orthodox ritual. The king returned an equivocal answer to this item in the boyars' articles and requests. He made no guarantee his son would abjure the Catholic faith.

The Tushino boyars insisted serfdom must remain sacrosanct. The agreement strongly recommended Wladyslaw not grant Russian peasants a right of departure, or free boyar slaves, or allow them to serve in fortresses. The future fate of the free cossacks was left open. The Tushino plan provided that Wladyslaw should rule jointly with the boyar and ecclesiastical councils. The upheavals during the Time of Troubles had expanded the purview of national assemblies. Russians now deemed it impossible to settle issues without them. Wladyslaw would be obliged to confer with the patriarch, the higher clergy, the boyars and "all the realm" on matters of great moment. The men from Tushino understood the last term to mean primarily gentry and leading merchants.[6]

They were concerned about impoverished gentry and were careful to insist that such persons be assigned modest holdings in terms of service, not birth. The instrument allowed gentry to go abroad for study and guaranteed that in so doing they would not lose their lands and property. There may have been advantages in the Smolensk covenant, but the undertaking was not worth the paper it was written on because King Sigismund had not given the men from Tushino real guarantees he would fulfill its terms. And there was no need: the government headed by Filaret Romanov and Saltykov fell the day after the agreement was signed. Saltykov and the other envoys sat in one of the king's carriages at Smolensk, where they had turned into lackeys of the foreign aggressors. The king employed the agreement to conceal the real reason he had undertaken the war, which was to seize lands along the border.

The Smolensk agreement enormously complicated the murky situation in Russia. Besides two tsars, the legal one in Moscow and the Thief in Kaluga, a third, "Vladislav Sigismundovich," had appeared like a mirage in a desert. Acting in his name, Sigismund lavishly recompensed the men from Tushino with lands in Russia that did not belong to him. The king considered the Smolensk agreement a credible device which would enable him to win control of the Muscovite realm. However, even he understood that the military situation did not favor his grand design. The siege of Smolensk had lasted more than six months. The king's army had suffered losses and had failed to make the Russian garrison surrender. Ruzynski and Jan Sapieha could not maintain themselves in the center of Russia. After fierce fighting Sapieha withdrew from the Trinity-St. Sergius monastery to the Lithuanian frontier. Ruzynski burned down the camp at Tushino and retired to Volokolamsk.

In March, 1610 the people of Moscow were delighted to extend a warm welcome to Mikhail Skopin and his army. The siege was over. Prince Skopin, the liberator of Moscow, enjoyed exceptional popularity. The gentry no longer trusted unsuccessful Tsar Vasilii and more and more placed their hopes in his energetic and authoritative nephew. Prokofii Liapunov was the first to say aloud what many were privately thinking. He wrote a letter to Skopin in which he sharply assailed Vasilii and hailed the young commander as the new tsar.[7]

Skopin refused to approve a palace coup and had Liapunov's emissaries arrested, but subsequently they were released. Partisans of the tsar found out about the matter. Their denunciations were taken seriously. The royal welcome Moscow had accorded Skopin intensified Shuiskii's suspicions. Tsar Vasilii attempted to have it out with his nephew in private. In a heated family quarrel Skopin reportedly advised his uncle to abdicate and allow the realm to elect another tsar capable of uniting a country torn by civil strife. The tsar's brothers fanned the flames and made no attempt to conceal their hatred of the liberator of Moscow. Arrogant, haughty Dmitrii Shuiskii hoped to occupy the throne when childless Tsar Vasilii died. Skopin's achievements threatened his plans. Watching Skopin's triumphant entry from the city wall, Dmitrii could not refrain from crying out, "There goes my rival!"[8]

Moscow and the boyars hailed the hero with genuine enthusiasm. He was invited to a new festivity every day. Skopin invariably assented and his complaisancy caused him great misfortune. At Vorotynskii's home wine flowed like water. Visitors downed bumpers to hail the commander. Suddenly the guest of honor was taken ill. Blood poured from his nose. His retainers rushed him home. For two weeks he ran a high fever and became delirious. Then he died. He was little more than twenty years old.

The young commander's inexplicable death puzzled people. It was whispered all over Moscow that Skopin had been poisoned by his aunt, Ekaterina Skuratova-Shuiskaia, but no one could say for certain whether poison or excessive drinking had caused the commander's death. Tsar Vasilii wept publicly at his nephew's grave but few believed he was sincere.[9] Skopin's death was a disaster for the army and for the country. Dmitrii Shuiskii immediately took his place. He was a man born, so contemporaries said, to bring disgrace, not glory, to Russian arms. His appointment provoked discontent among both officers and men. Tsar Vasilii had not forgotten Dmitrii's disastrous failures, but he had no choice. He believed only in his brothers. The rest of the boyars long ago had forfeited his trust.

A Swedish general, Jacob de la Gardie, had accompanied Skopin to Moscow. A showdown was imminent. Sweden had sent fresh reinforcements to Russia. A contingent of 1,500 men reached de la Gardie in Moscow, and General Horn hastened south with 2,000 soldiers to help him. Karl IX had sent two of his best generals to Russia at the head of some 10,000 men, a considerable portion of Sweden's army. At the beginning of summer the Moscow high command managed with great difficulty to muster the gentry levy and brought the army's strength up to 30,000 men. Skopin's associate Valuev, with an army of 6,000, relieved Mozhaisk and moved along the Smolensk highway to Tsarev Zaimishche, where he built a fort and waited for the arrival of the main force.

Zolkiewski, the Polish hetman, knowing the enemy force was divided, decided to take advantage of this circumstance to forestall an allied attack on Smolensk. After a stubborn fight he pushed Valuev back and surrounded his fort. Dmitrii Shuiskii and de la Gardie came to Valuev's aid. By the evening of June 23 the armies were bivouaced for the night in the village of Klushino. Next day the allies decided to attack the Poles and free Valuev from his beleaguered fort some thirteen miles away. The numbers of the Russo-Swedish army far exceeded those of the Poles but Zolkiewski managed to augment his strength with help from the men of Tushino. He was joined by Zarutskii with Don cossacks and by Ivan Saltykov and his forces. Zolkiewski planned to take the allies unawares. Leaving his infantry at Valuev's fort, he and the cavalry, proceeding by night, came out at Klushino before dawn on June 24. Valuev might have attacked the Poles from the rear at any moment but he decided not to risk it. Aware their opponents were few, the allies took scant precautions. They did not trouble to post sentries along the Smolensk highway. The Swedish commander-in-chief spent the night in Dmitrii Shuiskii's tent, boasting he would capture the hetman.

The Russian and Swedish armies passed the night at some distance from each other. Their men were still asleep during the predawn hours, when Polish mounted patrols suddenly appeared. The hetman had taken the allies by surprise but even so he could not launch a general attack. It was still dark; Zolkiewski's army was strung out along narrow forest trails, and his cannon were mired in a swamp. The Polish cavalry required more than an hour to reach the battle site.

The allies were aroused and their camps were filled with shouts and the neighing of horses. Russians and Swedes managed to accoutre themselves. Both armies rushed out to assume a defensive position before their respective camps. Wattles dividing peasant fields formed

the sole cover for the infantry. They hindered the enemy cavalry from
wheeling to attack until the Poles managed to cut wide swathes through
them. The field at Klushino sounded like the Tower of Babel. Commands, curses, and exhortations were heard in almost every European
language—Russian, Polish, Swedish, German, Lithuanian, Tatar,
English, French, Finnish, and Scotch. The battle lasted more than four
hours. The sun rose over the edge of the forest and its rays sharply
illuminated the knoll before Klushino.

Squadrons of heavily-armed Polish hussars made several attacks on
the Russians. Vasilii Buturlin, commander of the advance guard, was
wounded and Andrei Golitsyn's regiment was wavering. It was time
to bring on the main force, but Dmitrii Shuiskii preferred to skulk in
his camp. Receiving no help, Golitsyn's soldiers turned to flight and
disappeared into an adjacent wood. The Swedish infantry on the right
flank conducted light fire from behind the wattles at the enemy's
attacking cavalry. At the height of the battle the Poles moved up two
cannon and started shooting at the infantry. The mercenaries successfully abandoned their unsafe cover and retired to camp. Soldiers fled
into the forest. The allied ranks appeared broken, and to make things
worse de la Gardie and Horn, forsaking the infantry, retired with a
cavalry force to Shuiskii's camp.

Pressure from the Polish cavalry began to slacken and the allies tried
to seize the initiative. A detachment of mounted English and French
musketeers galloped over the Klushino fields to charge the enemy. The
musketeers fired and wheeled their horses to let the second rank move
forward. The Poles did not let them complete their maneuvre and fell
upon them with broadswords. Thrown into confusion, the musketeers
pulled back and hussars swept into Shuiskii's camp right on their heels.
Bombardiers and fusiliers held their fire for fear of hitting their own
men. Rushing at full tilt through the camp the hussars continued the
chase until their horses were exhausted. The camp fired at them while
they were returning and they had to use an unfrequented path in order
to get by.

Prince Shuiskii stayed with the wagons. He was joined by Andrei
Golitsyn and the men who had managed to assemble in the wood. More
than 5,000 fusiliers and soldiers were preparing for the final encounter.
They had eighteen field pieces. Dmitrii Shuiskii had ample forces in
reserve to mount an attack, but he waited and procrastinated. Fighting
stopped for a long time. The final result was unclear. The Polish cavalry
had sustained heavy losses and needed respite. The hussars had shot

their bolt and hurried to regroup behind the knoll. Without infantry the hetman could not attack the Russian camp bristling with artillery and he realized his cavalry would have difficulty getting at the Swedish infantry. Then he was suddenly informed that deserters had come.

Mercenary armies are notoriously fickle. De la Gardie had found it difficult to make his multilingual force obey him. The soldiers had mutinied just prior to the battle, demanding money. The tsar had supplied the general with vast sums but the latter had refrained from disbursing them, anticipating his ranks would be thinned considerably. The Swedish commander-in-chief's greed redounded on his own head. While he and Horn were absent the mercenaries mutinied. Zolkiewski appraised the situation and sent his nephew to the Swedish camp to cut a deal. French mercenaries were the first to go over to the enemy. Next a detachment of Germans started to waver. Dmitrii Shuiskii learned of the parleys and sent Gavrila Pushkin to promise the Germans an immense reward.

The Swedish commanders finally woke up, returned to camp, and tried to halt the mutiny, but it was too late. In an effort to save the Swedish army from complete collapse, de la Gardie betrayed his Russian allies. He met with Zolkiewski on the battlefield and concluded a separate truce with him. While he was doing so half his forces passed by him on their way to join the Poles. De la Gardie ran to the wagons and began to pay the Swedes the monies the tsar had just sent him. The English and French mercenaries demanded their share and almost killed their Swedish commanders. They got no money and so they plundered de la Gardie's wagons. Then they made for the Russian supply train and sacked it too.[10]

The Swedish army no longer existed. Karl IX was beside himself when he learned of the catastrophe. The collapse of the Swedish army fatally affected the Russian forces. Dmitrii Shuiskii issued an order to retreat, and the retreat became a disorderly rout. Soldiers ran to hide in nearby forests. In utter panic Prince Dmitrii spurred on his horse until the beast got mired in a swamp. Abandoning the animal, the craven commander barely managed to extricate himself from the quagmire. He arrived in Mozhaisk with no army. People were puzzled when they beheld a richly-dressed knight striking the sides of a scraggy peasant jade with his bare heels in an effort to make it move faster. A few who recognized the tsar's brother hastened to make the sign of the cross.

Hearing nothing from Dmitrii Shuiskii, three days later Valuev made a strong sortie from his fort. When the besieged learned the Russian army had been destroyed they began to waver. The hetman dispatched Ivan Saltykov to meet with Valuev. This man of Tushino swore that the king would lift the siege of Smolensk and restore the border towns as soon as Russia recognized Wladyslaw as tsar. Valuev yielded to persuasion and declared he would accept the Smolensk covenant.

Hetman Zolkiewski now had Zarutskii's cossacks and Valuev's soldiers under his banner, a force of several thousand Russians. He counted on swinging Jan Sapieha to his side but Sapieha's mercenaries, whom the king had not paid, went off to join the pretender in Kaluga. Russia's military situation was daily growing worse. With Sapieha's support Dmitrii renewed his attack on Moscow and occupied Serpukhov. Zolkiewski's army entered Viazma and approached the Russian capital from the west.

Tsar Vasilii asked the Crimea for help. Responding to his call Kantemir-Murza reached Russia with 10,000 knights. The Crimeans passed Tula on their way to the Oka. Shuiskii sent a courier bearing rich gifts and commissioned Prince Pozharskii to escort the treasure to the Tatar encampment. Prince Lykov and 400 fusiliers followed Pozharskii to the Oka. Kantemir-Murza, nicknamed "Bloody Sword," listened approvingly to what the tsar's representative had to say and accepted the splendid gifts, but he understood what was happening around Moscow. Having no intention of becoming entangled in a struggle with the men of Tushino and the Poles, these perfidious allies turned their weapons against Shuiskii's troops and drove Lykov's detachment away. Sapieha provided the finishing touch. Kantemir-Murza left the Oka for the steppe.

Shuiskii had suffered one defeat after another. After Klushino he no longer had an army. The tsar ordered another gentry levy and to prepare Moscow for a siege, but the days of his dynasty were numbered. The people rejected the Shuiskii family, considering its fortunes lost. The inhabitants of Moscow assembled in large crowds outside the palace windows, shouting at Shuiskii, "you're not our sovereign!" The terrified ruler was afraid to show his face. In vain did the autocrat keep sending couriers to the provinces, asking commanders for reinforcements. The Riazan gentry, who had helped the tsar endure the siege by False Dmitrii II, insolently refused his overtures. The mutiny was headed by the conciliar courtier, Prokofii Liapunov. Striving to bring

Shuiskii down as quickly as possible he secretly concerted with Boyar Vasilii Golitsyn and other opponents of Shuiskii in Moscow. To be on the safe side he also negotiated with the Thief in Kaluga.

The ambitious leader of the Riazan gentry earlier had tried to enlist Dmitrii Pozharskii in the conspiracy against Shuiskii. He had his nephew Fedor take a letter to him in Zaraisk. Pozharskii realized it was dangerous to carry out a palace coup while a foreign invasion was underway. He categorically refused to support the conpiracy, sent Liapunov's letter back to Moscow, and called for reinforcements.

The news that Dmitrii was on the move again provoked risings in Kolomna and Kashira. Commons and cossacks alike showed their support for the Lawful Tsar. The people of Kolomna stirred up the inhabitants of Zaraisk, but the commander there at the time was Pozharskii; it was folly to provoke him. Pozharskii shut himself up in the stone fortress and refused to submit. The fortress contained the town's provisions, and substantial citizens had deposited their valuables there. The commander's adamant stance produced division in his opponents' ranks. Pozharskii waited until the turbulence abated and came to terms with representatives from the town. The agreement accurately expressed Pozharskii's political sentiments: "If Tsar Vasilii is sitting on the throne of Muscovy as he has been, I shall serve him; if another should sit there, I shall serve him too."[11]

The Zaraisk commander acted boldly and vigorously to save Moscow from imminent danger. He sent soldiers to Kolomna and persuaded the people to change their minds and abandon the Thief. Moscow's military situation became somewhat better but only a miracle could save Shuiskii. His fall was inevitable.

Chapter Eight

THE COUNCIL OF SEVEN

The last days of Vasilii Shuiskii's reign were gloomy. Once he had lost the support of the leaders in the boyar council and the city population his mandate ceased to be viable. The inhabitants of Moscow had not been able to come to terms with the boyars of Tushino as long as they supported the pretender, but everything began to change after the Tushino people signed the Smolensk agreement. Wladyslaw's candidacy seemed equally acceptable to Prince Fedor Mstislavskii, leader of the council, and to Filaret Romanov, head of the Tushino government. Filaret was genuinely enthusiastic about the covenant with Sigismund. He left Tushino with the last Polish detachments to take refuge in the king's train at Smolensk, but he failed to attain his objective. Valuev's armies took him prisoner after a battle at Volokolamsk and sent him to Moscow.

Tsar Vasilii did not dare to try the Thief's patriarch and rashly let him stay in the capital. Hermogen hastened to announce that Romanov had been a prisoner sacrificed to Dmitrii and declared he was entitled to his former office as metropolitan of Rostov. Not expecting such a reception, Filaret soon recovered his previous assurance and began working indefatigably to restore the influence the Romanov circle previously had enjoyed. Supported by the great boyars and his brothers and nephews, Filaret quickly became, as an observer noted, the second most powerful man after the patriarch. The Shuiskii interests had acquired a formidable foe. The pro-Polish party in Moscow was careful not to reveal its aims. Mstislavskii and the Romanov group were cognizant of the fact that the people had no wish to see a foreign king on the throne. It was Golitsyn's partisans, not Wladyslaw's supporters, who took the initiative to overthrow Shuiskii.

Vasilii Vasilevich Golitsyn was the most influential of the Russians aspiring for the throne. He had been in quest of the crown for a long time. He had executed Tsar Fedor Godunov and had been primarily responsible for getting rid of False Dmitrii I. Now it was Shuiskii's turn. Golitsyn abandoned his previous caution when he became convinced he had support in the provinces. Prokofii Liapunov, who had stirred up the entire Riazan region against the tsar, entered into an arrangement with him. In July Liapunov sent Aleshka Peshkov to Golitsyn and to his brother, Zakhar Liapunov, urging them to make haste with their rising. Since the days of the siege many Riazan gentry had been living in Moscow. They were eager to support the conspirators.

On July 16, Dmitrii arrived in the vicinity of Moscow with 3,000 cossacks. He was accompanied by his *alter ego*, Boyar Prince Dmitrii Trubetskoi, and other men of Tushino who had stayed with him. Lacking sufficient forces to storm the capital, Trubetskoi and his associates opted for deception. They proposed the people of Moscow should dethrone hapless Tsar Vasilii, hypocritically promising to do the same to Dmitrii. Then, they declared, all could join together to elect a new sovereign and end the fratricidal war.[1] Vasilii Golitsyn and his friends favored the Tushino initiative; it was the best device to justify the coup they were meditating. Shuiskii's opponents decided to act without delay.

On July 17, Ivan Nikitich Saltykov, Zakhar Liapunov, and the rest of the conspirators assembled a large crowd in Red Square and called upon the townsmen to overthrow the tsar, who had brought the country nothing but ruin.[2] Fearing Hermogen's opposition, the mutineers burst into and occupied the patriarch's residence. Boyars were held hostage by the crowd; they were hunted down everywhere and dragged to the Place of Execution. Mindful of past failures, the conspirators left the palace alone and concentrated on the army, which would decide the issue. To neutralize the pretender the command massed its forces in the Transriver district[3] [which means, broadly, the area just to the north and east of Moscow—ed.], where Saltykov and Liapunov conducted the mob. They constantly tormented the aged patriarch and kept close watch on the boyars.

In the army camp outside Serpukhov gate a remarkable assembly was held, in which the council, higher clergy, and the rebellious people took part. The Golitsyn faction, Mstislavskii, and Filaret Romanov called for Shuiskii's ouster. Patriarch Hermogen tried to defend him but nobody would listen. A few boyars were rash enough to oppose the general will but they soon fell silent. The assembly sent Boyars Vorotynskii and Fedor Sheremetev, the patriarch and the whole ecclesiastical council[4] to negotiate with Shuiskii in the Kremlin. The emissaries sincerely tried to persuade the tsar to abdicate. His brother-in-law, Prince Vorotynskii, promised to assign a special appanage principality with its seat at Nizhnii Novgorod to Vasilii, but he would not listen and refused to give up the tsar's staff. After that they forced him to leave the palace and go to his old residence. His brothers were forbidden to come to council and placed under guard.

After overthrowing the tsar, the assembly sent representatives to False Dmitrii's camp near the Danilov monastery. They proposed that the Kaluga boyars should get rid of Dmitrii at once and join the whole realm in electing a tsar who would be universally popular. Their hopes were dashed. Prince Dmitrii Trubetskoi and the other men of Tushino declared the people should throw open the gates of Moscow to the True Sovereign. There could be no more illusions. Confusion was general. The Shuiskii faction closed ranks and tried to recover what it had lost. The patriarch issued an appeal, beseeching the people to restore the old tsar to his throne. Ivan Shuiskii, head of the Fusilier chancery, used trusty intermediaries in an effort to induce Kremlin fusiliers to carry out a counter-coup.

The conspirators resorted to extreme measures. Conciliar Courtier Gavrila Pushkin and local gentry met with Zakhar Liapunov. This time the conspirators avoided appealing to the assembly and went so far as to set aside decisions it had taken. With a few fusiliers and a band of Muscovites they went to Shuiskii's residence, bringing a monk from the Miracles monastery with them. Gentry restrained the autocrat, to whom they administered a drubbing, until the monk had completed the ritual of tonsure. Then the new monk Varlaam immediately was taken out of his chambers and removed in a covered cart to the Miracles monastery, where he was placed under guard.

The day of the coup Zakhar Liapunov and the men of Riazan proclaimed that Prince Vasilii Golitsyn should ascend the throne.[5] The conspirators had miscalculated. The boyar council, headed by Fedor Mstislavskii, categorically opposed Golitsyn's election. The pro-Polish party in council had the chance to deny a candidate it did not want but did not dare advance its own. The coup caused doubt and dissension within this group. Sensing the popular mood, Filaret turned away from Wladyslaw and tried to put his own son Mikhail, then fourteen years old, on the throne. Contemporaries felt Mikhail had the best claim because he was a nephew once removed of the last lawful tsar. The Romanov faction managed to drum up support among the people and Patriarch Hermogen, considering it necessary to choose a Russian as tsar, was ready to come out on their side.

None of the candidates obtained a majority in council or at the assembly. Members recalled that Shuiskii had been elected without support from the provinces and this was why he had often been called an usurper. They had no wish to repeat previous mistakes and voted to postpone the election until representatives from the entire realm could meet in Moscow.[6] Couriers hastened to the provinces with instructions to choose men of every rank to take part in an electoral assembly.

In accordance with ancient tradition, the council appointed an extraordinary comission of its members to rule the country during the interregnum. Following custom, the assembly consigned direction of affairs to seven chosen boyars until provincial representatives could meet. Thus was the notorious council of seven formed. It included Fedor Mstislavskii, Ivan Vorotynskii, Vasilii Golitsyn, Ivan Romanov, Fedor Sheremetev, Andrei Trubetskoi, and Boris Lykov. Gentry, chancellery officials, fusiliers, cossacks, merchants, and the commons quickly swore fealty to the provisional boyar administration. On their part the boyars bound themselves to guard the Muscovite land and prepare the whole realm to elect a new tsar.

Less than a week later the military situation in Moscow took a sharp turn for the worse. Zolkiewski reached the capital by the old Smolensk road. The Poles pitched camp at a place called Fair Meadows. The crown hetman initiated talks simultaneously with the boyars in Moscow and in Tushino. To the Moscow boyars he suggested they should associate themselves with the Smolensk agreement and swear an oath to Wladyslaw; to the pretender he offered his forces for the purpose of storming Moscow.

The council of seven sent a minor official to Zolkiewski with orders to play for time and prevent the two enemy armies from uniting. It was in vain the boyars tried to outwit the hetman. Mstislavskii ultimately had to go to Zolkiewski's quarters and negotiate with him personally. By coincidence Dmitrii had set fire to Moscow's suburbs in an attempt to sneak across the Moscow river into the Transriver district at the moment Mstislavskii was discussing the situation with Zolkiewski. Jan Sapieha and his Lithuanians were assailing Serpukhov gate. The Poles in Zolkiewski's army were not anxious to aid their own men but the Russians allied with the crown hetman rushed off to help the people of Moscow. Without asking Zolkiewski, Valuev attacked Sapieha and drove him back, away from Serpukhov gate.[7] This episode created a sensation. The feckless leader of the council of seven attributed the success to his diplomatic initiatives. Feeling more sure of itself, the pro-Polish party passed a resolution in council not to elect a Moscow boyar as ruler. The road to choosing Wladyslaw and making peace with Poland now appeared open.

Even during the reigns of Tsar Fedor and Boris Godunov proposals to unite Russia and the Rzeczpospolita had been discussed in the boyar council. Originally that body had rejected them, but the peasant war had caused the attitude towards union to change. Shuiskii had proven unable to cope with popular uprisings. The nobility saw a solution: to ally with the feudal leaders of the Rzeczpospolita. It seemed to the boyars that if Wladyslaw were elected they could count on the king's army to restore order in the country. Mstislavskii and many other influential boyars also dreamed they would obtain the same privileges Polish magnates had always enjoyed. The assembly supported the proponents of unification largely because these men had come forward as champions of peace. The gentry were heartily sick of war and believed a mere stroke of the pen would banish foreign intervention and domestic strife.

Sigismund issued manifestos promising to give freedom to the Russian gentry and deliver them from tyranny. Such promises meant little to Muscovites, who were far more concerned about land and peasants. Gentry representatives formed the largest bloc in the assembly. The final decision was theirs. Unwilling to leave matters in the hands of the council of seven, they voted to take control of negotiations with Zolkiewski. The hetman estimated that as many as 500 gentry, cupbearers, and lesser boyars had come to the Polish camp.[8] Almost all assembly representatives took part in the discussions. Prince Cherkasskii was their spokesman. Zolkiewski answered his questions. He was lavish with promises and his speeches produced a favorable impression on the Moscow assembly. During one session the hetman was quietly told a courier had arrived. He broke off the talks and requested a day for reflection.

The king had forwarded instructions from Smolensk. The hetman was told to arrange matters in such a way that Moscow would take an oath to Sigismund and his son jointly. When the Smolensk agreement was concluded Skopin's army had been pressing the Poles hard and the king's men had been wondering how they could bring the disastrous war to a speedy end. Zolkiewski's prowess and the overthrow of the Shuiskii group had altered the situation dramatically. Now Sigismund was prepared to tear up the agreement to elect Wladyslaw. He was ready to occupy the Muscovite throne himself by right of conquest.

Zolkiewski opposed nullification of the understanding with the Russians. After the victories he had won he hoped his policy to achieve unification would again prevail. This led him to conceal the king's instructions from the boyars and to continue negotiations. Circumstances compelled Zolkiewski to move quickly. He had no money for his army. The mercenaries were demanding their pay and might mutiny at any moment. The council of seven had agreed to supply Zolkiewski with money, but not until an agreement was signed. To make matters worse, dissension broke out in the Polish army. Valuev had attacked the pretender but earlier the Don cossacks had refused to obey the hetman and joined forces with Dmitrii's cossacks.

Ataman Zarutskii once had prevented the men of the Don from quitting Tushino for Kaluga, and he had delivered a detachment of 3,000 men to Sigismund. After entering the interventionists' camp the

cossacks turned on their chief. Summoning the king's soldiers, Zarutskii had put down the rebellion by force, helped Zolkiewski destroy
Shuiskii's army, and accompanied him to the outskirts of Moscow.

Zarutskii expected rewards, but he was bitterly disappointed. Patriarch Hermogen and Mstislavskii had no trouble forgiving erring brothers like Romanov, Saltykov and the rest of the men of Tushino, but
they categorically refused to tolerate Zarustskii, a cossack boyar and
Bolotnikov's former supporter. In their eyes he remained the devil
incarnate, a living reminder of the peasant revolt. Former courtiers of
the Tushino tsar, who so recently had fawned upon the ataman, now
avoided him.

Ivan Mikhailovich Saltykov made bitter fun of the cossack boyar
when Zarutskii mumbled something about precedence rights. The
quarrel with Saltykov shattered the ataman's ambitious dreams. He
asked Zolkiewski to back him up but the hetman had no wish to disturb
the boyar government and felt no qualms at sacrificing his ally. A reck-
less gambler, Zarutskii could see no solution save once again to make
contact with False Dmitrii II. The pretender's camp welcomed him
with open arms while high circles in Moscow greeted the departure
of the cossacks from Zolkiewski's camp with a sigh of relief. The last
obstacle to agreement with the hetman had been removed.

On August 16, 1610 Mstislavskii, Filaret Romanov, Vasilii Golitsyn, and the assembly ranks showed the final text of the agreement
to the hetman. The next day Zolkiewski's emissaries, Valuev and
Saltykov, came to the Kremlin and read out the text to the people. Muscovites of every rank promptly went to the Cathedral of the Dormition,
where they took an oath. Boyars, servingmen, and the populace then
proceeded from the Kremlin to New Virgin field, where Zolkiewski
and his officers were awaiting them. The hetman noted that more than
10,000 Russians were assembled there. The Russian and Polish leaders
solemnly ratified the covenant before the people. There was no unanimity among the assembled Muscovites. As a result, the boyar government refused to let them sign the accord. Mstislavskii, Golitsyn, and
Sheremetev affixed their seals to the document and two conciliar
secretaries appended their signatures. That was all.[9]

The Moscow agreement was a compromise unsatisfactory to both
sides. The boyar council and the patriarch had refused to entertain even
the idea that a Catholic sovereign might sit on the Orthodox throne.
Zolkiewski considered it grotesque to expect Heir Wladyslaw would
submit to baptism. The oath had two clauses. The first provided that

envoys should be dispatched to Sigismund with a request to send Wladyslaw to Russia. The second clause was an oath of fealty to Wladyslaw as tsar of Russia. In their haste the boyar regents had thrown caution and even common sense to the winds. There was logic in their actions, but it was the logic of men who were desperately afraid.

No matter how unpopular a tsar might be, the people always considered the wicked boyars as the incarnation of evil. When the boyars overthrew Shuiskii and demanded an oath be sworn to them, they aroused the suspicion that the country might never again have a proper ruler. The Moscow garrison numbered 15,000 men, while the pretender could muster no more than three to five thousand soldiers. However, the boyars by no means had forgotten Otrepev's triumphal entry into the capital. For almost two years they had used a lawful tsar to protect Moscow from a second pretender. With no tsar on the throne it would be far more difficult to contend with Good Dmitrii. This is what made the boyars decide to proclaim Wladyslaw tsar of all Russia as soon as possible. Unable to use the power that had fallen to them, they hoped they could pacify the people with a name: "Vladislav Sigismundovich," the lawful tsar. The council of seven had failed to reckon with the fact that their candidate was highly unpopular among the Russian people.

The Moscow accord forced a choice upon the people: either submit to the evil boyars and their foreign prince or cling to True Orthodox Dmitrii. The myth of Ivan the Terrible's Good Son once again seized popular imagination. The boyar regents were like men floundering in a swamp. The more convulsively they grabbed for power, the deeper they sank into the abyss. By proclaiming the election of Wladyslaw they alienated the people for good and all. Those who beheld events in Moscow unanimously declared that the commons was totally opposed to the boyars' intention to set Wladyslaw on the throne. In ordinary circumstances the council, relying on the national assembly, would have experienced little difficulty in deciding the succession question entirely on its own; the lower orders had no representatives in the assembly. But during the Time of Troubles the people's influence had increased enormously.

Few Muscovites had taken part in the procession to New Virgin field which the boyars had arranged. The day after the ceremony, the rank and file in the Simonov monastery sent a handful of monks to convey greetings to False Dmitrii II. Two days later a host of people in Moscow, refusing to accept a Catholic ruler, left the capital for the pretender's camp. The provinces had even better reason for being annoyed with the council of seven. The regents had flouted the assembly decree by refusing to wait until electors from the entire realm could come together. They had chosen a sovereign without the country's participation. The results were soon apparent. In August disturbances occurred in Tver, Vladimir, Rostov, Suzdal, and Galich. The commons in these towns sent representatives to take petitions to Dmitrii.

Wladyslaw's election caused the feudal leaders to close ranks. Many men formerly of Tushino and long in the king's service came to Moscow. The inhabitants greeted them with reserve; they had not forgotten the lean years of the siege. Everyone wanted to hear what the head of the church would say. He was a bitter opponent of the Tushino regime. One day Mikhail Saltykov went to the Cathedral of the Dormition to ask the patriarch's blessing. For the record Hermogen read him a stern lecture but then forgave his trespasses after he had tearfully and humbly repented. Gentry who had supported False Dmitrii II to the end followed Saltykov's example. They too returned to Moscow and swore an oath to Wladyslaw. But as gentry left the camp at Kaluga, Dmitrii acquired more supporters among the city poor, peasants, and slaves.

A formidable social explosion was once again imminent. The people had not forgotten Bolotnikov's rising and were ready to take up the cudgels again. Fear of potential revolt drove the boyars into the arms of the interventionists. They hoped the foreign army would help them check the peasants and cossacks. The Moscow accord contained one point which the boyars considered extremely important. They had insisted Zolkiewski should continue to operate against the Tushino enclaves until the Thief either was killed or captured and his camp no longer existed. Then the country would be at peace.[10] Once Wladyslaw was on the throne it would be time to decide what to do with the free cossacks.

At dawn on August 27 Zolkiewski surrounded the pretender's camp in the village of Kolomenskoe. Mstislavskii brought up supporting units. The hetman gave Jan Sapieha an ultimatum but the latter refused to abandon Dmitrii. Unwilling to shed the blood of fellow countrymen, Zolkiewski did not press the attack and entered into discussions with the Thief. In Sigismund's name he promised to grant him Sambor if he would stop interfering in the king's affairs in Russia. The pretender rejected the offer, slipped out of Kolomenskoe, and shut himself up in the adjacent Nikolskii monastery.

The boyars had drawn up 15,000 men in a field near the gate leading into Kolomenskoe, but they distrusted their own forces and again had to ask Zolkiewski for help. The hetman insisted they should conduct his men through Moscow by the shortest route. Night had barely fallen when guards threw open the fortress gate. Marching through empty streets Zolkiewski's forces linked up with Mstislavskii's unit and proceeded to the Nikolskii monastery. Warned in good time, the Thief fled to Kaluga before daybreak. The Polish forces returned to camp, going through the fortress a second time.

Zolkiewski told the boyars that Jan Sapieha would abandon False Dmitrii II if they gave him money. Mstislavskii hastened to agree. Sapieha's men left the outskirts of Moscow with 3,000 rubles. The hetman was playing an ingenious diplomatic game. The Polish units were much more reliable than the foreigners who had gone over to Zolkiewski at Klushino. The boyar regents were nervous when they beheld the men who had recently betrayed them. The hetman let the boyars know he would be glad to disband this mob as soon as he could pay them off. Mstislavskii and his associates again swallowed the bait. They offered massive subsidies. Zolkiewski once more had survived a crisis threatening to break up his army. He paid off the mercenaries. Reserving 800 of his most capable soldiers, he dismissed 2,500 German, English, and French mercenaries who had defected at Klushino. His army was reduced to six or seven thousand men.

After administering the oath to Wladyslaw, the regents designated ambassadors to conclude peace negotiations with the king in his camp at Smolensk. Zolkiewski used much persuasion and flattery to convince Golitsyn and Romanov to form part of the mission but he frankly admitted he was deliberately removing these men from Moscow. Filaret Romanov remained a strong champion of the Smolensk agreement, for which he was chiefly responsible, but after Shuiskii was overthrown he hoped his son Mikhail might mount the throne. He was playing a crafty game. Zolkiewski had been toying with the idea of sending Mikhail Romanov to the king, but the lad was too young to form part of the embassy. The hetman thus decided to send Filaret; this would make him a hostage. Golitsyn constituted an even greater danger to Wladyslaw than young Mikhail. It is understandable that Zolkiewski did not want him to remain in Moscow.

The ambassadors were escorted to Smolensk by some fifty attendants, representing all ranks and levels in the assembly. Some Moscow abbots and elders from the Orthodox clergy accompanied Filaret to the king. Besides Golitsyn, the council was represented by Associate Boyar Mezetskii, Conciliar Courtier Sulin, and two conciliar secretaries. Service ranks were represented by Moscow gentry, cupbearers, and picked gentry from Smolensk, Novgorod, Riazan, Yaroslavl, Kostroma, and two dozen other smaller towns. The Moscow garrison was represented by Captain Ivan Kozlov and seven fusiliers; the Moscow town quarter by a wealthy merchant, Ivan Koshurin, a tailor, a jeweler, and three traders. Many who had been extensively involved in the recent coup, including Zakhar Liapunov, also left Moscow with the ambassadors.

Muscovites had sworn fealty to a ruler of another faith in hopes the war soon would end, but peace still eluded the long-suffering country. The envoys heard disturbing rumors en route. The king's armies were still sacking and burning Russian villages and hamlets as though the Moscow covenant did not exist. Kozelsk endured a vicious raid. Kaliazin monastery was reduced to ashes. Moscow learned that Sigismund was planning to ascend the throne himself. The king was unpopular even among his own subjects; Muscovites hated the very sound of his name.

The boyar government could not bring peace to the country nor give it a popular dynasty. The people were utterly estranged. Everyone who was in Moscow during these crucial days saw what was happening. The nobility and Polish officers held parties in the Kremlin but outside the palace windows the commons was in ferment, threatening to settle accounts with the boyars. The king's supporters sent one report after another to Smolensk: there were people in Moscow planning to surrender the capital to the Thief; others wanted to become rulers themselves; everyone was on the verge of revolt.[11] Zolkiewski was equally alarmed. He wrote that the Moscow commons, prone to unruliness, might summon the deceiver, False Dmitrii II, at any moment. A monk in Moscow, Avraamii Palitsyn, recalled that many persons favored the Thief of Kaluga and made secret contact with his people.

Ironically enough, it was the former men of Tushino, Mikhail Saltykov and his associates, who were shouting loudest about the danger of a coup in favor of Dmitrii. They were deliberately trying to frighten the Moscow nobility with the idea that the commons might overthrow those in power and hand the city over to the Thief. Citing the danger of popular rebellion, Saltykov insistently demanded the hetman's soldiers should be admitted into Moscow.

The leaders of the council of seven had sufficient political experience to realize how perilous it would be to allow foreigners to intrude. By concluding the treaty with Zolkiewski they had tried to prevent the king's forces from entering the capital. The treaty provided that Zolkiewski's soldiers might visit the city, but only with special permission and in groups of no more than twenty. But the boyars themselves broke the accord they had signed when the specter of a coup filled them with dread.

Mstislavskii, Ivan Romanov, and two other boyars, enough to possess a firm majority in the council of seven, took the initiative and invited the mercenary forces into the Kremlin. Zolkiewski fully understood the motive of his new allies: the boyar regents were terrified of their own people and wanted his armies to keep them safe from the angry commons.[12]

Mstislavskii and his confederates failed to achieve their immediate purpose. They invited Colonel Gosiewski to the Kremlin and Russian escorts took him on a tour to inspect the places in which his troops would be billeted. Fearing the worst, the people of Moscow sounded the tocsin. Snatching any weapon they could lay hands on, they rushed to the Kremlin to prevent this attempt to introduce foreign armies into the fortress.

The king's party in Moscow was premature in claiming victory. This group could not consider itself successful until the assembly that had toppled Shuiskii had ceased to function. Zolkiewski knew the assembly had been important. He had done his best to include its most influential members among the complement of the embassy he had sent to Smolensk. The popular rising had momentarily revived that moribund institution, and assembly members tried to break free in order to oppose Mstislavkii's designs.

Patriarch Hermogen summoned two members of the council of seven, Andrei Golitsyn and Ivan Vorotynskii, and with their cooperation invited gentry and chancellery officials to his residence. He also sent twice for Mstislavskii and other leading boyars but they pleaded press of business. Then the patriarch lost patience and announced he would come with his retinue to the council in person. Mstislavskii and his associates appeared at the meeting. Zolkiewski reported that Hermogen had brought many people together, ordinary citizens, gentry, and servingmen. The atmosphere was electric. Forgetting diplomatic niceties, gentry bitterly chided the hetman for transgressing the agreement: in violation of the accord he had been distributing estates on his own authority without regard for property rights. Speakers cried out: "He wants to be tsar of Muscovy! He intends to bring his armies into the city!"[13]

Mstislavskii was given another opportunity publicly to display his ineptitude. Under universal attack, he thought only of himself. Adopting an air of injured innocence, he kept repeating the statement that he had never violated an oath and was ready to die for Tsar Wladyslaw.

Hermogen was chiefly annoyed because the Polish command had not made good its promise to exterminate the enclaves and capture False Dmitrii II. The gentry majority fully shared his sentiments. Zolkiewski had not lived up to expectations. But he had defenders. Ivan Nikitch Romanov declared passionately that if the hetman quitted Moscow the boyars would have to go with him in order to be safe from the rabble.

Supporters had contrived to inform Gosiewski about the meeting and he sent his agent, Prince Vasilii Cherkasskii, to the patriarch. Gosiewski swore that if the Moscow commanders would support him, the Polish high command would dispatch forces against Kaluga the following day. Gosiewski's assurances were false. He was preparing to seize Moscow, not to campaign against Kaluga. Mstislavskii loudly reiterated Gosiewski's lies and forced Hermogen to keep quiet. The boyars used this interlude to prorogue the meeting, and they severely criticized those who had convoked it: the patriarch should attend to church concerns and not meddle in secular matters. Priests had never been in charge of affairs of state.

This attempt to resuscitate the assembly proved abortive. Its influential leaders were absent from the capital; only a few of those remaining realized the great danger threatening the state. Hermogen and his circle were only interested in destroying the camp at Kaluga. They were anxious to prevent the king's army from occupying the Kremlin but they refused to ask for help from the one force that could retrieve the situation. The head of the church was too afraid of the commons to turn to it. Fear that the people might rise in revolt paralyzed the assembly.

After the session was over, Mstislavskii and Saltykov met with Gosiewski and ordered the arrest of four patriots who had resolutely defied their treacherous plans. The next day the boyars summoned the men who had convoked the meeting to Zolkiewski's headquarters. True to form, the hetman tried to sooth the jittery representatives. He justified his conduct and assured them he had no intention of taking control of the administration. Zolkiewski was all sweetness and light. He let Saltykov do the dirty work. The former man of Tushino heaped reproaches on the assembly members, openly declaring they were in revolt against Wladyslaw, the lawful tsar.

Many assembly participants refused to appear before the hetman, although the boyar regents kept pressing them to do so. On returning to the Kremlin, Fedor Sheremetev and Mikhail Saltykov canvassed the dissidents and reasoned with them. They scolded noblemen, but showed restraint. This was not true in the case of the commons. Their representatives were menaced with punishment and forced to beg the hetman's pardon. Boyar Andrei Golitsyn and Hermogen deserted the cause and no longer opposed Mstislavskii. Golitsyn and Saltykov walked along the streets, trying to calm the people and head off insurrection and bloodshed. After quashing assembly opposition, the boyars took the final step needed to admit the foreign force into Moscow.

The mercenary units entered the fortress quietly, with banners furled. Zolkiewski established himself in the Kremlin but kept only a few attendants by him. One regiment occupied the barracks in Kitaigorod; another, the one in White Town. The remaining force stayed at New Virgin monastery. The Muscovite embassy had by this time reached the king's camp at Smolensk, bearing rich gifts for Wladyslaw and his father.[14]

Polish champions of union between Russia and the Rzeczpospolita had been stressing the political benefits that would accrue from the alliance and insisting the obligations Zolkiewski had enjoined must be fulfilled, but they soon fell silent. Extraordinary news was emanating from Moscow: the boyars had become Wladyslaw's slaves. Protracted internal disorders had sapped Russia's strength. The boyar administration was through. This allowed the war party in the king's circle to surface, although its leaders had won no victories. Zolkiewski was alarmed and hastened to the camp at Smolensk. On taking leave of his soldiers he observed: "the king will not send Wladyslaw to Moscow unless I go to Smolensk at once."[15] Zolkiewski's return did not improve matters. Sigismund had no intention of sending Wladyslaw to Moscow. He intended to occupy the Muscovite throne himself, although so far he had been immersed in achieving immediate goals. He did nothing about the occupied Seversk lands; to take Smolensk was now a matter of personal pride.

His officials delivered an ultimatum to the Russian envoys, ordering them to surrender Smolensk at once and force its inhabitants to take an oath to Sigismund. Senators gloomily predicted to the Muscovites that Russia's total collapse was imminent. Zolkiewski made the boyars fresh promises: "Don't be stubborn; once Smolensk surrenders we'll draw up a treaty and remove the king's forces from Russia." The envoys replied that the hetman already had signed such an undertaking and displayed the concordat he had made with Valuev. Obviously embarrassed, Zolkiewski said that it was Russians who had drawn up the memorandum, which he had attested without scrutiny. Now he could not recall it. The envoys responded by reading out the clause in the Moscow accord that bound the king to vacate border areas he had seized. Zolkiewski merely advised them to admit the king's forces into Smolensk, as they had been into Moscow: "then perhaps the king will not demand the people of the city swear an oath to him."

The envoys were planning to raise the question of whether Wladyslaw would adopt their faith. Chancellor Lew Sapieha mocked them: "the heir already has been baptized; no other baptism has ever been recorded."[16] When Golitsyn and Filaret urged Wladyslaw be sent to his realm in Moscow they were fobbed off with vague promises. On November 18 Golitsyn called the assembly representatives together, including gentry, chancellery officials, fusiliers, and townsmen, to inform them negotiations had completely collapsed. The envoys were now virtually hostages but they refused to despair. After the meeting they voted to insist that the peace terms must be honorable, whatever the cost.

The Smolensk covenant, signed by the king's officials, had paved the way for negotiations about union. The Moscow accord, subscribed to by Zolkiewski, contained the idea of a personal union between Russia and the Rzeczpospolita. Sigismund rejected both agreements out of hand, considering them useless scraps of paper. As long as Smolensk held out, the king's army was pinned down on the frontier. To crush Russia it was necessary to take Smolensk. On November 21, 1610 Sigismund again tried to storm the Russian fortress. Shortly after dawn a tremendous explosion shook the area. A tower fell and part of the wall collapsed. Three times the enemy charged into the city and three times he was forced to retreat. The roar of cannon at Smolensk showed that the king was determined to prosecute the siege. By admitting the foe into Moscow the council of seven had betrayed the nation. The Russian people had to pay for their leaders' treachery in rivers of blood.

Chapter Nine

MERCENARIES IN THE CAPITAL

The lies and deceit did not become immediately apparent. False hopes of peace which the Moscow accord had conjured up were widespread throughout Russia. One provincial commander after another administered an oath to "Tsar Vladislav." Prokofii Liapunov administered it in Riazan and Prince Dmitrii Pozharskii did likewise in Zaraisk.

The boyars expected Wladyslaw would come to Russia with dispatch and they did what they could to inform him about Muscovite customs. Crown secretaries compiled a list for the young ruler in order to acquaint him with Muscovite ways. They glowingly sketched the fabulous riches the tsar's treasury contained, which would belong to Wladyslaw when he ascended the throne. Besides treasure he also would receive crowns, regal attire, gold and silver vessels, velvet, satin, garments sewn with gold, uncountable sableskins and dark felt cloaks, and last but not least, money. The note specified that the boyar council was the autocrat's advisory body: "the duty of boyars, associate boyars, and conciliar secretaries is always to be in Moscow at the sovereign's side, to sit in the palace, and to ponder issues the sovereign communicates to us that are pertinent to the Muscovite realm."[1] The authors of the document also tried to give young Wladyslaw information about the gentry levy and military dispositions, Muscovy's financial system, and principal Russian towns. The secretaries briefly outlined court ceremonial and the proper way to entertain the sovereign. Vessels for eating and drinking had to be brought to the royal board in sequence by chamberlains, courtiers, stewards, and cupbearers.

Foreigners were prone to criticize Muscovite food. The daily fare Russians ate was indeed unappetizing. People stuffed themselves with bread and groats. The only vegetables were turnip and cabbage; the most popular beverage was *kvas* [a grain-based fermented drink, something like beer—ed.]. The food was monotonous but it was fresh, and garlic and onions played a prominent part. Wladyslaw's supporters, afraid the young king might be put off by Russian cuisine, did their best to present the meat, fish, and pastry dishes as attractively as possible and delicately avoided allusion to strong drink.[2] Since crowned heads of Europe were passionately fond of hunting the secretaries dilated upon the many facilities for this sport available to the ruler. These included splendid preserves, an abundance of game, skilled hunters at court, and well-trained dogs.

It was useless for Sigismund's partisans to try and entice Wladyslaw by reciting the glories of the treasury, the palace kitchen, and the hunt. The king had no intention of allowing his son to go to remote Moscow. Sigismund had never set eyes on the place, even from a distance, but he felt he was already its master. He arbitrarily distributed lands to his Russian supporters, assigned his men to chancelleries, and removed money from the treasury.

Even before the Moscow accord was signed Sigismund had promised generously to reward Mstislavskii for past favors and to raise him higher than his fellow boyars.[3] After Mstislavskii helped Zolkiewski occupy Moscow the king recalled his promise. On October 16 he issued a special rescript awarding Mstislavskii the exalted ranks of Servitor and Master of Horse. No one had borne these titles save the regent, Boris Godunov, in Tsar Fedor's time until Mstislavskii assumed them. The appanage prince also received new revenues and lands.

The king handed out conciliar ranks indiscriminately, since it cost him nothing. He made Mikhail Molchanov, Fedor Meshcherskii, Ivan Rzhevskii and Fedor Zvenigorodskii associate boyars. Grigorii Valuev, Kornilii Cheglokov, Prince Aleksei Lvov, and Grigorii Rzhevskii became conciliar courtiers; Ivan Chepchugov an equerry, Ivan Bezobrazov a huntsman, and Lev Pleshcheev a steward. He made a Tushino secretary, Ivan Gramotin, keeper of the royal seal.

Sigismund lavishly rewarded the perfidious Mikhail Saltykov. He made his son, Ivan Mikhailovich, a boyar and his nephew, Ivan Nikitich, an associate boyar. On September 10 the king's chancellery granted Saltykov title to the large, rich Vaga district, which had once belonged to the regent, Boris Godunov. In addition, the Saltykov family was given the northern towns of Charonda and Totma. Mikhail Saltykov had garnered riches beyond his wildest dreams,[4] but he was still not satisfied. He thought he was close to his desired goal. All he had to do was to make a final effort and the helm of state would be in his hands.

The Time of Troubles had brought about numerous changes in the Moscow hierarchy. The head of the Fusilier chancellery, who had formerly been of little consequence, by now had become a key figure

in the administration. Picked fusilier armies numbering 7,000 men
guarded the Kremlin and the inner city walls. Anyone who commanded
the fusilier garrison was a man to be reckoned with. The king was
minded to put Ivan Mikhailovich Saltykov in charge of the Fusilier
chancellery but Zolkiewski was the arbiter in Moscow. With the con-
currence of Mstislavskii and some other members of the council of
seven he awarded the post to Colonel Alexander Gosiewski, who thereby acquired boyar rank and took a seat in council next to native-born
Russian nobles.

While Otrepev still held power Gosiewski had conducted clandestine negotiations with the boyars, who were even then offering the Russian throne to Wladyslaw. When he came to Moscow as the king's envoy he contributed to overthrowing False Dmitrii I. His interference
in Muscovite affairs cost the colonel dearly. His co-conspirator, Shuiskii, kept him in Russia two years, but this did give the envoy an opportunity to come to know the chief boyars and reach understandings with
them. After returning to Poland, Gosiewski urged the king to attack.
When he arrived in Moscow a second time he was open and friendly
on the surface but underneath he still considered Russians his sworn
enemies. When he took charge of the Fusilier chancellery he set about
weakening and disbanding the garrison entrusted to him. He handled
assignment of Fusilier chancelleries to the towns. A Polish officer
openly wrote in his diary: "this is how we weaken the enemy."[5] Without
support from the council of seven the small Polish garrison could not
have lasted more than a few weeks in Moscow, but as time passed the
ratio of forces continued changing to the Russians' detriment. The
approach of winter facilitated Gosiewski's plans. Gentry were accustomed to spend the winter on their estates. In spite of the alarming
situation in the capital they dispersed in droves to their homes.

Zolkiewski, a champion of unification, was waiting for Wladyslaw
to arrive in Moscow and doing whatever he could to prevent clashes
between the king's units and the population. Well aware of the character of the mercenary soldiers, he drew up a detailed rescript that threatened severe punishment for marauding and rape. At first the command
vigorously enforced it. A drunken dragoon on sentry duty publicly set
fire to an icon that hung above a gate. Moscow learned of the incident
at once. The city hummed like an angry beehive. The Poles hastily
summoned the army and sentenced the guilty party to death. The
dragoon's hands were cut off; he was thrown alive on a pyre, and his

hands were nailed to the wall under the icon of the Virgin he had destroyed. A military tribunal also sentenced some marauders to death. They were saved only when Hermogen interceded on their behalf.

Zolkiewski's good intentions failed to produce the desired results. He himself did not stay long in Moscow. Those who favored conquering Russia annulled the peace agreements. The unexpected allies whom the boyars had admitted into Moscow were the same as hostile occupants. Clashes between mercenaries and the people seemed unavoidable. Military requisitioning and imposts were a primary cause of the constant conflict.

Since its members had taken an oath to Wladyslaw the council of seven had to assume responsibility for maintaining the king's forces in Moscow. With little money in the treasury, the boyars decided to make the provinces pay for the mercenaries. They assigned several large towns to every unit. For example, one unit was to receive supplies from Suzdal and Kostroma. The soldiers sent out special collectors and foragers. A Polish officer tellingly described how mercenaries behaved in the towns assigned to them. He wrote that the soldiers knew no restraint. Not content with the patience the people of Moscow displayed, they arbitrarily took anything they pleased, carrying off Russian wives and daughters by force, including those from noble families.[6] The population fretted openly and the council of seven was forced to recall the foragers. After lining their pockets the mercenaries announced they were prepared to give up maintenance and receive wages in cash. In a few short months the Muscovite treasury, as Zolkiewski noted, paid his soldiers 100,000 rubles for food alone. The cost of maintaining the foreign force imposed a heavy burden on the commons, who paid the taxes.

The attack on Smolensk had dumfounded Muscovites, who had just taken the oath to Wladyslaw. The king's rude violation of the Moscow covenant divided the boyars. Saying farewell to Zolkiewski, Mstislavskii, head of council, declared he was ready to make further concessions: "let the king come with his son to Moscow; let him rule the Muscovite realm until Vladislav is of age." But not all boyars shared Mstislavskii's sentiments. Andrei Golitsyn was the first to speak out. Ivan Rzhevskii, an ordinary courtier, once came to council with news he had just been created associate boyar. Unable to contain his anger Golitsyn reproached Gosiewski: "Lord Poles! You are grossly deceiving us. We have accepted Vladislav as our sovereign but he has not come. The king writes to us in his own name and distributes honors in his own right. Base persons are made equal to us, who are mighty men." Golitsyn demanded Sigismund stop interfering in Muscovite affairs and send his son to Moscow at once, "otherwise Moscow will consider itself free of the oath to Vladislav and we shall take thought for ourselves."[7] Prince Ivan Vorotynskii supported Golitsyn.

Under pressure from Mstislavskii and Saltykov the boyar council decided to trust Sigismund and ordered the Smolensk garrison to lay down its arms without delay. This capitulation aroused patriots. Patriarch Hermogen refused to sign the boyar decree. Mikhail Saltykov threatened the stubborn old man with a knife but Hermogen was not cowed.

In the king's camp at Smolensk the envoys categorically refused to obey the strange order to surrender the city. "We have been sent by the patriarch, the entire ecclesiastical council, the boyars, all ranks, and the whole realm. This letter has been composed without the assent of the patriarch and without the knowledge of the whole realm. How can we obey it?" they declared to the king's officials.[8]

Vasilii Golitsyn, one of the envoys, informed Hermogen that Sigismund intended to occupy the Russian throne himself. The patriarch should not under any circumstances believe the king's promises he would send his son to Moscow. The envoy's revelation brought the situation to fever pitch. Growing uneasy, the king's partisans began searching for a pretext to settle accounts with the patriots. With Saltykov's help, Gosiewski contrived a lurid juridical trial in Moscow.

A certain cossack in the pretender's army fell into the hands of the authorities. Under torture the prisoner implicated Ilarion, a Moscow priest, who supposedly had conveyed to False Dmitrii II a letter from all ranks in the Orthodox capital purportedly inviting Dmitrii to Moscow, where everyone was ready to take an oath to him. The authorities launched an investigation. Information laid by a slave belonging to Boyar Mstislavskii was of considerable help. The slave told his master he had seen the suspected priest the day he left Moscow for Serpukhov. Testimony of witnesses conflicted. The cossack mentioned Priest Ilarion but the slave referred to a Priest Khariton. Such trifles did not bother the investigators. When Khariton was arrested, letters from the Thief were found on his person. They contained no appeals to Dmitrii from the Muscovites. Khariton had the sort of letters which were common in Moscow at the time. The pretender wrote scores of flattering missives promising to be generous to all and sundry. They were addressed to Hermogen and other individuals. The Thief's epistles did not implicate the patriarch, but the judges found a solution. They introduced depositions from a man who had once served Jerzy Mniszech. The servant deposed that together with Hermogen and False Dmitrii he had performed "treacherous deeds" for Wladyslaw.

Priest Khariton was tortured several times until he confessed to the crimes previously attributed to Ilarion and humbly repeated the words the executioners whispered to him. He affirmed that Boyar Ivan Vorotynskii and Prince Zasekin had often commissioned him to carry treasonous letters to Kaluga. On his way to Smolensk Vasilii Golitsyn had been in touch with Dmitrii. His brother Andrei had also been involved in the conspiracy with the Thief. The authorities circulated an official version they thought would expose the conspirators' plans. They were supposed to have carried out a coup three hours before dawn on October 19 in concert with the commander of Serpukhov, Fedor Pleshcheev, a supporter of the pretender. Pleshcheev and the cossacks were to wait at Pakhra until they received a prearranged signal. The minute bells rang out the rebels were to rush through a secret underground passage to the Kremlin, take control of Vodianyi gate, and admit the Thief's army into the fortress. They had planned to kill all the Poles except the most noble, and to "rob Prince Mstislavskii and take him to the Thief in nothing but his shirt."[9]

The instigators of the trial wanted to convince Mstislavskii that the conspiracy was directed against him personally as well as at the rest of the leaders in the capital. They declared the rebels had planned to murder boyars, pedigreed courtiers, and loyal Muscovites who had taken no part in the Thief's council, and to give wives, sisters, and the property of the slain to slaves and cossacks. The charges against the conspirators sounded familiar. The authorities had invariably recited such a litany against rebels, beginning with Bolotnikov. There was no doubt that Moscow was ripe for an uprising. Dmitrii's emissaries were openly agitating among the people against Wladyslaw. Guards and gentry would apprehend such persons in market squares but the crowds would chase them away. It was easy for Gosiewski to acquire all the proof he wanted that a rising might occur in the capital, but the truth of the matter was that neither the patriarch, nor Golitsyn, nor Vorotynskii had anything to do with the imminent explosion of the commons. They were more afraid of cossacks than they were of foreign soldiers.

Interest in the presumed conspiracy linking patriarch and boyars with the Thief was dying down when the affair was moved from torture chamber to court. Boyars, colonels, and other officers assembled there expected significant revelations. As soon as court convened, the principal witness, Priest Khariton, recanted his deposition, declaring it was fear that had forced him falsely to implicate the Golitsyn boyars. Khariton's repentance ruined the show but it did not make those who had initiated the trial abandon their intention.

The discovery of the supposed conspiracy gave Gosiewski a good excuse to introduce his men into the Kremlin. After that, German mercenaries stood beside fusiliers on guard at Kremlin gates. Keys to the gates were entrusted to a joint commission of representatives from the council of seven and the Polish high command.

Ivan Vorotynskii was not acquitted, but he was cooperative and after a brief detention returned to council. Andrei Golitsyn maintained his innocence at the trial, but since he was strongly opposed to giving the throne to Sigismund he was in effect deprived of boyar rank and kept under guard in prison until he died. The patriarch was charged with conducting secret correspondence with the Thief, although the two always had been sworn foes. The court ordered the patriarch's servants, including secretaries, undersecretaries, and courtiers, removed. This left Hermogen "with no one to write for him."[10] After that, the head of the church was attended exclusively by Gosiewski's minions.

Persecution of the patriarch lent strength to the rumors that he was an open opponent of the enemy, the foreign king. In the provinces people were saying Mikhail Saltykov purportedly had insisted that Hermogen should bless the oath to Sigismund and threatened him with bodily harm. The good shepherd presumedly was not cowed and summoned representatives from among Moscow's district elders, merchants, and traders to the Cathedral of the Dormition, where he enjoined them to refuse to take an oath to the king. Foreign units were stationed fully armed on horseback in front of the cathedral but Hermogen made no effort to conceal his actions. The patriarch had no need to make a public announcement. Even Saltykov would not have dared openly to demand an oath to the king. He was afraid the people would revolt. The traitor advised Sigismund to spread rumors he was intending to attack the Thief in Kaluga and then suddenly turn about and occupy Moscow with strong forces.

After this harassment of Dmitrii's real and fictitious supporters in Moscow, the boyar administration's armies, supported by the king's units, launched an attack on the pretender's camp. They drove the cossacks out of Serpukhov and Tula and threatened Kaluga. Dmitrii despaired and prepared to withdraw to Voronezh, closer to the cossacks. He ordered the fort there strengthened and filled with supplies. At the same time he dispatched couriers to Astrakhan in case Voronezh should not prove a safe refuge.

Four years earlier Astrakhan townsmen and free cossacks had acknowledged Good Dmitrii and departed from Moscow. The social movement was more pronounced there than in other towns. Astrakhan had provided Bolotnikov his best soldiers. Cossack units from Astrakhan constantly swelled the ranks of Dmitrii's army. On orders from his boyars and the hetman, the Thief of Tushino had executed several self-proclaimed heirs from Astrakhan but much had happened since and the pretender's camp again looked like a cossack enclave. Dmitrii was sure he would have something in common with the leaders of the Astrakhan rebels. He told them he and his entire family would come there soon. The boyars who had stuck with the pretender were becoming less reliable. Courtiers were executed on suspicion of treason, including Boyar Ivan Godunov, related to the Romanov family.

In the past Dmitrii had been eager to award lands to German mercenaries but now he no longer trusted them. In Kaluga he repossessed holdings from German landlords and ordered them killed. Queen Marina tried to intercede on behalf of the Germans but the pretender told her: "These accursed Germans shall die today or my name's not Dmitrii. If you provoke me concerning them I shall have you drowned with them."[11] Marina had to endure the insult. The queen and her Polish attendants long ago had forfeited trust among the cossacks.

False Dmitrii II, a nonentity, was only the nominal head of the camp at Kaluga. Ataman Zarutskii was in charge. Unlike the ruler, he had refused to give up and had started to fight the interventionists. The pretender's former hetman, Jan Sapieha, was wintering with his army near Kaluga. The king and the council of seven had assigned Sapieha to storm the cossack camp but Zarutskii stole a march on him. Late in November his armies fell on Sapieha and his men and early in December, 1610 defeated them again. Zarutskii conducted the struggle with his former allies decisively and mercilessly. Each day he sent out patrols from Kaluga. The interventionists believed they were masters around Moscow. They paid dearly for their arrogance and carelessness. Cossacks seized the king's gentry and soldiers in their winter quarters, took them to Kaluga, and drowned them. Merchants from Lithuania apprehended on the highway met the same fate.

King Sigismund had avoided making an agreement with the pretender although he was anxious to use him as a pretext for interfering in Russian affairs. After fleeing from Tushino to Kaluga, Lord Janikowski, one of Dmitrii's favorites, had let the king know that he and his friends were ready to assassinate the pretender and hold Kaluga until royal armies arrived. Sigismund had declined the proposal because he needed the pretender to counter Shuiskii. But after Wladyslaw was elected to the Russian throne the pretender became an obstacle to the king's plans. Late in November, 1610 Sigismund issued a rescript ordering the inhabitants of Kaluga to apprehend the Deceiver and send him to Smolensk.[12]

His rescript produced no results. The Kaluga camp fought the interventionists harder than ever. Secret steps were taken to get rid of Dmitrii. With Sigismund's approval, a service khan from Kasimov, Uraz-Mohamed, came to Kaluga. The khan had served in Tushino and gone on to Smolensk but his wife and son were still with the pretender. Uraz-Mohamed had taken part in the attempts to storm Smolensk and had shown himself a loyal servant of the king. It was agreed he should go to Kaluga because he missed his wife and son. Uraz-Mohamed might have gone there openly and been well received but he stole in stealthily, concealing his name. Kasimov Tatars formed part of the Thief's bodyguard; with their help the Kasimov khan might have seized Dmitrii and delivered him to the king. Uraz-Mohamed had no luck. He was recognized and after a short inquiry executed as the king's agent. His family was put under guard. Fifty Tatar bodyguards were detained briefly and then released. The pretender had managed to survive.

Then, one fine winter morning, December 11, 1610, following his custom Dmitrii went for a sleigh ride outside town accompanied by his jester, Petr Koshelev, and a bodyguard consisting of twenty Tatars. Some distance from Kaluga the captain of the guard, Petr Urusov, rode up to the sled, fired at the Thief and then, to show his loyalty, cut off the dead man's head. The jester galloped back to sound the alarm. Bells rang all over Kaluga. Townsmen ran out and found the naked headless corpse on a knoll by a fork in a road on the further side of the Yachenka river. The body was carried to the fortress and cossacks slew Tatar noblemen to avenge the sovereign's death.[13]

The murder of False Dmitrii II was the product of a conspiracy. Shortly before the attempt was made, Prince Petr Urusov and his confederates had been arrested, charged with complicity with Uraz-Mohamed, beaten, and tortured. Urusov was not related to the Kasimov khan and had no reason to avenge his death, but he did have contacts with the Poles. Zolkiewski made a curious observation in his notes: "Some thought I had suborned Urusov. They suspected me probably because I had dealt with Urusov in a polite and friendly manner after the pretender had fled from Moscow."[14]

Dmitrii and his wife had occupied the best accommodations available in Kaluga, known as the tsar's palace. Marina Mniszech was beside herself. When the fateful news reached the court the Queen, disheveled and pregnant, rushed into the street and made a frenzied show of grief. The square rang with her wailing and sobbing. Baring her breast, Marina asked to die with her beloved consort. The Poles in her entourage trembled for their lives. Grigorii Shakhovskoi intervened on their behalf but soon lost control of the people.

The few boyars left in Kaluga intended to go to Moscow at once and seek forgiveness. Ataman Zarutskii tried to flee the fort and hide in the steppe but the inhabitants refused to let him leave. Readying his forces to fight the cossacks, Jan Sapieha decided to use this opportunity to persuade Kaluga to surrender. He came up to the town and tried to open negotiations with the queen and the boyars. The people of Kaluga rejected his overtures. Anticipating treason, they set a guard over Marina and intensified their watch on the boyars. Alhough under house arrest, Marina hoped for support from her coreligionists. A stranger carrying a basket in which a candle was hidden entered Sapieha's camp. When the candle was carefully opened a note from Marina fell out: "Free me, free me, for God's sake! I have no more than two weeks to live. Save me! Save me! God will reward you throughout eternity."[15]

Sapieha did not dare to storm Kaluga and departed precipitately. The danger passed; the commons grew quiet. No one knew what to do next. A dead pretender was of no use. His corpse lay more than a month in a draughty church thronged with local inhabitants and visitors desiring

to see the severed head. After his death a Talmud and letters and papers
in Hebrew were found among Dmitrii's effects. This gave rise to the
notion that the murdered man had been of Jewish origin.

The men of Tushino left in Kaluga were genuinely anxious to
achieve an agreement with Moscow. The boyar government sent
Prince Yurii Trubetskoi to administer an oath to its inhabitants. The
fractious commons denied him entrance. They selected their own representatives "from the gentry and atamans, and cossacks, and from all
the people." The men chosen went to Moscow to find out what was
happening in the country and returned with disturbing news. The
cossacks and others had seen foreign mercenaries in the Kremlin and
a disaffected people ready to rise against their oppressors. After the
delegates returned from Moscow the people of Kaluga hesitated no
longer. No matter what the boyars said, the commons decreed not to
submit to Wladyslaw until he arrived in Moscow and the Polish troops
had been withdrawn from Russia. Boyar Yurii Trubetskoi, the council
of seven's envoy, barely escaped with his life. Revolutionary Kaluga
had challenged boyar Moscow.

Meantime Marina, fearfully awaiting her kinsmen, was successfully
delivered of a child. The Tiny Thief's birth was inauspicious. Otrepev's widow had never married the second pretender; many considered
her son illegitimate. Marina was universally scorned. Chroniclers reported she had had numerous affairs; contemporaries simply shrugged
their shoulders when asked who was the child's father. However, even
after Dmitrii died Marina thought she could still found a new dynasty
in Moscow. The queen had forgotten her devotion to the Holy See and
had become fiercely Orthodox. After her child was born she told the
cossacks and the people of Kaluga they might baptize her son in the
Orthodox faith and bring him up according to their customs. Her appeal
produced an effect.

The split with Moscow and the birth of the heir reminded the
commons that the pretender had not been buried. They solemnly
interred the body in a church. Next they baptized the heir, calling him
Ivan. Perhaps the movement had found a new standard-bearer. This
was what people at the burial and baptism thought, but their notion
soon proved illusory. The pretender's son was not destined to play a
part in subsequent events. The people were indifferent to him.

Moscow's ruling elite was delighted when Dmitrii died but the
nobles rejoiced too soon. Disaffection in the capital grew stronger

instead of abating. The trial of Priest Khariton and subsequent perse-
cutions in the town quarter had made matters worse. In Moscow a
social explosion had long been brewing. In order to stop it the boyar
government called in the king's forces. Interference by the foreigners
caused the conflict to assume a new form. The social movement took
on nationalist overtones. The wicked boyars were as hated as ever, but
the hostility was now more and more suffused with a sensation of
national degradation. The people felt it was intolerable for the boyars
to allow foreign aggressors to control the country.

Other reasons for quarrel and conflict were abundant. Moscow no
longer had access to cheap grain from the north. Disturbances in Riazan
proved the last straw. The price of food increased dramatically. People
had to do without, but the mercenaries, thinking themselves masters
of the city, had no intention of paying high prices. They made Moscow
traders accept what they offered or confiscated their goods. Markets
were the scene of quarrels and fights that might at any moment develop
into a general uprising. Bells often pealed in the city, summoning
aroused Muscovites to the square. Gosiewski had to keep his force in
a state of constant alert. A Pole noted that hussars often sat in the saddle
for days on end. Mercenary troops stood at the gates in military array.

Since the days of the siege, cannon had been mounted on the walls
of Wooden Town and White Town and others located near assembly
headquarters were ready to fire. The authorities decided to wheel the
cannon into the Kremlin and Kitaigorod, where they also transferred
powder they had seized from shops and manufactories. The boyars
feared domestic sedition more than foreign foes. The cannon in the
Kremlin and Kitaigorod now had the whole town quarter of Moscow
within range.

The council of seven encouraged Gosiewski to redouble his vig-
ilance. Hussars patroled Moscow's streets and squares. The authorities
decided to place barricades to close off streets at night. A curfew was
enforced from dusk to dawn. Often inhabitants on their way to market
in the morning would stumble over bodies of slain fusiliers or townsmen. Muscovites retaliated. Gosiewski reported that they would lure
foreigners to remote parts of town and kill them. Drovers enticed
drunken mercenaries into their sleds, took them to the Moscow river,
and dumped them in the water. For all practical purposes undeclared
war was raging in the city.

The boyar government lost far more than it gained by allying with the interventionists and handing Moscow over to the mercenary armies. The gulf between the prominent and the commons was growing wider. The Moscow accord had not brought peace; it had hobbled the country. The intervention had assumed more menacing proportions. The prospect of losing national independence greatly worried patriotic gentry. The overwhelming majority of the gentry believed peace was just around the corner, but a few perceptive officers foresaw a new crisis. Risking danger they tried to prevent removal of forces from the west. In October, 1610 Associate Boyar Artemii Izmailov went to Viazma and entreated the local commander to send 300 available Riazan serving men to guard Mozhaisk. His friend Dmitrii Pozharskii, commander of Zaraisk, sent men to urge Zarutskii's cossacks to come over to his side.[16] No commander had yet openly opposed the boyar government but some were trying to establish contact with the camp at Kaluga. It is difficult to say what immediate goals Izmailov, Pozharskii and their associates were pursuing, but they were the ones destined to do battle with the interventionists in approaching months.

In Moscow the patriotic movement among the gentry was headed by Vasilii Buturlin, Fedor Pogozhii and others who were not noblemen. In October this Moscow group made contact with Prokofii Liapunov in Riazan. From his brother Zakhar, who had taken part in the embassy, Prokofii had just learned that the peace talks in the king's camp had collapsed. Appreciating the danger, Liapunov at once sent a letter to the council of seven. It was extremely long and contained a host of quotations from holy writ. Liapunov inquired of the boyars whether the king had fulfilled the conditions of the agreement and when Wladyslaw would come to Moscow. Next Prokofii met with Vasilii Buturlin, who came to his estate at Riazan in autumn. He and the Moscow patriots agreed with Liapunov to make a concerted move against the interventionists.

The attack on Smolensk had aroused Russian anger and indignation. Prokofii Liapunov hurled down an open challenge to the boyar government. He sent another missive to the boyars, this time couched in harsh language. The leader of the Riazan gentry declared the king had broken the treaty and summoned patriots to war against the foreign aggressors. Liapunov threatened that he would soon come to Moscow himself to liberate the Orthodox capital from the Latins. Shortly afterwards

Liapunov sent a courier with a communication to Buturlin expressing his concern.[17] Agents of the council of seven arrested the courier and found the letter. The hapless servitor was impaled on a stake and Buturlin was tortured. He admitted he had been planning to raise a revolt and call in the men of Riazan to help the Muscovites in their struggle against the interventionists.

By opposing the plan to surrender Smolensk, Hermogen acquired patriots' sympathy. These obscure men were anxious to associate the patriarch's name with the liberation movement. They blanketed Moscow with an appeal that had a long florid title. Muscovites read "A New Tale of the Glorious Russian Tsardom, the Sufferings of Most Holy Hermogen, and New Treasons." The proclamation was considered an accusation against the council of seven. The authors of the Tale wrote: "Instead of upholding the realm the boyars have become its destroyers. They have exchanged their noble birth for base slave-like servitude to a grasping enemy. Our highborn leaders have become totally blind and mean-spirited; they have betrayed us all. There must be some of boyar rank who long to fight for the faith and for all of us but they are afraid to show themselves. They are not strong enough to fight for what is right." The broadside's authors sought to contrast righteous Patriarch Hermogen to the traitorous boyars. They called the citizens to arms: "Be brave; take up arms, and bethink how to deliver us from our enemies. The time for a rising has come!" The authors of the Tale strengthened Hermogen's authority but their reference to him could be interpreted in more ways than one: "What have they started; what mistakes have they made? Are you waiting for that mighty pillar (the patriarch) himself to order you to fall upon your enemies? You know yourselves where he stands on the question of shedding blood."[18]

During the Time of Troubles every rank put forward prominent figures. The clergy had given Russia a host of pretenders, and Hermogen too. At the time when the movement to liberate the land was gaining strength his blazing appeals to defend Russia's independence assumed great importance. The patriarch was filled with desire to prevent contamination of the pure Orthodox faith by the godless Latins. To do so he was ready to sacrifice his power and even his life. But the patriarch's office tied Hermogen tightly to boyar interests. His prejudices prevented him from grasping the changes that had occurred in society. The camp at Kaluga had long been waging a struggle against the aggressors. But the patriarch wanted nothing to do with Kaluga cossacks and the rebellious men of Riazan. This anomaly made the head of the church act inconsistently.

Lord Lisowski and Ataman Andrei Prosovetskii long had been fighting the Swedes around Pskov. Having begun his struggle with the interventionists, Zarutskii summoned the cossacks back from the frontier. Prosovetskii and Mishka Cherkashenin and the cossacks retired with their leaders towards Moscow. Lisowski tried but failed to plunder them. In the depth of winter the cossacks reached the outskirts of Moscow, where they unexpectedly learned of the death of Tsar Dmitrii. At a loss what to do, the atamans sent representatives to the head of the church. Hermogen refused to consider making an agreement with the cossack enclaves and he ordered Prosovetskii and Cherkashenin to take an oath to Wladyslaw at once.

While telling Prosovetskii he should serve Wladyslaw faithfully, the patriarch was secretly appealing to the people of Nizhnii Novgorod. In his communication he declared he was absolving the Russian people of their oath to Wladyslaw. Hermogen urged the people of Nizhnii Novgorod to devote their lives and resources to expelling the enemy from the country and preserving the faith: "A Latin tsar has been forcibly imposed on us: he is destroying our country. We must freely elect a tsar of Russian stock!"

The boyars had spies in the patriarch's court and soon learned of the prelate's rash act. After hearing from them, Gosiewski ordered barriers erected on roads linking the capital with the Volga towns. Vasilii Chertov, a courier who had volunteered to convey the patriarch's screed to Nizhnii Novgorod, was seized near a gate by Polish scouts. The boyar government, relying upon supporters and the mercenaries, declared the capital in a state of siege. Moscow patriots had to go underground. They sustained serious losses and could not unite their forces. That comic hireling, the Thief of Tushino, had long been a stumbling-block to the massive patriotic movement welling up from the lower orders in the Kaluga camp. With his death this obstacle to uniting the forces struggling against the foreign aggressors was removed.

The council of seven, doubting their own units, asked Sigismund to send troops to put down the rising. The king sent Zaporozhian cossacks to Tula and Riazan. The Moscow boyars dispatched Isak

Sumbulov with a detachment of Riazan gentry to help them. On December 26, 1610 Ataman Andrei Nalivaiko burned down Aleksin and menaced Tula. The rest of the Zaporozhians joined Sumbulov's unit at Riazan.

Liapunov's broadsides had produced a marked impression in the capital. But after proclaiming war on the boyar government, the conciliar courtier was slow to assemble an army. A number of principal Riazan gentry remained loyal to the boyar government. Petty servingmen, who predominated in the district, were ready to support Liapunov's patriotic appeal but to summon landholders from their estates in the dead of winter was not easy. The last independent duchy in Russia, Riazan had declined after it was united with Moscow. Its population of townsmen remained insignificant until the beginning of the seventeenth century. The ancient fortifications were in disrepair.

Liapunov possessed an hereditary patrimonial estate on the Prona river, where he apparently was when military activity started. The leader of the Riazan gentry managed to hide in Pronsk, where 200 armed men joined him in the fortress. Sumbulov and the cossacks tried to apprehend Liapunov. They surrounded Pronsk, an old border fortress girt with wooden walls. A redoubt protected by a moat and palings was attached to the fortress. The Pronsk gentry had a few dozen houses there in which to withstand a siege. Two fusilier and three cossack villages were located in the environs. Shut up and hard pressed in Pronsk, Liapunov dispatched many appeals for aid. The first to respond was Prince Dmitrii Pozharskii, serving as commander of Zaraisk. He added men from Kolomna and Riazan as he proceeded. The sudden appearance of a strong detachment to the rear frightened Sumbulov, who hastily withdrew without offering battle. Prince Dmitrii delivered Liapunov from encirclement and solemnly entered Riazan at the head of the united forces. The people greeted the warriors with enthusiasm. The local archbishop gave his blessing to Liapunov and Pozharskii because they were fighting the foreign aggressors. This was how a national army first came into being. Prince Dmitrii stood at its head.

The inhabitants of Zaraisk pressed the commander to return. Dismissing the men of Kolomna, Pozharskii took leave of Liapunov and went back to his post with a small force. Sumbulov had to leave the Riazan area. Zaraisk lay on his route. Unwilling to go back to Moscow with unwelcome news, Sumbulov decided he would attack Zaraisk and punish its commander and people for their disobedience. After dark the boyar government's army burst into the town. Pozharskii could endure any kind of siege in the stone fort but he preferred offense to defense. Right after sunup his soldiers fell upon the enemy and with help from the inhabitants drove them out. Sumbulov withdrew to Moscow and the Zaporozhian cossacks went back to the frontier. Pozharskii made no accusations against the boyar government but his decisiveness and energy had saved the day. His victories at Pronsk and Zaraisk heartened the rebels.

Jan Sapieha told the Zaporozhians to keep close watch on Liapunov and Zarutskii and be ready to destroy them. But his order was not carried out. Zarutskii ejected the Cherkassians [another name for cossacks from the Ukraine—ed.] from Tula and Pozharskii defeated them at Zaraisk. The patriotic movement was growing quickly. The struggle against the common foe originated in this example of military cooperation which the camps at Kaluga and Riazan had displayed.

Chapter Ten

MOSCOW BURNS

The revolt in Riazan acted like a spark thrown into a powder keg. The ground had long been prepared. All the way from the Seversk region to Kazan in the east and Vologda to the north, town after town came out in favor of the liberation movement. A military camp suddenly appeared. The people displayed unprecedented activity. Town quarter commons met and passed resolutions to reject the authority of the boyar government cooperating with the interventionists. When the outcome was peaceful, local commanders kept control of the movement but in a number of towns, such as Kazan, the insurgent people overthrew the boyars.

Kazan, once the heart of the khanate of Kazan, lay along the Kazanka river a short distance from the Volga. By the end of the sixteenth century a new stone fortress had been built there. The population of the town quarter and the fortress was now almost entirely Russian. Artisans and traders from Moscow, Riazan, Pskov, Kostroma, Vologda and other places moved there during the sixteenth century. The authorities maintained a very strong fusilier garrison in Kazan, consisting of three Fusilier units. The city contained more fusiliers and serving men than townsmen. Gentry were far fewer.

In December, 1610 the people of Kazan sent Crown Secretary Evdokimov to Moscow. The envoy failed to make contact with Hermogen or underground patriotic groups. This had serious consequences. The Kazan town quarter started turning to the Kaluga camp, considering it to be the one organized force engaged in opposing the aggressors. The secretary's tales about disasters in the capital had a shattering effect on the people of Kazan and caused them to revolt against the boyars and foreign conquerors. Not knowing what had happened in Kaluga, fusiliers and the lower orders administered an oath of loyalty to False Dmitrii to the inhabitants and vowed to fight the foreigners to the death. Local commanders proved powerless to check the flow of events. Their efforts to subdue the spontaneous rising ended badly: the eminent boyar Bogdan Belskii, a commander in Kazan, was murdered by a mob.

Coups were carried out peacefully and without bloodshed in Murom, Nizhnii Novgorod, Yaroslavl, and Vladimir. On January 24, 1611 the people of Nizhnii Novgorod informed Liapunov they had resolved, on the advice of the entire realm and with Hermogen's blessing, to proceed immediately to liberate Moscow from apostate boyars and foreigners. Commander Vasilii Litvinov Mosalskii, an associate boyar, came from Murom with gentry and cossacks to help them. Liapunov hastened to send a regular mission, headed by a relative, Steward Ivan Birkin, to Nizhnii Novgorod in order to devise a common strategy.

The Yaroslavl gentry overcame their scruples after Ataman Andrei Prosovetskii arrived with his cossacks. Supporters of the militia at last prevailed. They and the cossacks swore to cooperate in saving the Muscovite realm. The rebel towns had devised an uniform oath to swear fealty to Russia, but the Yaroslavl gentry introduced a significant reservation into its text: "If the king refuses to give us his son as the Muscovite sovereign...and does not withdraw his soldiers (from Russia) we shall fight him to the death."[1] The men of Kaluga and Riazan had pledged to wage war with the aggressors and their boyar confederates without reservation, but the people of Yaroslavl still cherished illusions of peace and felt agreement with the council of seven and Wladyslaw might still be possible.

Despite their illusions the men of Yaroslavl vigorously undertook military preparations. Under his banner the local commander mustered regional gentry, who were joined by 300 veteran cossacks. The army contained soldiers from adjacent towns and villages. Clever Yaroslavl smiths made them 2,000 iron axes. Cannon were found too: taken down from fortress walls, or removed from old factories and repaired. Lord Gosiewski sent 500 Moscow fusiliers to Vologda. The people of Yaroslavl called on them to help. The fusiliers broke with the boyar government and enrolled in the Yaroslavl contingent. The ancient towns of Vladimir and Suzdal ran up the flag of revolt. Associate Boyar Artemii Izmailov was in Vladimir and Ataman Prosovetskii and his cossacks were in Suzdal after January, 1611.

The boyar government had disposed of impressive forces until Gosiewski started to disperse parts of the capital's garrison throughout the towns. When the towns rose, the boyars lacked the power to suppress the rebellions. At the end of winter they put together a few units and sent them to attack Vladimir. This served a twofold purpose: to prevent mustering militia units for an immediate descent on Moscow and to guarantee the capital grain deliveries from Suzdal villages. Warned of the danger by the commander of Vladimir, Prokofii Liapunov moved a unit behind Boyar Kurakin, who was advancing from Moscow. On February 11, near Vladimir, Kurakin attempted to crush Izmailov's and Prosovetskii's units. The boyar government army fought without enthusiasm and took to flight after the first setback. Then they learned men of Riazan had intersected the great Vladimir highway and built a camp in the Undol region. In escaping, they had to move north quickly and use back roads to make Yurevets Polskii.

Liapunov frequently informed the towns he was determined to march on Moscow, but he kept putting the action off. By sending a commander with loyal troops to Kolomna, the boyar government had succeeded in holding that splendidly fortified town barring the way to Moscow. On February 13-14, 1611 the leaders of the Kaluga camp invited the men of Riazan to plan an attack on Moscow and to parley with Sapieha. The results of the Kaluga negotiations immediately became apparent. The pretender's former boyar, Ivan Pleshcheev, and the cossacks invested Kolomna, and with help from the populace succeeded in taking it. Learning of the fall of Kolomna, Liapunov had cannon moved there. He transferred a collapsible wooden fortress known as a Gulai-gorod to Kolomna on wagons. This joint operation by the men of Kaluga and Riazan brought thc militia another success. The boyar government held Serpukhov as long as Polish units were stationed there but as soon as the mercenaries abandoned the town the populace rose in revolt. Zarutskii sent cossacks to aid the rebels. Liapunov dispatched 500 Riazan and Vologda fusiliers.

After consolidating his position closer to Moscow, Liapunov sent missives to the towns outlining plans for a general assault designed to liberate the capital. Forces from Vladimir, Nizhnii Novgorod, and Kazan were to proceed to Kolomna and link up with the men of Riazan. Detachments from Tula, Kaluga, and the Seversk towns were to launch an attack on Serpukhov. Liapunov failed to accomplish his plan. Commanders north of Moscow declined to mass their forces in Kolomna, which ultimately proved highly unfortunate. The commanders had trouble overcoming their longstanding mistrust of the cossack enclaves in Kaluga. Furthermore, they were afraid to leave their towns undefended. Commander Kurakin received reinforcements from Moscow and operated between the Vladimir and Pereiaslavl highroads. It was not until March, 1611 that militia units from Pereiaslavl managed to defeat Kurakin's advance guard and compel him to retreat towards Moscow. The immediate threat to the towns north of Moscow was thereby eliminated.

Abandoning their intention to join forces in Kolomna, the militia commanders marched on Moscow, each taking his own route. Liapunov started on March 3. Izmailov, commander of Vladimir, Ataman Prosovetskii, and the men from Nizhnii Novgorod and Murom set out a week later. The Yaroslavl and Kostroma contingents were held up in Rostov until almost the middle of March.

In Moscow events were moving forward more quickly than the militia leaders had expected. The crisis was inexorably deepening. Saltykov and Gosiewski expelled Prince Andrei Golitsyn from the council of seven because he sympathized with the liberation movement. He was replaced with his brother, Prince Ivan, who submitted to the majority. The crushing of the opposition in Moscow produced a substantial impression on the envoys. Deprived of support from their confederates, Vasilii Golitsyn and Filaret began earnestly to seek an understanding with Sigismund. Early in February, 1611 they agreed to introduce 200 Polish soldiers into Smolensk and tried to get the garrison to accept the offer. Commander Shein and the people of Smolensk rejected their mediation. They fully understood that the issue was the surrender of the fortress. The envoys' concessions did not advance the cause of long-awaited peace.

Convinced the concept of union had collapsed, Hetman Zolkiewski kept urging the senators to undertake normal diplomatic discussions with the boyar government and conclude a profitable peace. But Sigismund, who had not won a single victory, imagined that he had already conquered Russia and refused to listen to the advice of his finest officer.

The envoys, like Hermogen, had totally dissociated themselves from the revolt in the towns. Although they had offered concessions over Smolensk, the king summoned them to his quarters in the middle of March and had them arrested. Guards later plundered the envoys' belongings and thrashed their servitors. The envoys were conveyed as prisoners to Lithuania. Disapproving of such behavior Zolkiewski quit the camp at Smolensk to return home. His departure freed the hands of those demanding Russia should finally be destroyed and partitioned. Their triumph had an immediate impact on the situation in Moscow. Gosiewski no longer stood on ceremony and spoke to the boyar rulers like a conqueror. Summoning council members to the Kremlin, he delivered a menacing speech. If they did not cow the insurgents at once, rivers of blood would flow. After terrifying the rulers, the colonel heaped reproaches on the head of the church. He displayed to the council incendiary letters his soldiers had intercepted.[2]

The patriarch's guilt was palpable and proven. Although old, frail, and with poor eyesight, nothing could stop Hermogen from justifying himself. Seated next to him, Archbishop Arsenios heard the stubborn old man repeatedly declare he had had nothing whatsoever to do with the popular rising.[3] In his own way the patriarch was correct. He had no connections with Kaluga and Riazan, the chief centers of the movement, and he had refused categorically to accept responsibility for the militia. The authorities might have put Hermogen on trial and deposed him. But they were swayed by the justification he made and allowed him to remain head of the church. His equivocal attitude had enabled the prelate to survive.

Late in February Gosiewski insisted the treasury expend large sums to pay the mercenaries and supply them with food because prices were high. Patriots learned of this and stirred up the people. While colonels were dickering with boyars in palaces some 3,000 men from the town quarter gathered in the square. They were noisy, demanding to settle accounts with Traitor Saltykov. The boyars were afraid to come out.

Units of fully-armed German mercenaries then arrived. They were preparing to charge the unarmed crowd but a clash was avoided.

The revolt in the provinces cut off Moscow's supplies. Prices in city markets began rising faster than they had before. The mercenaries resorted more and more to acts of violence in order to obtain food. In February a fight broke out in a market, involving Muscovites and the occupiers. The foreign guard charged the crowd with pikes. Fifteen Muscovites were killed on the spot. Many were wounded.

The approach of Easter, the supreme church holiday, invariably brought hordes of people to Moscow. Gosiewski demanded the Easter procession be cancelled but the council of seven ignored his representations. The boyars were afraid this would render the people more indignant and gain them a reputation as lackeys of godless heretics. They were also sure they could convince the populace that Hermogen, the pillar of Orthodoxy, whom the people considered a martyr, was still on their side as he had been before.

March 17 was Easter day. While hundreds of big and small bells tolled the holiday, Hermogen issued through the Kremlin gate at the head of a solemn procession. The custom was for the tsar to walk, leading a donkey with a saddle, on which the patriarch was triumphantly seated. In place of the absent Wladyslaw, a donkey bearing Hermogen was led by a courtier whom the boyars had assigned to perform the sovereign's duty. The splendid procession reminded Muscovites of the good old days. Everything looked the same. Twenty panoplied courtiers marched in front of the patriarch, covering his route with costly carpet. Behind the donkey came sleds and a tree full of apples. Youthful choristers sitting in the sleds chanted psalms. Next came clergy carrying crosses and icons, boyars, and finally the whole people. According to custom, Muscovites greeted one another and made the sign of the cross as a token of forgiveness and reconciliation. But faces displayed no joy or tenderness. Enmity and hatred, not peace, gripped the capital.

Mercenary cavalry and infantry units stood on full alert in the Kremlin and Kitaigorod. The boyars and the Moscow nobility were glad to see them. Bereft of popular support and without an army, they considered the mercenary force their last hope and refuge. An invisible barrier deeply divided the city. Those in power felt secure only in the Kremlin and Kitaigorod. A wall of hatred surrounded them in White Town and in the suburbs. The people made no attempt to conceal their feelings towards the godless foreigners and their boyar confederates.

In the city center there were no incidents on Easter Day but clashes occurred in White Town.

A crowd of gaily-attired citizens thronged the narrow streets of Kulishki. Suddenly a cart came through the city gate onto the street. An armed servitor tried to disperse the people and clear a way for the vehicle. Not wanting a clash with foreign guests, the people of the town let the cart pass but the driver dropped the reigns and fled. Boyar emissaries came to the place where the incident had occurred but were greeted with hoots of derision and hastily withdrew.

The Kremlin and Kitaigorod were only a tiny part of the area in which the Russian capital was situated. The Kremlin contained numerous edifices comprising the royal palace, the patriarch's residence, Appanage Prince Mstislavskii's residence, boyar abodes, chancellery edifices, homes of servants and chancellery officials at the foot of the hill, cathedrals in the central square, and two monasteries. The Kremlin was the city's administrative heart; Kitaigorod was its mercantile center. A large part of it was filled with individual shops and blocks of spacious stores. On holidays the whole of Red Square was thronged with shoppers.

Boyars, serving men, merchants, traders, and artisans lived in Kitaigorod. Houses were huddled closely together. The bulk of Moscow's population did not live in Kitaigorod but rather in White Town, Earthen Town, and the Transriver district. When he beheld these places in the late sixteenth century, an Englishman, Giles Fletcher, noted: "Moscow is somewhat larger than London."[4] Jesuits who visited the Russian capital a few years earlier than Fletcher asserted the city had been ruined and no more than twenty or thirty thousand pople were left in it. The population had increased by the end of the century but the cruel famine in Tsar Boris' time depopulated it again. The unhappy period that was Shuiskii's reign was not conducive to growth in the town quarter.

In the early seventeenth century population levels in White Town and the Transriver district varied considerably. West of the Kremlin lay Chertole, a large square intersected with ravines, in which the royal stables were located. Chertole and the area lying between Arbat and Dmitrovka and the tsars' gardens situated along the bank of the Moscow river were among the least inhabited sections. Population density was extremely high in centers of artisan production. Many armorers lived in Greater and Lesser Bronnyi streets near Cannon Court beyond

Lubianka; blacksmiths and boilermakers were found in Earthen Town beyond the Yauza river; and weavers in Kadyshev village in the Trans-river district. Fusilier villages were concentrated in White Town. The sectors that were thickly populated with the urban poor and lower orders had become the main centers of disaffection. Military settlements were close by. Fusiliers were petty traders. Reassignment of fusilier units to other towns meant that many families were left with no one to provide for them.

By March, 1611 the alienated people of Moscow were certain the days of the boyar government were numbered. Militia detachments were converging on Moscow from every direction. Patriots were diligently preparing for a rising in the city, gathering forces, and handing out weapons. Fusiliers were slipping into Moscow at night, using side streets. Citizens gladly concealed them in safe places. Donning civilian clothes, soldiers lost themselves in street crowds and had no trouble working their way inside the Kremlin fortifications.

The boyar government realized revolt might break out in the town quarter at any moment. It issued an edict depriving Muscovites of their weapons. Gosiewski enforced it. Boyar guards and soldiers confiscated pistols, swords, axes, and knives in the town quarter. Death was the penalty decreed for violators. Guards at the city's gates searched vehicles carefully. Sacks of grain in wagons often concealed pistols and swords. Weapons were collected and removed to the Kremlin; drivers were drowned in the river. But these executions could not halt the tide.

The morning of March 19, Mstislavskii, Saltykov and Gosiewski activated the interior fortification system. Soldiers dragged in cannon and mounted them on the walls of the Kremlin and Kitaigorod. The lower ranks openly abused and mocked the soldiers. An officer superintending installation of cannon near Vodianyi gate ordered carters watching the work from a distance to lend a hand. The carters knew whom the cannon would be fired at and refused. Mercenaries grabbed some peasants by the scruff of the neck. A scuffle ensued. The carters handled staves niftily but they were no match for swords and muskets. Many Russians were killed.

Kremlin sentinels told Gosiewski what was happening. Interrupting mass, he galloped through Frolov gate onto the square and tried to stop the brawl. But on seeing how many Muscovites were dead he waved his hand and, according to a Polish eyewitness, told the mercenaries:

"Finish what you have begun."[5] The clash soon turned into a pitched battle. Trumpets sounded in the Kremlin. Units lined up under their banners and charged the unarmed crowd. Mercenaries struck and slashed everyone they came across. They heaped mountains of corpses in the square and adjacent market corridors.

The capital had long been a tinder box. Popular disaffection had attained fever pitch. The encounter in Kitaigorod was the spark that ignited the train. In White Town, Earthen Town, and the Transriver district hordes of Muscovites seized arms. The fusiliers supported the insurgent people.

After disposing of the crowd in Kitaigorod, the mercenary units were ordered to occupy White Town. They immediately encountered organized resistance. The minute enemy soldiers appeared on a street Muscovites erected barricades. Every single person found something to do. People dragged bundles of wood out of houses and threw down barrels, tables, and counters. Impeded by these obstructions, the cavalry was forced to halt. The streets were narrow; some assailed the knights with slats torn from fences and showered them with stones while others kept firing rounds from roofs and windows. Sometimes inhabitants got hold of cannon and positioned them in the center of a street. The cavalry units were compelled to retreat to Kitaigorod and the Kremlin. German mercenary units, whose ferocity knew no bounds, took their place. When soldiers led by Jacques Margeret came back to the Kremlin after the encounter they looked like butchers: they were completely covered with the blood of Muscovites they had slain.[6]

This action by the king's mercenaries constituted a tragic and sanguinary event in the history of the Moscow troubles. Gosiewski and the boyars were equally responsible. Traitors like Mikhail Saltykov, the entire boyar council, many gentry, and merchants joined the enemy at the moment of crisis. Mstislavksii, Vorotynskii, Romanov, Sheremetev, Lykov, and the Golovin family vigorously helped Gosiewski crush the rising of the lower orders. From the first day of the rising people and rulers found themselves on opposite sides of the barricades.

The Moscow uprising was one of the most significant events of the civil war. Long anticipating an assault, the boyars were prepared to deal with it, but the rising took them unawares. Initially confusion reigned in high Kremlin circles but soon the boyars overcame their disarray, closed ranks tightly around Gosiewski, and began actively supporting him. At a meeting with the colonel, council members bitterly assailed "rootless people who would decide to revolt." Higher clergy shared their indignation. Archbishop Arsenios, who became one of the church's chief leaders after Hermogen was placed under official displeasure, did his best to convince Gosiewski that the town commons "had sounded the tocsin without the approval of boyars and church-men."[7] Moscow courtiers feared the lower orders far more than they did foreign soldiers. They vividly imagined what the people would do: they had murdered Boyar Petr Sheremetev in Pskov and Boyar Bogdan Belskii in Kazan. The courtiers believed that the triumph of the lower orders would destroy the realm.

Moscow was the home of hundreds of eminent courtiers. Only a few could be counted among the supporters of the insurgent people, but their ranks were now swelled by Prince Dmitrii Pozharskii, Ivan Mat-veevich Buturlin, and Ivan Koltovskoi. It is unclear why Pozharskii appeared in Moscow. By going over to Liapunov he had of course alienated Saltykov and Gosiewski, but the commander could have suc-cessfully survived difficult times in the fortress of Zaraisk. It was the decisive struggle that had broken out in Moscow which drew him there. It is unlikely that such a prudent man as Pozharskii would have risked his life merely to visit relatives. The capital was starving; gentry families preferred to winter in their rural retreats. If he had wanted to see his family Prince Dmitrii would have gone to Mugreevo, not to Moscow. The conclusion is inescapable that the Zaraisk commander, a leader in the militia, had gone to Moscow in order to prepare an up-rising. If a militia attack had been coordinated with a revolt inside the city the boyar government would have toppled. The rising provoked by the mercenaries wrought havoc with the patriots' plans.

On the morning of March 19 Pozharskii was in residence in Sreten-ka, near Lubianka. When bells rang in Kitaigorod he and his men rushed into the street. Instantaneously appraising the situation, the commander set out for a nearby fusilier settlement. Gathering fusiliers and townsmen, Pozharskii fell upon mercenaries who had appeared in Sretenka near Vvedenskii church. Next he sent his men to Truba, where the Cannon Court was located. Bombardiers straightway came to assist him, bringing a few light cannon with them. The mercenaries were met with fusillades and retired from Sretenka towards Kitaigorod.

Fusilier settlements became focal points of resistance throughout the town quarter. Fusiliers opposite Ilin gate found a leader in the per-son of Ivan Buturlin. Gosiewski's attempts to burst into the eastern part of White Town ended in failure. Buturlin pushed the enemy back in Kulishki and prevented him from reaching Yauza gate. Fusilier quarters on Tver street formed an impregnable barrier to the units trying to cut their way into the western part. The mercenaries could not get to Tver gate. They suffered losses and turned back. Ivan Koltovskoi spearheaded resistance in the Transriver district. Rebels threw up high barriers along a floating bridge and fired at the Vodianyi gate of the Kremlin from there. Thousands of Muscovites flew to arms. Their rage and anger made it seem they could clear all obstacles from their path. The mercenaries had sustained a decisive defeat in White Town. Hard pressed on all sides, they withdrew to Kitaigorod. Gosiewski informed the king: "Deeming the issue of battle doubtful, I ordered our men to set fire to parts of the Transriver district and White Town." Russian chroniclers assert it was Saltykov and his comrades who told Gosiewski to torch Moscow.

The treacherous boyars advised the enemy and actively assisted him. Mikhail Saltykov directed the struggle with the rebels in the area where his residence was located. When patriots began to get the upper hand the boyar ordered slaves to set fire to his house to prevent anyone's acquiring his riches. A conflagration broke out. The rebels were forced to retreat. Observing Saltykov's success, Gosiewski ordered his men to burn down the whole town quarter. It took his soldiers quite some time to fulfill his behest.

That year it seemed winter would never end. Cold frosts lasted until late March. The Moscow river was covered with ice, and snow lay everywhere. The chill sun did not warm the frozen beams of fences and buildings. Torches in hand, Gosiewski's soldiers tried to kindle the rubble but nothing happened. One of the arsonists wrote in his diary that they torched each building several times but in vain: the houses would not catch fire. The author of the diary expressed the naive sentiment that "the fire must have been bewitched."[8] But finally the incendiaries' efforts bore fruit. Columns of smoke were seen above various places in the town quarter. Soon flames engulfed whole quarters. Muscovites had to stop fighting and concentrate their energies on extinguishing fires. So many people poured out of their homes that it was virtually impossible to move along the streets. Women whose children were lost in the crowd cried out bitterly. Some people tried to drive cattle out of pasture while others were dragging their possessions away from the blaze.

The conflagration enabled Gosiewski to crush Muscovite resistance in Kulishki and at Tver gate. Winds blew the flames deep into White Town. Enemy soldiers rampaged over the burning areas, following directly after the ball of fire. The enemy failed to accomplish his ferocious purpose only in Lubianka. True to form, Pozharskii attacked the foes incessantly until he had bottled them up in Kitaigorod. Mercenaries refused to poke their noses outside the fortress. The area adjacent to Sretenka was saved from destruction.

All night bells clanged constantly in the city and Muscovites' warlike shouting was heard. Patriots asked Kolomna and Serpukhov for help. The national commanders responded at once. Ivan Pleshcheev hastily set out for Moscow from Kolomna with cossacks and men of Kolomna and Riazan. Fedor Smerdov Pleshcheev joined him en route. Fedor had been an associate boyar with the pretender. The boyars suspected he had been conniving with the Muscovites even while he was serving as commander of Serpukhov.

Militia units entered the Transriver district after dark. News of their arrival momentarily encouraged the capital and elicited a burst of enthusiasm. All night long the rebels got ready to renew the battle. At dawn their forces were massed in Sretenka and Chertole. At Chertole gate right by the Kremlin wall some thousand fusiliers had assembled. The inhabitants helped them erect barricades, over which banners fluttered, on the square.

Long after midnight Gosiewski held a council of war in the Kremlin. Many noble Muscovite courtiers were present. The members of the boyar government, receiving news from different parts of the city, were better informed about the actual state of affairs than the Polish command. They insistently urged Gosiewski to direct his blows at the Transriver district to interdict the circle of rebellious suburbs and clear a path for the king's troops advancing from the Mozhaisk region.

No one slept that night. Day scarcely had dawned when the Polish guard threw open the Kitaigorod gate, through which came boyars surrounded by attendants. The defenders on the barricades prepared to fire but lowered their weapons when they saw that no Lithuanians or Germans were accompanying the boyars. Approaching the ramparts, Mstislavskii and his comrades urged the Muscovites to cease their resistance and lay down their arms. Indignant shouts from the crowd drowned out their words. Townsmen uttered such expressions about the traitors that they preferred to clear out quickly. Bullets spattered behind them.

The boyars had been given the unenviable task of diverting the patriots' attention. While Mstislavskii was parleying with the people, German mercenary units advancing over the ice on the Moscow river fell in behind the fusiliers defending Chertole and set fire to the area next to the barricades. Cut off from their own men by a wall of fire, the fusiliers savagely fought the Germans but were unable to hold the position.

Taking the boyars' advice, Gosiewski ordered his soldiers to set fire to the Transriver district. At noon watchmen on Ivan the Great's belfry observed cavalry approaching from the west. A detachment led by Struys [a Dutch mercenary officer in Polish service who played a prominent part in the final phase of the Time of Troubles—ed.] could not enter Moscow because the Muscovites slammed the gate of Wooden Town shut in the hussars' faces. Gosiewski's incendiaries came to Struys' aid. Abetted by traitors, they secretly made their way up to the wall of Wooden Town and set fire to it from inside. The wall blazed up in several places and the fire leaped to adjacent areas in Earthen Town. Struys' unit was now in a position to force its way into the center of town and link up with Gosiewski.

During the first day of the uprising the fire burned only a small part of the town quarter, but next day the weather was windy. This made the arsonists' task easier. One of them wrote in his diary: "None of us failed that day to fight the enemy. Flames devoured one house after another. Impelled by fierce winds the flames drove the Russians away while we quietly followed, fanning the flames without interference. We did not return to the Kremlin until evening." Falling back before the bursts of flame, militia units and the populace withdrew from the Transriver district. No longer fearing attack from the south, Gosiewski renewed his efforts to destroy the rebel forces in White Town. His soldiers quickly advanced in Kulishki but at Sretenka the interventionists were taught a terrible lesson.

In the morning the Muscovites had managed to build a small redoubt at Sretenka near Vvedenskii church. For a day Pozharskii skillfully defended it. Disturbed by this nest of resistance in White Town, the Polish command moved reinforcements there from other parts of the city. The forces of the contenders appeared unequal. The mercenaries burst into the redoubt and the majority of its defenders perished. Struck by an enemy sword, Prince Pozharskii fell to the ground, severely wounded in the head. Blood streamed down his face. The patriots did not abandon their commander. He was carried, barely alive, from the battlefield, placed in a cart, and removed to a safe place. Next, Prince Dmitrii was transferred to the Trinity-St. Sergius monastery, which was protected by stout walls.

Moscow was on fire for several days. At night it was as bright as day in the Kremlin. The town quarter was burning over a vast area. The ruined city made contemporaries think of the Fiery Furnace. Buildings tottered and fell; fierce gouts of flame flared up into the air. By the fourth day no more than approximately a third of the town quarter was left undamaged. Gosiewski learned that militia units had appeared on the Vladimir highway. Fearing the Muscovites would renew their resistance, he sent out fresh bands of incendiaries from the Kremlin. The interventionists proposed to burn down the eastern part of the city to prevent the militia from establishing itself there.

The national army entered the Moscow suburbs after noon on March 21. Ataman Prosovetskii and his cossacks came first, followed by units led by Izmailov, Mosalskii, and Repnin. While waiting for the main militia force to arrive from the south, Izmailov and his comrades decided to dig in about five miles from the eastern gate of the capital, which the interventionists held. Militiamen hastily began to build fortifications but they did not complete their task.

Liapunov had failed to coordinate the attack on Moscow. Gosiewski adroitly took advantage of the Russians' disarray. He hurled almost all his available forces against Izmailov. The units from Vladimir, Nizhnii Novgorod, and Murom were undermanned, and alone they could not withstand the foe's superior forces. Supported by Struys' detachment, the foreign troops routed gentry cavalry and occupied the unfinished redoubt. Still fighting, the militiamen retired to a church standing alone in a field. Rebel infantry from Moscow rushed to their aid. The battle resumed with new ferocity. Militiamen and Muscovites trapped in the church fended the enemy off until all of them were destroyed.

The militia had not lost too many men but their banners, transport and cannon had fallen into enemy hands. Gosiewski complained that only nightfall had prevented his forces from destroying the Russians. The cavalry said it was the deep snow. In reality it was because the mercenaries wanted to finish off the battle as quickly as possible and return to the protection of the fortress, since the revolt in Moscow could flare up again in a matter of seconds.

The savagery displayed by the aggressors ruined thousands of peaceful inhabitants. Fate had played a cruel trick on prosperous

citizens who were not involved in the liberation movement. Many lost
their property and some their lives. Mercenaries charged into homes
of the wealthy and carried off everything they could find. Those who
resisted were cut down on the spot. Gosiewski saw a chance to get rid
of those who were of no more use to him. Boyar Andrei Golitsyn, under
house arrest, was brutally murdered. During the destruction of Moscow, Conciliar Courtier Ivan Mikhailovich Pushkin and many others
were cut down on the street. Yet the uprising saved many peaceful
inhabitants. The carnage the mercenaries were perpetrating in Kitaigorod abated as soon as they met with the setback in White Town. A
Moscow chronicler testified that the foreigners slew every Russian in
the Kremlin and Kitaigorod but few in White Town.[9]

The soldiers regarded the wealth of the royal city with greedy eyes.
They felt they had a right to it, and they had been waiting for an
opportunity to engage in pillage. The first day of the uprising they
plundered hundreds of shops and manufactories in Kitaigorod. The
officer Bussow, who was in Moscow, gloatingly observed that soldiers
that evening had acquired an enormous booty in gold, silver, and
precious stones.[10] In the space of two or three days the huge city had
become a pile of ashes. Row after row of fallen chimneys indicated
the places where only yesterday human habitations had been located.
Thousands of Muscovites, deprived of their homes and possessions,
scattered in all directions. A horde of dark figures obscured the snow
on the limitless plains around Moscow. The few inhabitants who had
barely survived the fire were left with nothing but their shirts; they had
no shoes or warm clothing. Many froze to death in the wind-swept open
fields during the first night.

A few days later an orgy of looting began in the spacious city
forsaken by its inhabitants. Nothing could have kept the mercenaries
in their barracks. In the morning they set out to pillage and towards
evening returned with sacks of booty. They rummaged in the cellars
of burnt-out dwellings in quest of hidden goods and wine. They sold
what they had taken in the units' stables. Marauders carried off gold
and silver utensils, gouged settings from icons, and destroyed the
shrines of the miracle workers in the church of Vasilii the Blessed and
others. After finishing with White Town, bands of plunderers essayed
a night raid on the Kremlin. Guards brandished weapons to ward them
off.

The mercenaries had subdued Moscow, but their triumph was
inglorious. They had not prevailed in honest, open battle. Plundering

ultimately demoralized the mercenary army. The conquerors staged an extraordinary celebration among the smoking ruins and unburied corpses. Wine flowed like water. At cards soldiers bet gold and Russian women they had violently seized on the streets. Bragging of their riches, drunken mercenaries charged their rifles with small jewels and fired them out of windows at those who chanced to be passing by.

The burning of Moscow shook the people's mind and soul. Thousands of impoverished refugees scattered all over the country. From them the rest of the people heard details of the unprecedented disaster. Their native land had been defiled. The tragedy aroused the populace to struggle and vengeance.

Chapter Eleven

AT THE BRINK

It was the end of March of 1611 but on roads around Moscow peasants still rode in sledges!

Nationalist units were approaching the capital along the last winter route. By March 23, in holy week, Prokofii Liapunov and the men of Riazan had reached the suburbs. Zarutskii and the cossacks and Trubetskoi and the serving men arrived shortly afterwards. They came up during Easter week, which began March 24.[1] The cossacks fought mostly on foot. Liapunov's gentry cavalry were more mobile than the infantry. It was not just the roads that delayed the cossacks. Jan Sapieha was in position a short distance from Kaluga. His army had rested well in winter quarters and was ready for summer campaigns. Sapieha and his men proposed an alliance with the militia but wanted too much in return. Zarutskii well understood how far he could trust such an ally. Sapieha might strike at the Kaluga camp from the rear at any moment.

Preparing to assault Moscow, the towns sought to encourage one another and inspire the enemy with exaggerated notions about the size of their forces. Liapunov spread rumors throughout the country that a horde of 40,000 men was on its way to aid him.[2] The Poles to some extent believed his broadsides. They assumed Liapunov had brought 80,000 soldiers to Moscow. They also calculated that Zarutskii had managed to collect 50,000, and Izmailov and Prosovetskii had 15,000, so that the militia complement amounted to more than 100,000 soldiers. Such a figure was absurd, but the mercenaries in the Kremlin thought they were being besieged by incalculable forces. The Swedes had more accurate information. Liapunov's emissary honestly told them the militia complement before Moscow comprised no more than 6,000 men. The actual number of militiamen was small, but the minute they approached the city Muscovites in burned-out sites and surviving villages flocked to their camp from all sides. The populace sought safety with the national militia. The flow of inhabitants made the besiegers' camp seem boundless in numbers. But appearances were deceptive.

Gosiewski managed to keep Moscow quiet, but only for a few days. His representatives fanned out all over the capital to administer an oath to Muscovites who had lain down arms. But the minute the people learned the militia commanders were approaching they rose again. The representatives barely escaped.

The boyar government failed to reestablish its power, even temporarily, in the southern suburbs. Rebel units under Commander Fedor Pleshcheev held the Simonov monastery firmly. After an unsuccessful battle Izmailov and Prosovetskii withdrew to the Andronov monastery, occupied it, and then linked up with Pleshcheev at the Simonov monastery. Zarutskii's men pitched camp by the Nikolskii-Ugreshkii monastery, located at the place where the Ugresha river empties into the Moscow river. This monastery, some nine miles from the fortress, had served as a shelter for False Dmitrii II during his final advance on Moscow.

On March 27 Gosiewski led his troops through the Yauza gate and tried to crush the militia forces and rebels around the Simonov monastery. He had no luck. A pitched battle was fought in the southeastern suburbs, lasting several days, but both sides avoided risking a major engagement. It was rather a trial of strength. The opponents were taking each other's measure.

The Russians enjoyed an appreciable success in this skirmish. Their vigorous combined onslaught made the mercenaries suffer losses and flee the battlefield. Chagrined at the failure, Gosiewski abandoned his plans for a new attack and did not dare even to defend the outer fortress walls. The night of April 1 militia soldiers crossed the Yauza river without encountering opposition and liberated almost all of White Town. Gosiewski now held no more than a small part of the White Town wall, from Nikitin to Chertole gate, and a few adjacent streets.

Spring came, and with it a long, tedious pause in military activity. It was more than two months before the militia was in a position to renew the attack. As early as the time of the first clashes Gosiewski's soldiers had noticed that the members of the national movement showed little trust in each other. Moscow chroniclers reported that their army lost a lot of time because its leaders were constantly bickering.[3] When the commanders met near Moscow they could not immediately overcome their mutual distrust or settle precedence accounts. However, it was not quarrels that caused the inexplicable inactivity.

The Moscow commons had been of great assistance to the militia, but the rebels lacked discipline and were poorly armed. The militia's resources were so meagre that its leaders could not hope for speedy success. To mount a proper siege of the fortress they needed ample forces. Liapunov and his confederates had neither large armies nor heavy artillery. Under such circumstances it was suicide to storm the Kremlin, which was remarkably well fortified, as was Kitaigorod. The interventionists had control of the best Russian artillery. Never before had so many cannon been deployed as were now to be seen along the Kremlin walls. The besiegers could never have endured their fire.

The militia did the best it could. Liapunov and the men of Riazan occupied the area around Yauza gate. Zarutskii and Trubetskoi helped fortify this vital point and then doubled back to Vorontsov field and deployed along White Town wall as far as Pokrov gate. The remaining units covered the White Town wall from Pokrov gate to Trubnyi square on the Neglinnyi river. The northern part of the wall was some distance from the cannon of Kitaigorod. Izmailov, Mosalskii and Repnin, the commanders who had just sustained a setback on the Vladimir highway, assumed responsibility for its defense. They were reinforced by other commanders who had recently arrived: Ivan Volynskii with men from Yaroslavl, Fedor Volkonskii with men from Kostroma, and Fedor Pogozhii with men from Uglich.

Liapunov's units contolled an essential communication line: the old Kolomenskoe road connecting Moscow with the Riazan region. The roads from the capital to Rostov and Yaroslavl also passed into the hands of the commanders in the Transriver district. Liapunov's position became the key one for the nationalist camp. From the first day it was fired upon constantly. The men of Riazan were exposed to an intense barrage. The enemy was determined to recover Yauza gate and prevent the soldiers from digging in near Kitaigorod and the Kremlin.

Militia commanders had to set up artillery under murderous fire. The Muscovites helped them plait gabions out of twigs and position a battery on a hill by St. Peter's church.

The nationalists set up another battery by Nikita church, nearer to the Yauza river. Balls rattled off the walls of Kitaigorod like peas, but without heavy siege artillery it was useless to think about knocking down the mighty towers. However, volleys from these batteries harassed the enemy and caused fires to break out in Kitaigorod and the Kremlin.

The militia leaders hoped the towns would come to their aid in time. All were impatient for the Kazan contingent to arrive. But the men of Kazan were delayed by internal friction and the start of the thaw. Heavy rains played havoc with roads and complicated movement of supplies. A harsh spring had set in.

Those who had acknowledged their responsibility and set out to liberate Moscow were experiencing difficulties. Even worse befell the heroic defenders of Smolensk. They were exhausted. The town had been under siege for nearly two years. No supplies were left. People were dying left and right of starvation. An epidemic was the last straw. At the end, no more than 300 or 400 persons capable of bearing arms were left in the town, but they continued the struggle with monumental stubbornness. The king's camp knew about the losses the Smolensk garrison had sustained and about the famine. Sigismund was waiting for an opportune moment to deliver a final blow to the long-suffering city.

At dawn, June 3, 1611 a mighty volley rocked the fortress. The walls around Kryloshev tower were demolished. Attack columns raced into the breach. Mercenaries advanced from several directions simultaneously. The garrison lacked the strength to repel attacks on the breach to the west, on the Bogoslovskii and Kryloshev towers, and on Abramiev monastery all at once. Most of the defenders of Smolensk perished on the streets with arms in their hands. A few survivors shut themselves up in a stone cathedral in the center of town. When the situation became hopeless, they blew themselves up with powder stored in the cathedral cellar so as not to fall alive into enemy hands. So ended the heroic defense of Smolensk, which had lasted almost two years. This was a magnificent achievement by people ready to defend the motherland. Smolensk had absorbed the main thrust of the attacking army. The town had devoured Sigismund's strength and had served as an insurmountable obstacle to his march on Moscow.

News of the fall of Smolensk flew the length and breadth of the country. Russians experienced feelings of alarm and despair. They expected Sigismund to occupy Moscow immediately with powerful forces. But the king hesitated to risk his hard-won victory and instead celebrated a triumph. His treasury was burdened with staggering debts. His army had sustained great losses and was in no condition to renew the attack.

Things were going worse for the interventionists in Moscow than on the western frontier. The Russian capital was spread over a vast area. The militia lacked forces to blockade the entire city but it controlled all approaches to Moscow except the one from Smolensk. The last links the boyar government had with the provinces were sundered and it was difficult to supply the Kremlin with provisions. In May the mercenaries informed Sigismund that they could not remain in Moscow longer than three weeks unless they received money and fodder for their horses immediately.

The enemy garrison held the Arbat and New Virgin Monastery, where the great Smolensk road started, but the road was not secure. It went through districts that were participating in the uprising. Risking their lives, peasants armed with forks, axes, and clubs formed units and struggled on. The enemy termed them rioters. In May these rioters plundered a gentry convoy and took away treasure the boyar government was pledging to Jan Sapieha.

Sapieha was making the boyars bid against Liapunov. Mstislavskii finally won by giving him 3,000 rubles, and he set out on campaign. Marching to Moscow, Sapieha and his men exchanged remarkable letters with the Polish garrison in the Kremlin. They demanded the garrison keep the treasury safe, refrain from appropriating money and treasure, and leave something for them. The knights in the capital replied that Sapieha's soldiers had no right to dispose of the Moscow treasury and could not withdraw money from it without the king's permission. Blinded by the glitter of Muscovite gold, the mercenaries were ready to tear one another to pieces for the sake of the booty.

The militia leaders were determined to prevent Sapieha and his men from entering Moscow. When it became clear they could not stop Sapieha's advance, Zarutskii decided to offer battle at the ford across the Ugra river at Kaluga. Liapunov preferred peaceful parleys.

The nationalists negotiated with the mercenaries for a whole month. They promised to discharge the pretender's debts, but they had no cash.

The boyars and Gosiewski outbid them by pledging as security tsarist regalia worth half a million Polish zloty to Sapieha and his men.

After reaching agreement with Gosiewski, Sapieha declared war on the militia. On June 23 his units fell on militiamen near Luzhniki. A week later Sapieha crossed the Moscow river and tried to get control of Tver gate. The battle was protracted. The militiamen routed Sapieha's German infantry and seized their standards. Skirmishing resumed two days later. For several hours the Russian army resisted the enemy attack. Mosalskii, the commander from Murom, was a hero who was killed in action while winning temporary military success.

To supply beleaguered Moscow grew more difficult. Gosiewski proposed Sapieha should lead a campaign to requisition grain in Pereiaslavl-Zalesskii. The boyar government instructed Commander Grigorii Romodanovskii with gentry and servitors to assist Sapieha; the Polish commanders assigned mercenary units and transport.

On July 5, 1611 the nationalist commanders took advantage of a decline in enemy strength and undertook a general storm. Liapunov's units concentrated on the corner tower in Kitaigorod near Yauza gate. Three hours before dawn soldiers closed in on the Kitaigorod wall, positioned ladders, and forced their way up. They managed to reach the tower, but it was easier to defend the inner fortress. Gosiewski hurled picked forces against Liapunov. The militiamen had to withdraw.

A fierce battle was fought in the western part of Moscow. Germans tried to hold the redoubt they had acquired by Koze swamp not far from the Neglinnyi river. Russian soldiers savagely fell upon them with such contempt for death that the Germans quickly left the redoubt in disarray and retired towards the Kremlin gate.

The Russians won Nikolskii tower. The 300 mercenaries holed up in it laid down their arms. The battle spilled over into the area by Trekhsviatyi gate. Militiamen managed to fire the powder cellar under the corner tower. An explosion followed and the tower was engulfed in flames. Few enemy soldiers succeeded in extricating themselves alive from the ruins. The nationalists had sustained heavy losses during the storm but reinforcements kept arriving from the provinces. The Kazan force finally reached Moscow in July. With its help Zarutskii occupied New Virgin Monastery after a fierce battle.

The July engagements significantly strengthened the militia's position around Moscow. The nationalists had won all White Town wall and had expelled the enemy from White Town. Henceforth the enemy garrison was trapped in the inner fortifications. Zarutskii had occupied New Virgin Monastery, where there was a strong fortress. He who held the monastery controlled the roads linking Moscow with the western frontier.

While the militia was battling at great odds to liberate Moscow, the military situation on the northwestern frontier around Great Novgorod was deteriorating. Next to Moscow, Novgorod for long was the most powerful city in the country. A large and wealthy trading and artisan population lived in its town quarter. The Novgorod militia was calculated at several thousand gentry. Moscow had to reckon with what might occur in one of Russia's most important regions.

Independent Novgorod had been hostile to the agreement the boyar government had concluded with Zolkiewski. The boyars were forced to send Ivan Saltykov and some troops to exact obedience from the city's turbulent population. Novgorod had refused to open its gates to Sigismund's representatives; only after lengthy persuasion did Saltykov prevail upon the inhabitants to admit him. Patriots made him swear an oath that he would not introduce foreigners into the city, but Saltykov had no intention of adhering to the obligation he had assumed. He made secret preparations to seize the fortress. The traitor fully understood where the foreign aggressors he served would encounter resistance and he acted ruthlessly. After Shuiskii had destroyed Bolotnikov's army he sent several hundred captives to Novgorod prisons, where they had been languishing for more than two years when Saltykov appeared. The boyar government's emissary ordered the prisoners executed. They were led out in batches, beaten with cudgels, and drowned in the Volkhov river.

The council of seven made Novgorod obey orders. The inhabitants there and in Toropets took the oath to Wladyslaw. Sigismund's units soon arrived in the outskirts of Toropets. Soldiers torched villages, seized residents, and carried them off as prisoners. The intruders showed no restraint. The people of Toropets let the people of Novgorod know what had happened to them. At the time a foreign detachment of 2,000 occupied Staraia Rusa and in March, 1611 drew close to Novgorod. The people repelled the attack. Boyar Saltykov had failed to accomplish his treacherous plans and secretly fled the city. Everywhere in Novgorod patriots rose up in anger against those who were cooperating with the aggressors. Saltykov did not get as far as Moscow.

He was recognized and brought back to Novgorod under guard. Patriots demanded a thorough investigation. The inquiry left no doubt that it was the council of seven's emissary who had invited the foreigners to Novgorod. Saltykov first was imprisoned and then impaled on a stake with his assistant, the courtier Cheglokov. What Mikhail Saltykov had managed to do in Moscow his son had failed to accomplish in Novgorod.

The news that the people of Novgorod had broken with the council of seven produced a strong impression. The city henceforward openly supported the liberation movement. Its inhabitants told Liapunov they would send commanders with troops and artillery to Moscow at once. But they could not do so because the Swedes were daily becoming more active in the area. The Swedes had not been able to save Tsar Vasilii. The actions of their king's mercenaries had ruined Shuiskii's fortunes. Nevertheless, the Swedes stubbornly insisted that the former tsar's pledge to surrender Korela should be honored. Nor did their ambitions stop there. Karl IX impatiently urged his commanders to take Novgorod. But they could not do more than their available strength permitted; thus their goals in the undeclared war were initially more modest. De la Gardie led the remnants of the Swedish army from Klushino to Novgorod. As his soldiers went along they plundered villages and took the inhabitants prisoner. On August 15, 1610 the mercenaries occupied and devastated ancient Ladoga.

After collecting troops, de la Gardie had fallen upon Oreshek and then occupied Korela. Tsar Vasilii had dispatched Commander Ivan Mikhailovich Pushkin to Korela with instructions to turn the place over to the Swedes and move its population inland. En route Pushkin learned that Shuiskii had fallen. He decided to defend Korela as best he could. Set on a granite crag in the swift-flowing Vuoksa river, nature had made the wooden fortress of Korela impregnable. Its walls descended almost into the water. A submerged tower made it difficult for enemy boats to approach the island. The lively river flowed strongly and seldom froze even in coldest weather.

For six months the Swedish army had been encamped before this formidable fortress. The heroic defenders of Korela had sustained losses, were ill with scurvy, and were suffering from hunger, but no one thought of surrendering. The garrison was greatly assisted by Russian and Karelian peasants. De la Gardie had to assign part of his force to fight partisans. By February, 1611 no more than 100 of the 2,000 men originally shut up in the fortress were still alive. Having no soldiers, Commander Pushkin began to negotiate with the enemy. He told de la Gardie he would blow up the fortress if the Swedes refused his terms. The Swedish command made concessions. On March 2, 1611 the handful of defenders left the fortress and made their way through the Swedish camp towards Oreshek. The local bishop brought church property with him. Pushkin took the commander's archive. Citizens carried their possessions on their backs.

Having taken Korela, the Swedish army fiercely stormed Oreshek but was completely defeated. Corpses of Swedish soldiers were loaded onto ten wagons and removed to Vyborg for burial. Many soldiers from all over Europe fought under de la Gardie's banner. The Swedes piled up those who were killed at Oreshek in a heap and pushed the bodies under the ice.

The savage war Sweden had unleashed against Russia had not gone well for the aggressors. Karl IX had to resort to diplomacy to improve his army's situation. The Swedish king sent one note after another to Moscow and Novgorod officials, couched in amicable terms. Pretending he was a friend and ally, he wrote as though Swedish armies had entered Russia for the sole purpose of using their available forces to help the Russians rid their country of the Poles. The king's assurances were patently false. Karl IX secretly had told de la Gardie to attack and take Novgorod as soon as possible. His last order was even more specific: "Everything we do has only one aim; to join Ivangorod, Oreshek, Yam, Kopore, and Kola to the Swedish crown."[4]

These friendly overtures from the Swedish king inspired Liapunov with hope. He knew nothing about the secret diplomatic agenda. The militia leader sent courier after courier to Novgorod, asking the people to arrange for de la Gardie to send Swedish auxiliaries to Moscow as soon as possible.

The men of Novgorod repulsed an attack by a strong Lithuanian force but the war was only beginning. Blows might fall simultaneously from several directions: from Livonia, where considerable troops were stationed, and from Lithuania, and from Smolensk. While preparing for a long struggle with Sigismund, Novgorod also had to be secure to the rear. Peace and an alliance with Sweden seemed the best way to do it. In March Karl IX sent another note to Novgorod, promising the people an alliance and aid against the Polish-Lithuanian armies. The onset of spring favored his deception: de la Gardie could not carry out the king's order to attack Novgorod. His 5,000-man force was encamped at Izhorsk, where it remained immobilized all spring. Soldiers plundered the whole area, searching for food and fodder.

Under pressure from Moscow and Stockholm, late in April the people of Novgorod sent envoys to the Swedish camp with a formula expressing full agreement.[5] They asked for ratification of a treaty of alliance between Russia and Sweden and for new joint military operations against the Rzeczpospolita. They requested de la Gardie to drive the enemy out of their territory and help them expel former men of Tushino from Ivangorod and a few other fortresses. In return for alliance and military aid the Novgorod authorities (Metropolitan Isidor and the commander, Prince Odoevskii), gentry, and men of all ranks agreed to "honor" Karl IX by ceding him several depots on the far side of the Neva river.

The spring thaw ended and de la Gardie launched a vigorous assault on Novgorod. On June 2, 1611 his army came right up to the fortress on the Volkhov. Lacking timely and accurate information about Swedish moves, Liapunov underestimated the threat they posed. Hewing to the line of the agreement with Sweden, the national council sent Commander Vasilii Buturlin to Novgorod. His choice as emissary was deliberate. Buturlin knew de la Gardie well and had been friends with him since the time the Swedes had helped Skopin liberate Moscow. The council wanted Buturlin to be a new Skopin. The commander was to bring de la Gardie's army to deliver the Russian capital a second time.

Buturlin showed himself to be an upright patriot. He rejected agreement with Sigismund out of hand. He had scores to settle with the Poles. Wounded in the battle at Klushino, the commander had suffered severely while a prisoner. On returning to Moscow he became involved in the patriotic movement. Gosiewski had him arrested and punished. With great difficulty Buturlin managed to escape from prison. He joined Liapunov's militia.

The council repeated Vasilii Shuiskii's mistake. Sure that the Swedes would help them liberate Moscow, the militia leaders were ready to sacrifice territory. They offered to compensate Sweden with Novgorod lands on the frontier. This at once aroused the people of Novgorod against them. They recently had been collecting forces to help the militia before Moscow. Now relations were strained and marked by mutual misunderstanding and distrust. The people of

Novgorod categorically rejected Liapunov's proposal to revise their ancient borders. Thus Buturlin was unable to come to terms with them about taking a common position in the upcoming negotiations with Sweden.

On June 6, 1611 de la Gardie received Vasilii Buturlin and Novgorod envoys on the outskirts of the city. Between the two armies drawn up in rows Novgorod commanders, courtiers, merchants, and town elders followed the Swedish commander-in-chief into a tent. Buturlin spoke first. In the name of the whole realm he asked his old friend de la Gardie to send troops to Moscow immediately, because Sigismund would undoubtedly soon be there with a huge army. The Novgorod envoys supported Moscow's request. They assured the Swede they would pay part of the mercenaries' salaries and temporarily pledge one border fortress to Sweden. The impatient Buturlin did not allow the men of Novgorod to finish their speech. Abruptly cutting them off, he asked de la Gardie what lands the king required.

Encouraged by Buturlin, the Swedes offered Novgorod totally unacceptable conditions. In addition to Korela, de la Gardie demanded Ladoga, Ivangorod, Yam, Kopore, and Gdov. The Novgorod envoys replied sturdily: "Better to die where we are than give up all our border forts."[6]

Buturlin undertook a dangerous ploy. He had established good relations with de la Gardie and obtained the right to negotiate with the Swedes in the name of the people of Novgorod. In private the Muscovite emissary informed his former friend in great secrecy of an idea that had been broached in Novgorod circles; namely, to offer the Muscovite throne to a Swedish prince. "There is no doubt," he added, "that all Moscow will agree if Karl IX will see to it that he is Orthodox."[7] The promise to elect a Swedish prince was designed to make the new ally more compliant. A seasoned diplomat, de la Gardie could scarcely believe his ears. He became unstinting in his tokens of friendship to the militia's emissary, held entertainments for him, and treated him like an honored guest.

The negotiations in the Swedish camp constituted a serious diplomatic defeat. Karl IX got what he had long coveted. The unoffical offer to seat a Swedish prince on the tsars' throne freed his hands. De la Gardie used the information Buturlin had given him in secret to bring further pressure on Liapunov. Swedish couriers hastened to Moscow. De la Gardie wrote in a personal communication to Liapunov: "As for your request to have one of his majesty's sons as your grand prince, his majesty has stated that henceforth you Russians will enjoy his mighty favor to a still higher degree."

Liapunov considered the Swedish project a device to obtain military aid. He was not anxious to discuss the project itself. He dismissed the Swedish couriers on July 16 and gave Buturlin new instructions. The militia leader proposed that his emissary should continue negotiating with the Swedes and as a last resort pledge Oreshek and Ladoga to the king. As for the dynastic parleys, Liapunov observed in passing: "We shall talk directly with Mr. Jacob de la Gardie here about choosing a Swedish prince as our grand prince." After the couriers departed, the national assembly was asked to discuss the issue of a Swedish candidacy. The military situation in Moscow was growing worse. Jan Sapieha's armies were fighting militia units in the western suburbs. Assembly members were afraid the enemy might transfer to Moscow forces made available by the fall of Smolensk.

Secretaries showed the council translations of letters sent by Karl IX and de la Gardie, and Buturlin's notes. The king's suave pronouncements made an impression on those present. However, many patriots strongly opposed the Swedish plan. They firmly pointed out that the Swedish king's words were very different from his deeds and they rejected all discussion concerning a Swedish heir. But Liapunov, still hoping for Swedish aid, favored a cautious stance. The assembly decided to send envoys to Sweden to discuss the election of a Swedish heir. They signed an assembly motion before the representatives set out. A decree stating a Swedish prince was worthy of election to the tsars' throne was a great diplomatic mistake. The assembly members were relying on erroneous information. There was no reason to assume Sweden would make an alliance.

De la Gardie fobbed off the people of Novgorod with words about how Russia and Sweden would soon form an indissoluble alliance. He promised Liapunov aid. But at the time he was massing his troops for an attack on Novgorod. The situation steadily deteriorated. The Swedes pitched camps all around the city. The hostile intentions of the foreign army were becoming constantly clearer. Swedish foragers roamed the Novgorod area, confiscating everything they could find. To be safe from pillage and violence the inhabitants sought refuge behind the fortress walls. The people kept calling for organized resistance to the interventionists.

Buturlin became convinced he had been cruelly deceived. He issued an ultimatum ordering de la Gardie to pull his forces back from Novgorod. The Swedes haughtily declined. Realizing the danger, Buturlin did not hesitate to ignore Liapunov's instructions and prepared to fight the aggressors. His fusiliers burned down wooden houses in the town quarter which obstructed cannon fire from the fortress walls. It was too late. Buturlin had been dickering with de la Gardie for such a long time behind their backs that the people of Novgorod lost faith in him. Buturlin obtained no support from Commander Odoevskii or church leaders, nor among ordinary citizens. Patriots suspected him of treason.

The protracted civil war long had divided Russian society. Novgorod contained many Pskov gentry and prosperous individuals who had been driven out of their city by the insurgent people. The authorities were fearful that what had happened in Pskov would be repeated in Novgorod if war broke out. The lower orders were turbulent and insisting war with the aggressors should be prosecuted vigorously. The upper orders preferred to come to an agreement. Novgorod merchants were taking supplies to the Swedish camp almost until the time cannon started firing. Substantial citizens were upset and complained when the fusiliers burned down the suburbs.[8]

Swedish soldiers roamed suburban villages. Patriots decided to teach them a lesson. They collected volunteers and made a sortie. Their force was small and their leadership inadequate, and the Swedes prevailed. Many Novgorod soldiers lay dead on the battlefield. The rest withdrew to the fortress. Their failure deepened the mood of general gloom. The chief commander, Boyar Odoevskii, summoned a council which gentry and church leaders attended. Views differed. Some called for energetic measures and organization to repel the enemy. Others cited the agreement the militia had made and proposed to extend the parleys with the Swedes and reach an understanding with them. Odoevskii and the churchmen were inclined to this policy. The council dispersed without coming to a decision.

By mid-June, 1611 de la Gardie had completed preparations for an attack. He knew how to rouse his men's spirits. The soldiers had been promised rich booty. The day before the attack de la Gardie made a feint. With the people looking on, squadrons of Swedes approached the bank of the Volkhov river at the southeastern end of the fortress, where his soldiers delivered boats from all over the Volkhov. At dawn on June 16 the Swedes launched a diversionary assault from the southeast. Attracted by firing and noise, the people of Novgorod ran from everywhere to the exposed towers. Then de la Gardie struck from the opposite side. In the morning murk German mercenaries pushed up to a gate and attempted to batter it down with a ram. Scotch and English troops hoisted a petard to an adjacent gate. Swedes clambered up the moat in the space between the gates. The people of Novgorod beat back the attack, fired on the Germans, and drove them away from the gate. But traitors helped the Swedes. One led the enemy to an unguarded gate. He wiggled under it on his stomach by a track which wheels had made and managed to open it from the inside. Swedish cavalry charged through the gate into the city. The Russians retreated along the wall to the towers, from which they kept firing for a long time. But Swedish forces already had penetrated far into the fortress. A fire broke out in the eastern part of the city during the battle. People took to flight and crammed the streets. The commanders were no longer in control of the situation. Soldiers blended with civilians in a great fleeing tide.

Mercenaries viciously struck and slashed everyone they came across. The battle was still raging when they turned to pillaging homes. Though they were separated, parts of the garrison tried to halt the onset in different places. Popular memory has preserved the names of outstanding leaders: Fusilier Captains Vasilii Gaiutin and Vasilii Orlov, and Ataman Timofei Sharov. They preferred death to capture. Crown Secretary Afinogen Golenishchev, a delegate from the national militia, kept on fighting until he was killed. Civilians helped soldiers. For a long time the Swedes could not take a house on a corner which contained Archpriest Amos and some townsmen. The Swedes tried to get them to surrender, promising to spare their lives. The men of Novgorod answered with fire. The soldiers burned the house down with its defenders inside it.

If they had possessed a unified command, the people of Novgorod might have been able to gather their forces and resist the enemy, but the city was badly prepared for defense. Noble Prince Odoevskii was a poor commander. He did nothing to save the city. Vasilii Buturlin tried to direct the struggle. His headquarters were in a large square near the Volkhov. Here the Swedes encountered their strongest opposition. Cossacks and soldiers fought the enemy to the death. The Swedes tried to surround Buturlin's division. The commander forced his way onto

the bridge across the Volkhov and went over to the Trading Side.
Enemy soldiers were following closely on his heels across the bridge.

The Swedes got control of the inner fortress on the Sophia Side.
They had achieved a success but it was a far cry from victory. Russian
standards still fluttered over the Kremlin, the impregnable citadel in
the center of the city. It was more strongly fortified than the inner city,
surrounded by a deep trench and equipped with drawbridges. Its high
towers and walls contained a mass of cannon. The Kremlin dominated
the city. It would be folly to storm it without siege artillery. However,
the Novgorod citadel was wholly unprepared to sustain a siege. The
Swedes were dumbfounded when later they inspected the entire Kremlin and found no food or powder there.

Novgorod leaders had fatally miscalculated the foe's strength. They
remembered the Poles had routed de la Gardie and his army at Klushino. They also recalled that de la Gardie had been unable to take
Korela by storm and had wasted six months before its walls. They knew
that he had been twice defeated at Oreshek. The Swedish general did
not have enough cannon or soldiers. The Russian command was sure
the enemy would never penetrate the inner fortifications. Thus they
dispersed the garrison all over the city wall. Their unjustifiable over-
confidence was succeeded by a mood of panic and despair when it took
the Swedes only a day to win control of the first line of defense.

Commander Odoevskii summoned a new council of war in the beleaguered Kremlin. Reports from secretaries, junior commanders, and
captains painted an alarming picture. Many soldiers and large numbers
of civilians had sought refuge in the Kremlin after the battle. There
was nothing to eat; the Kremlin granaries were empty. The artillery
was silent; there was no powder. Gripped by a wave of panic, the members of the war council decided to give up. After long deliberation with
Metropolitan Isidor, courtiers, and prosperous traders, Commander
Prince Odoevskii sent a delegation to the Swedes to surrender the
Kremlin. De la Gardie at once moved the king's bodyguard into the
invincible citadel.

The upper orders in Novgorod originally had broken with the boyar
government but then proceeded to imitate it. What had happened in
Moscow was repeated with only slight variations in Novgorod. The
Novgorod nobles betrayed the national interest as easily as the Muscovite nobles had done. In time they would try to blame the militia leaders for their actions. Two weeks before the assault a courier from the

national militia had come to Novgorod. Odoevskii and Metropolitan Isidor claimed he had brought a decree from the Moscow assembly authorizing election of a Swedish prince whom King Karl "might see fit" to bestow as ruler of the mighty Russian tsardom. Then, following the assembly's wishes, the Novgorod authorities concluded a treaty with Sweden to that effect.

Boyar Odoevskii and his confederates were behaving hypocritically. The Swedish translation of the decree of the Moscow assembly completely contradicted the version they had put forward: "All ranks in the Muscovite realm have recognized that the elder son of King Karl IX is worthy to be elected grand prince and sovereign of the Muscovite realm."[9] Recognizing a Swedish prince as a worthy candidate was of course not tantamount to election. The council of the people's militia remembered the unfortunate experience involving the oath to Wladyslaw. They were in no hurry to elect a Swedish prince to the throne.

After concluding the treaty with de la Gardie, Isidor and Odoevskii took the initiative and assumed responsibility for proclaiming a Swedish pretender as the Russian tsar. The treaty stated: "Metropolitan Isidor and the sacred council, Boyar Prince Odoevskii, commanders, princes, boyars, merchants, and peasants have elected a Swedish prince as tsar and grand prince of the Novgorod principality and also of the Vladimir and Moscow principalities, if the latter desire to associate themselves with the Novgorod principality."[10]

The text of the treaty was unequivocal. Novgorod nobles pretended they were merely executing the militia decree. In fact, they betrayed the liberation movement. A Novgorod state under the aegis of a nameless Swedish prince could form no part of Russia. Boyar Odoevskii, a descendant of appanage princes, emerged as nominal head of this state. A decisive struggle for Moscow lay ahead. The Novgorod authorities knew it but did not trouble to insert a clause into the treaty to the effect that they would send armies to help. The militia was left to its fate.

The people of Novgorod had striven to make de la Gardie acknowledge that the ancient boundaries of the Novgorod land were inviolable. The agreement did not even mention Korela and its environs; they were declared Swedish possessions. But the Swedes considered the whole treaty no more than a diplomatic subterfuge. De la Gardie had badly lost prestige over the Klushino debacle. He was ready to promise anything in order to bring the Novgorod war to a successful conclusion.

Odoevskii surrendered the Kremlin although he had no guarantee that the Swedes would preserve Novgorod's territorial integrity. Furthermore, his government had betrayed the towns that were still offering armed resistance to the foreign aggressors. The covenant stipulated that Swedish garrisons should occupy all border forts. The upper orders in Novgorod had envisaged that the peace treaty would bring the war to an end. All it actually had done was open the gate wide to the aggressors.

In a critical position, Vasilii Buturlin acted imprudently. Forced to quit the Trading Side, he gave vent to the resentment he had long harbored against Novgorod. Unwilling to leave rich booty to the Swedes, the commander ordered his men to smash shops in the marketplace and remove the most valuable merchandise from them. He retired to Bronnitsa, where he tried to resume the contest with the Swedes. Local gentry and soldiers flocked to his camp, but Odoevskii's treachery had nullified his efforts.

Novgorod leaders had promised the gentry their lands and homes would be safe under a Swedish pretender because Swedes would not receive lands around Novgorod. This proviso was embodied in the text of the treaty. One landholder after another abandoned Buturlin and joined the people of Novgorod in taking an oath to the nameless Swedish pretender. De la Gardie compensated Buturlin in his own way. He ordered property the commander had left in Novgorod found and restored to him. Forsaken by the gentry, Buturlin departed for Moscow.

Karl IX celebrated his victory with a solemn church service. He humbly thanked God for all he had won. The Swedish king was acting like his nephew Sigismund. Impatience and stubbornness were characteristics of the Vasa family. Karl respected the Novgorod covenant as little as Sigismund did the Moscow undertaking. He issued an order to appropriate Novgorod border forts for the Swedish crown, effective immediately.

Karl was not destined to enjoy the fruits of his victory. He died three months after the subjugation of Novgorod. The Swedish throne passed to his heir, Gustav Adolphus, aged 17 years. The son continued his father's duplicitous Russian policy. Loudly proclaiming his peaceful intentions and concern for Russian welfare, Gustav Adolphus kept on dismembering Russia and incorporated Novgorod and Pskov into Sweden. Appearing before the Swedish parliament, the new king uttered these remarkable words: "The proud Poles have often been defeated by the Russians. Greedy and cunning foxes, they have prevailed only when Russia has been beset by internal strife. In seizing a Russia torn by violence they have been behaving like ravening lions!"[11] Gustav Adolphus chose not to notice that the Swedes too were picking at Russia, not like foxes or lions, but like jackals. Once before, King John III had occupied Ivangorod, Narva, Yam, and Kopore, taking advantage of the fact that the garrisons of these towns had been absent, defending Pskov from Batory. Karl IX and his son acquired the whole of the Novgorod land only after the armies of the Rzeczpospolita had taken Smolensk and advanced on Moscow.

Sweden now assigned a low priority to the struggle with Poland over Livonia. Yesterday's sworn enemies concluded a truce there in order to concentrate almost all their forces against Russia. The cruel civil war had exhausted the Russian people and ruined the Russian armed forces. The country was faced with catastrophe. Enemies had seized Novgorod and Smolensk, two of its strongest places, the main defense points on the western and northern frontiers. One foe was ensconced in Moscow. Rent internally, the Russian realm seemed on the verge of collapse and dismemberment.

Chapter Twelve

DUAL POWER

The Moscow uprising had affected the fortunes of the leaders of the boyar council drastically. The barricades had split the boyar government hopelessly from the people. The council of seven now resembled a severed head. The number of its supporters, even in beleaguered Moscow, was steadily diminishing. Every day courtiers, fusiliers and undersecretaries fled from the Kremlin to the militia. Having completely forfeited the support of the capital population and the provinces the members of the council of seven had become lackeys of the foreign mercenaries.

Colonel Gosiewski had amassed considerable power. He proudly styled himself Elder of Moscow and distributed lands and treasure. A pack of traitors and jailbirds had clustered around him. The Elder was glad to make use of their services. Mstislavskii, Vorotynskii, Romanov, and other boyars assembled in the palace and solemnly discussed affairs of state. But their attempts to wield sovereign power were simply ridiculous. The boyars complained they could not hear a word of the discussions between Gosiewski and his confederates, Mikhail Saltykov and Fedka Andronov, nor the decisions they made in the council's name.

Fedor Andronov was the most colorful personage among Gosiewski's associates. His knavery had attracted attention even in Shuiskii's time. During Otrepev's brief rule Andronov had signed out valuable furs from the treasury. When Tsar Vasilii mounted the throne the trader fled to Tushino with his treasury goods. Fedka went from Tushino to Smolensk, where Sigismund designated him Treasurer of Moscow. The members of the council of seven shunned the society of the rascally trader but, not daring to disobey the king's mandate, they consigned the keys of the tsars' treasury to the new council member. Fedor henceforth joined High Treasurer Golovin. Every day both men appeared in the Treasury Court and sealed its doors with two seals when they left. Once, when the boyars came to the treasury, they found its doors sealed only with Andronov's seal. When they expressed annoyance Fedka soon quieted them by saying he had opened the treasury doors at the personal command of Gosiewski.

The colonel's head was turned by the sight of the great wealth in the Moscow treasury. The temptation was overwhelming and the Elder yielded. Chancellery documents reveal that "Lord Elder Gosiewski" removed velvet, golden satin, jewels, horse trappings, and other items valued at 698 rubles from the palace treasury.[1] Treasury books record only a trifling part of what the Moscow Elder appropriated. Andronov stealthily helped him filch many other objects. Ensconced in the treasury chancellery, Fedor Andronov finally was able to indulge his cravings. His father dealt in bast shoes; the son had hidden gold chains, emerald and ruby cuff links, jewelled necklaces, and many other precious objects.

The members of the council of seven cannot be charged with idly standing by while the tsars' treasury was looted. Each one of them tried his best to get his fair share. To accommodate them the treasury chancellery sold in the Traders' Court what the tsars had accumulated. Boyars, associate boyars, courtiers, and chancellery officials bought items at reduced prices, ostensibly to pay their debts. They were credited with many thousands of rubles, but even so they did not manage to discharge their obligations because "for our sins there is devastation in Moscow."

Over the years the Muscovite sovereigns, descendants of Ivan
Kalita, had acquired a great many valuable objects. The fabulous
wealth in the Moscow treasury was on Sigismund's mind. Gosiewski's
reports further excited his cupidity. He wrote that many articles in the
treasury could provide the king with revenue. All he had to do was to
send coiners to Moscow and mint gold and silver objects. Then he
could pay his mercenaries what he owed them. The Currency Court
in Moscow minted new coins. Precious silver vessels from the treasury
were given to the coiners. There was not enough silver; Gosiewski
decided to expropriate gold and silver plate from churches. Metal objects were melted down. The new coins were stamped with Tsar Wladyslaw's name. Incomplete lists show that Fedor Sheremetev and
Fedka Andronov sent the king in Smolensk sables worth 4,000 rubles,
obeyed his behest to distribute money and goods worth 6,000 rubles
to courtiers and officials, and gave Elder Gosiewski silver, gold, and
other objects worth 4780 rubles.

Gosiewski had been in the Kremlin a year. The boyar government
decided to inventory expenditures. The results were discouraging.
Otrepev had inherited a full treasury from Godunov but had managed
to squander millions within a year. Vasilii Shuiskii had been parsimo-
nious with his courtiers and had succeeded in refilling the treasury.
From him the boyar government had inherited some 120,000 rubles
in cash. Moscow was home to five permanent Fusilier chancelleries,
each containing complements of 2,000 to 3,000 men. The treasury had
expended 7392 rubles in order to maintain them. It spent somewhat
more on serving men, which was paid out to support those on home
and provincial duty. The boyars had spent 20,000 rubles on the Russian
garrison in goods and supplementary payments. This money was
essentially expended during the first six months because in March
fusiliers and many serving men favored the uprising and went over to
the militia.

The treasury gave out far more to foreign mercenaries than it did
to Russian armies. In a year 800 Germans received 35,000 rubles in
money and valuables. Simply for maintenance, the foreigners extracted 65,000 rubles in cash and goods from the treasury. The mercenary
army devoured the lion's share—more than 90,000 of the 120,000
rubles. Until autumn the boyars were able to supplement treasury revenues with tax receipts, but then remittances stopped. They had to resort
to the royal treasury. To pay salaries Gosiewski removed gold plate,

valuable crosses, rings, precious stones, jewels, gold chains, sable and other furs, tsaric robes, velvet, and cloth from the treasury. The boyars did not scruple to take gold ornaments from the icon of the Savior and rip the jewels off the coat lying on Tsar Fedor's tomb.

The Kremlin had become the site of a strange trade. Delegates from the mercenaries appeared in the Palace of Facets, demanding payment in full. The boyars offered them objects of value. The delegates would swagger and make a show of refusing to accept what was tendered. After they forced down the price of the valuables they would generously agree to accept them, but then they would come back and ask for additional subsidies. The cost of food went up in the besieged city while the price of gold went down. The treasurers had to estimate the precious metal at the lowest possible price, which was twice as low as usual. The treasury offered the foreigners 160,000 rubles in gold and furs. The delegates were not satisfied. They paid only 120,000 rubles for these valuables, thereby obtaining regal items for a pittance. In the course of a year the treasury sold goods for 232,000 rubles. Their full value would have been half a million.

When the towns rose in revolt the boyar government and the occupation authorities confiscated land from participants in the national liberation movement. Nobles, chancellery bureaucrats, and foreigners in the Kremlin saw a chance to acquire immense wealth. The boyars set an example to minor traitors. The traditional assignment of 1350 acres of service land was not enough for them. Boyars Fedor Shereme-tev and Boris Lykov obtained some 4,000 acres more than they had been assigned. Gosiewski strongly encouraged their speculations.

Gosiewski imprisoned Patriarch Hermogen after the uprising. The boyars soon started insisting he should be transferred to the residence which the Kirillo-Belozersk monastery maintained in the Kremlin, where his guards were Polish escorts. The boyar council had good reason to intercede on behalf of the aged prince of the church. Though Moscow was in ruins, Hermogen's attitude had not changed. He regarded the circle of cossack enclaves surrounding the city with anguished distrust. Prince Ivan Khvorostinin, one of the council of seven members, had a meeting with the patriarch at the time and noted down what he said. On one occasion the old man embraced the young courtier and said tearfully: "Our detractors speak ill of me, as though I were stirring up the soldiers and equipping the units comprising this strange force of many faiths. I have only one thing to say to everyone. Remain at your posts and pray!"[2] Free cossacks from remote regions had no churches and were careless of ritual. Besides them, the militia contained masses of Tatars, Chuvash, Mordvinians, Ukrainians, Belorussians, Poles, Lithuanians, and Germans. This is what Hermogen meant when he called the militia units a strange host of many faiths. As he was under guard, the patriarch was afraid to speak out concerning the villainies perpetrated by the foreign aggressors. However, with the boyars' approval he was happy to inveigh against licence, pillage, drunkenness, and immorality in the cossack enclaves around Moscow.

Hermogen's authority as head of the church was of considerable help to the council of seven, seeking to keep waverers in line. In the autumn of 1611 Hermogen again wrote to Sigismund humbly and submissively: "O king, give us your son; God loves him and has chosen him tsar in our Orthodox faith...."[3] The patriarch was fostering illusions held by those who, like the council of seven members, were trying to end the popular rebellion by seating a "lawful" tsar on the throne.

No matter what Mstislavskii and his comrades did, the Kremlin was a place of resignation and despondency. Chancelleries were not functioning. The few undersecretaries left in them wandered around empty offices with nothing to do. While the boyar government was declining, the rebel camp was growing stronger and acquiring new authority. In April, 1611 Liapunov, Zarutskii and other militia commanders administered an oath to their men. The soldiers showed emotion as they uttered the words of the exhortation. The oath legitimized their struggle. They undertook solemn obligations: to stand together as one with the towns against the king, the heir, and those who had thrown in with them; to rid Muscovy of Poles and Lithuanians; to refuse to obey the edicts of the Moscow boyars, and to serve a sovereign chosen by the whole realm.

Circumstances forced the national militia government to concentrate on military problems. Without fresh troops it would be impossible to rid the country of foreign conquerors and restore native sovereignty. The first thing the commanders did was to proclaim a general mobilization of gentry militia. They instructed gentry to appear in the besieging camp before Moscow no later than May, 1611. Those who refused to serve were threatened with prompt confiscation of their holdings. The gentry militia constituted the core of the Russian army, but the Time of Troubles had demoralized it. Many landholders had chosen to have nothing to do with the liberation movement and had tried to wait things out in remote places, but the militia's victories had made a deep impression on them. Serving men from faraway provinces came to Moscow. This responsible attitude affected even Moscow courtiers who had stuck with the council of seven through thick and thin. Many of them went over to the nationalist camp.

The national militia created an assembly that was in continuous session. The army was comprised of men from many towns and districts; thus, the militia assembly acquired the title of Council of the Entire Realm. Nobility, boyars, princes of the church, and great Moscow courtiers had invariably dominated previous assemblies. This assembly, riding on the crest of the liberation movement, excluded the official boyar and ecclesiastical councils. For the first time in many decades provincial gentry, lesser boyars, serving men, and free cossacks constituted a firm majority in a high representative national body.

In April and May the council passed many different resolutions, which were consolidated and triumphantly approved on June 30, 1611. The resulting decree essentially became the first militia constitution. Serving men from 25 towns, including Nizhnii Novgorod, Yaroslavl, Vladimir, Pereiaslavl-Zalesskii, Rostov, Kostroma, Vologda, Kaluga, and Murom, subscribed its text. Atamans, captains, and ordinary cossacks from various regiments signed the document along with gentry.

Those who held the majority could determine the decisions. The Time of Troubles had elevated people who previously had stood modestly apart in the shade. Serving men were no longer content to be the obedient foils they had been at former assemblies. In camp they showered Liapunov and other commanders with incessant petitions. The gentry wished to control their own affairs. This meant only one thing. The national government would have to seize the property of boyars and nobles cooperating with the enemy. A gentry group would carry out the confiscations and award such lands to impoverished serving men for their maintenance. Any militia leader who appropriated the patrimonial estate of a treacherous boyar should do so "on the basis of merit, not need." Distribution of boyar lands must also take service to Tsar Vasilii and the Thief of Tushino into condideration. What the Kaluga people had added to old land parcels was to be placed in a common fund. Non-noble gentry had long dreamed of equality in land. It was now possible to accomplish it. Gentry petitions formed the base of the militia constitution of June 30, 1611.

Land redistribution was central to the council decree. Three months of haggling at last had freed national representatives of any illusions about coming to terms with the boyar government. The language of the decree confiscating lands belonging to traitorous boyars was uncompromising and unequivocal: "He from here who consorts with foreigners in Moscow...and like a thief does not come to our forces will lose his service-tenure and patrimonial estates."[4] Land taken from the nobility had to go to patriots in the liberation movement.

The national government declared it was the protector of ruined petty serving men. It enacted that land should be given to "gentry and lesser boyars who are poor, destitute, and have no holdings or only dwarf holdings." Justice would triumph. First to receive land were those whom foreigners had ruined: "No one will be allowed to demand an allotment and no one will be enfeoffed until the poor and destitute are enfeoffed."[5] The assembly decree corresponded to the interests of petty gentry and the cossack upper orders. Many lesser boyars who had little or no land had long been serving as atamans and captains in cossack armies. Their outlook on life was much the same as the rest of the gentry. The June 30 constitution granted atamans and senior cossacks the right to have land, depending upon the size of their families and the extent of their service, or to receive a salary paid either in grain or cash. The assembly counted as lesser cossacks former slaves, indentured peasants, and the commons serving in the militia before the siege of Moscow began. Privileges conferred on serving men were not extended to them.

Gentry petitions were filled with complaints about peasant departure. The assembly affirmed that the system which had evolved since abolition of the right of St. George's Day was sacrosanct. Peasants who moved from estate to estate might be tracked down and returned to their original owners, as well as slaves who had fled to the towns. Fearing cossack wrath, the gentry did not dare demand that the peasants and slaves present in large numbers in the militia's cossack units should be enserfed.

The popular movement carried Liapunov and his confederates along with it. They were steadily growing more convinced that the success of the liberation movement depended upon involving all free cossacks in the struggle and retaining them and the gentry in the national army.

The civil war had aroused separatist tendencies on the periphery. Novgorod had been detached from Muscovy. Word was abroad that an independent Astrakhan was preparing to emulate Novgorod. For five years Astrakhan had been following its own bent, refusing to acknowledge Moscow's authority. The militia was concerned that the people of Astrakhan were covertly trying to persuade the people of Kazan to secede from Russia and place themselves under the protection of Persia.

Alarmed by such rumors Liapunov appealed to the people of Kazan to support liberation of the motherland. He tried to involve Kazan in talks with the Volga cossacks. Liapunov decreed: "in the name of the national government have the people of Kazan write to atamans and cossacks dwelling along the Volga and in the lower river regions. We call upon all of you to come to Moscow's aid. A salary, powder, and shot are waiting for you. Anyone senior who is indentured to boyars should come without fear or hesitation. Like other cossacks, you will be free and receive a salary. Boyars and commanders and the whole realm will issue you letters in accordance with the terms of the general agreement."[6] When sending proclamations to the borderlands the national government drew no distinction between junior and senior cossacks. It promised freedom to all, even those who recently had been slaves or serfs. This fiery exhortation provoked a response from those who had fled to the Volga and Don regions in order to escape the yoke of serfdom.

Men of the town quarters, who had been largely responsible for organizing the national movement, stood aside when the militia marched on Moscow. This enabled the war party to prevail in the assembly before the capital, to the detriment of urban dwellers. None of them was close to Liapunov and other assembly leaders. Townsmen always wanted returned taxpaying individuals who had fled ruined towns to live on feudal estates. Their demands were ignored.

The civil war had split the upper orders. Members of the same family could be found in either camp. One of the Trubetskoi boyars was prominent in the council of seven, while the other led the militia. Boyars Ivan Vasilevich Golitsyn and Fedor Sheremetev supported Gosiewski, while Courtiers Ivan Andreevich Golitsyn and Ivan Sheremetev served in the national militia. Two members of the Pleshcheev family were helping the insurgent Muscovites, while a third was assisting the foreigners to repress them. The national assembly contained but few eminent noblemen, and they did not put themselves forward. Younger members of boyar families had no objection to acquiring inherited patrimonies belonging to their older relatives, but the assembly gave them short shrift. The national government declared they might receive allotments from the fund of land confiscated from their kinsmen and courtiers fighting against Muscovy on the side of the foreigners. But that was all.

Boyar nobles and gentry often had tried to solve their problems by seizing church lands. The Council of the Entire Realm acted otherwise. Serving men now believed they could get the land they coveted from the enormous holdings belonging to the aristocracy; they refused to touch the church's patrimony. Russians thought a struggle for independence was inseparable from a struggle to preserve the faith of their fathers, of which the church was the repository. The assembly confirmed that the patriarch and the rest of the clergy had an indisputable right to their ancient patrimonies, but it did decree that church lands should make contributions to maintain an abode for soldiers.

Slaves to tradition, militia leaders regarded the national government as a kind of boyar commission. They issued decrees in the name of "the boyars and the whole realm." Few native boyars actually served in the militia. Conciliar Courtier Prokofii Liapunov was the most influential member of the council. As head of the liberation movement Liapunov had become very popular. Towns and individuals usually turned to him to decide important questions.

The provinces initially received charters issued in the name of commanders, boyars, and Conciliar Courtier Prokofii Liapunov. The council did not specify which boyars and commanders, because at first the boyars could not agree where each of them stood. Associate Boyars Izmailov and Mosalskii and Commanders Repnin and Bakhteiarov were unwilling to acknowledge that men who had been made boyars in Tushino outranked them. Tushino boyars were suspicious of those who had been named boyars by Tsar Vasilii Shuiskii.

By May the assembly had undertaken a reform designed to end divisiveness among the leaders. After much discussion it enacted that power should be concentrated in the hands of its three outstanding officers. Dmitrii Trubetskoi joined Liapunov. The Trubetskoi princes had long ago squandered their inherited resources; if they had not served in the oprichnina they would no longer have been boyars. Dmitrii Trubetskoi had obtained his rank from the Thief. He was the most pedigreed of the militia leaders. Liapunov deemed him a suitable associate because the boyar had little intelligence or character.

To choose the third figure presented the most difficulties. Leaders of gentry units around Moscow who had received conciliar rank could aspire to this office. However, Liapunov chose not one of these but

Zarutskii, head of the cossack hosts, as his associate. A non-noble cossack boyar was something Russia had never seen. In recognizing Zarutskii's boyar rank the council acknowledged that cossacks were equal partners in the militia. The formation of the triumvirate strengthened the alliance between gentry and chiefs of the cossack enclaves.

Cossack leader Zarutskii possessed more extensive military experience than the other commanders. Liapunov sought to establish a close relationship with him. The illiterate ataman had Liapunov, not his Tushino comrade Trubetskoi, sign the assembly decree for him. The assembly granted no privileges to the triumvirs. They were assigned boyars' estates of the traditional size they had been under previous rulers. Other wealth obtained from the pretender was distributed to everyone. The triumvirs could not decide high affairs of state alone, nor could they pass death sentences without council approval. Their plenipotentiary powers were temporary. The assembly had the right to substitute another person, more devoted to the national cause, for a member of this "boyar commission" at any time.

In its work the triumvirate relied on chancelleries such as Service-Tenure and Military Affairs, etc. It was not difficult to organize them. The Kremlin contained old, well-constructed chancellery buildings but, as secretaries informed the boyars, only Poles and Lithuanians were working in them; undersecretaries had gone over to "the Thief's units."[7] Warm chancellery offices had been converted into barracks; the few remaining secretaries wandered about with nothing to do. New militia chancelleries were established outside the Kremlin walls, but quite near the old ones. People in the militia chancelleries set to work in cramped houses and dugouts. They lacked even rudimentary equipment like tables, benches, paper, and ink, but these difficulties failed to daunt the representatives of the new order. Crowds of people were always clustered about the entrances to these uncomfortable, squalid edifices. They pulsated with life. Secretaries from the camp at Kaluga worked side by side with Moscow officials in the militia chancelleries. The second group looked to Liapunov; the first, to Trubetskoi and Zarutskii. Three Moscow secretaries close to Liapunov drew up the text of the June 30 decree under his supervision.

The militia decree, for all its positive qualities, contained one glaring error. It had not spelled out the procedures for electing a tsar. As the towns prepared for the campaign they automatically assumed the Cap of Monomakh would pass to a true Orthodox Russian. The abbot of the influential Solovetskii monastery best expressed the universal

attitude. He wrote in reply to a question put by the Swedes: "Our realm
is unanimous in wishing to choose a tsar from among its native boyars.
It wants no foreigners of a different faith from another land." When
the militia entered Moscow it was forced to revise its thinking with
respect to the succession. The highborn boyars among whom alone a
candidate for the throne could be sought were under siege with the
foreigners and had no intention of coming over to the national liberation movement. All hope of reaching agreement with them was finally
dashed. People reluctantly began to doubt: have nationalists shed blood
merely to surrender the crown to an abettor of a savage foe?

To select a tsar proved enormously difficult. As soon as assembly
members got down to discussing specific candidates, the nobles in the
militia became bitterly divided. To avoid a split, the council decreed
negotiations with Sweden should resume. Liapunov's associate Buturlin clearly explained the situation to the Swedes: "Our experience
has convinced us that fate does not want Muscovy to have a tsar of
Russian blood. He will not be strong enough to cope with the rivalry
among the boyars, because no noble will admit another is worthy to
hold the lofty office of tsar."[8]

The militia leaders agreed to discuss a Swedish heir only after the
military situation had deteriorated sharply. Smolensk had fallen and
Sigismund might move his forces against Moscow at any time. Jan
Sapieha's armies were operating around the Russian capital. Liapunov
was afraid he could not repel Sigismund without Swedish help. His
prognosis was totally wrong. After taking Smolensk, the Polish king
had disbanded his army and rejected a plan to advance immediately
on Moscow. The Swedish king was pretending to offer an alliance to
the national government but was in reality intending to wage a major
war of aggression against Russia. Of all the mistakes Liapunov made,
the Swedish one was the worst. He hoped a Swedish candidate would
help him put an end to internal strife. In fact, he was pouring oil on
the fire. Relations among the triumvirs became strained.

Zarutskii decided to tie his fate to Marina Mniszech. This forced
him to oppose a Swedish candidate for the Russian throne. Refusing
to accept the council decree, he secretly tried to incline the cossacks
to support Heir Ivan Dmitrievich. This shows that the ataman had never
abandoned his dream that the Tiny Thief might ultimately win the
throne. This would mean that Marina's lover could count on serving
as regent during the sovereign's minority. The dashing cossack Ivanka
Zarutskii had long been married to a woman of similar background.

But after receiving boyar rank and rising high he began to think of marrying a noblewoman. At the first favorable opportunity Zarutskii got rid of his wife, who had grown hateful to him, and packed her off to a nunnery. He then straightway assigned his son to Marina's residence in Kolomna. The ataman's detractors floated rumors that he wanted to marry Marina and sit on the throne with her. Zarutskii was exceptionally ambitious but even he would never have dreamed of aspiring so high.

The boyars and the patriarch were carefully following developments in the militia. As soon as the disgraced Hermogen learned that Zarutskii was agitating on behalf of the Tiny Thief he heaped obloquy upon him. In a circular letter to the people of Nizhnii Novgorod he adjured the flock not to allow Marina's "accursed son" to occupy the throne and to repudiate him if the cossacks should arbitrarily elect him tsar.[9] The decree asserting it was possible to elect a Swedish prince finally ruined Liapunov's reputation and brought down the wrath of the cossacks and the Moscow commons upon his head. The country had no sooner managed to get rid of one man of different faith than it was to be saddled with another. Ordinary people vented their annoyance. A disturbance broke out in the militia. Men who had served for years under Good Dmitrii's banner were ready to support the Orthodox heir close by in Kolomna in preference to a Swedish heretic.

Liapunov had been the first to discern that all patriotic elements should be united. His name was synonymous with national unity. But the task proved too much for him. He could not overcome his distrust of the cossacks. He could not attract even gentry. On the other hand, nobles in the militia openly expressed displeasure that this non-noble member of the gentry had acquired such great power. A Moscow chronicler subsequently wrote: "Liapunov had risen too high and became haughty. He shamed and insulted old native houses, lesser boyars and boyars themselves."[10] A proud, stern man, Liapunov did not show favor to nobles. Those whom he was willing to receive often had to cool their heels for a long time at his headquarters.

Noble courtiers might overlook Liapunov's uncouth ways and conceit but they were far less tolerant when his talk turned to dividing up power and land. Many items in the June 30 constitution displeased them greatly. Unwilling to accept their defeat in the assembly, they formed a conspiracy to overthrow Liapunov. Informed contemporaries spoke about it quite freely. Prince Dmitrii Pozharskii wrote that Liapunov was slain at Ivan Sheremetev's initiative. Some sources state that

Princes Grigorii Shakhovskoi and Ivan Zasekin and Commander Ivan Pleshcheev joined Sheremetev in the conspiracy. Their service in Tushino and Kaluga had made these men well known to the enclaves. Cossacks would listen to them. The conspirators suborned others to deal with Liapunov.

From the first days of the siege the national government had encountered great difficulties in supplying the army before Moscow. The region around the capital was devastated; it was not easy to find provender. Commanders supplied their units as best they could. Liapunov dispatched gentry to command posts in towns and villages. Zarutskii sent cossacks to find food on taxpaying and court estates. The council told the triumvirs to organize regular food collections. Cossack atamans were ordered to stop their men from requisitioning. The task of collecting food from estates was assigned to what were called honest gentry. Cossacks were not to exact food without their permission.

Rich gentry received supplies from their estates. Poor serving men had to tighten their belts when grain deliveries were interrupted. The cossacks were very badly off after the authorities forbade them to make independent collections of food. Need led to excess. Episodes of violence occurred in the area around Moscow. A strong current in a river channel will cause silt to rise from the bottom. Something like this happened in the national movement. Unstable forces prone to revolt surfaced again. They began by requisitioning. Next, finding it worked well, they started to plunder the populace. Prosperous peasants were tortured in villages. Such actions caused the national militia immense harm. Wagons from the provinces could not reach their destination. Robbers seized them on the highway. In the confusion of the civil war impoverished gentry learned how to wield a club as niftily as a cossack.

Commanders resorted to brutal measures in an effort to stop the pillage. A Tushino boyar, Matvei Pleshcheev, stationed with a unit in Nikolskii-Ugreshkii monastery, ordered 28 cossacks drowned when they were caught red-handed with spoils, but the atamans were informed and they rescued the guilty men. The cossacks summoned a conclave to protest Pleshcheev's action. Their representations led the national assembly sternly to forbid commanders to execute anyone without its authorization.

Liapunov frequently called Zarutskii and Prosovetskii to the Military Affairs chancellery to confer with him about how to stop arbitrary requisitioning. The atamans convoked numerous military conclaves and finally promulgated a statute designed to halt plundering and unauthorized descents on villages. The militia leaders might easily have restored order in the regiments if they had been able to guarantee supplies but they could not accomplish their goal. In despair, Liapunov threatened he would declare local authorities expelled from the national movement if they did not arrest the general deterioration. His words had little effect. Soon the militia commanders officially informed the provinces that serving men, fusiliers, and cossacks were submitting insistent petitions to receive salaries and maintenance but there was nothing to give them.[11] By July the situation had become so menacing that the commanders asked the abbot of the Trinity-St. Sergius monastery to make a desperate appeal to the towns: "Help the militia with men and money so that the Orthodox army before Moscow will not have to disband because of need."[12]

Lack of supplies and the need this caused intensified turmoil in the enclaves. The cossacks held Liapunov responsible for their misfortunes because he had persecuted them for making arbitrary requisitions but had proved unable to keep the army supplied. Hostility towards Liapunov became more intense after the enclaves learned about his most recent rescript. Liapunov told the towns to check theft and brigandage, apprehend cossacks who were stealing and slay them on the spot or ship them to Moscow. A storm of protest erupted when his charge was read out in the enclaves. The cossacks were supported by many who wanted to settle accounts with Liapunov. Assembling a large conclave, they demanded an answer from the commander. Ataman Sergei Karamyshev entered his tent. Liapunov scornfully declined an invitation to meet with the cossack host. Next the conclave sent to headquarters two lesser boyars, Silvestr Tolstoi and Yurii Potemkin. They assured the commander the army would do him no harm. Believing them, Liapunov set out for the cossack camp, attended by a few gentry. When he appeared the conclave was thrown into angry uproar. Atamans openly called him a traitor. Liapunov was furious and started shouting at them.

Liapunov could never transcend his past. People had not forgotten that he had betrayed Godunov. Bolotnikov's followers remembered who it was that had forsaken them at the height of the siege of Moscow. Shuiskii had rewarded Liapunov generously but he had betrayed the former tsar too. It was not surprising that cossacks would believe charges levelled against Prokofii, even though he was not guilty of them.

The exchange between Liapunov and the atamans ended when the
alleged traitor was handed a letter subscribed in his own hand. He carefully examined the signature and muttered, with signal lack of confidence: "It looks like my writing but I never signed it." His words were
drowned out in the ensuing uproar. Cossacks unsheathed their weapons
and shouted to kill the traitor. In the confusion Ataman Karamyshev
hurled himself on Liapunov and struck him with his sword. Covered
with blood, he fell to the ground. Courtiers standing nearby finished
him off. Ivan Rzhevskii displayed presence of mind. He was a foe of
Liapunov but he was troubled by the nature of this kangaroo court.
Rzhevskii shouted that a national commander was being killed for a
trivial, ridiculous reason. In the heat of the moment the cossacks slew
him too, after which they rushed to Liapunov's camp and wrecked the
Military Affairs chancellery.

For three days the mangled corpses of Liapunov and Rzhevskii lay
in a field near a redoubt. Swarms of flies settled on them. At night they
were gnawed by gangs of homeless dogs roaming about the burned-
out site. On the fourth day the bodies were slung into a cart and removed
to an adjacent church. Thence the corpses were taken to the Trinity-
St. Sergius monastery, where they were buried without honor. A curt
inscription above their stone grave proclaimed: "Prokofii Liapunov
and Ivan Rzhevskii, slain July 22, the year 7119."[1611. This is the
system of reckoning from *anno mundi* in use in Russia at the time—
ed.].

Monks found no words to celebrate these fighters for the national
cause. But they were not forgotten. Many years later the people composed a song about them. It was crude but it rang with praise for Liapunov and cursed the faithless boyars.

Many Russian boyars gave themselves to dishonor,
   Gave themselves to dishonor, apostasized from Christ's faith.
Now one boyar, a little conciliar commander, sturdily kept his faith,
   Sturdily kept his faith, drove out traitors.
...When Gzhmund (Sigismund) learned from his traitorous boyars
   That Liapunov had dispatched couriers to the towns,
couriers to the towns, to call commanders to come here with an army:
   He became angry, he flew into a rage, base Gzhmund:
   In his rage he ordered the little commander slain,
   That very commander, Prokofii Liapunov.
   Sly traitors slew the little commander.

The report that Liapunov had been murdered produced a bad impression on patriots everywhere. Many were of the opinion the commander had been undone by the militia leaders, who had conspired with the cossacks and forged an ill-fated letter attributed to Liapunov. Some named Ivan Sheremetev as leader of the conspiracy; others, Zarutskii. The witnesses to Liapunov's fall were misled.

The truth did not come out until associates of Gosiewski published accounts. One of them, a certain Marchocki, told the world that his colonel, lacking strength to defeat the militia in open contest, decided to destroy Liapunov, "that upright man," by stirring up the cossacks against him. Gosiewski had many secretaries and scribes at his disposal; they had no trouble drawing up the letter he needed. In Liapunov's name its compilers issued a call to kill and drown men of the Don wherever they were. They promised to eradicate that "evil nation" as soon as the Muscovite realm was calm again. Liapunov's signature on the document was a clever forgery. A certain Ataman Sidorka undertook to deliver the letter to the enclaves, and Gosiewski ordered his adoptive father released from captivity. The Moscow chronicler knew nothing of the revelations made by this member of the Polish gentry. But he was aware that Ataman Sidorka Zavarzin had brought Liapunov's fictive letter to the conclave. The identity of the names supports the veracity of the Polish version.

Since he was in the Kremlin, Marchocki was in a position quite carefully to describe how the triumvirs behaved when the disturbance broke out. Zarutskii and his attendant equerries were so frightened by the insubordinate cossacks that they took to their heels. Contrary to what Russian contemporaries suspected, neither Zarutskii nor Sheremetev had anything to do with the unfortunate letter. Gosiewski alone was responsible. He filled the streets of Moscow with blood and his ploy almost toppled the shaky national government.

Liapunov's death deprived the militia of its most authoritative leader. The Nizhnii Novgorod town quarter was shaken by the news of their leader's presumed treachery. The courtier Birkin, a relative of Liapunov and his personal emissary, was there at the time. He tried to prove that the head of the national government had been basely betrayed. The Nizhnii Novgorod town quarter was once more in ferment. Again citizens assembled at meeting places to discuss the alarming and appalling news. The wounded Pozharskii refused to believe it when he was told about the tragedy in the militia. No one could explain what had happened. It was Liapunov and Prince Dmitrii who had run up the banner of national struggle. Together they had overcome initial difficulties. Now his former confederate had been slain by his own men. What Pozharskii had fought for was melting away before his eyes.

Chapter Thirteen

CONFLICT

The militia leaders feared the king would bring his army from Smolensk to attack Moscow. After the conquest of Smolensk Sigismund had actually returned to Poland. He intended to appoint Zolkiewski to finish his eastern campaign but the Polish crown hetman declined. The king then entrusted the task to Jan Karol Chodkiewicz, hetman of Lithuania. There was a particular reason for this. Lithuanian magnates and gentry were urgently demanding they be given preference in the distribution of booty in the occupied Smolensk and Seversk lands. They insisted Polish gentry should not receive service-tenure allotments in Smolensk. Bowing to their wishes, Sigismund agreed to incorporate Smolensk into the grand duchy of Lithuania.

Hetman Chodkiewicz had acquired a reputation as one of the best commanders in the Rzeczpospolita. With 5,000 soldiers he had routed a Swedish army of 8,000 in Livonia. Karl IX, leader of that army, had barely escaped capture. At a meeting with Sigismund in summer, 1611 Chodkiewicz formulated final plans for the Moscow campaign. There was a small but chosen Livonian army, and the king placed more than 1,000 hussars, drawn from the forces that had been besieging Smolensk, under the hetman's command. Preparations for the campaign cost Chodkiewicz a good deal of time.

The boyar government in Moscow hoped the king's army would help them put down the national liberation movement but Chodkiewicz was delayed and the council of seven members had to make do with what troops they had. The boyars used them in an attempt to assert their authority in the towns around Moscow. The arrival of Jan Sapieha's army before Moscow facilitated their efforts. From the Kremlin Mstislavskii dispatched Boyar Romodanovskii and a gentry detachment loyal to the boyar government to assist Sapieha. Reinforced by the council of seven's men, Sapieha took Suzdal and Rostov and marched on Pereiaslavl-Zalesskii in an effort to clear a path to Yaroslavl.

Nationalist enclaves sought to neutralize the enemy. Ataman Prosovetskii and Commander Bakhteiarov hastened north. Prosovetskii encountered Sapieha approaching Pereiaslavl and kept him away from the Yaroslavl highway. For a fortnight the two sides skirmished before Pereiaslavl's ancient walls. The cossacks effectively harassed Sapieha's men; their leader decided not to try and storm the fortress. Early in August Sapieha and Romodanovskii returned to the Moscow area with a huge load of provisions. Delighted by the report of Liapunov's demise, Sapieha resolved to get control of a cossack redoubt on the other side of the Yauza river and clear a way to the Kremlin. He seriously overestimated his strength. The cossacks easily turned back Sapieha's and Romodanovskii's army. Then, bypassing nationalist army fortifications, Sapieha's men came out on the western approach and at twilight suddenly fell upon militiamen in the Arbat region. A fierce battle raged all night and into the next day. At a crucial moment Gosiewski's forces attacked the Russians from the rear. Caught between two fires, the militia retired, leaving Arbat and Nikitskii gates in enemy hands.[1] The enemy garrison in Moscow profited from breaking out of encirclement but disturbances soon broke out among the mercenaries. Discipline was virtually non-existent. German mercenaries carried out plundering raids in broad daylight. Gosiewski needed soldiers but he was forced to disband a detachment of German knights demoralized by pillage. When they left Moscow, Captain Jacques Margeret and a few hundred of his soldiers took away many precious objects from the Moscow treasury and a wagonload of stolen property.[2]

Russians were convinced the days of foreign domination were numbered. Cracks were appearing in the boyar government. Rats were scurrying to abandon the sinking ship and seeking refuge. On September 11, 1611 Boyar Mikhail Saltykov, Yurii Trubetskoi, Mikhail Nagoi, and Fedor Andronov abandoned the city they had betrayed. The traitors hoped they could escape inevitable retribution by hiding abroad. Mstislavskii made it easy for them to leave by designating them ambassadors plenipotentiary. Saltykov promised he would make "Tsar Vladislav" come to Russia soon. On the other side of Mozhaisk the boyars encountered Chodkiewicz and his army proceeding towards Moscow. The hetman had already assumed he was the arbiter of Russia's destiny. He detained the ambassadors and demanded that in the name of the boyar government they must recognize Sigismund as tsar. Certain he would quickly triumph, Chodkiewicz dreamed of bringing off a masterly diplomatic coup. He hoped to lay the tsars' crown as spoils of war at the king's feet. The hetman poorly understood the country where he had been called upon to fight. The council of seven members, terrified as they were of Gosiewski, refused to execute his demand. Mstislavskii tearfully tried to convince the colonel that renouncing the oath to Tsar Wladyslaw, whom an assembly had elected, would make even Russians still loyal to the boyar government rise up against it. To surrender the throne to Sigismund would completely ruin their common enterprise.

Chodkiewicz made Mikhail Nagoi and Fedor Andronov go back to Moscow but he allowed the others to proceed. After the boyars arrived, former patriarch Ignatii turned up in Poland as well. The interventionists were planning to get rid of Hermogen and bestow the patriarchal office upon their trusted acolyte, but Ignatii had incurred such universal odium that the aggressors had to abandon their design. Saltykov had brought many valuables filched from the treasury. Chodkiewicz controlled the Smolensk highway; the boyars had no trouble reaching the frontier. The former patriarch was less fortunate. As soon as the army wagons disappeared in the distance irregulars came out on the road, ambushed the Greek, and took away his ill-gotten gains. Ignatii lost his chattels and his clothing too. He arrived in Lithuania frozen and barely alive.

The militia leaders knew Chodkiewicz's army was approaching and attempted to immobilize the enemy garrison before the hetman arrived. On September 15, 1611 they moved ten mortars close to the walls and peppered Kitaigorod with fiery balls. One hit a shed full of straw, a vast amount of which Gosiewski had put by to feed the hussars' horses. A column of flame shot up from the storage depot. Strong winds bore pieces of blazing straw all over Kitaigorod. Nationalist soldiers immediately rushed in to storm the place; they got control of the gate. The mercenaries sought refuge from the fire in the Kremlin. The long-awaited moment of victory was at hand, but the fire caused problems for the nationalists as well as the foreigners. As they picked their way through burning streets Russian soldiers tried to extinguish fires and help the desolate population. The interventionists took advantage of the pause to regroup their forces. Cannon on the Kremlin wall rained down murderous fire on the militia. When the conflagration abated the enemy made a sortie and drove the Russians out of Kitaigorod. The cossack enclaves could not render timely assistance to their allies because Jan Sapieha had attacked them from the rear.

Many soldiers fell in the battle for Kitaigorod but the enemy had sustained appreciable losses and his morale was badly shaken. Zarutskii's cossacks again occupied New Virgin monastery and tightened the blockade around Moscow. If Chodkiewicz had not arrived, the occupation regime would have collapsed swiftly. The Lithuanian hetman was sure the militia, rent by internal strife, could never withstand his army, which was splendidly equipped and battle hardened. Chodkiewicz was a brave man. He longed for a decisive encounter. The Polish-Lithuanian command was certain the war would be over after a single engagement. The hetman was encouraged, recalling the brilliant victories his soldiers had recently won. But he overlooked the fact that this time he was facing an armed people. Russian soldiers knew their country's future depended upon them. They accomplished what the entire realm expected of them.

Late in September, 1611 Chodkiewicz pitched camp south of Moscow. His force was substantially augmented when Jan Sapieha and his men joined him. Chodkiewicz's army marched in full panoply past the Andronov monastery and stormed a cossack redoubt on the Yauza. The soldiers suffered losses but they charged the earthen rampart again and again. Shots rang out. Clouds of smoke rose into the sky. The cossacks fought with such frenzy that they inspired terror in Chodkiewicz's veterans. The hetman realized he might lose his whole army and sounded the retreat. Zarutskii appraised the situation and tried to seize the initiative. The cossacks isolated a hussar cavalry unit from the main force and pursued it to the Yauza. The hussars attempted to cross the river but its banks were slippery and marshy. The heavily-armed knights and their horses drowned in a quagmire.[3]

Chodkiewicz could not achieve a single one of the goals he had set. He was unable to crush the national militia and drive it from the walls of Moscow. Sigismund's aggressive plans had aborted. The Russian liberation movement had achieved a decisive military and moral victory that had far-reaching consequences. The hetman was powerless to relieve the Kremlin garrison. The mercenaries refused to obey their commanders and threatened to quit Moscow. There was incessant looting and pillaging. Chodkiewicz tried to prevent garrisons from marauding. He summarily punished a few German mercenaries but his rescript almost caused a riot. He had to give up his determination to introduce order in his army. He augmented the garrison with his and

Sapicha's soldiers, increasing its complement to 2,500 men. Detachments plagued by desertion were permitted to leave Moscow and return home.

The autumn weather had been unpleasant for a long time. Cold rains fell for days on end. Fog rose from the ground. At night the soil froze. Winter was at hand. Chodkiewicz had hoped he could dispose his army in Moscow and allow his soldiers to enjoy much-desired rest but he was unable to do so. The fire in Kitaigorod had destroyed most supplies and fodder. The houses in which his men had been quartered had gone up in flames. In chilly and inclement weather the hetman transferred his army to Rogachevo, where he pitched his winter camp. His departure from Moscow was ignominious. The interventionists stripped villages north of Moscow and soon gathered abundant supplies for Gosiewski but partisans joined cossacks in ambushing the convoy. They destroyed several hundred wagons. Only a few supplies reached the Kremlin. Hunger forced the enemy garrison to take the blockade seriously. In the Kitaigorod market the price of rye bread rose to three rubles per loaf. Swarms of loudly-croaking crows hovered above the Kremlin. Soldiers shot and sold them for considerable sums. Sparrows fetched almost as much. Famished men carried off carrion and devoured it.[4]

It seemed that all Russian arms had to do was to make a final effort to expel the enemy from Moscow. But the militia had exhausted its strength and resources. The September battles were its last gasp. The militia had inflicted severe defeats on the foe but had paid too high a price. Losses had been staggering. Soldiers were overcome with fatigue. Service-tenure militiamen simply disappeared. Contrary to legend, Liapunov's murder did not occasion mass gentry flight from Moscow. Even Prokofii's son felt it was safe to remain among the enclaves after his father was killed. During summer the besiegers' camp had welcomed individual serving men and large gentry units. It was not until autumn that dissolution set in. From time immemorial gentry had fought in clusters, plying their weapons on horseback. Well mounted and wearing heavy armor, a member of the gentry surrounded by fighting servitors on the battlefield felt he was in full control of the situation. His slaves protected him with their bodies; his shield warded off enemy blows, and his trusty horse saved him from pursuit. The general ruin undermined the confidence service-tenure landholders had formerly possessed. Many had lost their slaves and had not succeeded in obtaining fresh stocks of weapons after the long fierce battles.

Wretchedly accoutred on a poor mount, a landholder felt helpless and vulnerable.

The constitution of June 30, 1611 had promised benefits to impoverished landholders who joined the liberation struggle. Liapunov had vowed land grants for them would be the first order of business. Serving men deluged Service-Tenure chancelleries with petitions. Afraid to estrange the gentry, the council attempted to meet their demands. Chancelleries were constantly issuing charters granting them service-tenure estates. The feudatories hastened to them in order to demonstrate right of ownership and to recoup lost fortunes. In November, 1611 the Military Affairs chancellery drew up a list of gentry who had served with Boyar Dmitrii Trubetskoi. It was soon filled with references to men who were no longer present. They had left to recover from wounds, to take part in land distributions, or because they had been given leave by their commanders. Many simply deserted without permission from their superiors. The components of the service-tenure contingents once again had demonstrated their inveterate failing. Their units were dissolving, and with them the rock on which the nationalist gentry government rested.

The composition of the Council of the Entire Realm was changing. Liapunov, the man who had epitomized it, was dead. One after another, his coadjutors among the gentry quitted the scene. Some, like Associate Boyar Mosalskii, perished in the savage battles. Others, like Associate Boyar Artemii Izmailov and Andrei Repnin, went home to their towns. Fear of the cossacks scarcely explains why these commanders fled. Izmailov's son Vasilii continued to serve. When Ivan Sheremetev was designated commander in Kostroma, his cousin, the steward Vasilii, immediately took his place.

Depleted gentry units were on guard in the western and northern sections of Moscow. Commander Miron Veliaminov and his troops held the position at Tver gate. Steward Isak Pogozhii and the men of Uglich were dug in at Truba, near Petrovka. Steward Izmailov's unit stood next to them. The national militia's main position lay to the east, in the quarter near the Yauza gate. Cossacks had established a large camp there and surrounded it with high earthen ramparts in preparation for further struggles. The number of cossack units now far exceeded gentry detachments. Their preponderance was bound to affect the militia's command structure.

Prince Dmitrii Trubetskoi, the noblest boyar in the militia, was its titular head as he had been in Liapunov's time, but everything was in the hands of the ubiquitous Zarutskii. He had become the real leader of the national government. Observers in Moscow who endured the siege by the militia asserted that Ataman Prosovetskii, who was popular among the cossacks, had emerged as the second most influential personage. It is unclear whether the army chose him or whether he won the place next to Zarutskii because of his military prowess. Two atamans at the head of the national army was too much for the gentry. The council looked more and more like a cossack conclave. Prosovetskii demanded resolute action to bring the enemy down at once. By early December he had completed preparations to take the offensive. His actions did not go unnoticed. The mercenaries found out in good time where he planned to strike.

A person entering Moscow saw nothing but a huge pile of ashes. Heaps of burned wood, out of which jutted lonely chimneys, were strewn about wherever one looked. Only the Kremlin towered above the charred ruins. The boyars had surrendered the citadel to the enemy together with a mass of cannon and powder. The Russian army had long prided itself on its artillery. Now Russian cannon were firing murderous salvos at Russian soldiers.

Early in December, 1611 Prosovetskii led out his men to mount an attack. Forcing open one of the Kitaigorod gates, cossacks and soldiers rushed into the fortress but were stopped by volleys. Aware of Russian intentions, the enemy had disposed thirty cannon behind the gate, barrel to barrel in a semicircle. The cossacks swept forward in a display of vigor and enthusiasm but the withering fire mowed down row after row of them. The attack was an utter failure. The disaster reflected badly on Prosovetskii and his supporters. It was rumored he had quarreled with Zarutskii. Poles reported that Prosovetskii quit the main camp and intended to hole himself and 1,000 cossacks up in the Simonov monastery on the Kolomenskoe road. Zarutskii and his army ran to overtake them and forced him to parley. In front of everyone Prosovetskii supposedly asserted that Zarutskii was not fit to command such a large army, which contained members of old and worthy princely houses. The quarrel between the atamans aroused the commons. Zarutskii was said to have been assassinated and Prosovetskii named to his place. The Poles considered Zarutskii the most dangerous of the militia commanders and were delighted to credit rumors he had fallen, but the reports had no basis in fact.

Winter was well advanced. Deep snow covered the fields around Moscow. The cold caused great hardship for the militia and the people of Moscow but they displayed a rare devotion for their native region. They endured severe trials but refused to abandon their city. To take the place of their former homes they built huts out of boards and mud. These habitations lay close to the national militia's fortified enclaves. Witnesses told stories about how Muscovites, including the commons, traders, and merchants, lived outside the city with the troops, sustained themselves, and kept abundant provisions by them. Towards the end of winter of 1611-1612 food supplies in the dugout villages in the town quarter were almost depleted. It was not infamous cossack banditry but the utter devastation of the area that caused famine in the quarters of Moscow that had been liberated. Cossacks followed the gentry's lead and went off to winter in distant places. Military activity in Moscow ceased until spring.

Chapter Fourteen

FALSE DMITRII III

Several years earlier a bitter civil war had been fought in the Pskov district, where many exciting events had occurred since. The local commons had been among the first to rise against Vasilii Shuiskii. In fall, 1608 they had admitted Fedor Pleshcheev, False Dmitrii II's commander, into their citadel. Pleshcheev at once released 400 supporters of Bolotnikov from Pskov prisons. These men had been sent to Pskov after the peasant war met with defeat. They left immediately for Moscow and entered the enclaves at Tushino.[1] Commander Petr Sheremetev, who had oppressed the people, was impaled on a stake. A revolt broke out after a serious fire had occurred in the city. The commons was determined to get rid of rapacious gentry and merchants.

Many prosperous people had fled to Novgorod and lost no time summoning troops loyal to Shuiskii. Gentry remaining in Pskov intended to admit them into the city, but the conspiracy was discovered and the traitors punished. Authority passed to the radical poor led by Kudekusha Trepets, who personally supervised the tortures. Many gentry had their ribs broken. The poor did not remain in power for long. Kudekusha and other members of his clique were stoned and hurled into the moat surrounding the fortress. Prosperous people arrested earlier were freed and the poor and the hungry were put in the same places as their predecessors had been. Priests now supervised the torture. After interrogation, an executioner beheaded numbers of townsmen, whether guilty or innocent. Others were were beaten with knouts in the marketplace.

In spring, 1610 the local commander, supported by clergy, gentry, and merchants, had tried to make Pskov swear an oath of fealty to Vasilii Shuiskii. The inhabitants, calling in fusiliers to help, expelled him. Three hundred gentry and members of the upper orders fled Pskov and sought refuge in Novgorod. More than 200 members of the upper orders remaining in Pskov were called traitors and confined in cellars and prisons.[2] Nowhere did social strife become so intense as it did in Pskov. The poor put an end to the power of the propertied upper orders. After Shuiskii fell, the people of Pskov refused to take an oath to the boyar government or to Heir Wladyslaw. But when a new pretender, False Dmitrii III, was proclaimed in the Pskov area the city's inhabitants were unwilling to acknowlege him immediately.

The story of False Dmitrii III is quite simple. As soon as the people of Kaluga handed the remains of the second pretender over to the nationalists another adventurer turned up in Moscow and undertook to continue the interrupted farce to its conclusion. The identity of the new pretender is unknown. Russian chroniclers are contradictory whenever the subject of False Dmitrii III comes up. A court chronicler during the first Romanov years asserted he was from Moscow: "a deacon, Matiushka, or Matvei, came to Ivangorod from the part of Moscow on the far side of the Yauza river and called himself Tsar Dmitrii." Contemporaries suspected the new Thief came from a clerical background, but even so were unable to establish his name precisely. The aforementioned chronicler unexpectedly entitled his account of False Tsar Matiushka "about Sidorka, the Thief of Pskov." This means the last pretender was called either Matvei or Sidor. This is all that is known about him. Arriving in Novgorod the pretender became a petty trader. He got some knives and a few other trifles and planned to dispose of this merchandise profitably. His scheme soon failed and Matiushka was forced to beg to avoid starvation. One fine day he took courage and revealed his regal name to the people of Novgorod.[3] A crowd jeered and mocked the freshly-minted tsar. Many recognized the itinerant peddler. The hapless pretender beat a hasty retreat. He had, however, managed to attract a handful of followers, who accompanied him to Ivangorod.

Former men of Tushino still held this town and the Swedes had been
besieging it for months. No one had responded to their appeals for help.
Finally Lisowski arrived from the south. The inhabitants were afraid
to admit such a doubtful ally into their fortress. The area around Ivangorod was full of strange rumors. To the question "who is with you"
the inhabitants replied cryptically: "we shall not favor Shuiskii nor
Dmitrii; we are hoping for something else. Ere now princes were
chosen in the depth of night; now soon we shall have a protector upon
whom it will be worthwhile to look in the light of day and under the
sun. He will forthwith give us a happier kingdom."[4] It is not clear
whom these people considered sovereign for several months before the
Kaluga pretender fell, but when a Good Dmitrii again appeared and
banged on Ivangorod's gate, the former men of Tushino welcomed him
as a long-awaited savior. The people of Ivangorod joyfully discharged
cannon three days in a row, starting March 23, 1611. Simple folk
considered this tsar to be one of them. Foreigners found him secretive,
of an impetuous nature, and an effective speaker. Matiushka never tired
of relating the incredible tale of his fourth manifestation to anyone
willing to listen. He had been wounded in Uglich but escaped death.
He had been mangled and cremated in Moscow and this time he arose
from the dead. He had been beheaded in Kaluga, but now here he was,
standing before the world alive and well!

The new pretender was singularly amiable and ready to cooperate
with anybody. His further plans were soon revealed. Having obtained
no support from Novgorod, the Thief approached the Swedish governor of Narva and through him asked the Swedish king to come to
his aid with an army. Karl IX felt honored by this personal appeal but
de la Gardie wanted nothing to do with a baseborn sojourner and preferred to find common ground with the Novgorod gentry.

Reports that a new tsar had appeared were disturbing. The cossacks
in Pskov were restless. In April they announced they intended to proceed against Lisowski. As soon as the fortress gate closed behind them,
the cossacks wheeled about and raced to Ivangorod. On reaching the
town they assured Matiushka that Pskov would welcome him with
open arms. The Thief believed them and early in July pitched camp
in a Pskov suburb. His emissaries asked for the keys to the city. The
people of Pskov long debated what action to take. They finally decided
they had no need of the Thief. Matiushka had ruined his chances by
ordering animals from the city's herd to be slaughtered so that he could
splendidly entertain his army. For six weeks the pretender hung around

the fortress and then suddenly disappeared. The Swedes had frightened him. Swedish units and the Novgorod gentry militia were approaching Pskov along the Novgorod highway. A fair number of Pskov landholders joined them. The Pskov commons, knowing they would be given no quarter if they were defeated, stoutly rejected offers to surrender. Representatives of the so-called Novgorod sovereign state vainly tried to persuade the people of Pskov to follow their example and place themselves under Swedish protection, but the people of Pskov refused to become traitors. They had not risen against Wladyslaw only to acknowledge the authority of a nameless Swedish prince.

Supported by Novgorod and Pskov gentry, the Swedes tried forcibly to gain control of the fractious city. September 8, 1611 they battered down the fortress gate and strove to attack from the Velikaia river side. Recalling how they had taken Novgorod, the mercenaries expected to win easily and they were getting ready to plunder the ancient city. But the people of Pskov had long since driven out those who might be willing to help the enemy, and the Swedish soldiers met with no success. Their attack was repulsed. The enemy beleaguered the fortress for five weeks and then retired to Novgorod.

Pskov was like a jutting crag in a seething ocean. The Swedes constantly invaded its territory from the north and east while Lithuanian units came from the south and west. Lisowski allowed the people of Pskov no respite. Sigismund had sent Hetman Chodkiewicz's army, stationed in Livonia, against the city. Chodkiewicz had laid siege to the Pskovo-Pecherskii monastery. Heavy guns bombarded it for a year and a half. The fortress wall cracked in some places and collapsed. But fusiliers, monks, and neighboring peasants entrenched in the monastery refused to despair. They beat back seven enemy attacks and forced Chodkiewicz to lift the siege and retire to Livonia.

Popular sovereignty was firmly established in Pskov. The city had long since indicated it supported the national liberation movement. The citizens had been preparing to send forces to hasten the deliverance of Moscow, but instead they had to ask for help from the national militia in order to survive the unequal contest. The Pskov commune wrote to the militia leaders: "We have been attacked everywhere many times, but no aid reaches us."[5] The council responded. Commanders Nikita Veliaminov and later Nikita Khvostov with a cossack detachment entered the city.

Liapunov's death freed the hands of those in the militia before Moscow who favored pretenders, but they were disunited. The Swedes received trustworthy information that Zarutskii was trying to persuade the cossacks to elect Ivan Dmitrievich tsar. The Tiny Thief was an infant; everyone knew his mother Marina would rule in his name. The widow of the two pretenders enjoyed no popularity among the people. News that a new Dmitrii had shown himself around Novgorod briefly aroused the cossacks but the reports died down: the story was simply incredible. The enclaves harbored too many veterans who had personally beheld the sovereign's severed head. However, after a while tales of Dmitrii's activities started to circulate again and to intensify. It had taken time, but credulous people were more and more inclined to think that Ivan the Terrible's genuinely immortal son had been saved once again. Cossacks and Moscow rebels who had never seen the dead Thief swallowed the bait. A great band of new converts joined the force the militia leaders dispatched to Pskov.

The arrival of False Dmitrii's partisans in Pskov changed the picture. Stimulated by their agitating, the Pskov commons demanded the True Sovereign be acknowledged immediately. They sent envoys to Ivangorod who handed the True Sovereign an invitation from the Pskov commune. Matiushka did not wait to be asked twice. He set out at once. The Thief and his suite took remote country roads, thereby managing to elude Swedish guards. The cavalcade reached Pskov on December 4, 1611. The inhabitants found it within themselves to forgive their Sovereign for the cows in the city herd he had slain and welcomed him joyfully. The commanders had no means to check the outpouring of popular sentiment. Matiushka rewarded them for their submissiveness. Commanders Prince Ivan Khovanskii and Nikita Veliaminov were awarded boyar rank and sat in places of honor at the side of the pretender. As soon as he was ensconced in the Pskov citadel Matiushka sent Ataman Gerasim Popov to appeal to the veterans of Tushino in the enclaves before Moscow.

The Sovereign's appeal stirred up the populace of Moscow and the cossacks. People now hoped for a miracle. They longed for an Orthodox Russian on the throne. The assembly's decision to invite a Swedish prince had deeply offended nationalist sensibilities. The new explosion of sympathy for Dmitrii was a reaction to the attempt to foist on the country another foreign tsar of a different faith.

The cossacks convoked a conclave and carefully listened to what Ataman Popov, the Sovereign's legate, had to say. Some participants openly expressed doubts about Dmitrii's miraculous deliverance. The

pretender's zealous supporters demanded the cossacks take an immediate oath to the Lawful Tsar. The majority adopted a cautious stance.
Their influence decided the conclave to dispatch a special delegation
to Pskov in order to take a look at the new tsar. Avoiding this dubious
distinction, False Dmitrii II's old boyars assigned the task to Kazarin
Begichev, a former fusilier captain, who had held conciliar rank at the
court of the Tushino Thief and had executed his commissions in Pskov.
People there knew him well. A Tushino conciliar secretary and a cossack detachment accompanied Begichev. False Dmitrii III received the
militia envoys splendidly. When admitted to his presence, old cossacks
knew the man standing before them was a pretender, totally unlike the
former Thief. But Matiushka's armed guard surrounded his throne and
the cossacks had no choice but to hold their tongues. No one dared
expose this Thief. The people of Pskov made the envoys send the
militia an attestation affirming this man was True Dmitrii.

This charter, sent by plenipotentiary envoys of the Entire Realm,
created a sensation. Commons and cossacks wanted to believe their
Good Tsar had been saved again from the "wicked boyars." Subsequent events unfolded as they did because unrestrainable elemental
energies had been unleashed. On March 2, 1612 a cossack conclave,
which many Muscovites attended, announced that the Pskov pretender
was the Sovereign. The militia leaders, Zarutskii, Trubetskoi, and
others, remembering what had happened to Liapunov, accepted the
decision. Along with the cossacks they took an oath to False Dmitrii
III and returned to their headquarters, accompanied by a triumphal
procession and an artillery salute. The people made the gentry they
found from Trubetskoi's detachment kiss the cross.[6] The swearing-
in met with failure among militia units stationed at a distance from the
enclaves. Commanders Miron Veliaminov, Isaiia Pogozhii, and Izmailov, occupying positions at Tver gate and in Truba, fled in fear of their
lives.

Liapunov some time ago had succeeeded in bringing disparate
forces together in the movement to liberate Moscow. The oath to the
new False Dmitrii destroyed his fragile coalition. The split Liapunov
had feared had come about and the Moscow commons and the cossacks
were responsible. Even as late as the end of the year 1610, and even
with help from the mercenaries, the boyar government had barely
managed to check the elements supporting the Kaluga pretender. It was
now a year and a half later. Moscow had been devastated; towns were

in ruins. The people hated the aggressors and their accomplices more than ever. The commons hoped the reincarnated Dmitrii would help them settle accounts with the "evil boyars" once and for all.

Zarutskii, leader of the militia, was powerless to stem this spontaneous tide. He bowed to the insurgent people, but he strove to place his own interpretation on the oath. Directly after what had happened, the commanders serving "Mitka the Slave," Trubetskoi and Ivashko Zarutskii, sent a petition to "Sovereign Marina Yurevna and Sovereign Heir Ivan Dmitrievich of all Russia."[7] Zarutskii was looking to Kolomna, the residence of Marina and her son, not to Pskov. He was slowly taking steps to set the Tiny Thief on the throne.

The new uprising found support in southern and Seversk towns previously inclined towards Kaluga. These contained a goodly number of atamans and cossacks who had been in Bolotnikov's army. To the east, the Pskov pretender's authority was quickly recognized in the small towns of Arzamas and Alatyr. The people of Arzamas were as revolutionary as the men of Pskov. Local peasants, supported by rebellious fusiliers, hunted out gentry, tortured and hanged them. Arzamas rebels had initially been inclined to kiss the cross to the Thieves' widow, Marina, and her son. Later they joined the Moscow enclaves in proclaiming adherence to False Dmitrii III.

Nizhnii Novgorod, Kazan, Yaroslavl, and Kostroma had been angry when their people learned the council was negotiating to place a Swedish prince on the throne but they considered the elevation of False Dmitrii III an illegal act in violation of the will of the Russian realm. Nizhnii Novgorod, Yaroslavl, and Kostroma categorically refused to recognize the Pskov pretender. An internal struggle between supporters and opponents of False Dmitrii III threatened to destroy the national liberation movement.

Chapter Fifteen

THE SECOND NATIONAL MILITIA

Men of the town quarters had begun to lose faith in the national government after Liapunov, the militia's most popular leader, was assassinated and Zarutskii, who took his place, proposed to set the pretender's son on the throne. The people of Kazan were the first to cause trouble. In August, 1611 they combined with the people of Nizhnii Novgorod and worked out an agreement. The proclamation from these two powerful towns was a fearsome portent for the nationalist authorities before Moscow. The townsmen warned they would not tolerate a change in the commanders they had sent to liberate Moscow nor would they acknowledge appointments made by Zarutskii and the cossacks on their own recognizance. The townsmen expressed doubt that the militia would ever be able to elect a tsar and declared they would reject any sovereign the cossacks might place on the throne without the consent of the realm. Their distrust of the national government had become so intense that the two communes decreed they would refuse to admit cossack detachments from the enclaves into their towns.[1] The understanding between Nizhnii Novgorod and Kazan was a prolog to the formation of a second militia. The people of Kazan, initially active, then stepped aside, but the people of Nizhnii Novgorod soon passed from words to deeds. They were about to accomplish a formidable task.

With no bishop of its own, Nizhnii Novgorod was supervised directly by the patriarch. This was why the people of Nizhnii Novgorod decided to seek spiritual guidance from Hermogen, their patron. They dispatched an emissary, Moseev, to the Kremlin bearing a petition asking for advice. The envoy stared death in the face many times before he managed to insinuate his way into the beleaguered Kremlin, where Hermogen lived under official displeasure. The aged patriarch passed his days in want and misery. Gosiewski's attendants had taken away his sacred robes and confined him to the Miracles monastery.

Hermogen listened attentively when Moseev asked him to support the Nizhnii Novgorod enterprise. The dethroned patriarch's appeal to Nizhnii Novgorod became his political testament. Hermogen had not forgotten the fate of Andrei Golitsyn; a martyr's crown held no attraction for him. In a rescript to the people of Nizhnii Novgorod he made no reference to boyar treason nor to the mercenaries' excesses but he was rabid in his indictment of the cossacks. The patriarch suggested convoking the bishops to bring pressure on the national government before Moscow. He called upon the men of Nizhnii Novgorod to establish connections with the metropolitan of Kazan, the bishop of Riazan, and hierarchs in both towns. These princes of the church would compose letters of instruction for the nationalist boyars, which would then be collected. Hermogen urged Moseev, as a neutral, to disseminate these letters around Moscow and publicize them even if the cossacks threatened him with death. This was the way in which the head of the church sought to influence the election and prevent Zarutskii and the cossacks from setting a pretender on the throne. Hermogen angrily wrote: "Marina's accursed son is unfit to rule. He stands condemned by the ecclesiastical council and by us."[2] Moseev hid the patriarch's missive and managed to deliver it to the place it was supposed to go. But the national liberation movement had no intention of following Hermogen's prescriptions. It was the townsmen of Nizhnii Novgorod, not the prince of the church, who took charge of events.

Nizhnii Novgorod was still one of the great towns of Russia in the early seventeenth century. Travelers who visited it estimated the population to be at least 8,000. Town life was vigorous. Local blacksmiths kept some 30 shops but could scarcely cope with the volume of orders coming in from everywhere. Nizhnii Novgorod carpenters were famous throughout the region. Many were shipwrights. They would take axes, chop down trees in the dense forests surrounding the town, and build boats on the banks of the Volga and the Oka. Some of these boats could handle almost eighteen tons of freight. Thirty local merchants and prominent traders sailed the whole length of the Volga, conducting a great deal of business. Smaller traders worked in the town market, each man to his own stall. A customer would inspect rows of shops before he managed to fill his basket with a variety of foodstuffs. "He would go from and the Groats and Onion stalls to the Bread, Fish, and Meat stalls, and from there to the Salt row. Shoe, Hat and Fulling stalls were also at his service."

Nizhnii Novgorod was situated at the intersection of great trade routes, the place where the Oka empties into the Volga. The main Vladimir highway, popularly known as *Vladimirka*, led from Nizhnii Novgorod to Moscow. The town served as a link between the capital

and the heartland, the lower Volga region, the Perm district, and
Siberia. Marine flotillas from Nizhnii Novgorod moved down the
Volga to the Caspian sea. The fields at Nizhnii Novgorod were
thronged with traders from all over Russia on fair days. One might find
a merchant from Yaroslavl in a caftan, an Englishman in a smock, or
a Persian in a jacket and fez. Nizhnii Novgorod was the sixth largest
trading center in the country. The town had no bishop of its own but
the wealthy Pechorskii monastery was located on the Volga heights
near the town quarter. Just before the Time of Troubles began, a
landslide detroyed its stone cathedrals and other edifices. The monks
moved their cells to another place, where they had only started to
rebuild.

Prosperous townsmen were far more influential in Nizhnii Novgorod than the military-feudal complex. Rural gentry were neither rich
nor of noble birth. Most of them lived outside Nizhnii Novgorod on
service-tenure estates. No more than 100 of them could withdraw into
the fortress in an emergency. Five hundred fusiliers constituted the
main force in the Nizhnii Novgorod garrison. Like the townsmen they
were engaged in trade and manufacturing and they lived comfortably.
The disastrous Time of Troubles immensely harmed town quarters
throughout Russia but Nizhnii Novgorod was less afflicted than others.
Trade and manufacturing slackened during the civil war and population declined but the town was relatively free from pillage and assault.
Revolts occurred elsewhere in the district and in minor town quarters.
The people of Nizhnii Novgorod frequently beheld detachments from
Tushino and from the foreigners before their walls but they never
managed to take the town.

Nizhnii Novgorod possessed an excellent defense system. The town
was located on a promontory between the Oka and Volga rivers. To
the north it was bounded by the Volga escarpment; on the west a moat
had been dug to take advantage of Pochainyi brook. Few Russian towns
had a stone fortress equal to the Nizhnii Novgorod Kremlin. Its thick
walls, covered with planks, rose gradually in the air or lowered to the
river. Innumerable towers had been erected wherever the defense line
was vulnerable. The chief thoroughfare in the Kremlin, Great Bridge
Street, started at the gate by the four-cornered Ivanov tower and led
up to the main square. Spaso-Preobrazhenskii cathedral, built of white
stone, was situated in the middle of the square, surrounded by a number
of little wooden churches. From the west, broad town quarters intruded
upon the Kremlin. They were protected by a fort that had wooden

towers and a moat. The town quarters were full of tumbledown huts. Homes of the rich had women's quarters that were topped with tenting.

A council chamber stood in front of the main Kremlin cathedral. In it the local authorities dispensed justice amd meted out punishments. When the Time of Troubles was at its worst, elected townsmen acquired exceptional influence. The town commune was usually in session during autumn, the first days of the new year. At that time years were computed from the creation of the world and a new year would be celebrated on the first day of September. The commune elected elders, chancellery officials, and other office-holders. Those possessing substantial means regularly held these posts. Most of these individuals were usually returned to office but in times of tribulation townsmen would choose elders for reasons other than their money. In fall, 1611 patriots put Kuzma Minin in office.

He was a prosperous member of the town quarter. His father, Mina Ankudinov, lived near Nizhnii Novgorod in Balakhna. He was a salt panner. Kuzma's brothers inherited their father's enterprise. Kuzma moved into Nizhnii Novgorod and opened a butcher shop. He had a stall in Butchers' Row, where he worked with his adult son Nefed. This business enabled the family to live well and save money, but Minin was not the sort of man for whom the acquisition of material goods constituted the chief goal in life. He would not hesitate to sacrifice his own and his family's comfort or his savings if a higher cause should require it.

Feudal society was cruel to the millions of common people who paid taxes to the crown. They were not allowed to become active in politics, for prejudice against them was intense. A man had to be singularly courageous in order to transcend this limitation. Minin well remembered the fierce internal struggle it cost him to become involved in affairs of state. Monks who set down Kuzma's reminiscences infused them with religious overtones. Minin recalled that in late summer he often would leave his stifling dwelling for the garden and spend the night in his summerhouse. He dreamed the same dream three times while he was there. He seemed to be marching with a host of soldiers to purge Muscovy. Even the thought of such activity long upset him but he refused to admit it, even to himself. A sensible individual, he was a realist; whenever he awoke from the dream he was seriously alarmed. "Should I not pay attention to my own affairs?" he would ask himself. He was tormented by doubts. The proprietor of the butcher stall realized he had no military experience and that he was only an ordinary taxpaying citizen, not a member of the town establishment. He felt intolerably burdened; his stomach was queasy and he could barely get out of bed, but eventually he came to believe it was fate itself that was calling him to rise up on behalf of the motherland. He could never forget the words that had come to him in his dreams: "If elders, gentry and commanders will not act, ordinary taxpaying men will have to do so. Their initiative will be good and lead to a successful outcome."[3]

Kuzma considered his election as a town elder to be the beckoning finger of fate. After he took his seat on it, the council became a center of patriotic activity. Nizhnii Novgorod townsmen intently followed the battles in the Moscow suburbs during autumn. Monks from the Trinity-St. Sergius monastery let them know in time that the militia was in danger of disbanding due to heavy losses, famine, and want. The citizens knew at first hand how critical the situation was in Moscow because after every engagement wounded soldiers were brought to them.

The news from Moscow caused Nizhnii Novgorod commanders and chancellery members to despair. They were at a loss what to do. It was not they but Town Elder Minin who proposed a resolution to organize a new militia. Kuzma, immediately becoming the leader of those who still had courage, demanded new sacrifices for the fatherland. As they daily discussed the position of the militia, patriots grew convinced that the creation of a strong new force would determine the outcome of the contest for Moscow.

Council meetings were constantly attracting larger audiences. With tears in his eyes Minin tried to persuade his fellow citizens that Nizhnii Novgorod could not escape destiny and its future would be determined in Moscow: "Muscovy is in ruins; men have been killed and captured; our misfortunes are incalculable. God has preserved us from attack but the enemy is plotting to destroy us too. We do not take this seriously and are failing in our duty."[4] Masses of people from every walk of life thronged the hall. Some approved of the new elder's speeches but other reviled and spat upon him. Men of means feared the cost. They remembered that it required considerable outlays to organize military forces. Minin found most of his supporters among the commons. Young people were inspired by the elder's zeal. After a meeting they would reproach their parents for their parsimony: "What use is our wealth? When the enemy comes and takes our town, do you think he won't destroy us as he has done the others? Will our town be the only one left?"

Crowds of people assembled in the square in front of the town hall. A decisive moment was at hand. Minin cried out: "If we want to help the Muscovite realm we must not spare our resources or our lives. It's not just a question of our money. We shall have to sell our estates, and consign our wives and children to slavery!" The elder's appeal was distasteful to the prosperous but the commons would no longer pay attention to the upper orders. Patriots dominated the town assembly and then and there in the crown chancellery their leaders drew up a decree authorizing a financial levy to outfit soldiers. In accordance with tradition, Minin circulated the decree for everyone to sign and thus the entire town attested it. The motion invested the elected elder with broad powers. Kuzma was instructed to impose an extraordinary levy on Nizhnii Novgorod traders and people of the district and to determine the amount each should pay in terms of his income and expenditures.

The first contributions were voluntary. Minin set an example for others. Contemporaries were not unanimous on this subject. In his notes one gentry witness had the elder say: "Brothers, we shall divide our estates into three parts. Let us give two to the army and keep one for ourselves." If this is valid, Kuzma would have given two-thirds of what he had to the treasury. Others declared the elder told the commune he had 300 rubles, and laid out 100 rubles to meet the assessment. One late tradition states that Kuzma gave up all his money, removed the gold from his icons, and threw in his wife Tatiana's jewelry, consisting of necklaces and pendants sewn with gold thread.

Minin was but one of many. Nizhnii Novgorod people brought whatever they could to the council chamber in the square. Their generosity fired contemporary imaginations and created a legend, the tale of the Rich Widow. She inherited 20,000 rubles from her husband and gave 10,000 of them to the nationalist leaders. The self-sacrificing gesture by this pious woman, contemporaries observed, inspired fear in many.[5]

Voluntary contributions served as seed money for the new militia. Minin and his cohorts calculated carefully because they knew that to fight would require a great deal of money. They promulgated a statute which decreed an exceptional levy. The people of Nizhnii Novgorod genuinely sacrificed their "stomachs," the word then used to denote property. They had already spent a lot to outfit the original militia. The town commune now approved a collection of one-fifth of the area's entire revenue to pay for soldiers. This levy was conducted in the town and throughout the entire region. Supply wagons moved into Nizhnii Novgorod, sent by peasants in the trading village of Pavlov, beekeepers in Mordva villages, and the rest of the populace. Wealthy monasteries and crown peasants were also obliged to contribute to the fund.

The townsmen for some time had been pondering the question of who was to be in charge of the army they were setting out to organize. Their original commander, Prince Aleksandr Repnin, enjoyed an undistinguished reputation; the national council had removed him him from Moscow to Sviiazhsk, near Kazan, and sent Prince Vasilii Zvenigorodskii to take Repnin's place. The people of Nizhnii Novgorod distrusted and were even hostile to their new commander. He was closely related to the traitorous Mikhail Saltykov and had received associate boyar rank from Sigismund. Andrei Aliabev for a long time had been serving as adjutant to the Nizhnii Novgorod commander and had rendered the commune a number of services, but he was of humble birth and low rank. Aliabev only recently had risen from the rank of crown secretary to become a Moscow courtier. The elected nationalist authorities fully understood that the enterprise they had undertaken would fail unless they could find a leader popular with the army and in the country. The townsmen wanted an upstanding man familiar with military matters, experienced, and, above all, one who would not sell them out.[6]

During the Time of Troubles only a few courtiers holding the rank of commander had preserved their reputations intact. Most had been compromised; honest men were few and far between. The people of Nizhnii Novgorod were faced with a difficult decision. They came to the conclusion they should rely entirely on their own experience and seek a candidate among serving men they knew personally. Kuzma Minin first advanced the name of Dmitrii Pozharskii. The commune supported him. Prince Dmitrii was recuperating in the village of Mugreevo, near Nizhnii Novgorod. The commander had been wounded many months ago. Nature had not endowed Pozharskii with a robust constitution. His recovery was slow. His serious head injury had caused Prince Dmitrii to suffer from epilepsy, the "black ailment," as it was then called. The seizures and convulsions of those afflicted with this malady frightened superstitious persons; they called epileptics unburied corpses. Simple folk felt sorry for them but tended to avoid them.

The epilepsy delayed Pozharskii's recovery. When Nizhnii Novgorod emissaries arrived, Dmitrii did not return them a clear answer. The envoys departed empty-handed. Recalling the incident later, Prince Dmitrii was fond of saying that the entire realm had strongly urged him to undertake the task, but had one of the great leaders like Boyar Vasilii Golitsyn been available at the time, he would have stepped aside and refused to assume such a responsibility in a boyar's stead. His remarks about boyars were simply an excuse. Vasilii Golitsyn was a prisoner and the other "great leaders" were with the Poles in the Kremlin. Nizhnii Novgorod had to send emissaries many times before Pozharskii would agree to accept their invitation.[7] Prince Dmitrii could not violate canons of etiquette by agreeing when first contacted, and he was concerned about his health. Furthermore, Mugreevo had heard that the people of Nizhnii Novgorod would not obey their commanders; Dmitrii was anxious to determine in advance the nature of his future relations with the town commune. Kuzma Minin had to go to Mugreevo in person to allay the prince's fears. Both men were inspired by the same aims and goals and soon found common ground. The chief problem Minin and Pozharskii had to solve was how to get money. Commanders were not normally required to worry about financial matters. They were supported by the tsars' treasury. Now finances were in the hands of the council of seven and the foreigners. Pozharskii agreed to assume command of the militia, but he insisted the commune must designate as his assistant a treasurer of its own, with broad powers.

To conclude negotiations Nizhnii Novgorod dispatched to Mugreevo an upright member of the gentry, Zhdan Boltin, Feodosii, abbot of the Pechorskii monastery, and elected townsmen. Pozharskii informed them he was ready to lead the militia but again demanded they name a treasurer. His request initially puzzled the senior envoys. It was hard for them to entertain the notion that an army could be led by an elected townsman as well as by the prince. The commander's request flew in the face of time-honored custom that sternly forbade townsmen to assume military responsibilities. The abbot unequivocally refused to accept Pozharskii's proposal, declaring there was no suitable individual at hand. Then Pozharskii put forward Minin's name. The junior envoys made no effort to conceal their delight. Minin did not immediately accept the distinguished office tendered to him. He had his reasons. He agreed to take the post only on condition that the commune would grant him extraordinary powers to collect revenue in order to provide soldiers with weapons and supplies.

The town commune accepted Minin's terms and the nationalist headquarters quickly passed decrees in the spirit of the general resolution. Nizhnii Novgorod townsmen pledged unreservedly to serve the man they had chosen and to provide money for soldiers. Townsmen's ears still rang with Kuzma's fiery exhortations to make any sacrifice necessary to succor their prostrate realm. They inserted into the decree a proviso to the effect they would donate their estates for the benefit of the army and in event of extraordinary need to indenture their wives and children in order to raise money. The minute the decree was signed and ratified national headquarters rushed the document to Pozharskii.

While the discussions were taking place in Mugreevo, the commune invited representatives of the Smolensk gentry to come to Nizhnii Novgorod. The fall of Smolensk had compelled local serving men to leave the area occupied by the enemy and move towards Moscow. The refugees had petitioned Liapunov and Zarutskii to assign them estates. A council decree authorized the serving men to proceed to Arzamas and the adjacent towns of Kurmysh and Alatyr, where they could settle on gentry lands. Local peasants were furious at the thought they would be returned to the status of serfs and refused to admit the uninvited landholders. An uprising broke out. Despairing of a resolution of the issue, in the fall some gentry withdrew to Nizhnii Novgorod. The remainder continued fighting the rebels. Eventually they managed to win control of two rebel forts and destroy their forces.

In Nizhnii Novgorod the commune welcomed the Smolensk gentry representatives warmly and provided them with supplies. Some men of Smolensk accompanied the townsmen to Mugreevo to meet with Pozharskii. The gentry begged the commander to hasten to Nizhnii Novgorod. The arrival of the Smolensk soldiers encouraged Pozharskii. Besides them he called upon landholders from Viazma and Dorogobuzh stationed in crown villages at Yaropolk. This was close to Mugreevo; many Viazma landholders escorted Pozharskii while he rode to Nizhnii Novgorod in a wagon.

Clergy, gentry, and townsmen came out to greet Pozharskii and his force, carrying icons and bread and salt. The nationalist unit was reinforced by 150 fusiliers from the local garrison. However, it took a lot longer to muster soldiers than the people of Nizhnii Novgorod had expected. The Smolensk gentry refused to campaign until the question of their lands was settled. Their representatives reached agreement with Minin by the end of October, but the soldiers were not actually enrolled in Nizhnii Novgorod until January 6, 1612. Brought in from villages, where they had endured a harsh winter, the Smolensk serving men presented a sorry sight. Some were riding old nags; others in tattered clothes were walking, followed by peasant carts. The population sympathized with the men of Smolensk and escorted them in a crowd to the command post. From on high Minin strikingly adjured the new arrivals: "You are our brothers. You have come to us to succor our town and to purge the Muscovite realm!"[8]

The men of Smolensk were heartened by the sincerity of their welcome, which involuntarily reminded them of better times. Minin was a practical man and realized that words alone were not enough. Many years later serving men were still telling stories of Kuzma's astonishing generosity. There were justifiable reasons for it. The ruined landholders were simply unfit to fight. They would have to be properly equipped and reliably mounted before they could go off to battle.

Pozharskii held a review and divided the gentry into three categories. Landholders in the first categories received twenty to thirty rubles each; lesser boyars in the third category got fifteen rubles. Besides this allocation, national headquarters distributed money to buy horses and procure equipment for all of them at once. News of what was happening in Nizhnii Novgorod soon spread to adjacent areas. Masses of petty serving men entered the nationalists' profitable service. In addition to Kolomenskoe and Riazan landholders, Pozharskii enrolled gentry, fusiliers, and cossacks from border fortresses.

Pozharskii planned to raise forces everywhere as quickly as possible and set out at once to relieve Moscow, but to accomplish this task proved unexpectedly difficult. The men of Nizhnii Novgorod soon realized they could not go it alone. Minin and Pozharskii had to look for support from towns and districts near and far, and this was bound to lead to conflict with the other national government. The boyars and chancellery officials before Moscow believed that only they possessed the right to levy soldiers and provide equipment. Minin's and Pozharskii's enterprise threatened to upset their complex structure. The people of Nizhnii Novgorod had to devote much time and effort to restoring good relations with local militia commanders and officials.

For ages Nizhnii Novgorod had served as a magnet to adjacent towns and regions. Tsar Ivan had given the heirs of what he termed the grand duchy of Nizhnii Novgorod lands and roads, the towns of Balakhna and Vasilsursk, and control of the Mordva and Cheremis peoples. One small town in the region was Kurmysh. Trubetskoi and Zarutskii sent Lesser Boyar Elagin to command there. He was unable to win the serving men's support. Hearing of Pozharskii's appeals, the men of Kurmysh sent him a petition criticizing Elagin. When he received it Pozharskii told the Kurmysh commander to pay the gentry at once, give fusiliers a small sum beyond what they had been assigned, and cossacks a ruble if they served in the cavalry. After they were paid their salaries the Kurmysh soldiers were ordered to proceed forthwith in a body to Nizhnii Novgorod and then march against the foreigners in Moscow. If his orders were not obeyed, Pozharskii asked the soldiers to send him new petitions and he promised to assign another commander to Kurmysh. Elagin refused to do what Pozharskii had asked him. He had a rescript from Trubetskoi and Zarutskii empowering him to raise revenue, pay serving men's salaries and send them to national service before Moscow directly, not through Nizhnii Novgorod. Some time later the Nizhnii Novgorod national council tried to remove Elagin. A member of the Nizhnii Novgorod gentry, Dmitrii Zhezdrinskii, went to Kurmysh but his mission was a failure. The town refused to admit the new commander.

The original national government had high hopes of the Nizhnii Novgorod force but as in the past it demanded all revenue raised in the provinces should be sent to the treasury. It frowned upon any expenditure of money locally. The undertaking by the people of Nizhnii Novgorod would inevitably have foundered if they had not been supported by the towns in their quarrel with the boyars before Moscow. Volga towns had furnished supplies and men to the first national militia, but they had no representatives on the national council. The council decree of June 30, 1611 made no reference to townsmen; this was bound to provoke ill-feeling. The boyars before Moscow regarded wealthy townsmen exclusively as a source of income. They insisted imposts be paid promptly. Nothing else interested them. Ultimately they were to pay dearly for their shortsightedness.

The provinces had good reason to fear that Moscow would elect a tsar without consulting them, as had often happened before. Early in winter Zarutskii expressed annoyance that Nizhnii Novgorod, Kazan, Kurmysh and other towns were issuing what he termed "meaningless" charters of their own about electing a tsar. Quarrels broke out in the enclaves around Moscow. Some wanted to listen to the provinces; others voiced indignation that anyone would wish to do so. Minin's and Pozharskii's appeal refrained from attacking the national government headed by Trubetskoi and Zarutskii, but it alluded extensively to cossack banditry. Atamans Zarutskii and Prosovetskii were the leaders of the enclaves around Moscow; cossacks predominated in the ranks. The provinces were greatly concerned that the cossacks might launch another intrigue involving a pretender.

In a letter to Vologda townsmen, the nationalist authorities noted two ominous portents: the appearance of a new Thief, False Dmitrii III, in Pskov and the fact that Marina was disseminating "dark charters" in the name of Heir Ivan Dmitrievich. The people of Nizhnii Novgorod made their views on pretenders crystal clear: "To our dying day we shall not consent to the election of the Thief of Pskov nor of the Tiny Thief of Kolomenskoe." In supporting Nizhnii Novgorod the towns were indicating how much they disapproved of the cossacks for having murdered Liapunov and maintaining ties with pretenders. The people of Nizhnii Novgorod were expressing attitudes with long histories in the provinces. A short time later, in a circular letter to the people, Prince Pozharskii publicly declared that all towns, whether to the south, on the north coast, or along the Volga, as well as Riazan, were to make all their remittances exclusively to Nizhnii Novgorod in preparation for the campaign to free Moscow. The citizenry was again taking control of the liberation movement.

Political calculations influenced the military policies adopted by the Nizhnii Novgorod leaders. Soon after January 6, 1612 they informed the towns they intended to relieve Suzdal, which was under siege by the foreigners. Suzdal was the site where Pozharskii proposed to establish his staging area, in which the militia from towns north of Moscow as well as Riazan would assemble. When inviting the inhabitants of Vologda to join the Suzdal campaign, the nationalists tried to allay their concerns and revealed their innermost feelings: "Look you, sires, you must be aware of rapacious attacks by the cossacks, but you need not be afraid. We are going to summon all the towns of the upper and lower regions and we shall convoke a Council of the Entire Realm to deal with this, and we shall not allow Thieves to cause any harm. We shall not allow any one before Moscow to cause harm by concerting with Marina and her son."[9]

Minin's and Pozharskii's plans were now clear and precise. They would concentrate town militias in Suzdal and use them to check the pretenders' partisans in the cossack enclaves. They intended to summon a new national assembly in Suzdal in which the entire realm would be well represented. This assembly would be asked to determine procedures for electing a tsar. The people of Nizhnii Novgorod wrote: "When we all come together from the upper towns and the heartland, all of us in the land will elect for the Muscovite realm the sovereign God shall give us."[10] Associate Boyar Artemii Izmailov was the commander in Vladimir, not far from Suzdal. Boyar Vasilii Morozov was at Yaroslavl, in the central region north of Moscow. Pozharskii was counting on their help. He knew the Pskov pretender would receive little support from the gentry with Trubetskoi before Moscow and hoped to win this group over.

Minin and Pozharskii had devised a careful plan to attack Suzdal and then convoke the assembly there, but they were unable to overcome the opposition of the other nationalist government. Zarutskii stole a march on the men of Nizhnii Novgorod. When Sapieha's army took Rostov, Zarutskii lost no time sending Atamans Andrei and Ivan Prosovetskii with cossacks to attack it. The Prosovetskii brothers forced Sapieha to vacate Rostov and late in winter to withdraw to Moscow. Zarutskii began to group units loyal to him in the Vladimir-Suzdal area. The national government taught the men of Nizhnii Novgorod an obvious lesson. In January, 1612 Arzamas heeded that government's injunction and dispatched reinforcements to the Prosovetskii atamans dug in at Vladimir and Suzdal. The men of Nizhnii Novgorod tried vainly to win over detachments from Arzamas, Kurmysh, and other towns. The Kazan authorities, who had helped the people of Nizhnii Novgorod form the new militia, strove to assist Minin and Pozharskii. They threatened they would come in full force against the people of Kurmysh and besiege the local commander unless he submitted to the Nizhnii Novgorod council, but they could not make good on their threats. The original national government was still strong in the provinces.

Zarutskii's agitation on behalf of the Tiny Thief and the dispatch of the delegation to False Dmitrii III in Pskov intensified the contest within the militia and hastened the demarcation of respective spheres of influence. The national government and the Nizhnii Novgorod council fell to open quarreling, like two brothers. The occupation of Suzdal by cossack detachments made it impossible for Minin and Pozharskii to convoke a new land assembly there. They then started eyeing Yaroslavl. Zarutskii understood the importance of Yaroslavl; it was the key position in the entire region north of Moscow. After expelling the Poles from Rostov he was able to establish direct communications between Moscow and Yaroslavl. Beyond Yaroslavl lay Kostroma. The local commander there was loyal to the boyars before Moscow; it was easier to subject Yaroslavl. Zarutskii assigned the task to the Prosovetskii brothers. Cossack scouts soon appeared in Yaroslavl. The local commander and the authorities in the town quarter earlier had entered into close contact with the Nizhnii Novgorod council. As soon as cossacks appeared in the town, Morozov, the Yaroslavl commander, sounded the tocsin and asked Pozharskii for reinforcements.

Minin and Pozharskii realized that delay would be fatal to their enterprise. They had to accept Zarutskii's challenge or else give up. The Nizhnii Novgorod council ordered an immediate advance. There was now no way they could carry out their former plan of marching on Moscow by the shortest route via Vladimir and Suzdal. They had to detour along the banks of the Volga. They also had to win over hostile Kostroma and send aid to their allies in Yaroslavl. The struggle for the capital began with a struggle for the provinces.

Winter was coming to an end; the people of Nizhnii Novogord had to speed up their campaign because the spring thaw was imminent. Pozharskii put forth great efforts but he failed to assemble a significant number of troops in Nizhnii Novgorod. Only a few men of Smolensk and a handful from Viazma turned out. Contemporaries estimated the men of Smolensk at Pozharskii's side numbered less than 2,000. In fact, the men of Smolensk had been dispersed all over the country; there were no more than 1,000 gentry from Smolensk and Viazma left in Nizhnii Novgorod.

The artisans of the town quarter were hard put to provide Pozharskii's forces with arms. The men from Smolensk had been in Nizhnii Novgorod a month and a half. During this time many had repaired their weapons and armor and acquired good mounts. This well-accoutred cavalry unit and the fusilier infantry became the core of the Nizhnii Novgorod militia. Pozharskii hoped that a detachment would arrive from Kazan to bolster his army but his emissary, Birkin, could not bring up the men of Kazan in time. Kazan disappointed the hopes the Nizhnii Novgorod council had placed in it. With a heavy heart Pozharskii gave the order to advance without waiting for his nearest allies. He entrusted command of the advance guard to his brother, Prince Dmitrii Petrovich Lopata Pozharskii. Lopata coped with his responsibilities effectively. He reached where he was to go by the shortest possible route, avoiding major towns. Digging in before Yaroslavl, Lopata occupied the place with support from the local population. The commander imprisoned cossacks he captured. Advancing on Yaroslavl from the south, Andrei Prosovetskii thought better of clashing with Lopata and turned aside.

The main Nizhnii Novgorod militia force moved on Balakhna February 23, 1612, the day of a great fast. The town of Balakhna had a rectangular-shaped fortress with wooden walls and towers. It was protected on the north by a small brook, a tributary of the Volga, and by a lake to the east. The local garrison met Pozharskii at the gate. Commanders and gentry were lodged in redoubts in the fortress. The rest of the soldiers spent the night in the town quarter.

Pozharskii's campaign served to unify the forces opposing Zarutskii. The prince was joined by Matvei Pleshcheev in Balakhna. This commander had acquired distinction in the first national militia. During Liapunov's lifetime he had tried to check cossack licence in the regiments. After Liapunov's murder he was obliged to flee the militia and rusticate on his patrimonial estate in Kostroma. However, his encounter with Pleshcheev did nothing to improve Pozharskii's temper. The future of the liberation movement appeared vague and uncertain.

Leaving Balakhna at dusk the army proceeded to Yurevets. The soldiers had just disposed themselves for the night when an alarm suddenly sounded. A cavalry detachment was approaching the town, moving rapidly along the road. Sentries reached for their rifles, but they did not have to shoot. An emir was admitted to the fortress. He stated he had brought a Tatar unit to serve the national cause. After Yurevets the force halted in the village of Reshma. In the morning a courier came, sent by Artemii Izmailov in Vladimir. He brought unwelcome news. Izmailov informed Pozharskii, his old companion in arms, that ordinary cossacks before Moscow on March 2 had perpetrated a coup and elected False Dmitrii III, the Thief of Pskov, as tsar. The news had a bad effect on the Nizhnii Novgorod soldiers. Deep concern replaced the animation they had displayed during the first days of the campaign. Not knowing exactly what had happened, the militia leaders could not comprehend why the boyars before Moscow had decided to hurl down a challenge to the country and elect a tsar without taking counsel with the towns and representatives of the entire realm.

After Reshma the army stopped in Kineshma. The inhabitants of this small place greeted the men of Nizhnii Novgorod politely and offered them money. From Kineshma Pozharskii pushed on towards Kostroma. As they were approaching it the militia leaders received Kostroma townsmen, who warned Pozharskii that Ivan Sheremetev, their commander, had decided not to admit the men of Nizhnii Novgorod into the place. Kostroma was situated on the left [west] bank of the Volga at the point where the Kostroma river flows into it. In the center of the town lay a modest fortress surrounded by a moat. The town area was rather small, containing no more than 500 houses. The Time of Troubles had ruined Kostroma. Many homes had been destroyed. No services were held in the churches.

The first national government had sent Ivan Sheremetev as commander there. He had no intention of submitting to Pozharskii. Local gentry were divided. Some had gone over to Matvei Pleshcheev and Pozharskii; others had shut themselves up with Sheremetev in the fortress. Finding the fortress gate closed, the soldiers had to bivouac in the town area outside. Pozharskii stayed his hand and showed no hurry to storm the citadel. He displayed good judgment. A rebellion broke out in Kostroma. People besieged Sheremetev in the commander's residence and would have killed him if Pozharskii had not come up. By ordering his soldiers to arrest the commander Pozharskii saved Sheremetev's life. On quitting Kostroma Pozharskii left Prince Roman Gagarin as commander.

Yaroslavl was now close by. The town was rightly considered one of the great trading and artisan centers in the country. Urban life quickened perceptibly in the early seventeenth century. The town quarter expanded rapidly. Many boats were built on the banks of the Volga. Yaroslavl anchorages functioned as transfer points for goods on their way to Moscow, Arkhangelsk, Siberia, and Astrakhan. Companies of foreign merchants understood Yaroslavl's importance and opened trading depots there. Even after the vicissitudes of the Time of Troubles the town area still contained some 800 taxpaying households, although by the end of the Troubles half of them consisted of impoverished families.

The ancient Yaroslavl fortress, situated on a high promontory lying between the Volga and the mouth of the Kotorosl river, could be seen from far and wide. The town quarter, protected by external fortifications, stood next to it. Since the place had been quiet for a long time the wooden structure had deteriorated. Timbers had rotted and crumbled; the rampart was weak. The sole imposing stone edifice was the wealthy Salvation monastery right next to the Kremlin. Monks had built a thick stone wall around it. Commanders kept the treasury and maintained the fusilier garrison in the monastery, not in the outmoded Kremlin.

The people of Yaroslavl had often risen against the men of Tushino and the foreigners. The enemy had burned down the earthen town and the fort but had never managed to get control of Salvation monastery or the Kremlin. The town area had been gutted long before but as soon as the enemy withdrew the populace joined together to rebuild. Large forests abounded. A new town quarter would arise from the ashes. Unlike Nizhnii Novgorod, Yaroslavl was not primarily an abode of townsmen. Numerous gentry lived there. The first national government had tried to incorporate Yaroslavl into its defense system before the men of Nizhnii Novgorod took the initiative. During the struggle with Chodkiewicz, Boyar Andrei Kurakin and Crown Secretary Mikhail Danilov went to Yaroslavl, charged to recruit a supplementary army and bring it quickly to aid Moscow. Vasilii Buturlin was to do the same in Vladimir. With no money or authority, Kurakin and Buturlin failed to accomplish their missions. They lacked the qualities with which nature had abundantly endowed Kuzma Minin, who had risen from the lower orders. It seemed as though nothing more could be done in Yaroslavl. Commanders were unable to secure the cooperation of the town population in order to ensure the general welfare. The report that the enclaves had recognized the pretender and Commander Lopata Pozharskii's arrival made a strong impression on the elderly Commander Kurakin. He resolved to break with the first national government and throw in his lot with Pozharskii.

Nizhnii Novgorod units entered Yaroslavl to the sound of bells. Townsmen welcomed the soldiers with bread and salt. On that festive day no one had any idea Pozharskii would have to remain in Yaroslavl for four long months.

Chapter Sixteen

THE YAROSLAVL GOVERNMENT

No one has ever been able to wage war without money. Pozharskii was successfully recruiting serving men but resources were required to maintain them. Money collected earlier was rapidly disappearing; it proved difficult or almost impossible to find new sources in the desolate country. The financial system long ago had ceased to function. Constantly exposed to pillage, the people concealed what they had and husbanded their resources, for they saw that every new government laid on fresh imposts. Town inhabitants scattered among villages. Trade had declined drastically.

It took Kuzma Minin many weeks to persuade frugal rich men in Nizhnii Novgorod to contribute substantial sums. At home the elder was well known and could count on support from the entire town commune, but elsewhere Kuzma had to establish his authority all over again. He locked horns with the local saltpanners of Balakhna, including his own brothers. The oratory of the people's tribune had no effect on limited minds. These people were not anxious to part with their hard-earned money. Minin had no time for protracted discussions; the Nizhnii Novgorod detachment was preparing to depart. On one occasion in Balakhna Minin poured out the anger that possessed him. He made a long speech to the citizenry in which he labeled as common criminals traders trying to conceal their property to avoid the levy and refusing to make sacrifices for the army. Such guilty skinflints deserved to have their hands cut off![1] Minin spoke with such force that his speech overwhelmed those who heard it. They realized the elder would sacrifice even his brothers for the national cause. Wealthy merchants were ashamed and brought cash contributions to the council hall.

The same scenario was repeated in Yaroslavl. Minin called upon local merchants to contribute money to free Moscow but they turned a deaf ear to his appeals. The rich merchants Nikitnikov and Lytkin declared their bailiffs already had done their duty for the militia treasury in Nizhnii Novgorod. The upper orders in Yaroslavl looked askance at the elder. In him they saw a trader like themselves; they could not understand why they should have to obey him. Protracted discussions at national headquarters ensued. Kuzma long sought to sway the men of Yaroslavl with soothing words but when they produced no results Minin showed everyone it was dangerous to make a fool of him. He sent for fusiliers and told them to surround national headquarters. Nikitnikov and other traders were arrested on a charge of dishonor and conveyed to the commander's residence. Before commanders and chancellery officials Minin recited the merchants' culpability and demanded they be stripped of their possessions. Pozharskii supported him with his authority. Faced with what they felt was Kuzma's "brutality" and "wrongdoing" the prosperous traders fell on their knees and begged for mercy.

Minin and Pozharskii had no idea they would have to spend so much time in Yaroslavl. The rising that had occurred in the camps at Moscow upset their plans. Hopes were fading that Moscow would soon be liberated. Pozharskii could not advance on the capital as long as the

pretender's partisans were in charge there. Traitors refusing to acknowledge Good Dmitrii were threatened with death. The siege of
Moscow had immobilized Zarutskii. This gave Pozharskii a chance to
establish himself in the towns north of Moscow without too much
difficulty or effort. Emissaries already had come from Suzdal to Pozharskii while he was in Kostroma, begging him to send a commander
and soldiers to expel Prosovetskii and the cossacks. The people of
Nizhnii Novgorod at once dispatched Prince Roman Petrovich Pozharskii. Prosovetskii was unwilling to start a fratricidal war. When he
learned Pozharskii's force was approaching he withdrew towards Moscow.

Minin's and Pozharskii's army was firmly ensconced in Yaroslavl
but cossack bands loyal to Zarutskii were still operating along the roads
north of the town. Dmitrii sent Lopata Pozharskii and a force to Poshekhone with orders to clear a way to the north and the coastal region.
The commander defeated the cossacks he found there. Their ataman,
Vasilii Tolstoi, fled to Kashin, where Commander Dmitrii Cherkasskii
and his men were stationed. Cherkasskii had been in service in the
enclaves before Moscow but he soon came over to the Yaroslavl
militia. In May, 1612 the inhabitants of Pereiaslavl-Zalesskii asked
Pozharskii to protect them from Zarutskii. The council dispatched
Commander Ivan Naumov, who drove the cossacks out and established
himself in the town. He did so without bloodshed.

Yaroslavl had become a powerful magnet, attracting towns that
refused to support the Thief. Towns north of Moscow, along the Volga,
and on the northern coast kept sending armed detachments to Yaroslavl
or else asking for commanders and reinforcements to come to them.
Pozharskii dispatched soldiers to places such as Tver, Vladimir,
Rostov, and Kasimov. They secured the communication lines linking
Yaroslavl with the north. The coastal region and the northern towns
by now had become supply bases for the new national militia.

The split in the liberation movement had decreased the size of the
territory the new government controlled, but the Yaroslavl council had
brought many towns under its banner. It had no choice but to administer
them. Chaos and dissension, as usual, characterized the changeover,
but the wave of patriotic sentiment rose even higher despite the confusion. Kuzma Minin rode the crest of it. The humble Nizhnii Novgorod townsman was the heart and soul of the new government. His
title sounded strange but inspiring: "The Man Chosen by the Entire
Realm." Minin possessed inexhaustible energy. He and his close

associates had their work cut out for them. In a short time they had again to establish a government in the extensive territory that refused to recognize False Dmitrii III.

A Service-Tenure chancellery, a Kazan bureau, and a Novgorod office began to function in Yaroslavl. Gentry, fusiliers, and bombardiers poured into the town. The commanders inspected the new arrivals and paid them salaries. When handing out money they insisted landholders must offer surety and give written pledges to perform, not avoid service. The Service-Tenure chancellery set about distributing lands to impoverished gentry. Unlike the secretaries assisting him, Kuzma did not tread the long slippery halls of bureaucratic chancelleries. He was a stranger to pettifoggery. Whenever a desk worker threw up his hands in the face of monumental problems, Kuzma instantaneously cut the Gordian knot. It normally required a tremendous amount of time to compile land survey books, but within a matter of days Minin had dispatched surveyors to Suzdal, Kineshma, and Torzhok. Such prompt action enabled the Yaroslavl council to make attractive offers to taxpayers.

The new authorities looked for revenue wherever they could find it. A Monastery chancellery was established in Yaroslavl, headed by a judge, Timofei Vitivtov, a man of unblemished reputation. He had been made a conciliar secretary while serving in the first militia before Moscow. Monasteries possessed substantial wealth. Minin was eager to obtain loans from them. The Solovetskii monastery agreed to make funds available but voiced reservations about the plenipotentiary powers possessed by Minin, a man who held no rank. The monks insisted Pozharskii countersign the loan papers. The Stroganov family, merchants and saltpanners, proved more amenable than the monastery elders. At Minin's insistence their officers loaned the militia 4,000 rubles. Kuzma negotiated a loan with three Moscow and four Yaroslavl merchants, thereby acquiring another 1,000 rubles. He pledged to repay the money when Nizhnii Novgorod's revenues started to come in, but the war went on; outlays increased and devoured the new contributions. The militia leader had to worry about taking out new loans, not about repaying old ones.

Voluntarily people had made sacrifices to keep the national treasury steadily replenished, but Minin again and again appealed to them, urging them to compete with one another for the sake of the motherland, make further contributions to the national government, and tax themselves to the extent each could for support of the troops. His adjurations produced results. Of their own free will towns sent money they had collected to Yaroslavl. In addition to these cash offerings, the militia was given numerous objects made of silver. Kuzma at once appraised the situation and built a Coinage office in the town. Coiners melted down the valuables and fashioned coins the treasury used to pay the troops. Minin possessed the skills of a born organizer and knew how to subordinate everyone, even his enemies, to his will and point them in the desired direction. Nikitnikov and other Yaroslavl merchants were imprisoned briefly, but afterwards Kuzma persuaded them to enter nationalist service. They took seats on the council.

The second national government maintained close ties with town quarters and rural communes, which gained an opportunity to influence council activity through those representing them, Minin, traders, and important secretaries. When it undertook to amass contributions from different rural communes, the council would invite commune elders and prosperous peasants to come to a conference. When deciding substantive issues the council summoned regional representatives to Yaroslavl, demanding their principals provide them with written instructions. Towns then obtained an order in the name of their particular council to send two or three individuals chosen from all ranks, who would attest documents with their signatures on their councils' behalf.[2] Men chosen by their localities were constantly visiting Minin and Pozharskii. The leaders would retain them in Yaroslavl or assign tasks to carry out back home. In May an archpriest, two townsmen, and a peasant from the taxpaying crown communes of Beloozero came to Yaroslavl. Minin dismissed the townsmen but kept the archpriest and the peasant to serve on the council.

The second national government had innumerable ties with the first one. Many of its prominent leaders came to Yaroslavl from the camps before Moscow because they would not take an oath to False Dmitrii III. There came Commanders Miron Veliaminov and Isak Pogozhii with many lesser boyars, undersecretaries, and prosperous traders. Men who had organized the first militia, such as Artemii Izmailov, commander of the Kostroma gentry Fedor Volkonskii, and the leader of the people of Uglich, Fedor Pogozhii, also appeared in Pozharskii's camp.

The Yaroslavl council had its own style, which was different from the one the council headed by Liapunov had adopted. The split in the national government tended to polarize the armies. Cossacks remained before Moscow; lesser boyars flocked to Yaroslavl. Courtiers were experiencing similar changes of feeling. By spring, 1612 the council of seven had lost what little influence it had enjoyed previously. The nobility earlier had shunned the national movement but was now not so sure. Pozharskii did everything he could to form a broadly-based national coalition in Yaroslavl. Such a policy was bound to affect the composition of the Yaroslavl levy. Unlike Liapunov's council, Pozharskii included more nobles and representatives from the towns. Boyar Prince Andrei Petrovich Kurakin, Vasilii Morozov, Prince Vladimir Dolgorukii, and Associate Boyar Semen Golovin were senior council members. Relatives of Kurakin and Golovin were serving the council of seven; Dolgorukii had been confined in the Kremlin with the foreigners until March, 1611. Prince Nikita Odoevskii, whose brother headed the so-called Novgorod state, Princes Petr Pronskii and Ivan Cherkasskii, Boris Saltykov, Princes Ivan Troekurov and Dmitrii Cherkasskii, the Sheremetev brothers, and others also became council members in Yaroslavl.

This influx of wealthy nobles had far-reaching consequences. Not having forgotten how they had been humiliated by Liapunov's council, they strove to acquire privileged positions in the new assembly. Their pretensions caused trouble and dissension in the militia. Open quarreling broke out after the Kazan contingent arrived. Along with the men of Nizhnii Novgorod, men of Kazan had taken the initiative in organizing the new militia. While still in Nizhnii Novogorod, Pozharskii had named Courtier Ivan Birkin a principal coadjutor, charged with recruiting and delivering a detachment from Kazan. Birkin went there as the Nizhnii Novgorod council's chief representative, accompanied by Savva, a local archpriest, and a number of elected Smolensk gentry. The nationalist government placed high hopes in Kazan. When dealing with the Swedes, Pozharskii always emphasized that the towns of the Moscow and Kazan "realms" were on his side. As veterans of the movement, the men of Kazan expected they would play a prominent role in Yaroslavl, but they soon realized their error.

In Nizhnii Novgorod, Birkin had been an outstanding figure among Pozharskii's associates, but in Yaroslavl Birkin and even Pozharskii were lost in the throngs of boyars and noble courtiers. Birkin came to the council and in the name of the men of Kazan asked to be restored to his previous office, but the boyars and commanders cut him short. If this had been an ordinary precedence matter, the quarrel would have been confined to the chancellery, but other interests were involved. The men of Kazan, Smolensk gentry, and Nizhnii Novgorod fusiliers, who knew him well, all supported Birkin. Boyars and Yaroslavl and other gentry were ranged against him. The factions almost came to blows. the Kazan party was ready to fight, until good sense at last prevailed.

Social contrasts were sharper in Kazan than they were in the towns north of Moscow. After Boyar Belskii was murdered, the town administration had passed to Shulgin, a lowborn secretary. Boyar Vasilii Morozov, the local commander, went off to campaign before Moscow and decided not to return to Kazan. Now a commander in Yaroslavl, Morozov received the men of Kazan coldly. Liapunov had known how to handle Kazan. In dealing with its inhabitants he spoke their language. The first militia leader had ordered the Kazan commune to stir up the Volga cossacks to fight the aggressors, promising freedom to those who recently had been slaves. Birkin was Liapunov's personal emissary in Nizhnii Novgorod. After leaving the town he was obliged to spend considerable time in Kazan. Like Liapunov, he had managed to reach an excellent understanding with the Kazan town quarter, but the nobility in Yaroslavl had no respect for Liapunov's relative and former emissary. A chronicler spitefully observed that the boyars "fobbed off" Birkin.

He kept Kazan abreast of developments in Yaroslavl. Acting in the name of the local authorities Crown Secretary Shulgin recalled the Kazan contingent. The order provoked a split in the army ranks. Thirty landholders and some emirs leading a Tatar detachment refused to obey and entered the service of the Yaroslavl militia. The rest of the soldiers went home. Birkin's failure signaled the defeat of the groups in Kazan that earlier had instigated the march on Moscow. Pozharskii had to be very patient in order to avoid further divisions of this nature.

Minin and Pozharskii did not ask the Yaroslavl council to grant them full powers. They recalled Liapunov's fate and had no intention of reviving a triumvirate. Pozharskii had no ambition to be a dictator. He was the tenth to sign charter texts, thereby acknowledging that nine nobler boyars and stewards outranked him. Kuzma Minin's signature was the fifteenth. Pozharskii's restraint mollified the nobility but undermined his unique position.

In April the nationalist council formulated a new plan to proceed against the foreigners. Almost all existing militia forces were to take part. The nobility categorically refused to serve under an unpedigreed commander. To avoid precedence disputes, the council entrusted the operation to another commander, Prince Dmitrii Cherkasskii, not to Pozharskii. Cherkasskii's past was murky. He had served in the camp at Tushino for a long time; then he went over to the foreigners, and was a latecomer to the national militia. He was, however, a distinguished nobleman and stood high on the precedence ladder. By offering him such an important post the council finally managed to entice Cherkasskii from the camp before Moscow into service at Yaroslavl.

In the depth of winter military activity was largely confined to the traditional frontier. Lithuanian detachments supported by Atamans Shirai and Nalivaiko tried to take Sebezh. Unable to do so, the cossacks made off for Staraia Rusa and Toropets. On the way the Swedes attacked Nalivaiko, who withdrew to the Antonev-Krasnokholmskii monastery in Bezhetsk. The appearance of the cossacks alarmed Yaroslavl. From Bezhetsk, Nalivaiko might proceed to Volokolamsk and link up with Chodkiewicz's army in winter quarters there. The Yaroslavl council resolved to prevent the enemy forces from coalescing. Commanders were instructed: "Move against Hetman Chodkiewicz and the Zaporozhians." The primary purpose was to crush Nalivaiko. If they succeeded, the commanders were then to attack Chodkiewicz.

Commanders Prince Semen Prozorovskii, Leontii Veliaminov with cossacks, Lopata Pozharskii with men of Smolensk, Petr Mansurov with men of Vologda, the remainder of the Kazan contingent, and Tatars from Romanov came to Cherkasskii's headquarters in Kashin. In April Cherkasskii set out on campaign, but his own unit harbored a renegade: Yurii Potemkin, one of the men who had murdered Liapunov. Changing horses several times en route, the traitor warned the Zaporozhians of their danger. Nalivaiko quickly withdrew west. Prince Cherkasskii made no attempt to pursue the enemy and returned to Kashin. The Zaporozhians remained undefeated and eventually joined Chodkiewicz.

Cherkasskii acted indecisively because cossack units loyal to Zarutskii were in Uglich to the rear. The national council hoped to avoid conflict and persuade the cossacks to serve in the Yaroslavl militia. Prince Cherkasskii was told to win over the atamans and escort them to Yaroslavl. His army approached Uglich. Four atamans came over at once. The others reluctantly took the field and started fighting the gentry but they sustained a defeat. Cherkasskii carried out the national council's charge half-heartedly. He did not pursue the Zaporozhians after the battle at Uglich.

The issue of relations with the cossack camp was a subject of protracted discussions among the leaders of the new national government. In early April, 1612 the council sent a communication to the Stroganov family in Sol-Vychegodsk. It sounded like a veritable declaration of war on the cossacks. Its authors painted the history of the first militia in somber colors: the Tushino atamans, those inveterate inciters to evil, and the cossacks with their leader Ivan Zarutskii had assassinated Prokofii Liapunov, placed the gentry in deadly peril, and engaged in robbery and murder. This had caused gentry to disperse from Moscow; next, Trubetskoi, Zarutskii, and the cossacks had sworn an oath to the Thief of Pskov. "Their original wicked counsel has caused the death of boyars, courtiers, and men of every rank. All over the country they have plundered and slain and seized property from the upper orders in their rapacious cossack way."[3] Those responsible for the broadside were deliberately trying to frighten the Stroganov interests with the specter of peasant war. Liapunov had invariably invited atamans and cossacks to sign important assembly decrees. Cossack signatures were understandably absent from the Yaroslavl rescripts flaying cossack banditry.

The coup in favor of False Dmitrii III had terrified many courtiers. Some were anxious to break with the cossacks and exclude them from the liberation movement. Minin and Pozharskii took a different position and their point of view won general acceptance. By June, 1612, seventeen atamans and cossack encampments had taken up service in Yaroslavl and become identified with the Council of the Entire Realm. The departure of these cossacks from the enclaves around Moscow for Yaroslavl had a considerable effect on the results of the pretender's intrigue.

The liberation movement involved the entire population of Russia. Ukrainian cossacks, Belorussians, Tatars, Mordvinians, and Chuvash fought side by side with Russians in the national army. One Zaporozhian cossack leader in the militia was Ataman Taras Fedorovich Chernyi, later a hero in the struggle of the Ukrainian people to achieve national independence. Pozharskii was keen to cooperate with anyone who might be of genuine assistance. He eagerly welcomed Captain Chmelewski and his Poles, who were destined to render outstanding service to the liberation movement. Ivan Pagalevskii and his Lithuanians also served in the Yaroslavl army.

Pozharskii was concerned when a courier dispatched by Captain Margeret and other mercenaries in western Europe appeared in Yaroslavl. The Polish command had dismissed the sturdy Frenchman when it broke up the detachment of German mercenaries in the Kremlin.

Margeret had left for Holland in the fall of 1611 and then gone on to England. His tales of fabulously profitable service in Russia attracted a small number of soldiers of fortune who were subjects of the British and Austrian crowns. They were ready to serve anyone who would pay them well. In their missive the mercenaries swore to serve faithfully but they did not specify whom. They addressed the note to "Great and Noble Princes and His Majesty." A communication like this would have been satisfactory to the new False Dmitrii, the Tiny Thief, or the council of seven.

Margeret, who had given himself the rank of colonel, expected to be welcomed in Muscovy with open arms. He was wrong. Prince Pozharskii had not forgotten how savagely Margeret had repressed the popular rising in Moscow. He referred the question of hiring foreign mercenaries to the assembly. Its members sharply rejected Margeret's offer: "We do not need hired German [foreign—ed.] soldiers. They are unreliable and cannot be trusted."[4] A secretary in the Military Affairs chancellery informed the condottieri in a letter that Russia no longer required foreign assistance because the people were united and now had Dmitrii Pozharskii as their leader. Stressing Pozharskii's importance, the secretary stated that he had been chosen for his intelligence, goodness, and bravery. As he was reciting what he had written he hesitated, struck out the words "for his goodness and bravery," and substituted "for his righteousness." The correction accurately expressed the relationship Pozharskii had forged with the national movement. Prince Dmitrii possessed neither lengthy pedigree nor high nobility, which were considered a commander's principal adornments, but he was wise and bold and above all unswervingly championed what was right.

Since the time of the Moscow rising Pozharskii had acquired a reputation as an eminent fighter for liberation. The nobility had to reckon with it. Despite his lofty pedigree, Cherkasskii had demonstrated he was an unsuitable leader for the popular militia. The intensity of the struggle made it necessary to set precedence aside. Pozharskii prevailed over more pedigreed commanders because he enjoyed the country's trust.

Minin and Pozharskii, the leaders of the second militia, bore ingenious titles. The more influential a sovereign, the more comprehensive his title. Pozharskii's title might have made any powerful man proud, but it expressed an entirely different concept. He was the soul of the liberation movement and incarnated the triumph of the representative principle. His unprecedented title ran: "Steward and

Commander Prince Pozharskii, Elected by the Whole People of the Muscovite Realm and All Ranks of the People, Military and Civilian." While in Yaroslavl the nationalists devised a new coat-of-arms. Otrepev and the other pretenders invariably employed a two-headed eagle. The militia came up with another emblem: a lion. The great national seal bore a representation of two lions rampant; the lesser court seal depicted a single lion. Since the Yaroslavl council was responsible for foreign policy, Pozharskii requested a personal seal with its own coat-of-arms. It was very striking. It was adorned with representations of two lions supporting a heraldic shield on which a raven was depicted smiting an enemy head. A fire-breathing dragon lay underneath the shield. At the edge was a signature: "Steward and Commander and Prince, Dmitrii Mikhailovich Pozharskii of Starodub." The head of the national government included the allusion to his remote ancestors, who were appanage princes of Starodub, in order to fend off charges of humble birth which aristocrats leveled at him.

In its communications to the towns the national council in Yaroslavl constantly reiterated that the realm must elect a lawful tsar at once: "Gentlemen, you yourselves know what our position now is, standing without a sovereign against our common foes: Poles, Lithuanians, and Germans, as well as Russian Thieves. Without a sovereign how can we deliberate about our country's major affairs with neighboring sovereigns, and how can our realm remain strong and steadfast in the future?"[5] "We must make haste to deliver Muscovy from the disasters facing it. If we have no sovereign our realm may completely fall apart."

The Yaroslavl authorities made concrete preparations for electing a tsar. They suggested the towns draw up special resolutions (called decrees) which their representatives should bring "so that we (the assembly) may have the advice of the entire realm in the matter of choosing a sovereign with general consent."[6] Striving to unite the nationalist forces, the assembly recommended no candidate for the throne and was content merely to call upon everyone to oppose the Thief. In Yaroslavl no one even knew the new pretender's real name. People dubbed him Sidorka, equating him with the cossack ataman.

The efforts to unify all elements in society affected relations between the Yaroslavl council and the chief Moscow boyars. Liapunov had pilloried them as traitors and proposed to deprive them of their lands. The Yaroslavl council laid the blame for the ruin of the realm on the traitor, Mikhail Saltykov, and said nothing about the crimes of the council of seven. Council members wrote that Liapunov had besieged the foreigners in Moscow and pressed them hard. Members of the boyar government otherwise would never have fought against the nationalists. Unlike Liapunov, nobles in the national movement considered it impermissible to exclude great boyars from the process of electing a tsar. Ivan Sheremetev, whom the council of seven members had praised for his zeal, championed this point of view with exceptional energy. Minin and Pozharskii were obliged to take conservative attitudes into consideration and were careful to remove unflattering references to the council in Moscow from assembly resolutions.

Some noblemen had sat on Liapunov's council but the church hierarchy had been conspicuous by its absence. Hermogen was annoyed and attempted to guide the nationalist movement in new directions, but his counsel fell upon deaf ears. Like Liapunov, Minin and Pozharskii showed no enthusiasm for inviting princes of the church to join the national assembly. Former Metropolitan Kirill was an exception. The authorities invited him to Yaroslavl in hopes he might prove able to compose the serious difficulties that existed between the boyars and the rest of the people. Churchmen had been highly prominent in previous electoral campaigns. In Yaroslavl their voice was scarcely audible.

Intractable problems arose as soon as the Yaroslavl council took up the question of candidates for the throne. Vasilii Golitsyn was languishing in Polish captivity. The influential Romanov faction had no leader, because King Sigismund was holding Filaret Romanov in Poland as a hostage. Filaret's closest relatives, Princes Ivan Cherkasskii and Troekurov, Boris Saltykov, and the Pogozhii and Mikhalkov courtiers, were active in Yaroslavl and had no objection to supporting the election of Mikhail Romanov, but the assembly would not name as tsar a man in Tsar Wladyslaw's service who was cooperating with the council of seven. Mikhail was in the Kremlin with the family of his uncle, Ivan Nikitich Romanov, who was working closely with the interventionists. According to the concepts of those days people were classed as adults when they reached the age of fifteen. Mikhail had barely attained his majority; allusions to his age did not help the cause of those advancing his candidacy. Many of Mikhail Romanov's contemporaries had left the Kremlin and enrolled in the national militia. Mikhail's partisans in the movement showed unusual interest in coming to terms with the council of seven. The national council was sure the election of a tsar would enhance the spirit of unity in the nationalist forces, but the desired goal proved unattainable. The electoral campaign in council served only to inflame passions.

With support from the assembly and people, Minin and Pozharskii energetically set about organizing units in the new militia, filling up the gentry cavalry, and enrolling men from the towns among the fusiliers and as tillers of the soil. By the end of spring the results were evident. The thaw was over. Mud had dried and roads were again passable. Nationalist soldiers were actively preparing for the long-awaited march on Moscow when circumstances arose that occasioned further delay. A sickness broke out in Yaroslavl at the very end of spring. Soldiers were crammed into huts in the town quarter. This factor contributed to the rapid spread of the pestilence, which assumed menacing proportions after May 15, 1612. It was impossible to bury the dead. The people were frightened. To calm the town, Pozharskii appealed to the clergy, who suggested a religious procession. The morning of May 24 Pozharskii led a procession from the main cathedral to the suburbs and traversed the town walls. The pestilence prevented prompt dispatch of the army to Moscow. Many gentry went off to their estates to save themselves from disaster. When summer came the epidemic ceased. To commemorate their survival, in a single day the people of the Yaroslavl town quarter built a tiny wooden church, which they called "Universal Salvation."

Minin and Pozharskii concentrated their attention on recruiting and equipping the new nationalist force, but they could not send it to Moscow as long as they were threatened from the rear by war with Sweden. The metropolitan and boyars who had surrendered the Novgorod Kremlin to the Swedes were imitating the Moscow council of seven. Moscow's tragedy was repeated in Novgorod. Envoys went to Sweden to escort a Swedish prince to Novgorod, where he would be placed on the throne, but they were detained six months in Stockholm. Karl IX died and the throne passed to Gustav II Adolphus. De la Gardie swore the Swedish government would honor its undertaking and send Prince Karl Philip to Novgorod, but Gustav, like his cousin Sigismund, wanted the Russian throne for himself. Early in March, 1612 he told the people of Novgorod he would soon arrive in person in order to discover ways to pacify the Russian realm. He said nothing about sending Prince Karl Philip to Novgorod. The Novgorod authorities were alarmed to think their so-called state would become a Swedish province occupied by the king's armies. Gustav's meddling ruined the diplomatic game de la Gardie was playing. It required considerable time for him to calm the apprehensive people of Novgorod.

Gustav's senior officers behaved in the same way in Novgorod as Sigismund's colonels had in Moscow. They lavishly rewarded boyars

with land for betraying their people. De la Gardie gave the chief commander, Prince Ivan Odoevskii, an enormous tract comprised of more
than 2,000 acres of farmland not far from Novgorod. Scorned by the
people, the Novgorod leaders soon became totally dependent on the
Swedish military authorities. Boyars and the metropolitan tearfully
begged de la Gardie not to leave Novgorod. They declared that if he
did so dissension would inevitably break out between the army and
the people; no one would be able to stop it and the people would turn
against Sweden.

The boyars assisted the Swedes in establishing dominion over the
extensive Novgorod territory. When persuasion failed, the Swedes
used force. All over Novgorod territory riflemen mowed people down.
Left to their own devices, border castles were unable to stand alone.
General Horn directed the campaign to subdue them. At Klushino he
had been at least partially responsible for the Swedish army's defeat.
Now in Novogord he was hailed as a hero. Ranging throughout the
Novgorod land he sowed death and destruction everywhere. Quick to
appreciate his services, the king promoted him to field marshal.

The defenders of ancient Oreshek desperately resisted the aggressors until no more than 200 out of 1,300 soldiers remained alive. The
men in the fortress garrison then announced they would become part
of the so-called Novgorod state. Tikhvin and Ladoga surrendered after
the Swedes brought heavy artillery to bear upon the fortress. The
Swedes threatened to occupy the northern Russian coastline. Early in
1612 Swedish Commander Monk delivered an ultimatum to the
commander of Fort Sumskii on the White Sea. He vowed he would
devastate the entire region if the Russians refused to surrender the
redoubt. Monk made no secret of his plans. He assured the Sumskii
commander that powerful Swedish forces would come to his aid from
Novgorod. He and they would campaign in the trans-Onega district
and move against White Sea towns. Supplementary forces would then
come from the north and occupy the Kola peninsula.

The Swedish high command was obliged to divide its army because
it had occupied key points all over the Novgorod territory and had sent
men to attack Pskov. This meant commanders were unable to find
enough soldiers to undertake an expedition against the coastal towns,
but de la Gardie did not abandon hope he might acquire the Russian
north with help from Novgorod. Minin and Pozharskii were fully aware
of what was happening in the so-called Novgorod state. Vasilii
Buturlin and Leontii Veliaminov, members of the Yaroslavl council,

were able to deliver a lengthy report concerning the terrible slaughter that had attended the Swedish capture of Novgorod. Refugees from Novgorod villages and hamlets who had refused to accept foreign domination flocked into the area north of Moscow. Information about Swedish plans to occupy the north and the coastal region came into Yaroslavl from everywhere. In April, 1612 Pozharskii learned the Novgorod authorities had suggested to Beloozero and the Kirillov monastery that they should unite with the Novgorod state and acknowledge a Swedish prince as their sovereign.[7]

The national militia was preparing for its Moscow campaign. Pozharskii knew he should never divide his forces, but the menace from the north was real; the national government had to strengthen its defenses in that area. Commander Lopata Pozharskii, the ablest of Prince Dmitrii's associates, and a detachment were instructed to take up positions in the Ustiug area so that they might help the people of Beloozero in event of a Swedish attack from Tikhvin. The Yaroslavl council sent an official to Beloozero with orders to construct a new fortress and supply the garrison with powder and shot. War with Sweden might break out at any moment. Cherkasskii's units clashed with the Swedes but then the latter turned to destroy Nalivaiko and his cossacks. Swedish sources reported that Nalivaiko, hard pressed by Horn, announced he was ready to serve the Swedish lord of Novgorod. When nationalist armies appeared, the cossacks retired to Torzhok. Cherkasskii made no effort to pursue Nalivaiko because the Swedes were menacing his rear. Nationalist armies were instructed to avoid encounters with them.

The international situation was becoming steadily less favorable for realization of Minin's and Pozharskii's goals. Sweden and the Rzeczpospolita temporarily set aside their differences over Livonia. Chodkiewicz was able to leave Livonia and conclude a truce with Sweden. The two countries, so recently mortal enemies, were in a hurry to profit from Russia's parlous condition and carve up the Russian borderlands. The Thief of Pskov for some time had been struggling unsuccessfully with Sweden. The camps before Moscow had recognized him as tsar, which made direct conflict with Sweden highly likely. When the cossacks had rejected resoundingly the Swedish heir's candidacy they had given scarcely any thought to the diplomatic consequences of such a step.

Pozharskii and other leaders of the Yaroslavl militia understood how dangerous it was for the national liberation movement to wage war with the Rzeczpospolita and Sweden simultaneously. They could not begin their campaign to liberate Moscow as long as an immediate threat existed that the Swedes might seize the Russian north. The far-northern region had been less ravaged than the area directly north of Moscow. If the far north were lost, the Yaroslavl militia would lose its main supply base. Pozharskii embarked upon a complex diplomatic maneuvre designed to neutralize the danger to the rear and at the same time to avoid confrontation with Sweden. He decided to initiate peace negotiations with the Novgorod state and use them to tie Sweden's hands.

Acting on Minin's and Pozharskii's proposal, the national council dispatched a special embassy to Novgorod. Pozharskii could have called upon a number of noble courtiers but he considered it best to entrust the matter to Stepan Tatishchev, a provincial gentryman who held a modest post as judge in the Monastery chancellery, accompanied by fifteen representatives from various towns and a host of traders. As they went along they were joined by a number of refugees who were anxious to return in safety to their homes, but de la Gardie was obviously exaggerating when in May he informed the king that envoys from Yaroslavl had come to Novgorod attended by a suite of 2,000 people.

Pozharskii knew the Swedes had not honored the terms of the agreement to elect a Swedish heir to the throne. Nevertheless, he charged his envoy to ask the Novgorod authorities to draw up a formal account indicating the extent to which the Swedes had complied with the clauses of the understanding. Tatishchev was to inquire when the heir would come to Novgorod and when he intended to be baptized in the Orthodox faith. In Novgorod the envoy openly declared Russia would never agree to elect a Protestant; all Russians of high and low degree would fight to the death to have an Orthodox ruler, not someone of a different faith. Minin and Pozharskii informed the people of Novgorod the national council would soon hold meetings in Yaroslavl to choose a lawful sovereign for the entire realm. The envoys asked Novgorod to send representatives, two or three men from each rank, to this assembly. Russia stood on the verge of collapse and ruin. Nationalist diplomats had to undertake desperate measures in order to obtain an alliance or even a truce with their neighbors. The obvious weakness of their position made success seem remote. Their sole remaining advantage consisted of the issue of who was to sit on the tsars' throne. The diplomats, though somewhat inexperienced, often played this card.

Fate brought a certain Gregory, an Austrian subject, to Yaroslavl. He regularly traveled to Persia and was on his way home. The national council decided to take advantage of his presence and initiate diplomatic relations with Austria. Pozharskii invited Gregory to a meeting and held a long conversation with him. The commander was aware that moves had been afoot for a good while to elect a member of the house of Habsburg to the Russian throne. Such a project had been under discussion in Moscow even in Tsar Fedor's time. When Gregory spoke of the Holy Roman Emperor's brother, Maximilian, who had been a contender for a number of crowns, Pozharskii hesitated only slightly before observing that Maximilian would be most welcome in Moscow.[8] The reason Prince Dmitrii was interested in a scion of the Habsburg dynasty is not difficult to grasp. The Yaroslavl government was seeking an alliance with Vienna in hopes of taking advantage of Austrian mediation to incline the Rzeczpospolita to negotiate peace with Russia.

Pozharskii held out the same inducement in his diplomatic game with Sweden. Recalling Liapunov's disastrous failure, he avoided direct negotiations with Sweden and made full use of Novgorod. Envoy Tatishchev strove to convince leaders of the so-called Novgorod state that the Yaroslavl council was on the verge of electing a baptized Swedish prince. The national leaders wrote that as soon as they learned the Novgorod treaty was being observed and a decision to rebaptize the prince had been taken, they would confer with Novgorod representatives and dispatch envoys of the entire realm to petition the king to send a sovereign heir and would pass necessary resolutions pertaining to "affairs of state and the entire realm."[9]

Tatishchev casually interjected another demand: the people of Novgorod should refrain from proposing that towns further north and on the coast be joined to the Novgorod state unless the Yaroslavl council was informed. It was hinted that if Novgorod and the Swedes controlling the city agreed to these stipulations the main purpose of Tatishchev's mission would have been accomplished. The discussions pertaining to the future election of a Swedish heir were nothing but window-dressing. A Protestant Swedish prince was no more acceptable to Pozharskii than a Catholic Austrian archduke, but such arguments had to be employed.

Envoy Tatishchev successfully concluded the difficult negotiations and returned to Yaroslavl June 1, 1612. His report produced a depressing effect on council members. He stated unequivocally that the prognosis for Novgorod was poor. If the council made public honest information about the Swedish intervention, further negotiations with Novgorod would be impossible. The nationalist leaders realized this and published a version of the mission to Novgorod which was not true and was designed for diplomatic consumption. The council declared: "When questioned, Stepan Tatishchev stated that the Swedes will not harm the Orthodox faith in Great Novgorod; Christians are under no constraint; everybody is happy; Prince Karl will come soon to Novgorod at the invitation of the Novgorod state, and the people of Novgorod will welcome him joyfully."[10]

On June 10 Pozharskii informed the towns that negotiations with Novgorod had started and asked them to send two or three men from all ranks to Yaroslavl at once to attend a general national council. They should bear instructions concerning election by the entire realm "of the tsar God grants." The Novgorod authorities had promised Tatishchev they would send plenipotentiaries to Yaroslavl without delay to participate in the election of a tsar, but their representatives were delayed almost two months. Finally de la Gardie permitted Novgorod to form an embassy and dispatch it to Yaroslavl. It was led by Prince Fedor Obolenskii and Smirnoi Otrepev, uncle of the first pretender.

Prince Dmitrii Pozharskii received the Novgorod envoys and conducted negotiations with them personally. During the sessions the envoys swore that the Swedish government had decided the question of the prince favorably; Karl already had reached Vyborg on June 24, or was expected there around June 29. Asked when the sovereign would arrive in Novgorod, the envoys were unable to return a satisfactory answer. They merely said that when the heir arrived the people of Novgorod would approach him and ask him to adopt the Greek rite. Pozharskii patiently listened without interrupting to Obolenskii's confused speeches, after which he made a remarkable reply. He categorically rejected any notion of having the national council dispatch envoys to Stockholm to negotiate directly with the Swedish king. Moscow, he declared, already had sent envoys in quest of the Polish heir and they were languishing in captivity in a foreign land. After the Swedish heir arrived in Novgorod and changed his religion, the militia would be ready to discuss unification with the Novgorod state, but Russia would never accept a prince of another faith.

Pozharskii was expressing diplomatically the hostility he felt for the treaty struck between Novgorod and Sweden. He declared the nationalists might not object to unification with Novgorod but experience had convinced him it was idle to rely on foreign rulers. Sigismund supposedly wanted to put his son on the Russian throne but a year had gone by and he had not done so, and "you people of Novgorod know what the Poles are doing to the Muscovite realm." Pozharskii ended his speech with a telling observation: "The Swedish king Karl supposedly has intended also to send his son soon to the Novgorod state but in these regions a year has passed and there is no sign of a Swedish heir in Novgorod."[11]

In a letter to the people of Novgorod Pozharskii repeated what he had said to the envoys. Nevertheless, he sought to foster their illusions that an emissary from the Swedish pretender would appear. He wrote that the national government would wait until the end of the year. If the candidate did not come to Novgorod during the summer when traveling was easy the people in all Russian towns would begin to have doubts, because it was "impermissible for a mighty realm to remain for so long without a sovereign."[12] Pozharskii was trying to sooth the people of Novgorod but yet let them know the situation was so complex that the question of electing a Swedish pretender in the weeks ahead might become moot.

The Swedish royal family had no intention of sending Prince Karl Philip to Novgorod or of allowing him to be baptized in the Orthodox faith; Pozharskii and the Novgorod leaders were engaged in a kind of shadow-boxing. The real issue was which side would reap the greater benefit from this diplomatic intrigue.

Pozharskii was conducting these discussions with Novgorod in order to accomplish several purposes. He wanted to avoid confrontation with Sweden, stop the Novgorod state from trying to subjugate north Russian towns, and bring about a truce on the Novgorod border. He achieved all his goals. The negotiations with Obolenskii laid the groundwork for a formal truce. On June 26, 1612 the envoys left for home, accompanied by nationalist representatives Sekirin and Shishkin. Pozharskii empowered these men to sign a truce with the Novgorod state: until Karl Philip arrived, Novgorod was to live in peace and amity with the Russian realm, not to absorb Muscovite towns into the Novgorod state, and to refrain from fomenting incidents on the frontier.

Once the danger of Swedish invasion was removed, Pozharskii set out with his main forces for Moscow. He was sure the Swedes would not attack the militia from the rear, or at least not for a while.

Chapter Seventeen

GOSIEWSKI'S FLIGHT

When the winter of 1612-1613 began the field of battle shifted from Moscow proper to the vast expanses around the capital. People took up arms in many parts of the country. The largest number of partisan bands operated along the highway to Smolensk and around the places in which Chodkiewicz's armies were spending the winter.

Sigismund's forces controlled the Smolensk highway but snow and partisans made it difficult for them to move along it. Armed peasants from the villages bravely challenged regular enemy detachments. Mercenary commanders felt alarm when they looked at quiet snowy forests. The forests suddenly would come alive; hosts of peasants on skis brandishing axes and pitchforks would rush out. They attacked soldiers stealing horses and fodder and disappeared as quickly as they had come. Columns straggling along the road could not manage to assemble in one place. [Thus, earlier in 1612, in February, Colonel Strumps, who had returned to Smolensk, and some soldiers came to aid Chodkiewicz.] Partisans fell upon them as they were proceeding; Struys lost many men and barely escaped capture himself. Peasants tore off his fur coat. The soldiers retired, abandoning their equipment. In March Struys tried again to force his way to Moscow. This time he got as far as Viazma, but still could not attain his goal.

Chodkiewicz pitched his camp at first in the hamlet of Rogachevo, some 45 miles north of Moscow. His foragers soon stripped the entire district bare and the hetman was obliged to transfer his headquarters to a better endowed area. Chodkiewicz decided to take up a position closer to the Smolensk highway. He repaired to Fedorovskoe, a short distance from Volokolamsk. Only a few soldiers managed to find warm quarters in the hamlet. The others were dispersed throughout various small villages. Some had to go as far as Rzhev, Staritsa, and Kozelsk in search of shelter. Partisans never granted the uninvited guests a minute's respite. They attacked the enemy in the hamlet of Rodnia in broad daylight. Caught unawares, soldiers fled on unsaddled horses without arming themselves properly. The partisans got their rifles and the goods they had stolen.

No matter how many supplies foragers exacted from the populace, they seldom managed to deliver all of them to the garrison in Moscow. Early in March, 1612 a big sledge loaded with provisions came out of Fedorovskoe, escorted by as many as 300 soldiers and wagon attendants. The detachment was not far from the camp when partisans charged down upon it from all sides. The mercenaries were more anxious to save their own skins than to fight and took to flight at once. Russian peasants in the convoy turned to help the partisans and blocked the road with their sleds. Hussars jumped off the road and immediately they and their horses sank into snowbanks. Those in front lost their carts but were able to push on a little further. The rest struggled back to Fedorovskoe.

Shouting and cursing, the advancing soldiers made their way to the tiny village of Vishentsa, which was buried in snow. They seized an elderly peasant and told him to lead them to Mozhaisk without going through Volokolamsk, where Russian forces were stationed. The peasant had no choice but to put on a coat and set out. The short winter day grew to a close. Although the Poles were exhausted, they decided to continue their journey in the bright moonlight in order to pass the danger point as quickly as possible. The peasant turned off a forest path and led the unit along a road going directly to Volokolamsk. The unsuspecting soldiers had not gone another mile before they entered the Russian army zone. Pure chance saved them. A Polish officer was returning to his quarters in Ruza; he followed and overtook them. Summoning up their last ounce of strength the soldiers fled Volokolamsk, abandoning their weary horses on the way. The mercenaries dealt cruelly with this courageous Russian patriot. They beheaded him in a forest. No one has ever discovered the name of the unknown peasant from Vishentsa. His exploit was by no means unique. The populace had risen up in struggle to liberate their native land.

The aggressors brutally attempted to smash the partisans. When spring came and the snow melted, those who had survived the winter beheld a dreadful scene. Corpses lay unburied in many villages. The Trinity-St. Sergius monastery assigned monks and servitors with carts to inter the remains of Orthodox dead. The company collected bodies in adjacent villages and then in outlying ones. The brothers uttered prayers in the monastery every day. A monk wrote: "We ourselves and Brother Simon buried 4,000; then on the abbot's orders we scoured the villages and hamlets and estimate that in six months we buried more than another 3,000." The winter had been appalling. The enemy had ravaged the Russian land, leaving villages in ashes. Women, children, and old people perished from hunger or froze to death in the forests because they were left without a provider, or bread, or meat.

When winter came to an end and the warm spring season began, the partisans fell on evil times. A large unit comprised of several hundred men who had been operating along the Smolensk highway all winter decided to make its way to Pskov and enter Dmitrii's service. In mid-May, 1612 they unexpectedly encountered Colonel Struys' detachment. Struys was well prepared; he had 1,200 soldiers and 3,000 Zaporozhians under his command. The partisans could not resist such a force and dispersed after a brief battle. Among others the partisan Ivashka, the standard-bearer, was taken prisoner.

After taking over Struys' detachment and withdrawing soldiers from their winter bivouacs, Chodkiewicz returned to the Moscow area. Aware dissension existed in the militia and that some nationalist commanders and numerous gentry had quitted the camps and gone to Yaroslavl, the hetman was minded to test Zarutskii's strength again. This time he attacked from the hamlet of Nekhoroshevo. At an agreed signal Gosiewski's soldiers made a sortie from Kitaigorod. Dug in at their fortified camp across the Yauza the cossacks and nationalist soldiers endured the onset.[1] Mindful of their previous defeat, the foreign mercenaries were cautious. They scrambled up the sides of the redoubt but fell back under the blows of sharp cossack swords and abandoned the assault. Their losses were minimal, but Zborowski, one of the best Polish officers, was among the wounded.

Realizing the end was approaching, Alexander Gosiewski and his mercenaries forsook the city they had burned and sacked. Before quitting the Kremlin the Moscow Elder [Gosiewski] insisted that Mstislavskii must settle accounts in full with the hired knights. His army deputies ransacked the Treasury chancellery. Nothing escaped their covetous grasp. They removed tiny, ancient gold icons artistically adorned with stone and bone carvings of saints, two small royal tables with gold inlays and black incisions, Shuiskii's molded silver seal, a Cherkassian cap, old shields and armor, carpets, pitchers without tops, and even fox furs that had begun to decay.

In an effort to keep the mercenaries in Moscow Gosiewski had announced several times that he would raise their salaries. Hetman Chodkiewicz retained Sapieha's men by pledging in writing that he would pay them for their service with the pretender, going back to January, 1610. No one bothered to consult the boyars. They were merely tendered the bill. The amounts assumed fantastic proportions. Gosiewski's assistant made an entry in the treasury records: "Dragoons are to receive 300 rubles a month." Among Russians the treasury had paid 300 rubles to no more than a handful of members of the boyar council, and this was not per month but for a year. The soldiers treated Moscow like an occupied city. The salaries they paid themselves had long ago become a legalized form of theft.

When the treasury was bare the mercenaries turned to the palace, the chambers of the Muscovite sovereigns, and monasteries. In the palace they tore out beautifully sculptored adornments from "the tsar's place," staffs, horse trappings, armor, and even from a massive inkstand they found. Priceless products of the jeweler's art were reduced to lumps of gold and silver. To compensate the foreigners, treasurers dug the gold out of palls of tsars' tombs in Archangel Cathedral, despoiled the shrine of the wonderworker in the cathedral of the Annunciation, and removed utensils from monasteries.

When settling up with the foreigners, the Moscow Elder made an expansive gesture; he paid them more than 300 rubles in cash from his private purse. His unexpected generosity is not hard to explain. The imperious foreigners, considering they had been victimized, threatened to revolt against their leader. The mercenaries took the tsars' regalia from the treasury and distributed it among themselves. Gosiewski and the soldiers leaving Russia appropriated the two finest crowns. One had belonged to Boris Godunov; the other was destined for Otrepev but had not been finished.

What was called the "Cap of Godunov" was set off with two massive stones sparkling with perfectly-formed facets. The treasury described one stone as an azure sapphire, the other as dark blue. It contained extremely rare sapphires mined long ago in Ceylon. One stone was valued at 9,000 rubles; the other at 3,000. Their real worth was much greater. The crown was topped wih two gold hoops, apples, and crosses lavishly studded with large diamonds, rubies, jewels, and emeralds. Otrepev's crown contained a diamond of exceptional size. It sparkled and threw off fiery rays of different colors in every direction. A truly remarkable emerald shone in a nest above the diamond. False Dmitrii's unfinished crown was appraised at 8,000 rubles; Boris' crown at 20,000.[2]

Besides the crowns, Gosiewski took a gold staff adorned with brilliants, two single horns, and other valuables. The authorities usually called on Moscow merchants who understood the jewelry market to appraise treasury objects. The knights did not. They entrusted the appraisal to a jeweler named Nikolai, who came up with a figure of 250,000 rubles. The actual value of the tsars' regalia was far higher. Adam Zolkiewski, who chanced to behold the royal treasure, could not contain his admiration for one rhinocerous horn. In medieval Europe such horns were considered a great rarity and only eminent persons were privileged to possess them. The hetman's nephew said he had once held a single horn worth 200,000 Hungarian gold pieces in his hands. The rarity he had beheld was badly damaged at one end. The untarnished horn discovered in the Moscow treasury was worth much more. The mercenaries took both.

The boyar government dared not cross Gosiewski and agreed with ill grace to surrender these items to the mercenaries before paying their salaries. The agreement contained no provision for taking tsarist regalia abroad. However, on quitting Moscow Gosiewski insisted the treasury had not paid his soldiers in full and announced he would take the regalia away with him. He declared that if the boyars sent the money straightway to the frontier he would return the pledges. Of course the colonel had no intention of giving up these treasures. The Moscow Elder had simply robbed the treasury. After they had gotten the objects safely abroad the soldiers divided the treasure amongst themselves. The crowns and other valuables were broken up. Gosiewski appropriated the largest stones from the tsars' crowns and the tsar's gold staff for his own use.

Moscow patriots managed to advise partisans about the time when the convoy escorting these treasures was to leave Moscow. A large band of armed peasants gathered in one spot and set up an ambush in a forest defile. When the enemy infantry appeared on the road, uttering loud yells the partisans broke cover and assailed the foe from all sides. Cavalry came to the infantry's aid. The peasants could not sustain the cavalry attack. Gosiewski ordered hundreds of prisoners impaled on stakes to terrify the partisans. Moscow was abandoned by Gosiewski and almost all the soldiers who had come there after the battle of Klushino. Sapieha's men and the soldiers led by Struys, who previously had participated in the siege of Smolensk, took their place. Hetman Chodkiewicz's chief duty continued to be supplying the garrison. The situation inside Moscow was steadily deteriorating but Chodkiewicz had to leave the enfeebled garrison and go again to Volokolamsk in order to collect supplies.

Zarutskii kept close watch on what was happening in the enemy camp and took advantage of the first suitable opportunity to pass from defense to offense. Two weeks after Chodkiewicz's departure he tried to crush the garrison the hetman had been obliged to abandon and ordered a general assault. Several thousand cossacks and soldiers advanced on three fronts in an effort to gain control of the walls of Kitaigorod. At the height of the battle reserve units struck on the fourth side. The savage battle now engulfed the whole fortress. The cossacks fought, showing contempt for death, but they could not penetrate impregnable Kitaigorod. Ever since Musovite artisans had carefully built the stone towers and walls of the interior fortress, no one had succeeded in forcing his way inside that strong place. The attackers endured staggering losses from cannon volleys.

The camps around Moscow were decimated. Unaided they were powerless to liberate the Kremlin, but Zarutskii had his own scores to settle with Yaroslavl. He had hoped to achieve a stunning victory before Minin and Pozharskii could arrive.

Once more cossack blood had drenched the Muscovite land.

Chapter Eighteen

A SPLIT IN THE NATIONAL GOVERNMENT

To proclaim False Dmitrii III tsar was a form of revolution. Immediately after the oath to him was administered, secretaries in the chancelleries before Moscow started issuing charters in the new tsar's name, but their enthusiasm soon waned. After years of pretenders the name *Good Dmitrii* had lost its earlier magic. Many Russians had long considered it a symbol of dissension, not unity. Those who had brought about the coup were deceived in their expectations. People in towns north of Moscow—Riazan, Tver, and many others that earlier had concerted with the camp at Kaluga refused to kiss the cross to the pretender. Monks in the Trinity monastery were convinced the oath was ineffective even in Kaluga, Tula, and Serpukhov.

In Moscow people had little time to rejoice over having found a sovereign. Everyone sobered up after the grand celebration. Cossacks and the humble people of the capital were forced to realize that the provinces definitely had rejected their choice. Hopes that the Thief might liberate Moscow proved illusory; in Pskov, False Dmitrii III could not even handle Lisowski. The consequences of his elevation soon became apparent. The Nizhnii Novgorod force, whose arrival was impatiently awaited in Moscow, remained in Yaroslavl, refusing to come to the aid of the enclaves. Minin and Pozharskii, the leaders of the new militia, made a show of force against Prosovetskii's cossacks in order to demonstrate once and for all they would not tolerate a pretender on the throne.

The coup in favor of False Dmitrii III caused division and trouble even in the camp before Moscow. Boyar Trubetskoi and the courtiers attending him were frightened and attempted to organize a conspiracy against the pretender. Late in March, 1612 Trubetskoi dispatched two courtiers, the Pushkin brothers, to the Trinity-St. Sergius monastery. Through these emissaries he asked the monks to help him conclude an agreement with Pozharskii so that together they might outwit their enemies "who have been causing trouble." Conciliar Courtier Vasilii Sukin, who was in the monastery, the local abbot, and the elders eagerly supported the intrigue. The elders sent Pozharskii an extensive communication containing a proposal for him to meet Trubetskoi "in a place God wills you to," and take wise counsel concerning "the sovereign our God will bestow upon us," since many towns had not yet sworn an oath to the Thief and the soldiers before Moscow "have not lost the great stone city or the fortress, or their discipline through division."[1]

Minin and Pozharskii displayed remarkable forbearance in their efforts to avoid clashing with the cossack enclaves that supported the Thief of Pskov. They rejected an accommodation with Trubetskoi, who had acquired his boyar rank in Tushino and enjoyed a reputation of having been one of False Dmitrii II's most devoted minions. Minin and Pozharskii did not trust him. They also knew Trubetskoi was weak and that Zarutskii, not he, wielded the real power and influence in the camps. Pozharskii also understood that if he made a swift strike against the cossacks' pretender he would merely unite them and civil war would break out again. He decided to bide his time. Ensuing events demonstrated the wisdom of his decision.

Ataman Zarutskii was in a somewhat different position from Trubetskoi. The coup had caught him unawares, although his agitation in favor of the Tiny Thief of Kolomenskoe had unwittingly paved the way for False Dmitrii III. The oath to the new pretender opened the way to Moscow for the Thief of Pskov. He was preparing to arrive in the capital and claim Marina as his wife and the mother of his child.

Heretofore the ataman had enjoyed unrestricted influence over Marina. Seeing him as her last hope, the queen had become his mistress. The resurrection of a lawful husband threatened to undo all that Zarutskii had achieved, but he was not a man to hand his mistress and his power over to an unknown wanderer and sojourner without a struggle. It was not only personal motives that made the ataman refuse to support the new Thief. Zarutskii was a sufficiently astute politician to understand that any attempt to foist the Thief of Pskov on the country would shatter the authority of the original national government. The ataman needed False Dmitrii III solely for the purpose of placing Queen Marina and Heir Ivan on the throne.

In mid-March, 1612 the militia resolved to dispatch another embassy to Pskov. False Dmitrii III's partisans insisted that 300 cossacks should escort the envoys in hopes of ensuring that their sovereign might reach Moscow safely from Pskov. Knowing his power depended upon the support of the cossack enclaves, Zarutskii did not try to prevent this, but he arranged to have Ivan Pleshcheev head the delegation. A former favorite of the Thief of Tushino, Boyar Pleshcheev had served under Zarutskii and was considered one of his supporters. The designation of Pleshcheev provoked the wrath of Trubetskoi and his co-conspirators. In a letter to Pozharskii the Trinity elders asserted that Pleshcheev (they omitted the name of his patron, Zarutskii) had administered the oath to the Thief of Pskov but had called him a miscreant and apostate.

Trubetskoi did not trust Zarutskii and Pleshcheev and would not make them privy to his plans. In turn the cossack ataman and his associates organized a conspiracy of their own without Trubetskoi's knowledge. No one knew what Pleshcheev and Zarutskii said to one another before the former set out. One thing is certain: Zarutskii was the real power in the force before Moscow. Pleshcheev, his puppet, would never have dared arrest a sovereign confirmed by oath unless Zarutskii had expressly authorized him to do so.

Pleshcheev's mission was complex. When he departed, the cossacks swore a public oath they would again observe the Pskov Tsar closely. If he was not the man he claimed to be they would reject him, but if he was the True Sovereign they would escort him triumphantly to the capital. The nationalist embassy reached Pskov April 11, 1612. Whatever his instructions, Pleshcheev moved cautiously and took no chances. He had no desire to place himself in jeopardy; when he bent over the Thief's hand he loudly declared the man was the True Dmitrii.

For more than a month the former Tushino boyar zealously played the part of devoted servitor while secretly preparing a coup.

It was easy to see that the pretender was distinctly unpopular among the people of Pskov. Mishka had quickly squandered the money he had found in the city treasury and then began thrashing innumerable persons in order to extort more. Citizens of substance, burdened with exactions, angrily noted that the Thief paid lavish salaries to cossack brigands, former criminals, and boyar slaves. The people of Pskov had invited the sovereign in hopes he would protect them from their foes. Even a trifling success would have bolstered his prestige, but unfortunately Mishka was totally lacking in military experience. His efforts to expel Lisowski from the Pskov area invariably met with defeat.

Seated on his ephemeral throne Matiushka displayed the same qualities as his predecessors. He rushed to live life to the full. On the streets his minions seized local beauties who caught his eye and brought them to the palace at night to be debauched. Matiushka caroused and publicly indulged in lewdness. The fugitive deacon was an inept pretender. Thousands of eyes were watching him; he needed constantly to concoct fresh proofs he was Ivan's genuine son but he merely repeated his oft-told tale, which everyone found irritating. As the months went by many realized the game was up.

There were plenty of disaffected people in Pskov. Pleshcheev found it easy to organize a broad conspiracy against the Thief, involving a number of senior commanders, gentry, and Pskov merchants annoyed by the Thief's exactions. In May the Swedes were besieging the suburb of Porkhov. The conspirators used this opportunity to remove cossack detachments loyal to the pretender from Pskov. Sensing something was amiss, Matiushka tried to flee but the people would not let him leave the citadel. The pretender was aroused in his residence during the night of May 18, 1612. Someone smashed in the gate. Matiushka jumped on an unsaddled horse and fled from the fortress in just his overcoat and without a hat, accompanied by Prince Khovanskii and a few cossacks. The fugitive was unaware that Khovanskii, who was spending the night in the palace, was one of the chief conspirators. Losing control, and not knowing the road or where to turn, the Thief raced past Porkhov and found himself on the road to Gdov. One attendant after another fell away. Some men's horses could not keep up the furious pace; other men refused to risk their lives.

Pursuers ordered out from Pskov soon discovered the Thief's tracks and had no difficulty in apprehending him. Like a prisoner the pretender was conducted through the city streets chained to a horse. The people of Pskov immediately confined Matiushka under guard to what was called his palace.[2] This happened on May 20. Pleshcheev dispatched a courier to Moscow to inform the national government that the pretender had been arrested. The authorities gave False Dmitrii III's partisans no chance to organize. Early in July, 1612 the council ruled that the oath to the Thief of Pskov was invalid. The brief reign of False Tsar Matiushka was over. In fear of uprisings government leaders at first decreed the Thief should be detained in Pskov. He was brought, under heavy guard, to Moscow only on the first of July. On the way the convoy was ambushed. Lisowski almost rescued the pretender from the soldiers. The cossacks in their camps refused to condemn the pretender to death but they fastened him to a chain and put him on public display.

The council before Moscow lost no time dispatching an envoy, a courtier, Cheglokov, and four atamans, bearing a charter of submission, to Yaroslavl. On June 6 the envoys had an audience with Minin and Pozharskii, in which they communicated the substance of the council decree: boyars in the regiments before Moscow, Trubetskoi, Zarutskii, and the estates (including commanders, courtiers, atamans, cossacks, ordinary serving men, and inhabitants of Moscow) informed the Yaroslavl council that False Dmitrii III had been overthrown. They swore an oath not to put forward another Thief and to renounce Marina and her son. They suggested the Yaroslavl government should straightway join a "universal council" in which all would work together in order to elect a tsar for the whole realm.

The appeal from the authorities before Moscow evoked disagreement in Yaroslavl. Angry words rang out in the national council. Its members were divided. Some called for agreement with the enclaves, whereas others categorically rejected alliance with the cossacks and the ataman. Zarutskii's opponents attributed the basest motives to the enclaves. The gentry observed: "The cossacks are trying to lure Prince Dmitrii to Moscow. They intend to assassinate him, just as they did Prokofii Liapunov."[3] Dismissing the envoys from the Moscow camps, Prince Dmitrii assured them he had no fear of or wrath against the cossacks and that the Yaroslavl armies would do their duty and come to purge the Muscovite realm.[4] However, the dissension in the national assembly tied Pozharskii's hands and he was unable to designate a specific time to start the campaign. In a farewell audience Minin and Pozharskii generously rewarded the atamans.

The elevation of False Dmitrii III had made it impossible for the national council to come to terms with the cossack leader. It publicly labeled him Liapunov's murderer. The pretender's arrest had no effect on the attitude the Yaroslavl commanders had developed towards Zarutskii. In June they sent rescripts to northern and border towns, again exhorting them to abandon the Thief, Marina, and her son. Minin and Pozharskii were making a final effort to undermine Zarutskii's influence in areas which had long known and supported him. They charged the ataman with appropriating monies the towns had sent to the area before Moscow. Members of the gentry had deserted their units, it was now explained, because Zarutskii had refused to pay them and had reduced them to penury.

The Yaroslavl council met with some success. During the summer Ivan Dubina Begichev brought soldiers from border towns and Peremyshl to the area before Moscow. Unable to reach accommodation with Zarutskii, he decided to seek redress against him in Yaroslavl. Appearing before Minin and Pozharskii, Begichev complained he could not obtain salaries from the national treasury and that his men needed supplies and were hard pressed. Seeing the poverty of the soldiers who had come with Begichev, Minin immediately gave them money and material for clothing. They were happy when they returned to Moscow, but Zarutskii regarded their appeal as tantamount to open revolt. He ordered cossacks to attack them. Begichev's soldiers only saved themselves from Zarutskii's wrath by fleeing from the camps to their towns. Pozharskii's refusal to negotiate with Zarutskii and the cossack chieftain's response wrecked any chance of compromise between the two national governments. Despite his deviousness, Zarutskii's services to the liberation movement were indisputable. He knew how to rally the cossack enclaves and inspire them with the belief they would prevail. The cossacks had been besieging the once formidable enemy for over a year. Ties of blood linked them to the Muscovite realm; no losses could dim their yearning for victory.

Zarutskii sent the Yaroslavl leaders an exculpatory letter and did everything in his power to establish good relations. His efforts proved unavailing. The charges the Yaroslavl council leveled against him infuriated the ataman. He resolved to proceed against those who had spurned his overtures. There were rumors that Zarutskii sent warlocks to Yaroslavl to harm Prince Dmitrii by casting wicked spells upon him. "And to this very day," a contemporary wrote, "that illness, the dark fever, lies upon him."[5] Such claims were baseless. They merely proved that the ataman had many enemies who wished him no good. Zarutskii was indeed plotting to exterminate the leader of the Yaroslavl militia, but he employed secret assassins, not warlocks.

Pozharskii recovered from an attack of epilepsy and returned to his regular duties. One morning he looked in on the council chamber to decide pressing issues. After conferring with secretaries he made his way to the square in front of the Military Affairs chancellery to inspect cannon on which gunsmiths were working. It was time to move artillery to the Moscow area and the mounts and wheels had to be in order. After inspecting the weapons the commander returned to the porch of the Military Affairs chancellery and started pushing his way to the door through a crowd, escorted by a cossack, Roman, who was holding his arm. Suddenly the man at his side let go of the prince, groaned aloud, and fell awkwardly on his side. Not at once grasping what had occurred, Pozharskii kept on trying to get through the crowd, unaware of danger. People clutched him, densely packing about him on all sides. Men shouted: "They have tried to stab you with a knife!"[6] A bloodstained knife was discovered beside the wounded man. Its owner, who had not managed to escape, was apprehended. From everywhere soldiers and townsmen ran to the scene of the crime. The accused was brutally tortured; he soon told his name and implicated his confederates.

Zarutskii had assigned the task of assassinating Pozharskii to two cossacks, Stepan and Obrezek. After arriving in Yaroslavl, these men must have been able to involve Smolensk gentry and fusiliers in their conspiracy. They had enjoyed Zarutskii's protection while they were serving Sigismund in his camp before Smolensk and stood indebted to him. Zarutskii had miscalculated. The cossack Stenka had met with a lesser boyar, Ivan Dovodchikov, a fusilier, Shalda, and four other Smolensk men, but their talks had not led to action. Zarutskii's emissaries next tried to suborn Senka Zhvalov, one of Pozharskii's slaves. This man had long-standing accounts to settle with his master and soon consented. He agreed to sneak into the bedchamber at night and dispatch the prince while he was asleep, but he lost courage at the last minute and refused to take part in the conspiracy. Then Cossack Stenka decided to assassinate Pozharskii himself on the crowded street. Espying his victim near the council chamber he unsheathed his knife and stealthily attempted to thrust Pozharskii in the stomach from below. Striking from a wrong angle, he missed, and drove the knife into the ribs of the cossack attending Prince Dmitrii.

The conspirators were tried by judges named by the national council. They all confessed. Pozharskii took the cossack Stenka and his closest confederates to the Moscow area so as to implicate

Zarutskii; the rest of the conspirators were sent to various prisons. Prince Dmitrii was unwilling to put them to death. Zarutskii's intrigue had backfired. His position was tenuous. The ataman long since had ceased to trust Trubetskoi, his co-commander, who was negotiating secretly with Yaroslavl. Trubetskoi and the gentry were now ready to sacrifice Zarutskii in order to obtain aid from the second militia and end the war more quickly.

Zarutskii was like a cornered animal; he could see no solution. Aware of his problems, Chodkiewicz urged him to defect. A scout appeared in the nationalist camp with a letter from the hetman, which he delivered to Zarutskii. The ataman made no reply but he left the scout at liberty and allowed him to remain among the camps as though he were in nationalist service. His secret plans became known. The scout had confided in several Poles in the national service. One of them, Colonel Chmelewski, sounded the alarm and was not afraid to inform Trubetskoi and members of the national council before Moscow about what he had learned. The scout was tortured to death in an effort to hush up the matter; Chmelewski was forced to flee to Pozharskii in Yaroslavl, but rumors that Zarutskii was guilty of high treason constantly grew stronger.

The cossacks had not forgotten the terrible losses of life Zarutskii had caused them when he conceived the notion of taking them over into the king's service before Smolensk. They had begun to lose confidence in Zarutskii for other reasons as well and no longer were willing to forgive their leader merely because he was exceptionally brave and daring. The laws of the free cossacks enjoined that an elected ataman should be considered first among equals. That had once been true, but with the passage of time no traces of equality were left.

The cossacks had passed a hard snowy winter in hastily dug earthworks. They were hungry and lacked clothing. They felt their ataman was indifferent to their concerns and had used these difficult times shamelessly to enrich himself. His exceptional services had rewarded Zarutskii with the own-ership of the extensive Vaga district that once had belonged to the regent, Boris Godunov. The leader of the enclaves had summarily nullified the June 30 agreement he himself had attested and besides Vaga had acquired other lands too. Minin and Pozharskii had reason to reproach the ataman with misconduct.

Zarutskii had diverted revenues arbitrarily from the towns earmarked for the national treasury and assigned his own men to towns and court and taxpaying rural communes in order to collect money and supplies. The unequal distribution of revenue intensified the want felt by ordinary cossacks and rebels in Moscow. Those who yesterday had been slaves, ne'er-do-wells, and serfs and who now called themselves cossacks no longer regarded Zarutskii as one of their own. Now a great lord, the ataman had become a regular boyar. It was hard to recognize him. The power and wealth which the doughty cossack had acquired had completely transformed him. Now a mighty proprietor, Zarutskii had forgotten anti-feudal slogans, but the mass of the cossacks was still attracted by them.

At the end of June the authorities at the Trinity-St. Sergius monastery tried to speed up the second militia's advance on Moscow. A cellarer, Avraamii Palitsyn, came to Yaroslavl. The elder conferred at length with Minin and Pozharskii. He employed his great oratorical skills, quoted all the saints, and finally wept as he begged them to make haste to the Tsarist City. However, it was word that new foreign armies had arrived before Moscow, not Avraamii's speeches, that influenced the militia's plans.

Minin and Pozharskii had to overcome substantial difficulties in organizing the campaign. The nobles assembled in Yaroslavl were eager to function in the national council and signed its appeal, but as soon as Pozharskii began assigning commands they became agitated. Boyar Morozov, Cherkasskii, and the Sheremetev brothers unanimously demanded that each receive the highest position. The council had yielded to them already when it commissioned Cherkasskii to destroy Nalivaiko. The experience had proved abortive and it was decided not to repeat the previous mistake. Minin and Pozharkii were to be in charge of the Moscow campaign, but as soon as report of this spread through the town, noble courtiers quickly began leaving Yaroslavl. Some wangled command posts in distant towns; others withdrew to their estates. All Pozharskii had left were his brothers, his brother-in-law Ivan Khovanskii, and the secondary commanders Turenin and Dmitriev.

In mid-July Pozharskii dispatched 400 gentry cavalry to Moscow, led by Mikhail Dmitriev, who harbored no aspirations to a high precedence position. A man of advanced years, Dmitriev came over to the militia in Liapunov's time and was well known in the camps before Moscow. He was instructed to occupy a position between Tver and Pokrov gates, where the camp of the Yaroslavl and Nizhnii Novgorod commanders had once been situated. On July 24 Commander Dmitriev reached Moscow and fought a hard battle with Poles who had made a sortie from the fortress. The arrival of armies from Yaroslavl precipitated the division that had long been simmering in the enclaves before Moscow.

On the night of June 28 Zarutskii ordered the cossacks to leave their camps and proceed along the Kolomenskoe road. But the ataman no longer enjoyed his previous unquestioned authority and his order was not carried out. Fulfilling their patriotic duty, most cos-sacks refused to abandon the position before Moscow. Even with the assistance of loyal atamans Zarutskii failed to attract more than 2,000 men.

Five days later Commander Prince Lopata Pozharskii approached Moscow with 700 gentry cavalry and took up a position between Tver and Nikitskii gates. The struggle to liberate Moscow had entered a definitive stage.

Chapter Nineteen

CHODKIEWICZ'S ROUT

Unaware that Zarutskii had fled to Kolomna, Pozharskii and the main force were advancing from Yaroslavl. He had just finished the complex negotiations with the Novgorod envoys and was now fully convinced he was not threatened by a Swedish attack from the rear.

Vast wagon trains and cannon slowed the movement of the national army. Roads were in appalling condition and cannon would fall into deep ravines or break through flimsy bridges crossing fords. The army had first halted less than five miles from Yaroslavl. After covering another thirteen miles the militia pitched camp again. While the force was slowly advancing on Moscow, Pozharskii turned over command to his two adjutants, Kuzma Minin and Prince Ivan Khovanskii, while he and a small retinue hastened to Suzdal to pray for victory by the family tombs in the Spaso-Efimev monastery.

Burdened though he was by a host of concerns, Prince Dmitrii seldom resorted to churchmen. Too many hierarchs had made common cause with the boyars in the enemy camp. Patriarch Hermogen had died in captivity still hostile to the original national militia. Isidor, metropolitan of Novgorod, who ranked next to the patriarch in the church, had entered into treasonous dealings with the Swedes. The metropolitan of Kazan had expressed sympathy with the national movement; the national council was disposed to acknowledge him as the chief prince of the church but the militia leaders never sought to bring him to Yaroslavl or to the Moscow area. The eparchy of Rostov and Yaroslavl had no incumbent because Filaret Romanov was a prisoner in Lithuania. False Dmitrii I had deposed Kirill Zavidov, Filaret's predecessor in Rostov. Minin and Pozharskii summoned Zavidov from the Trinity-St. Sergius monastery where he was staying, and restored him to the rank of metropolitan.

Pondering the future, Pozharskii came to the conclusion that support from the church hierarchy was essential to the national movement. Meantime in Moscow the metropolitan of Krutitsa, Pafnutii, who always had stood next to the patriarch in the capital, died shortly after Patriarch Hermogen. Pafnutii, Grishka Otrepev's former patron, had remained loyal to the boyar government in the beleaguered Kremlin to the end. Hearing of Pafnutii's death, Minin and Pozharskii were determined to make a man on whom they might rely metropolitan of Krutitsa At Sheputskii posting-station, not far from Yaroslavl, Pozharskii had an undersecretary take down a screed to Efrem, metropolitan of Kazan, in which he asked the prelate to consecrate Isaiia, abbot of the Savvin-Storozhevskii monastery near Zvenigorod, as metropolitan of Krutitsa. In the absence of a patriarch the Krutitsa metropolitan was in charge of the patriarchal residence. The militia leaders needed to have this office in the hands of a patriot. However, they failed in their endeavor, for the metropolitan of Kazan refused to honor Pozharskii's request.

After his visit to Suzdal Prince Dmitrii departed for Rostov to rejoin Minin and Khovanskii and the army. Ataman Kruchina Vnukov and his comrades came to the Rostov headquarters. The cossack council had sent him to inform Pozharskii of Zarutskii's flight and to find out whether the Yaroslavl commanders were planning to pursue the cossack army. Minin and Pozharskii rewarded Vnukov and sent him back to the enclaves with friendly words.

Many gentry from surrounding estates assembled in Rostov. Commanders dispatched agents everywhere with instructions to impress local serving men. As Pozharskii was on his way to Pereiaslavl a courier brought him unwelcome tidings: Cherkassians and Lithuanians unexpectedly had attacked Beloozero and taken it on July 30. Commander Chepchugov, whom Zarutskii and Trubetskoi had sent there earlier, had fled without offering resistance to the enemy. Pozharskii at once assigned four cossack atamans with their hosts, 100 fusiliers, and a unit of foreigners in his service to proceed to the relief of Beloozero.

In mid-August the militia struck its camps around the Trinity-St. Sergius monastery. Pozharskii had been detained there four days. An experienced man, the prince knew it was vital to have the cossack camps agree to a unified command before they marched on Moscow. The army could not have two commanders-in-chief at the same time. Boyar disaffection threatened the entire enterprise. An effort to reach an accommodation with Trubetskoi proved fruitless. The advance commanders informed Pozharskii that the capital was daily expecting the arrival of Chodkiewicz's army. After consulting with Kuzma Minin, Prince Dmitrii sent Prince Vasilii Turenin ahead, telling him to take up a position by Chertole gate in hopes of establishing a total blockade of the enemy garrison in the interior fortresses.

On August 18 Pozharskii left the camp at Trinity escorted by the entire local population. Monks sprinkled holy water on the soldiers as they passed by. Crowds urged the warriors to stand firm for their native land. In the morning the weather turned windy. Heavy gusts almost blew the aged abbot off his feet. Strong retainers had to hold both his arms. Gentry cavalry units were the first to set out along the road and disappear in clouds of dust. Fusilier infantrymen and cossacks were soon out of sight around a bend. Those who had been pressed into service followed the noisy crowd. Hundreds of wagons brought up the rear. The soldiers moved along, bucking wind squalls and swallowing dust. While the final units were leaving the monastery's town quarter the wind suddenly changed. Now savage gusts smote the departing throng from behind. The men guarding the wagons could scarcely sit on their saddles.

The shift in the wind was considered an auspicious omen which made it easier for the soldiers to proceed, and they unwittingly increased their pace. The force halted for the night some three miles from the capital on the river Yauza. Spies sent on ahead passed Lopata Pozharskii's camp and reconnoitred the area by the Arbat gate. The commanders proposed delaying the march on the capital for two days. By the end of the second day the whole army had reached the Yauza. Although it was no more than three miles to the city, evening had come and Pozharskii issued an order to prepare to bivouac. Some soldiers built bonfires; others cleaned their weapons. The activity discernible around the commander's tent was unusual. From the enclaves Trubetskoi had lost no time sending emissaries to invite Pozharskii to his camp. The cossacks had been more than a year before Moscow and had succeeded in fortifying the Yauza redoubt with high ramparts. Their camp contained many deserted tunnels, huts and houses. The Yaroslavl soldiers were welcome to occupy them. Trubetskoi's offer appeared attractive but Minin and Pozharskii unequivocally rejected it, for the idea of concentrating their forces in the eastern suburbs beyond the Yauza was unacceptable to them.

Chodkiewicz was approaching Moscow from the west; hence, Prince Dmitrii resolved to dispose his men in the western parts of the city beyond the Arbat to deny the foe access to the Kremlin. Political considerations led the second national council to approve Pozharskii's decision. Offices of the original national government continued to function in the enclaves, where their boyars remained in charge at headquarters and their secretaries held sway in the chancelleries. At the Yauza site members of the Yaroslavl government would have had to be content with a secondary role. Given their stance, to remove to a strange monastery was risky.

A year and a half earlier Pozharskii had left a Moscow in flames. The mute ruins served as dire testimony of the disaster that had overwhelmed the city. Nevertheless, the enemy had not succeeded in conquering or destroying the capital. Its inhabitants stubbornly clung to their ancestral abodes. Life went on. As soon as it was light the sound of axes was heard everywhere. It seemed as though Moscow had been invaded by a band of friendly woodpeckers. The inhabitants worked hard during the last days of summer to replace their temporary quarters with warm residences. Many smiths opened their shops. Markets were crowded. A sea of humanity clustered around whenever a hawker or peasant started trading from his cart. On holidays bells rang discordantly in the capital. But this picture of peaceful life was deceptive. The enemy controlled no more than a tenth of the city but the free areas were within easy range of Kremlin cannon. A puff of smoke would rise above the Kremlin wall and the sound of a shot would reverberate through the city. Now and again enemy units approached Moscow and the ruined city became a battleground.

Their experiences had tempered the Muscovites. No feelings of despair or doom were visible. The city had no room for the timid or the weak. Such people long since had packed their knapsacks and dispersed to the villages. The only ones left were those who were not afraid to fight and were inured to living under fire. Foreigners were astounded at the endurance and remarkable patience the people displayed. They would see a Russian extract a pinch of flour from a bag, moisten it with water, and make do with such rations. Resting after a cup of soup around a fire, someone would produce a pipe, another would start to dance, and a third would strike up a song.

When Pozharskii's forces approached Moscow, Trubetskoi accompanied by his courtiers came out to meet the commander. The encounter between the two men produced no results. Boyar Trubetskoi, the senior in terms of rank and pedigree, intended to adopt a supercilious tone but was quickly cut off. He was beside himself when Pozharskii, as was his custom, turned to consult Minin. The aristocrat's anger shone through what he said. The account is legendary but accurately reflects the nature of the participants: "Here is a peasant trying to usurp our exalted position. Is our service and zeal to go for nought?" The commanders separated and after this interruption the regiments were on the move again. Soldiers immediately set about constructing fortifications near Arbat gate in White Town. They worked until late at night erecting a wooden redoubt and digging a moat to surround it. A host of Muscovites armed with spades and other tools helped them.

The Russians were expecting the attack to come from Dorogomilov posting-station, the start of the main highway to Smolensk. Pozharskii disposed his own detachment in the most dangerous location. The units of Prince Lopata and Commander Dmitriev were on his right. To his left Vasilii Turenin's force took up a position in Chertole, reinforced by Artemii Izmailov, who had reached Moscow with the Vladimir militia. A decisive struggle was at hand. Russia's future depended upon the outcome. The people of Moscow and the soldiers showed an unbridled determination to fight to the death.

Hetman Chodkiewicz, who had studied the lessons of previous encounters, had tried to increase the size of his infantry. King Sigismund had sent 1,500 men as reinforcements. Some 8,000 Zaporozhian cossacks led by Atamans Zaborovskii, Nalivaiko, and Shirai took part in the attack. Chodkiewicz was in constant communication with the commanders of the beleaguered garrison, who were to fall upon the Russians from the rear at the crucial moment.

No more than three or four thousand soldiers and cossacks remained in the camps with Trubetskoi. No precise estimate of the number of men in the Yaroslavl army can be made, but since Pozharskii's advance guard did not exceeed 1,000, the whole army probably consisted of no more than 10,000 men. The core was comprised of gentry cavalry, fusilier infantry, and cossacks. They were supported by a host of poorly-armed auxiliaries. The Polish gentry besieged in the Kremlin scornfully told Pozharskii to send his men back to plough the fields[1]. It is true that the militia before Moscow included many peasants and townsmen who had no previous military experience. Feudal concepts excluded them from military service. But the war in Russia had touched everyone. Men in the militia were animated by an awareness that they had a great patriotic duty to perform. They were fighting for their country.

When night fell the Poles lit up Poklonnyi hill with innumerable bonfires. Chodkiewicz's army was resting after its march and preparing for battle. From Poklonnyi the hetman could strike over the shortest distance at Pozharskii's position or he could turn to Donskoi monastery and force his way into the Kremlin through the Transriver district. Trubetskoi and his forces were disposed around the Crimean court. He dispatched patrols to Donskoi monastery. Pozharskii sent scouts to New Virgin monastery. Fearing the cossacks could not withstand an attack by the foreigners, he moved five picked gentry bands across to the right side of the Moscow river to reinforce them. The morning of August 22 Chodkiewicz's cavalry forded the river near New Virgin monastery. One row of knights followed another. The rays of the rising sun caught the sheen of the knights' brilliant armor while wind ruffled plumes on their steel helmets.

Pozharskii was the first to attack. His cavalry charged the enemy several times. The struggle on the field at New Virgin monastery was protracted[2]. The hetman sent in infantry to assist the cavalry. Unable to sustain the onset, the gentry bands retreated to the redoubt. The burned-out city quarters were ill-suited for cavalry operations; Pozharskii ordered the gentry to dismount and fight on foot. In the afternoon Chodkiewicz hurled all his forces into battle in an attempt to breach the Russian defenses around Tver gate and the Arbat. Fusiliers entrenched in the moat and on the walls of Stone Town kept up a murderous fire on the attackers, who took heavy losses before withdrawing.

The struggle had become critical when Struys made a sortie and attacked the militia from behind by Alekseev tower and Chertole gate. Pozharskii had been expecting this and had kept back a large number

of fusiliers on the inner defense circle to repel the attack. They had
not been involved in the fighting with Chodkiewicz's men; knowing
how hard a time their comrades were having, they were growing
impatient. Demoralized by the siege and by hunger, the garrison units
fought badly and fled back to the fortress under the blows delivered
by the Russians. Another sortie the Poles made through Vodianyi gate
and along the bank of the Moscow river was likewise unsuccessful.
All morning the Kremlin artillery had been bombarding Pozharskii's
position from behind but when hand-to-hand combat began the Polish
cannoneers had to cease firing for fear of hitting their own men. During
the sortie the garrison endured staggering casualties. Colonel Budzillo
wrote: "At that time the miserable men under siege suffered the worst
losses ever."[3] During the battle Pozharskii's forces seized several
enemy standards.

The struggle before the Kremlin itself lasted almost seven hours,
during which time Trubetskoi remained completely inactive in the
position assigned to him. Zarutskii's flight had deprived the enclaves
of their one capable leader. The crisis demonstrated that the Tushino
boyars among the camps were utterly ineffective. Rifle fire intensified
until it became a torrential roar. The ground shook under the fire of
the heavy cannon on the Kremlin walls. Tufts of smoke obscured the
battlefield across the river. Chodkiewicz managed to push some
Russian soldiers to the bank of the Moscow river. Cut off from their
own men, they tried to swim across to safety. Those who managed to
reach the opposite bank were a sorry sight. Many had lost their
weapons. Water streamed from their clothing. The appearance of these
fugitives caused Trubetskoi's headquarters to despair. Commanders
of the units Pozharskii had sent to the Transriver district demanded
prompt assistance, for their men were growing exhausted, but Trubetskoi refused. Never known for his bravery, the boyar was concerned
only with saving his army from defeat. Gentry units ignored the cowardly commander's order. In full battle array they left their positions
and set off for the ford.

The cossacks were in a ferment. Some atamans supported Trubetskoi's decision. They did not care if the force from Yaroslavl were
defeated. They shouted: "The rich have come from Yaroslavl and some
of them do not support the ataman!"[4] Despite their backing Trubetskoi
failed to make the cossack masses obey him. Filat Mezhakov and three
other atamans made a blazing appeal to their comrades: "Out of
hostility to Pozharskii this boyar is destroying the Muscovite realm!"

Disobeying Trubetskoi's order four cossack units left the Crimean court and followed the gentry detachments across the Moscow river. The arrival of fresh forces numbering at least 1,000 men decided the outcome of the battle. Experiencing a sudden flanking attack, Chodkiewicz broke off and quickly withdrew his forces.

Pozharskii employed the respite to flesh out his depleted units. As soon as the sun set the nationalists went out to clear the battlefield and bury the dead. The moats contained heaps of broken bodies from both armies. Priests and soldiers buried their own men and removed the others in carts and piled them into hastily dug pits. The losses both sides had sustained were massive.

After this reverse Chodkiewicz withdrew behind New Virgin monastery, where he made camp. At this difficult juncture the Moscow council of seven and its adherents came to his aid. The courtier Grigorii Orlov arrived at the hetman's headquarters. A year ago this traitor had given information to Gosiewski and was rewarded with Pozharskii's estate. Now he was doing all he could to serve his masters. Orlov undertook to lead a Polish division into the Kremlin. At night 500 dragoons left the camp and trying not to make any noise tiptoed along the bank of the Moscow river to the center of the city. The enemy successfully avoided the burning walls of Wooden Town. Circumventing places where cossack sentinels were posted, they pushed deep into the Transriver district as far as Egorevskii church. Before dawn, with help from the fortress, from several sides dragoons attacked the cossack redoubt that barred their way. Taken unawares, the cossacks could not beat the enemy back.

Trubetskoi had failed to pay proper attention to a report that Polish infantry had appeared to his rear and did not try to win back the redoubt. His indifference encouraged the hetman. On August 23 he transferred his camp to Donskoi monastery and started preparing to strike at the Transriver district. But after the fierce battle his soldiers needed rest. Chodkiewicz lost a whole day restoring order in his disheveled army.

In the Transriver district Russian positions were less well fortified than in the western parts of the city. The walls of Wooden Town had been burned to the ground. All the Russians had was a low rampart and a ditch to serve as a first line of defense. A cossack redoubt was located beyond Serpukhov gate in the center of Bolshaia Ordynka. Built in a burned-out area, it occupied considerable space, from Ordynka to St. Clement church in Piatitska. The redoubt was constructed in such a way as to dominate the main road in the Transriver district, that ran from Serpukhov gate to Stone Town. A second redoubt, which had protected cossack positions from the Kremlin, was now in Polish hands.

Trubetskoi had refused to come to the militia's aid, declaring that his men had to guard the Transriver district. Now it was his turn. Chodkiewicz's army threatened an all-out assault on his position. Pozharskii had not forgiven the boyar for his cowardly, near-treasonous behavior but he had to think of the future, not dwell on the past. He came to Trubetskoi's assistance and in effect assumed personal charge of the defense of the Transriver district. Cossacks maintained a defense line running from Bolshie Luzhniki near the village of Kolomenskoe to the Crimean court. Pozharskii remained on his side of the Moscow river at the church of the Prophet Elijah in Ostozhenka. Commanders Lopata Pozharkii and Turenin crossed to the Transriver side. Infantry occupied positions in the moat near the burned-out walls of Wooden Town.

Pozharskii divided his forces just before the decisive battle. He had little choice. If the whole Yaroslavl army had moved to the Transriver district nothing could have prevented Chodkiewicz from seizing the Crimean ford and forcing his way into the Kremlin through Ostozhenka. By straddling the ford Pozharskii was in a position to offer aid either to his advance guard in the Transriver district or to the units in Chertole if they should be assailed.

At dawn on August 24 Pozharskii dispatched cavalry units to engage the hetman. They joined battle with Polish cavalry and the Zaporozhians in the field lying between Donskoi monastery and Earthen Town. Trubetskoi attacked from the village of Kolomenskoe but acted feebly and indecisively. This allowed Chodkiewicz to hurl most of his men against Pozharskii. In order to withstand the pressure brought by the Polish cavalry, the Zaporozhians, and the foreign infantry, Pozharskii committed all his forces. The Russians fought with frenzy. Even in retreat they launched desperate counterattacks. Around noon the Russians, driven back to the bank of the Moscow river, began a disorderly retreat to the river's left bank, but the hetman failed to take advantage of his success and pursue the fugitives: Pozharskii barred the way at the ford. Prince Dmitrii's own unit, in the words of a chronicler, could barely withstand the enemy. Pozharskii encouraged his soldiers by his own example. Poles saw him close at hand in the front line of skirmishers. In Chodkiewicz's camp a rumor found currency that Pozharskii had been shot in the hand during the fighting.

While the national militia was locked in this fierce battle on the right flank, Trubetskoi's units on the left flank were unable to endure the enemy's onset and fell back to Bolshie Luzhniki. Grajewski's Hungarian infantry and Niewerowski's Polish infantry set out to storm the central Russian position near Serpukhov gate. Cossacks and fusiliers placed cannon on the rampart and fired on the advancing infantry. After a series of abortive attacks Grajewski asked Chodkiewicz for reinforcements. This forced the hetman to wind down the fighting around the Crimean ford and dispatch men to Serpukhov gate at the center. The cavalry made haste to bolster the infantry. Having received no timely assistance from their own men, the Russians started to abandon the rampart. The hetman lost no time taking advantage of his success. He told Grajewski to push the attack far into the Transriver district and press towards the Kremlin through Bolshaia Ordynka.

For many months cossacks from the enclaves had been fortifying the Clement redoubt in Ordynka, which was even equipped with artillery. They manfully beat back the Hungarians and Zaporozhians, inflicting heavy losses upon them. Urging one another on with shouts, soldiers packed the south wall of the redoubt; they failed to notice that the enemy was forcing his way there from the north. The fateful consequences of Trubetskoi's decision now stood revealed. The dragoons who had just taken the redoubt by the bridge over to the Transriver district now hit the cossacks from behind. The redoubt's defenders took to their heels. The Poles seized a few cannon and hoisted their standard to the belfry of the church of St. Clement as a sign of victory.

Chodkiewicz enjoyed greater success in the Transriver district than he had won in the western sectors two days earlier. Russian contemporaries paid him tribute. A chronicler wrote: "He rode everywhere among his troops. Like a lion roaring at its cubs he ordered his men to wield their weapons more vigorously."[5] After a stubborn battle lasting five hours the hetman forced open a route to the Kremlin. Not wasting a minute, he decided to use his advantage and brought wagons loaded with provisions for the beleaguered garrison to the Transriver district. The huge convoy, comprising more than 400 vehicles, filled Serpukhov square and the whole of Ordynka to the Clement redoubt. When firing around the fort suddenly intensified the train halted, jamming the entire street.

Chodkiewicz threw all his energies into the attack. He kept receiving reports from everywhere that the Russians had been defeated and were dispersing along the principal roads. The hetman erred in assuming the battle was won. The Russians were not beaten. Driven back from the redoubt, the cossacks waited out the storm behind barriers and in ditches. They were looking for an opportunity to renew the conflict. When the foreigners raised their banner over the church of St. Clement the cossacks realized they could waste no more time. The Clement redoubt blocked the way into Ordynka. Chodkiewicz's wagons could not get by. Soldiers had to break down the redoubt's gate in order for the wagons to pass through and deliver the supplies to the Kremlin. The cossacks were quick to take advantage of the enemy's oversight. Creeping up closer, they rained down rifle fire. Frightened horses overturned carts and knocked people down. Benefiting from the general confusion, the cossacks forced their way into the fortifications. They cut the enemy down instantaneously. The mercenaries fell back and tried to escape to the hetman's quarters but only a few managed to return to their own lines. A band of soldiers was locked up in the church over which their banner continued to wave. Their fire seriously wounded a cossack, Mishka Konstantinov, who had run ahead of his comrades holding a standard in his hands.

The inhabitants of the Transriver district ran up from everywhere to help the cossacks. Hearing heavy firing in the eastern sectors, Pozharskii made ready for a new assault and tried to establish contact with Trubetskoi. He sent a gentry unit, to which Avraamii Palitsyn was attached, to the cossack enclaves. The Trinity monk was well known in the enclaves before Moscow and had been seeking to play the part of intermediary between the Moscow and Yaroslavl factions. The gentry reached the Clement redoubt, beheld many dead foreigners, and saw cossacks standing under arms. Reaching agreement concerning a general attack, Pozharskii's emissaries set out for a place on the Moscow river facing the church of St. Nikita where cossacks had thrown up a floating bridge resting on barrels. Palitsyn and the gentry did not have to cross the river. Rumors that the Poles had been defeated at the Clement redoubt immediately spread throughout the enclaves and the cossacks, needing no exhortations from Palitsyn, rushed in a body to help their comrades in Ordynka.

After noon, military activity ceased for a considerable time. Having dispatched 500 soldiers from Niewerowski's regiment to assist the garrison and having lost almost all the Hungarian infantry, the hetman was beginning to run short of troops. The severe losses lowered the soldiers' morale. One more encounter and Chodkiewicz was in danger of having no army in the heart of enemy territory. After losing the Clement redoubt the hetman hesitated to commit his surviving forces to immediate battle. He gave them rest and food. Chodkiewicz had not abandoned hope the fortress garrison would come to his aid but the men were demoralized by the severe defeats they had suffered at the time of the sortie. From the high fortress walls garrison soldiers saw Russian troops assembling in gardens on the other side of the Moscow river opposite the Kremlin. Bells were ringing in surviving churches on the Yauza and in the Transriver district. The tocsin encouraged patriots while sounding a death-knell to the men shut up in the fortress.

It was evening when Pozharskii heard from his emissaries; he decided to renew the attack on the hetman in the Transriver district. Commanders at headquarters who had taken part in the morning fray appeared exhausted. Experienced in military affairs, they understood it would be difficult to defeat the foe once he had penetrated the entire Russian defense line. Finally Pozharskii yielded to Minin, without whose advice he had not undertaken any initiatives for a long time. Kuzma volunteered to lead the advance guard and engage the enemy. At first his words aroused general amazement: a man without field experience should not meddle in military matters, and the elected elder was so old that a chronicler was moved to call him feeble. Even so, he was more capable of realizing the proposed plan than were the commanders. After the morning failure they were overwhelmed with weariness and doubts, but Minin was confident that victory was at hand. His fanatical faith inspired the others. When he asked for men Prince Dmitrii replied briefly, "Take whom you will."[6]

After a quick review Minin chose three gentry units that had sustained fewer losses than the rest during the morning encounter, to which he added Colonel Chmelewski and his soldiers. With these modest forces he crossed the river and fell upon enemy troops stationed in the Crimean court. The mercenaries had no inkling of the attack. They turned and fled. Observing the confusion in the enemy ranks Russians jumped out of their dugouts and burrows and launched an attack. Cossacks harried the foe from Luzhniki and the Clement redoubt, while fusilier infantry that had withdrawn deep into the Transriver district fired across the river. Cellarer Avraamii personally witnessed the bravery of the cossacks as they went into battle: some in bare feet, others naked, clenching their weapons in their hands. They cut down the enemy everywhere at once. The vast army could not withstand an aroused people.

Chodkiewicz's soldiers were afraid of the foe. Although the Russians had lost almost half their army and were retreating in all directions they still continued to attack fiercely. The picked units that once had defeated the king of Sweden had finally lost their will to win. Chodkiewicz could no longer expect to overcome the Russians; he could only make desperate efforts to save his equipment. The Polish infantry had great trouble holding the Russians off while carters were turning their horses around and trying under fire to remove their wagons to a field outside Serpukhov gate. Neighing horses, shouting soldiers engaged in hand-to-hand combat, and clashing swords drowned out the crack of rifles. The hetman's order was not obeyed. Cossacks descended upon the wagons scattered about Ordynka and destroyed many of them. They got most of the wagons, tents and other property abandoned in the enemy camp.

It required all the skill Chodkiewicz possessed to save his army from utter disaster. Russian soldiers, bubbling with enthusiasm, rushed on to fight and insisted on pursuing the enemy. But the commanders ordered them to take up positions in the moat. "There cannot be two joys in one day," they told the impatient men. Even after the hetman's departure crossfire did not abate for another hour. Puffs of smoke from the powder rose into the air. Frequent volleys shook the environs. From afar it seemed as though the ruins in the Transriver district were again engulfed in flames. Fierce salvos made the hetman's troops keep a safe distance from Russian positions.

At dusk Chodkiewicz withdrew to Donskoi monastery. His cavalry passed the night on the alert in anticipation of further assaults. Later the hetman transferred his camp to Sparrow Hills; from there he headed for the Lithuanian frontier along the Smolensk highway.

The defeat of the Rzeczpospolita's field army in Moscow was the turning point in the Russian people's war of liberation. Chodkiewicz's retreat doomed the garrison occupying the Russian capital.

Chapter Twenty

THE LIBERATION OF MOSCOW

The cossack camps had contributed to the victory the national militia had won, but as soon as the struggle was over feuding between the two factions broke out once more. Minin's efforts had furnished the nationalists with adequate provisions and clothing. Kuzma realized it would be difficult to retain gentry in the besiegers' camp during autumn and had lavished money upon them. The situation among the cossacks was very different. They were in desperate straits. For a year and a half they had been living in siege earthworks and rarely given money. Later they received no salaries at all. Their clothing was now little more than rags and their shoes had worn out. As long as the weather stayed warm soldiers could fight naked and barefoot, but once the autumn winds began to blow and the cold set in the cossacks grew restive. Their need for food was of paramount importance. Hunger drove them to seize supply vehicles on their way to the militia. The downtrodden ranks that had borne the brunt of the struggle with the enemy were annoyed as they beheld the well-dressed, well-fed gentry who had just pitched their tents before the besieged fortress. Not envy but desperate need compelled the cossacks to protest the privileges the nationalists enjoyed.

Trubetskoi's headquarters harbored people who were deliberately fanning the flames of cossack discontent. One such was Ivan Sheremetev. He had refused to serve under Pozharskii and as soon as he arrived before Moscow he learned that the decisive battle had been won. Though a member of the Yaroslavl council, Sheremetev put himself under Trubetskoi's patronage. Sheremetev immediately attracted to his side many Tushino veterans, including Servitor and Boyar Prince Grigorii Shakhovskoi, Boyar Ivan Pleshcheev, and Prince Ivan Zasekin. Minin and Pozharskii were alarmed at this sinister alliance. A year earlier with their intrigues these former men of Tushino had prepared the ground for the assassination of Prokofii Liapunov. Now they were at it again.

Sheremetev and his supporters were free with promises in their efforts to win over the cossacks. Declaring the position was unfair, they urged the impoverished cossacks to send men to Yaroslavl, Vologda, and other towns to reestablish the original national government in those places and arrange for supplying the enclaves with money, provisions, and clothing. The agitation conducted by the Tushino boyars intensified divisions existing in the national army and threatened to lead to civil strife. The danger became so great that Minin and Pozharskii adopted stern measures against the malcontents. Early in September the national council revealed the extent of their conspiracy in circulars sent to the towns, charging the dissenters were plotting to assassinate Pozharskii and that their agitation had aroused the cossacks once again to commit robberies along the roads.[1] It was difficult for two national governments to coexist in one camp. Reports from the capital again confused the sluggish provinces. On September 12, 1612, Prince Vasilii Tiufiakin brought 300 knights from Odoev. Not knowing to whom to report he pitched his camp behind the walls of Wooden Town some distance from the primary one.

The dissension that had ruined the original militia once more bedeviled the army before Moscow. The traitors in the Kremlin foretold the collapse of the liberation army. But their joy was premature. Pozharskii warned them unequivocally. Early in September he sent a message to the besieged garrison: "Moscow traitors tell you that disagreements with the cossacks have arisen in our ranks and many soldiers are leaving us. Don't listen to what they are trying to insinuate to you and are prompting prisoners to say. Everybody knows that many people are coming to us and still more will be arriving soon. If we should have a real quarrel with the cossacks, we have forces to array against them and they are adequate."[2] Pozharskii was understandably attempting to play down the troubles he had to contend with, but Avraamii Palitsyn described them quite graphically. He asserted that great disorder had arisen before Moscow. Among the hungry some were threatening to abandon the enclaves while others were proposing to kill members of the gentry and seize the property of those who had grown rich by appropriating numerous estates.[3]

The Trinity-St. Sergius monastery, which had spent considerable sums supporting the original national government, tried to employ its influence to stop the disturbances in the camps. The monastery's financial resources were exhausted; the monks had no choice but to dip into their stores of clothing. They brought out precious robes from hiding places, put them carefully into carts, and delivered them to the enclaves. Monastery representatives summoned the cossack assembly and asked the soldiers to accept the garments as a pledge. The monks then stated that as soon as the monastery received quitrent from its peasants they would immediately redeem the pledge for 1,000 rubles. The cossacks needed adequate food and warm clothing. Golden robes were of no use to them. Such a pledge did not relieve their dire need. The council decreed the objects should be restored to the monastery treasury at once. Two atamans went to Trinity bearing a letter for the abbot in which the cossacks wrote that no adversity or disaster could force them to abandon Moscow.

During the fighting before Moscow, Prince Dmitrii Trubetskoi had confirmed his long-standing reputation as an untalented and inconsequential individual. The victory belonged to Minin and Pozharskii. Nevertheless, the pedigreed Trubetskoi would not even hear of acknowledging the authority of a non-noble steward and actually insisted that Pozharskii should obey his orders. The Trinity monks tendered their good offices in hopes of reconciling the rival commanders. Abbot Dionisii addressed a long communication to the two Princes Dmitrii. He alluded to all the saints and sought at great length to convince the commanders to come together: "O pious Princes Dmitrii Timofeevich and Dmitrii Mikhailovich! Spread love throughout the Russian land. Summon everyone to love you by the example of your own love."[4] Rhetorical appeals to love one another made little impression on the commanders. Reality was more compelling than preachments.

The cossack camps had sustained fewer losses than had the Yaroslavl army and so they were the first to renew the struggle. Early in September cossacks mounted cannon in the Transriver district and began bombarding the Kremlin with fireballs. They managed to ignite the court belonging to Boyar Mstislavskii. His residence was located behind a wall facing the tsars' gardens in the Transriver district. Three days later they ran shouting to storm the Kremlin but could not prevail against its invincible fortifications. As long as the two armies fought separately they achieved little success.

Everyone by now was convinced that only full unification of all military forces would ensure victory. Representatives of the national council and the enclaves negotiated for several days until the two sides reached agreement. Trubetskoi had to abandon his pretensions. He could no longer insist that Pozharskii come to his headquarters to hear his dispositions. The decree creating a unified command enjoined the commanders to establish a new headquarters at a place on the

Neglinnyi river at Truba. The site of a new Military Affairs chancellery was the place where the commanders were now to meet and resolve pending issues.

At the end of September, Trubetskoi and Pozharskii announced to the towns that they had combined their forces in accordance with an agreement of all ranks of the people. There was talk that another triumvirate had been formed. The commanders wrote: "Now we twain, Dmitrii Trubetskoi and Dmitrii Pozharskii, aver that the Muscovite realm is in the hands of ourselves and Chosen Elder Kuzma Minin."[5] Trubetskoi's name came first. He retained the nominal title of commander-in-chief but his actual influence was no greater than it had been before. For all practical purposes the triumvirate was headed by Minin and Pozharskii, who cooperated fully. The triumvirs took no direct part in devising the instrument of reconciliation. It was not they but assembly officials who signed the document, mostly men on the Yaroslavl council, Pozharskii's adjutants, including Commanders Prince Vasilii Turenin, Mikhail Dmitriev, and Vasilii Buturlin, Boyar Vladimir Dologorukii, Prince Dmitrii Cherkasskii, and Matvei Pleshcheev.

Unification constituted a defeat for the former Tushino boyars. Pozharskii assailed Boyar and Servitor Grigorii Shakhovskoi, Boyar Ivan Pleshcheev, and Prince Ivan Zasekin as inveterate fomenters of sedition. They had served in Zarutskii's regiment until he fled. That decided their fate. None of them signed the reconciliation document. Ivan Sheremetev was the sole exception. He was too eminent; the nationalists had no intention of expelling him from the militia. Besides Sheremetev, Tushino Associate Boyar Fedor Pleshcheev and Courtier Danila Mikulin also signed. The noble courtiers Dmitrii Golovin and Prince Andrei Sitskii, former armorer Ivan Izmailov, Nikifor Pleshcheev, town gentrymen Ivan Zybin, Lavrentii Novokreshchenov, Berkut Bludov, and Prokofii Sokovnin, Fusilier Captain Ivan Kozlov, Secretary Ivan Efanov, and other officals sat on the unified national council. Yaroslavl and Nizhnii Novgorod merchants, who had played a significant role in the national council when it was first formed, remained at home to collect revenues and for other purposes. As for Moscow merchants, some were under siege with the boyars while others were engaged in trade in the provinces. Their participation in the assembly was no longer discernible.

Formation of a unified command stepped up the pace of siege operations. With the people of Moscow cooperating, soldiers dug positions in three places to hold batteries: Cannon court, Ivanov meadow in

Kulishki, and at the Georgiev nunnery in Dimitrovka. Bombardiers methodically shelled the towers and gate of Kitaigorod. Batteries installed in the tsars' gardens reopened fire on the Kremlin.

The militia had beaten back Chodkiewicz's attack but danger of another assault from the west still existed. Several weeks later Moscow was filled with rumors that the hetman had acquired new transport and was proceeding at top speed to rescue the garrison. Minin and Pozharskii lost no time fortifying the defense line in the Transriver district. The whole army turned out into the field next to the burned-out fortress. Using spades and picks, soldiers made moats deeper, and built a double fence on top of the rampart, which they reinforced with earth. Anticipating a sudden strike, nationalist units posted sentries on the ramparts in round-the-clock shifts.

Early in September Pozharskii had urged the Polish garrison in the Kremlin to surrender. He indicated their position was hopeless; they should not count on help from Chodkiewicz after his defeat, and they would die of starvation. Prince Dmitrii wrote: "Save yourselves; send men to negotiate with us. Your lives will be spared. May I die if I fail to keep my word. I entreat all you warriors. If hunger prevents some of you from walking or you have no vehicle to ride in, we shall provide transport when you leave the fortress."[6]

The Russian command's appeal was couched in proper, indeed polite language, beginning with the words, "Prince Dmitrii Pozharskii addresses a petition to all knights." The mercenaries did not appreciate Russian good manners. Their answer was rude and offensive. The colonels wrote: "In future don't show us any more of your crude Muscovite antics. Pozharskii, you'll be better off if you send your folks back to the plough. Let slaves till the land as they always have; let priests stay in their churches, and let Kuzma go on with his trading!"[7]

The haughty Polish gentry wanted to insult and degrade the militia leaders. They twitted Minin for being a trader. They scorned Pozharskii because his origins were humble and he held the modest rank of steward, and they called the rank and file militia soldiers cowardly donkeys and rodents lurking in burrows. The knights obviously had forgotten that these rodents had just routed Chodkiewicz's formidable army and inflicted a defeat on them. The garrison command categorically rejected the proposal for talks, alluding to their unshakeable devotion to King Sigismund and their chivalric exploits in quest of immortal renown. The knights' bombastic, boastful reply struck the Russian camp as ironic. Minin and Pozharskii knew that back in summer soldiers from Budzillo's regiment had come together and told

Chodkiewicz they intended to leave the king's service by the end of August. They would have done so, save that they were caught in a trap.

Writing to the king, the mercenaries cleared up a mystery surrounding what was left of the tsars' treasure in Moscow: "Leaving the capital, our brothers were ready to take regalia required for coronation in this realm and other valuables in payment for their services."[8] The authors of the letters went on to say: "But we pledged these objects to the hetman." This was a clumsy attempt to implicate men who were no longer in Moscow. Gosiewski had not merely planned; he had actually removed the most valuable crowns. All that was left for the knights who took his place were some less valuable items like Ivan the Terrible's crowns. The knights, who boasted of their devotion to the king, had stolen treasure that should have been the property of Wladyslaw after he was crowned. With brazen impudence they hinted that Sigismund would need tsaric regalia at his son's coronation and suggested their sovereign should issue instructions to redeem the items from them by paying the money due them.

The mercenaries were not interested in historical objects. Since the days of Ivan Kalita, grand princes had bequeathed a golden cap along with the principality to their successors. The Austrian envoy Herberstein had seen Vasilii III wearing it. This was the oldest Muscovite crown. It was circular and completely covered with gold coins. Whenever a prince moved his head the coins would chink quietly. At the destruction of Moscow the treasury lost the Cap for good. Its fate was sealed the moment the soldiers caught sight of it. They appropriated the coins; the cap itself was discarded as useless junk. The impoverished Polish gentry, who sold their services to the highest bidder, coveted the treasure, which up to then they had beheld only from afar. Greed, not devotion to the king, made them refuse to capitulate. If they did so they would at once lose the wealth they had illegally acquired. After looting the Treasury Chancellery, the aggressors decided to live off the possessions of their Russian allies and supporters. As a result of the protracted siege only a handful of Russians were left in Kitaigorod and the Kremlin. Anyone who wished had a chance to go over to the militia. One had merely to climb over the fortress wall to reach the other camp. The Kremlin contained only a few men still loyal to King Sigismund III.

The garrison commanders had wanted to hold boyar families, gentry, and merchants as hostages in the Kremlin, but when famine broke out in the fortress Colonel Struys decided to get rid of these supernumeraries. Fedor Andronov and Ivan Bezobrazov agreed to implement the order. Accompanied by soldiers they visited homes of boyars and merchants in the Kremlin and conducted a general survey. On leaving someone's home the mercenaries would take old men, women, and children with them. A large crowd was soon assembled in the square, which was rent with weeping and wailing. Life may have been harsh in the beleaguered city but uncertainty inspired even greater fear. From the outset of the siege the patriarch and the lay authorities incessantly had impressed on the besieged that cossacks and boyar slaves were waiting for the opportunity to filch wealth from the rich and snatch away their wives and children. Alarmed for those dear to them, Mstislavskii and other members of the boyar government sent a special delegation to Minin and Pozharskii to entreat the nationalists to receive members of their families with honor.

As early as Liapunov's time cossacks and the Moscow commons had been demanding condign punishment for treacherous boyars and their families. As soon as the cossacks learned there were plans to remove the boyar families from the Kremlin they proposed confiscating their property, the usual way traitors had been dealt with since time immemorial. Feudal chroniclers have sternly indicted the cossacks and slaves, ascribing to them the intention of killing members of boyar families, but this is an unfair slander on the soldiers. Pozharskii was careful to welcome the boyar families with appropriate honors. He came to the fortress gate in person and escorted a throng of women and children to the nationalist camp. The fugitives were distributed among nationalist gentry and people from the town quarter in accordance with kinship and condition. It goes without saying that none of their wealth was left.

After the Russian families had departed the Kremlin, the colonels ordered a general requisitioning of supplies. After inspecting homes, the mercenaries took food, gold, silver, jewels, velvet and other valuables from the Russians. The aggressors showed no mercy to merchants and gentry. They were more polite to boyars and higher churchmen but plundered them too.

Patriarch Hermogen did not survive the second siege. He died in captivity under guard on February 17, 1612. His successor was the Greek, Arsenios, who had served as archbishop in charge of the tsarist tombs in the Cathedral of the Archangel. This foreigner had sought fame and fortune in Russia. Byzantine prelates acquainted with him referred to him as a dishonorable and covetous man. Arsenios had served Gosiewski faithfully and honestly. He had urged the defenders of Smolensk to surrender and cursed the patriots. But his treachery had not brought him the expected rewards. The day came when the Greek would write bitterly in his diary: "Elder Struys, soldiers, and Russians associated with Fedor Andronov and Ivan Bezobrazov have expelled helpless people, the old, women, boys, and girls, from Moscow, and have requisitioned the Russians' provisions and other items such as silver, gold, woven gold and silk garments. They also have appropriated the revenues of the most blessed archbishop of Archangel Cathedral, as well as many of his appurtenances and his money."[9]

By early September famine in the Kremlin had assumed catastrophic proportions. Its first victims were the Russian people, who lacked access to any food. Next it was the dragoons and the foreign mercenaries. The price of goods rose to unprecedented heights. An oxhide sold for one and a half rubles and then for three rubles. A small loaf of bread cost more than three rubles. Eventually there was no more bread and people would pay approximately a ruble for a tiny piece of swan. Famished men devoured dogs and cats. They scoured meadows and yards in search of swans and nettles and stripped bark from trees. Soon the first instances of cannibalism were observed. A foreign merchant returning home from service in the Cathedral of the Dormition pulled a sack out of a pit. He shook it open and out fell human heads and legs.

After September 4 the soldiers the hetman had introduced into the Kremlin started dying of starvation. They had come without supplies or money and the colonels in effect threw them to the wolves. Witnesses reported that the new infantry died almost to a man during the first weeks of the famine. Early in October snow fell and grass and roots that had survived here and there were buried under the drifts. Even a mouse was now considered a rare delicacy and people would pay something like a ruble for a dead crow. It was no longer safe for Russians to leave their homes. At night mercenaries would fall upon them and slay and eat them. In an effort to prevent the garrison from succumbing to utter disaster the colonels resorted to measures that confounded even those who had seen every kind of rapine. They had captives brought out from prisons, beaten to death, and allowed the dragoons to devour the corpses.

Cannibalism did not save the mercenaries; it merely compounded the misery. First it was prisoners; then soldiers maddened by hunger started killing each other. The bodies were hacked to pieces and salted down in barrels. Colonel Budzillo noted that on days when hunger was acute his "infantry devoured itself, hunted others down, and ate them."[10] This admission is highly significant because it emanates from one of the commanders of the beleaguered garrison. The hoary Kremlin walls witnessed frightful scenes. The strong devoured the weak. Soldiers fought over corpses. As soon as a dead man's comrades in his platoon were preparing to devour his body, his relatives would show up to claim it. A referee would first try to adjudicate among the contenders but then would fall silent when he beheld eyes blazing with frenzy. Seizing an opportune moment he would run away because he feared that those annoyed with his decision might eat him too. To save themselves from death some soldiers tried to clamber over the fortress walls and surrender. They had to escape after dark and many of them were dashed to pieces falling off the wall or died under the blows of night sentries apprehending an attack.

Augmented by Niewerowski's infantry, the Polish garrison had amounted to some 3,000 men. Two months later no more than 1,500 were left and they had lost their ability to fight. The mercenaries were utterly demoralized and in total disarray. What had once been an army was now a gang of predators and cannibals who killed friends not enemies. The Moscow boyars, the aggressors' allies, feared for their lives. Bandits even assailed the head of the council of seven. Two soldiers burst into Mstislavskii's residence and made a shambles of the place, searching for food. The boyar tried to reason with them but received a blow to the head that nearly killed him. Struys ordered the robbers hanged because they had gone too far, but their execution did not improve the situation.

The thugs had no idea that by striking Mstislavskii they were rendering him an inestimable service. This accomplice of the foreign aggressors used the incident to portray himself to his fellow countrymen as a victim. Shortly afterwards Mstislavskii informed Pozharskii he was being held in the Kremlin against his will: "Foreigners have struck me with pieces of iron and wounded me in the head in numerous places."[11] He was lying, even about minor details. His wounds were caused by brick shards, not pieces of iron. This memorable blow brought the appanage prince to his senses and put an end to the council of seven's inglorious history.

Archbishop Arsenios had fawned on Gosiewski as much as he had on Mstislavskii. His hope of receiving ample rewards was ultimately dashed when soldiers confiscated much of his property. Faint with hunger and afraid the aggressors might devour him, the bishop devised a scheme to deliver himself from inevitable retribution. One morning he informed his cellmate, Elder Kirill, that he had experienced nocturnal visions in which a remarkable man had visited and spoken at length with him. The heavenly envoy had explained to the anchorite that God Himself had heard Arsenios' prayers and would deliver the Muscovites from the tyranny of the hostile Latins.

If Arsenios actually prayed for anyone during the siege it would have been for the Latins, but Kirill was so simple that he took the bishop's affirmation seriously. After discussing the appearance of the "remarkable man" the friends both came to the conclusion that none other than the shade of Sergii of Radonezh had visited their cell. Nothing more splendid could be imagined. Sergii had founded the Trinity-St. Sergius monastery that had taken a prominent part in the national liberation movement. Arsenios intended to employ this contrivance in order to avoid a charge of treason and to win influential intercessors on his behalf among the Trinity monks.

As long as they remained in the Kremlin, Mstislavskii and Arsenios bent over backwards to prove their devotion to the aggressors. Some members of the council of seven were less cautious and suffered accordingly. Colonel Struys placed Boyar Prince Ivan Golitsyn under house arrest. The disaffected fell silent, but not for long. As soon as they felt the sting of want the so-called leaders at once insisted the Kremlin should be surrendered. Only Ivan Bezobrazov and Fedor Andronov, who feared the vengeance awaiting them, continued urging the Poles to hold out even if it meant the destruction of the garrison. Struys and his attendants had not been inclined to listen to the boyars, but as soon as all available supplies were used up they sang a different tune. The Poles suggested the commanders initiate discussions and they sent Colonel Budzillo as a hostage to the militia. On October 22, 1612 Pozharskii sent Commander Vasilii Buturlin as a hostage to the Kremlin. The talks produced no results. The Russians insisted on unconditional surrender, whereas the knights, who still preserved a few traces of their former honor, demanded various concessions.

The cossacks and the rank and file were furious when they learned the mercenaries were asking for concessions. A Polish witness declared that the Muscovites were annoyed because the knights and their captains were spinning out the parleys and stalling while they waited for the king's armies to appear. No one knows how long these fruitless negotiations would have dragged on if the people had not taken a hand. The cossacks were the first to lose patience. Ringing bells and raising their standards they marched in full force to Kitaigorod. Their action took the foreigners and the Russian commanders by surprise. A chronicler reported that when the commanders met to negotiate with the enemy someone called out the cossacks stationed in Ivanov meadow by All-saints church at Kulishki.[12] Colonel Budzillo noted that the Russians activated one of Trubetskoi's batteries.

The cossacks made numerous assaults on Kitaigorod, losing many men, but this time fortune favored them. Setting up ladders, soldiers scrambled over many places in the fortress wall. The mercenaries were terrified at their ferocity. Some were killed on the spot; those who had any strength left managed to hide in the Kremlin. This defeat completely sapped the garrison's morale. The colonels lost no time arranging to surrender. This time it was Colonel Struys who led the delegation from the garrison while Mstislavskii represented the boyar government. They left the Kremlin and encountered tribulation in a meeting with Pozharskii and Trubetskoi. Abandoning his previous arrogant attitude, Mstislavskii admitted his errors in a petition to the entire realm.

In an alley by the smoking Kremlin wall Pozharskii came to an agreement with the boyar government that determined the future of the tsarist throne. Compromise was inevitable. Unless they reached an understanding with the nobility, the national leaders could not achieve their original goal, which was to elect a sovereign from among the great boyars who were native Russians. They had no choice but to make peace with the boyar council. The danger from abroad drastically curtailed their freedom of maneuvre. They kept hearing that extensive military preparations were underway in the Rzeczpospolita. Heir Wladyslaw was planning a campaign to occupy the Muscovite throne. Russia could not finally rid itself of foreign tsars as long as the boyar council considered Wladyslaw the legitimate ruler of the realm.

After three days of negotiations the nationalist chiefs and the boyar government concluded a treaty and attested it with an oath. The boyars were guaranteed their patrimonial estates would be safe. In making this concession to the nobles the militia leaders secured an enormous political benefit. The boyar council, the monarchy's highest body, agreed to abjure the oath its members had sworn to Wladyslaw and break off relations with Sigismund III. The national commanders paid lip-service to the fiction that the foreigners had constrained the boyars against their will during the entire siege of Moscow.

The treaty provided that boyars, courtiers, secretaries, merchants, and others who had stayed with the foreigners in the Kremlin

immediately should return the money and valuables removed from the
crown treasury or from the realm. The dispositions Wladyslaw and
Sigismund had made were declared null and void. This was the undertaking Russians negotiated with Russians. The agreement with the
foreign garrison consisted of a single clause. Budzillo wrote: "We had
to come to terms with the Russians without any concessions save that
they would allow us to live."[13] This meant unconditional surrender.

On October 26, 1612 the mercenaries let the boyars and other Russians leave the Kremlin. A heavy iron gate screeched open and the band
of renegades appeared on the stone Trinity bridge. Mstislavskii led the
way, a bandage around his head and supported on both sides. Ivan
Vorotynskii, Ivan Romanov, and his nephew Mikhail followed closely. The boyars were afraid of the angry people and kept tightly together
like a flock of frightened sheep. Behind the nobles men resembling
living skeletons crawled out. Hunger had robbed them of strength and
even of human appearance. From the high stone bridge the boyars carefully scrutinized the national commanders on horseback and the gentry
units standing close behind them. Pozharskii had promised the boyars
they would be safe. They could rely on him, but Pozharskii could not
control everything.

At a distance from the bridge the bank of the Neglinnyi river was
packed with cossacks and the Moscow commons as far as the eye could
see. The cossack units had turned out to encounter Mstislavskii in full
panoply, their banners unfurled. As the boyars proceeded along the
bridge the menacing cries of the crowd grew louder. These traitors had
burned down Moscow; now they should receive the punishment they
deserved. The people longed to settle accounts with those responsible
for their anguish. The pitiable throng on the bridge walked more and
more slowly and finally stopped altogether. Pozharskii made no move;
as was his custom, he had decided to wait things out. Gradually
passions began to cool. The cossacks kept on shouting and brandishing
weapons for a fairly long time. Then they grew quiet. The boyars had
survived.

The following morning the enemy garrison surrendered to the
national commanders. Soldiers from Struys' regiment were escorted
by Trubetskoi's detachments into Kitaigorod, where cossacks disarmed them. Budzillo and his men, who originally had come to Russia
with Jan Sapieha, went from the Kremlin to White Town, where they
surrendered to Pozharskii. The garrison commander, Colonel Struys,
fearing for his life, remained as long as he could in Godunov's old

court, guarded by retainers. He surrendered there to the commanders. Regimental ensigns were turned downwards in the center of the square, where muskets, swords, and halberds that had belonged to the surrendered soldiers were piled. As they were led along the streets, hostile Muscovite throngs followed the captives. They would not forgive the mercenaries for the misery they had caused and the destruction of their city.

A strange sight greeted Muscovites who passed through the Kremlin gate. Everywhere was gloom and emptiness. Churches had been stripped and defiled; most wooden edifices had been smashed and burned. On the streets Muscovites stumbled over bodies of men who had died the previous night. They found barrels and tubs which contained preserved human flesh in chancellery offices which had been used as barracks. The people of the town quarter immediately set about totally to rid the Kremlin hill of everything that reminded them of the aggressors. It took a little time to realize what had happened. When the people were finally sure that not a single enemy soldier was left in the heart of Moscow their joy was unconstrained. Individuals and whole groups streamed up to the open Kremlin gate. Once more bells chimed in the Kremlin belfries. People wept, embraced, shouted, laughed, and sang. The inhabitants heretofore had been constantly expecting volleys of shot from which they would have to hide. Now the battle was won. The ghastly year was over.

Minin and Pozharskii shared the festive attitude. A parade was held in honor of the victory. The national army assembled in the Arbat and made its way in triumphal procession to Kitaigorod. Trubetskoi's troops massed behind Pokrov gate and entered the fortress simultaneously from the other side. The two armies blended in the square beside the Place of Execution and then passed through Spasskii gate into the Kremlin. This was their shining hour. The ancient capital of the Russian realm was entirely rid of foreign conquerors.

Chapter Twenty-One

THE NATIONAL ELECTORAL ASSEMBLY

King Sigismund had become drunk with military success. Politicians and poets vied with one another to praise the conqueror. Hetman Chodkiewicz had entered Warsaw in triumph and in the presence of the national assembly handed over the Muscovite tsar to the king as a prisoner. The assembly listened to innumerable warlike speeches.

Sigismund soon had to sober up after his wild fling. The aggressive war, which was not in the interest of the Polish people, grew unpopular. The assembly became increasingly unwilling to prolong the war and, in particular, to levy further extraordinary imposts. The cost of maintaining the mercenary force bankrupted the royal treasury and was a factor in the accumulation of a huge debt. The armies in Russia joined together and handed the king an ultimatum. Men returned to Poland and threatened to seize the royal estates in order to force the king to pay their salaries. Such activities intensified anti-war attitudes. The defeat of Chodkiewicz's army spread alarm and despair among those who recently had supported Sigismund's expansionism. Many senators advised the king to turn his attention to the Turkish danger and hasten to make peace in the east. Sigismund was too stubborn to listen to these voices of moderation but he was forced to abandon his efforts to sit on the Muscovite throne and number Russia among his possessions by right of conquest. To overcome Russian opposition the king declared he intended to bestow the Muscovite throne on his son Wladyslaw.

This decision caused further problems for the royal family. Sigismund was intensely concerned about his son. To ensure his safety [in Russia—ed.] the father was ready to destroy his actual and presumed opponents. They included the Shuiskii brothers languishing in prison. If the boyars should choose to dethrone Wladyslaw they might very well remember his predecessor Shuiskii, the lawful autocrat. Vasilii Shuiskii and his two brothers were conveyed in deepest secrecy to Gostun castle, where they were held under heavy guard. People who saw Vasilii at this time described his appearance. He was stocky and swarthy, with a shovel-shaped beard heavily streaked with grey. Small inflamed eyes peered out dejectedly from beneath thick eyebrows. His aquiline nose appeared unusually long and his mouth extraordinarily wide in his round face. Vasilii was confined in a cramped stone chamber above the castle gate. He was not permitted to see his relatives or his Russian attendant. Prince Dmitrii Shuiskii lived in a low stone room. The brothers were of different ages and their health was not the same. Nevertheless they died almost simultaneously. The tsar expired on September 12. No one close to him was present. Dmitrii died five days later. The jailers allowed the prince's wife and servants to watch his last agonies.

Guards were forbidden to utter the names of the prisoners. An official wrote: "The deceased, so rumor has it, was the Grand Tsar of Muscovy." Striving to dissipate suspicion that Vasilii had met with foul play the composers of the protocol added: "The deceased was approximately seventy years old."[1] In fact, the tsar had just turned sixty; his brother was a few years younger. The bodies were buried in secret in order to conceal the location of their graves. Ivan Shuiskii, the youngest of the three brothers, was spared. Later he said: "The most gracious king has granted me life instead of consigning me to death." The Shuiskii who survived had to endure the fate of an anonymous prisoner. He was obliged to forget his true name and origin and was henceforward known as Ivan Levin. The cost of his incarceration was reduced to three rubles a month. Any valuables he had left were consigned to the royal treasury. Sigismund tried hard to hush up the incident but rumors of the secret crime reached Russia. Muscovite chroniclers were certain the Shuiskii brothers had met a violent end in Lithuania.

Sigismund set out on his Moscow campaign on August 18, 1612. As had been the case prior to the Smolensk expedition, he was afraid to convoke the national assembly for fear it would oppose him. The majority view did not favor such adventurism. On the frontier an army consisting of 4,000 men was waiting for him. Hetman Chodkiewicz and his forces joined him in Viazma and the Smolensk garrison provided more than 1,000 cavalry. Sigismund planned to take the shortest possible route to Moscow but the region abutting on the old Smolensk road long since had been devastated and the royal army could not maintain itself there. Chodkiewicz suggested the regiments should leave Viazma and repair to the hamlet of Pogorelyi, then come out on the Rzhev road, and make for Volokolamsk. At the end of October Sigismund was still unaware of the catastrophe that had befallen the garrison in the Kremlin. However, the national government likewise had no idea that enemy forces had reached close approaches to Moscow. News that they had done so threw the nationalist government into confusion.

The situation in Moscow was difficult enough. As was usual in autumn, gentry started leaving their units and scattering to their estates. Directly after the liberation of the Kremlin Pozharskii and Trubetskoi despairingly appealed to the towns to send supplies: serving men had not spared their lives to free Moscow. Now they were starving to death while on national service. The commanders allowed gentry to disperse in order to decrease the demands for supplies. After the weeks in question less than half of the 4,000 gentry remained in Moscow. But furloughing a part of the army did not solve the problem. The capital had scarcely any provisions and might have to undergo another siege.

The minute he crossed the frontier Sigismund directed an appeal to the Muscovite population. He reiterated that his forces would bring Russia peace and prosperity. After three years of grueling warfare his words sounded hollow. Approaching Moscow the king communicated with Mstislavskii, indicating he would set Wladyslaw on the throne as soon as the boyars sent envoys to parley with him. The king's addresses provoked anger and irritation in the capital. Long ago Sigismund had torn up the Moscow accord. He had not kept Zolkiewski's promises to withdraw troops and stop aggressive warfare. His forces had taken Smolensk and the Seversk towns. Russian ambassadors were in his prisons. Now Sigismund wanted new envoys.

On November 19 enemy advance units reached Ruza. Their ranks contained Associate Boyar Mezetskii, once a member of the boyar government. He was to serve as intermediary in talks with the Muscovites. With foresight Sigismund had brought the deposed patriarch, the Greek Ignatii. His task would be to crown Wladyslaw in the Cathedral of the Dormition in the Kremlin. Moscow patriots refused to countenance renewal of treasonous negotiations with the aggressors. Wladyslaw's couriers who arrived in the capital were arrested. People from every walk of life arose to defend Moscow. The lower orders instinctively understood that only the sternest measures would avail. The people stubbornly insisted that the council of seven members were secretly preparing again to hand Moscow over to the king. Filosofov, a member of the gentry in Pozharskii's unit fell into Polish hands. Under examination he said: "In Moscow boyars who served the king and the more prosperous people wish to have the Great Hospodar, Heir Wladyslaw, son of Sigismund, as their king but they are afraid to speak out for fear of the cossacks."[2]

At this dangerous moment cossacks and people from the town quarter burst into the Kremlin in an attempt to settle accounts with the traitors whom they had besieged in the fortress for a year and a half. Seated in the Kremlin, Prince Trubetskoi and his courtiers interceded on behalf of the boyars. The cossacks then started threatening to settle accounts with Trubetskoi as well. The affair almost came to bloodshed.

A unit consisting of 1,200 knights advanced from Ruza towards Moscow and occupied Tushino. The king's mercenaries suddenly descended upon Vagankovo, turned, and tried to penetrate the town's fortifications. A fierce battle ensued. The hostage, Colonel Budzillo, wrote: "Our men engaged the Muscovites closely and fell back; at that very moment cossacks in the camps slew most of our unhappy prisoners."[3] The willful murder of the captives was caused by a panic among the cossacks. The enclaves held some 700 prisoners, who expected the rapidly-approaching armies of the king would free them at any moment. The cossacks could not assign enough men to guard them because one unit after another was told off from the camp to go to the western suburbs, where a fight had started. Fear arose that the mercenary prisoners would overcome the scanty guard, seize the enclaves, and try to help their own men. Yielding to panic, cossacks began killing prisoners. As always, Pozharskii showed restraint and composure. He would not permit acts of violence against enemy soldiers held in his camp.

In his new war of conquest the king met with hopeless failure at every turn. His soldiers were even beaten back from the tiny fort of Pogorelyi. Perhaps the local commander was serious or he may have been jesting when he advised the king to head straight for Moscow. He said: "Be on your way to Moscow. Moscow will soon be for you and we are ready to be for you too."[4] The commander ordered his men to greet the uninvited guests with fire from their weapons.

The battle of Vagankovo ended with the withdrawal of the king's advance units. Chodkiewicz already had experienced how hard Pozharskii could strike. For this reason he avoided a general confrontation. Instead of proceeding to Moscow as quickly as possible, the hetman invited Sigismund to his old camp in the village of Fedorovskoe, where he had spent the previous winter. The location in Fedorovskoe could give the Poles access to the trans-Volga region and other areas of the country which had been furnishing requirements to the militia.

There was one vulnerable spot in the position at Fedorovskoe. The fortress of Volokolamsk stood astride the road from Fedorovskoe to

Moscow. The king issued an order to take the fortress no matter what it cost, but although they did their best the mercenaries had not the slightest success. Cossack atamans Neliub Markov and Ivan Epanchin were in charge of the defense of Volokalamsk. Three times the king's soldiers hurled themselves against the place; three times they were repulsed, leaving their dead behind. Finally the cossacks made a bold sortie and carried away several enemy cannon.

The aggressors were greeted with hatred everywhere. The nearby Russian population concealed grain and hid in forests. Every effort to requisition supplies for the army failed. The chancellor of Lithuania wrote home from Fedorovskoe: "We are in dire need; the Germans are wilting from hunger and cold; horses are running away due to lack of hay, oats, and straw. There is almost nothing left to keep us going; we eat and drink from our wagons and now everything is coming to an end."

Heavy frosts set in and snow fell; foragers were afraid to poke their noses outside the camp. They feared hunger but were terrified of partisans. The war the whole people was waging threatened the aggressor on all sides. The unbroken string of disasters undermined the army's morale. On November 27 Sigismund gave the order for a general retreat. The journey to Smolensk was exceptionally difficult. Several times frosts were followed by thaws and snows by torrents of rain. Many brooks and marshes were hard for the transport to get through. The mercenary army quitted Russia ingloriously; along the way it lost men and abandoned wagons and equipment on the highway. The news that the enemy forces had withdrawn produced joy in Moscow. The nightmare of two years of street warfare and unprecedented misfortune and hardship were now things of the past.

The national government was faced with much pressing business. The army and the people of Moscow had to be supplied. Moscow contained 2,000 nationalist gentry, 1,000 fusiliers, 4,500 cossacks, and several thousand armed citizens drawn from rebel units. Winter portended hunger for the impoverished rebels and cossacks. Minin adopted desperate measures to maintain them in the capital. Pozharskii wrote to the towns: "If hunger compels the cossacks to leave national service, the mighty achievement of the nation will suffer irreparable damage. There will be no one to defend Moscow." The national council first defined cossack service. It decreed lists of senior cossacks should be drawn up in order to separate the regular cossack army from what were termed "disorderly elements."

Cossacks placed on the register obtained the right to collect food in towns and districts assigned to them. The national council preserved the order the original militia had proved unable to maintain in Zarutskii's time. It empowered atamans personally to supervise food collections. Zarutskii's distinguished comrade, Stepan Tashlykov, and his unit of 1,140 men received Balakhna for this purpose. Other atamans collected supplies in Vologda and other northern areas. Pozharskii proposed that Vologda secretaries should issue letters of authorization to cossack atamans, permitting them to distribute what they had collected among the peasants.

Kuzma Minin at once provided senior cossacks with a salary of eight rubles per man in money and kind. The national treasury was almost bare; thus junior cossacks not on the register were paid no salaries, but they did not feel badly used. Minin and Pozharskii made good on the promise Liapunov had made to the rebellious people. Former serfs and indentured servants who had served in the national militia obtained their freedom. The council acknowledged their services to the liberation movement and voted to build them houses in which they could live either in Moscow or in other towns. Furthermore, they were exempted from paying their debts and crown taxes for two years.

The intense social conflict in the country had not abated. Serfs urged cossacks to attack gentry estates. Such occurrences caused panic in Moscow. Landlords everywhere decried cossack arbitrariness. In November, 1612 Filosofov, a member of the gentry, was plainly irritated when he said: "The cossacks are stronger than the boyars and gentry in every way and act as they please. Boyars have no wish to free slaves in reward for military service nor to allow cossacks to collect supplies, but they have to keep quiet about it, at least for the present."

The relationship between the new national government and the previous council of seven remained complex and vague. Minin and Pozharskii kept their word. No great boyar was subject to prosecution. However, by popular demand the authorities arrested the traitor Fedor Andronov (Fedka Andreev), Conciliar Courtier Ivan Bezobrazov, and a few secretaries.

Kuzma Minin conducted an inventory of the property found in the Kremlin and initiated a search for items that had disappeared from the tsars' treasury. Now he understood why the colonels had remained in the Kremlin for days after the boyars had surrendered and why they had kept Andronov and some other trusted persons at their side. Hidden from general scrutiny, Struys and his associates apparently had discovered a secluded place and built a receptacle in which they concealed what was left of the tsars' treasure and other valuables they had stolen. Pozharskii and Minin ordered secretaries tortured in order to find out where the treasure was hidden. Three traitors died under examination. Fedor Andronov had influential patrons and managed to escape from his guards. Patriots aroused Moscow to hunt down the king's acolyte. Andronov met with the retribution he deserved. Brought to torture a second time, he disclosed the hiding-places in the Kremlin his masters had told him to build. They yielded up old tsars' crowns and other property Struys' and Budzillo's men had appropriated when the treasure was apportioned out. Minin spent most of the money he recovered on salaries for nationalist gentry and cossacks.

The leaders of the national militia could not imagine Russia without pedigreed boyars. They had no intention of dissolving the boyar council, but merely to rid it of individuals whom the foreigners had appointed. The chief nobles greeted these measures with approval. Amid general satisfaction Associate Boyars the Princes Zvenigorodskii, Prince Fedor Meshcherskii, Timofei Griaznoi, the Rzhevskii brothers, and Chamberlain Bezobrazov were expelled from council. Boyar Romodanovskii was demoted to associate boyar. Ivan Saltykov and Nikita Veliaminov were deprived of rank.

Once Moscow had been liberated from the interventionists, the nationalists were free to elect a head of state. In November, 1612 Filosofov told the Poles that the cossacks in Moscow favored a Russian: "They are inclined to Filaret's son and the Thief of Kaluga." Senior boyars were for electing a foreigner. The cossacks recollected Heir Ivan Dmitrievich at the moment of greatest danger. Sigismund III was standing before the gates of Moscow; the members of the council of seven who had surrendered might at any time switch to his side. Zarutskii and his army were backing the Heir of Kolomenskoe. The atamans hoped that at this critical juncture their old comrades in arms might come to their aid. But any calculations that Zarutskii might return proved mistaken. When the stakes were highest the ataman did not scruple to instigate civil war. Marina Mniszech, her young son, and Zarutskii appeared before Riazan and tried to take it. Mikhail Buturlin, commander of Riazan, confronted him and put him to flight. Zarutskii's attempt to acquire Riazan for the Tiny Thief proved abortive. Much earlier the towns had indicated they were hostile to Ivan Dmitrievich's candidacy. Agitation on his behalf in Moscow died down spontaneously.

No election of a tsar could be legally binding without the participation of the boyar council. The maneuvring in council seemed likely
to last for years. Many noble families were vying for the crown and
no one was willing to yield. Ever since Tsar Fedor died Prince Mstislavskii and members of the Romanov family had sought the throne,
and the electoral struggle later included the Golitsyn family. Mstislavskii had been badly compromised by his trafficking with the interventionists. There was no hope that Vasilii Golitsyn would return from
captivity in Poland. Prince Ivan, who worked with Mstislavskii, had
taken his brother's place in the council of seven. Ivan Golitsyn was
considered a possible candidate but he enjoyed little support.

Gentry who had been part of the liberation movement were willing
to have one of the national commanders, whom they knew well, acquire
the throne. These candidates included Princes Dmitrii Trubetskoi and
Dmitrii Cherkasskii. A baptized Kabardian, Emir Kanshov (known as
Dmitrii Mamstriukovich Cherkasskii), could boast of kinship with
Ivan the Terrible's line. He had rendered some service to the liberation
movement but his popularity was minimal. Dmitrii Trubetskoi and
Mikhail Romanov were slightly stronger contenders but senior boyars
looked down their noses when they uttered the names of such men.

The leaders of the national militia insisted that the decree the national assembly had adopted in Yaroslavl must be implemented. They
believed that the entire realm should be involved in electing a head
of state. Early in November Minin, Pozharskii, and Trubetskoi dispatched numerous letters to the towns in order to inform them a national
electoral assembly would be convoked in Moscow. Local administrations and the people were to choose ten men who were "substantial,
intelligent, and steady," and give them " a full, firm, sufficient mandate" to deliberate concerning the election of a tsar "openly and
impartially."[5] The quarrel with the council of seven had moved the
national council to seek support from as many levels of the population
as possible. Town quarters and peasants on crown and taxpaying lands
as well as gentry and clergy were to send representatives to the capital.

The national authorities understood that they had to proceed with
the election as quickly as possible in case intervention continued. December 6, 1612 was designated as the first day on which the assembly
should meet, but by then no more than a handful of electors had made
their way to Moscow. It was not only poor roads and great distances
that delayed them. Local administrations had greeted Minin's and
Pozharskii's dispositions with massive opposition. Commanders in the

towns simply could not understand why the commons and taxpaying people should be involved in electing a tsar.

At what was dubbed the Great Assembly Council of December, 1612 the ranks voted to summon Muscovite boyars and gentry who "lived in the towns" to the capital. At the same time they enacted that representation from the estates should be considerably expanded. Previously they had requested ten men to come to Moscow; now it was thirty. They asked the Dvina region to send twenty town dwellers and taxpaying peasants, five fusiliers, and five clergy. The provinces, as always, were slow to respond and the patience of the authorities in the capital was clearly wearing thin. Minin and Pozharskii at last resorted to ill-concealed threats to make the provincials take part in electing a tsar: "If you do not send chosen men to the annointing at the national assembly in Moscow we shall have to assume you need no sovereign in the Muscovite realm. When misfortune befalls for our sins, God will requite you." The assembly was put off a month to enable persons from remote towns to hasten to the capital. When early frosts set in, it could be postponed no longer and the body got down to discussing candidates.

A few days later electoral zeal had reached fever pitch. Electors split into a host of factions; everyone lobbied for his own candidate. Witnesses wrote: "All were mightily exercised. Everyone wanted to prevail; each spoke in favor of his own man."[6] Candidates lacking oratorical skills tried to grease the wheels. A chronicler noted that numerous nobles wanting to be tsar offered bribes, "giving and promising many gifts." There were some who actually said Pozharskii had spent 20,000 rubles "to buy the realm." This was a base slander which his opponents circulated many years later. At the time the assembly was in session Prince Dmitrii made no effort to secure the throne. He had no money. However, many nobles removed cash they had secreted in repositories in the belief that to win was worth any amount they spent.

The militia leaders were afraid that foreigners might again try to interfere in the electoral contest. The peace on the Swedish border was unstable; the nationalists had to undertake diplomatic maneuvres once more. In January, 1613 the government sent a Swedish agent to Novgorod from Moscow. De la Gardie had once sent this man to the capital, where he fell into the hands of the cossacks and was kept prisoner in the camps. When he reached Novgorod the agent informed the Swedish authorities that the Muscovite boyars were disposed to ask Prince Karl Philip to mount the throne. Most likely the nationalist commanders had carefully provided the Swede with misleading information concerning the electoral struggle in Russia. Fear of Swedish intervention remained strong; Prince Dmitrii was merely advancing the intrigue he had begun in Yaroslavl. The Swedish agent was still there when two Russian merchants from Moscow brought Novgorod more accurate details about Russian affairs. They reported the cossacks favored Mikhail Romanov but the boyars were opposing him at the recently-opened assembly. In addition, Romanov himself was not anxious to accept the offer tendered to him. These considerations had led the boyars to look for a foreign sovereign.

Obviously Mstislavskii and his associates were ready to repeat the maneuvre to which they had resorted after Vasilii Shuiskii was ousted. On that occasion they had forced the national assembly to pass a resolution not to elect a Russian to the throne, thereby forestalling the ambitions of the Romanov and Golitsyn families. The pedigreed boyars refused to accept defeat and tried to utilize the electoral campaign to win back their power. As soon as their intentions became known, a wave of indignation swept over Moscow. In November, 1612 Minin, Pozharskii, and Trubetskoi had asked all ranks in the towns whether Prince Fedor Mstislavskii and his associates should be allowed to enter the council and the assembly. A month or so later the answer was in. Obeying the will of the assembly representatives, Minin, Pozharskii, and Trubetskoi carried an extraordinary resolution. When the electoral campaign was at its height they made Mstislavskii and his associates leave the capital forthwith. This action taken against the former council of seven members met with universal approval. A Moscow chronicler wrote: "The whole country was up in arms against them. They had no right to be with Trubetskoi and Pozharskii in the council."[7] Hesitating to sever relations with the boyar council completely, assembly leaders widely proclaimed that the boyars had gone on a pilgrimage. But witnesses affirmed they had been forced temporarily to drop out of sight; the commons was hostile to them because they had cooperated with the interventionists. In the boyars' absence the national assembly passed a motion not to allow a Polish or Swedish or service Tatar prince or any other foreigner to sit on the throne. This was the first step towards arriving at a consensus.

After the liberation of Moscow Prince Dmitrii Pozharskii lived in Vozdvizhenskii monastery in the Arbat, to which he recently had moved from his cramped quarters. Trubetskoi had taken up residence grandiosely at the court in the Kremlin that once had belonged to Boris

Godunov. He was an avowed candidate for the position of regent. The minute Mstislavskii and his associates quitted the capital, Trubetskoi showed who held real power there. The national assembly and the clergy declared he was now the owner of the Vaga land in hereditary proprietorship.

The Time of Troubles had immensely complicated land-tenure relationships. Members of the council of seven had nakedly used their power for personal gain. Had the boyars managed to put their own man on the throne or bring back a boyar government to the country they could have preserved their gains, all or in part. When the liberation movement began, the national assembly had declared land belonging to traitorous boyars confiscate and also had forbidden boyars and commanders in the movement to enrich themselves unduly. Nationalist boyars had no right to own more land than the lawful tsars, Ivan IV and Fedor, had allotted all boyars. Acquisitions made by the men of Tushino which exceeded the allotment were to be reassigned to needy gentry patriots. This law, embodied in the June 30, 1611 constitution, had not been implemented. The former Tushino nobility, led by Trubetskoi, desired to hold onto the wealth its members had acquired. The national government at Moscow had allocated more than their fair share of villages and districts to noble courtiers serving in the militia in order to retain them.

For his devoted service Tsar Vasilii had awarded Vasilii Buturlin 675 acres of land from the crown estates at Riazan in hereditary tenure, and Zarutskii and Trubetskoi had granted him 1,620 acres around Murom. For fighting against the men of Tushino, Commander Prince Aleksei Lvov had been awarded no more than 250 acres, but upon conclusion of the 1610 Moscow agreement Sigismund III had raised him to the rank of conciliar courtier and assigned him a large estate. Lvov soon broke with the interventionists and joined the militia. He had squandered what the king had given him but the nationalist boyars bestowed more than 1,350 acres of crown land upon him.

Pozharskii had obtained no benefits from the king or the Thief of Tushino. The council of seven members had deprived him of Lower Landekh, his best village, and handed his service-tenure estate over to one of Gosiewski's supporters in order to punish him for having participated in the Moscow uprising. While in Yaroslavl Prince Dmitrii had declined Trubetskoi's offer to compensate him with another estate. By that time the second national government had already restored Landekh to Pozharskii, now as a patrimonial holding, not in service-tenure.

In recognition of his loyal service, the national assembly also transferred to him the wealthy trading and artisan village of Kholui. The purview of the respective national governments had not yet been defined; secretaries deemed it necessary to cite the authority of Vasilii Shuiskii when ratifying the national assembly grant. This tsar supposedly had awarded Lower Landekh and Kholui to Pozharskii "for enduring the siege of Moscow," as a patrimonial estate, not a service-tenure one. In fact, Pozharskii controlled fundamentally the same amount of land he had possessed in Shuiskii's time; only the title changed when part of his service-tenure estate became hereditary. In 1613 secretaries noted: "He has his old patrimonies plus approximately 2,000 acres assigned to him in Tsar Vasilii's time." Prince Dmitrii's new acquisition was the little town of Kholui, which had a thriving salt-panning industry; land there suitable for tillage amounted to no more than 80 acres. To celebrate the victory over the enemy the national government bestowed a new summer residence on Pozharskii: "The boyars and the whole realm gave it to him when they took Moscow. In Suzdal he has received a patrimonial estate consisting of crown villages and some 2200 acres and a service-tenure estate of 1,200 acres."[8] Both Lower Landekh and Upper Landekh were assigned to Prince Dmitrii. These two hamlets were considered suburbs of the large crown village of Myt, which had become one of Pozharskii's service-tenure holdings. The rest of them were located near Balakhna and Nizhnii Novgorod.

Men who had served in Tushino and the camps made large acquisitions of land during the Time of Troubles. The well-known courtier, Prince Fedor Boriatynskii, a Tushino boyar, was given 1,875 acres of service-tenure land by the boyars before Moscow. Another Tushino boyar, Prince Dmitrii Cherkasskii, who had possessed no more than 540 acres before the Troubles, obtained 4,500 acres around Suzdal and Meshchera. At the start of his service Mikhail Buturlin had an allotment of 945 acres. During the Troubles this favorite of the pretender acquired amazing wealth and went on to increase his fortune under the original militia. The boyars assigned him a holding and crown villages in the neighborhood of Kostroma and Riazan with arable lands totaling more than 5,800 acres. Buturlin now was also the proprietor of Sapozhek, a small fortified town in the Riazan region. He had won control of no less than 16,000 acres of hereditary and service-tenure land.

Prince Dmitrii Trubetskoi outdid them all. As leader of the Tushino boyar council he obtained boyar rank and vast territories from the Thief. By the time Moscow was liberated it was reckoned he was the

proprietor of 17,000 acres he had recently acquired in Riazan, Meshchera, and elsewhere. Even this did not satisfy him. For a long time the
real bone of contention in council had been the hereditary principality
of Vaga. This rich area had not been ruined; it attracted covetous boyars
like a magnet. King Sigismund granted the traitor, Mikhail Saltykov,
a choice piece of it. The national government proclaimed the land
escheated to Boyar Zarutskii. Saltykov had gone abroad and Zarutskii
had broken with the liberation movement. Vaga was left without a
proprietor; Trubetskoi demanded it. Mstislavskii and his associates
were beside themselves, for Vaga always had been more desirable than
their own ancestral holdings. The council tried to restrain Trubetskoi.
Next, the head of the national government vigorously supported the
suggestion that council leaders be banished from Moscow.

The grant deed for Vaga read like an assembly decree. Trubetskoi
was to receive the land from the clergy, service Tatars, boyars, stewards, gentry and lesser boyars, merchants, traders, and "all ranks in the
Muscovite realm." The formal copy of the deed was adorned with gold
writing. However, only a few gentry and clergy signed the document.
This revealed the depth of the cleavage existing among the leaders of
the liberation movement. Nationalist boyars who had received rank in
Moscow, not Tushino, thereby indicated where they stood. The deed
lacked the signatures of Boyars Prince Andrei Petrovich Kurakin,
Vasilii Morozov, and Vladimir Dologorukii, Associate Boyars Se-men
Golovin and Artemii Izmailov, national courtiers and commanders
Prince Fedor Volkonskii, Ivan and Vasilii Sheremetev, Isak Pogozhii,
Prince Ivan Odoevskii, and many others.

Prince Dmitrii Pozharskii, Vasilii Buturlin, Liapunov's supporters
Princes Ivan Andreevich Golitsyn, Yurii Suleshev, and Ivan Birkin,
former Tushino boyars Mikhail Buturlin, Prince Dmitrii Cherkasskii,
and Prince Fedor Boriatynskii signed Trubetskoi's deed. Only one
member of the regular gentry was allowed to sign the charter. He was
the impoverished Ignatii Mikhnev, who had been one of False Dmitrii
II's favorite chamberlains. Showing his contempt for petty traders, the
highborn Trubetskoi refused to permit Kuzma Minin, merchants, or
cossack atamans to take part in the ceremony. Trubetskoi was sufficiently powerful in Moscow that churchmen had no desire to cross him.
Elderly Metropolitan Kirill, Trinity Abbot Dionisii, Feodorit, archbishop of Riazan, and numerous monks did sign the grant deed.

The churchmen and national commanders bestowed the deed upon
Trubetskoi at the altar in the Cathedral of the Dormition. The solemn

Kremlin ceremony was designed to pave the way for electing the militia leader to the throne. The deed deliberately began with the words that Vaga had once belonged to Tsar Boris. This was not an auspicious comparison; Boris had also risen from regent to tsar. Trubetskoi possessed manifest advantages when contrasted with the humbly-born Boris. He was descended from the grand princes of Lithuania. Royal blood flowed in his veins. Trubetskoi had become the largest landed proprietor in the realm. He had the strength and means to win electoral assembly support, but he lacked the political wisdom and character Boris had possessed. This was the cause of his failure.

Liapunov once had promised to confiscate land held by traitorous boyars and to distribute it to impoverished petty gentry. Trubetskoi refused to follow Liapunov's example. The national assembly annulled assignments and awards made in "Tsar" Wladyslaw's name but did not touch the holdings of the former council of seven members and their supporters. Witnesses devastatingly observed: "They gave the boyars back their old patrimonial and service-tenure estates." Poor gentry and cossacks did not forgive Trubetskoi for conniving with traitors or for his passion for wealth. They had no wish to see him mount the throne.

The national assembly had been meeting in Moscow for three weeks. It was almost the end of January, but a Swedish agent who witnessed the event noted that its members had failed to reach agreement. The circle of candidates had been narrowed but no faction could obtain a majority. Dmitrii Trubetskoi's candidacy provoked sharp criticism. Many stated openly that he was incapable of ruling. During the discussions the assembly also rejected the candidacy of Mikhail Romanov. This youth, aged sixteen, attracted little attention. Fedor Boborykin, a man who observed the electoral process, wrote that the nationalists and the boyars had no respect for Mikhail. Boyar Ivan Nikitich Romanov had always cooperated with Mstislavskii; he had been particularly insistent that the mercenaries should be invited into the Kremlin. Mikhail had spent the entire siege there with his uncle. He was mortally afraid of the people and had shown no desire to struggle with the aggressors. Trubetskoi, Pozharskii, and other assembly leaders rejected Romanov's candidacy out of hand, but Mikhail had supporters as well as opponents among the nationalist commanders. Relatives of the Romanov family, including Commander Prince Ivan Borisovich Cherkasskii, Boris Saltykov, Prince Ivan Fedorovich Troekurov, and the Mikhailov courtiers, agitated insistently on his behalf.

The voting was split. An assembly member proposed to elect the tsar in the same way as the patriarch: name three candidates, cast lots among them, and wait and see whom God would deign to vouchsafe as sovereign. The majority rejected the proposal. Voices at once demanded the assembly be kept in session until a consensus emerged: "They are proposing a rule forbidding us to move from this spot until a tsar is chosen for the Muscovite realm." The electoral contest had become critical.

On February 2, 1613, the Romanov faction achieved its first modest success. The national government sent a courier to Poland with instructions to try and secure the release of Filaret, Vasilii Golitsyn, and their associates from captivity. Filaret had played no part in organizing the national liberation movement but he had been courageous enough to oppose the council of seven's decision calling for Smolensk to surrender, thereby acquiring popularity among patriots. Cossacks from the Tushino camp were well acquainted with Filaret. It was there he had assumed the office of patriarch. His popularity contributed to the suc-cess of the Romanov faction's agitation at the assembly. Three of the Romanov electoral campaigns had ended in failure but each setback brought the family a bit closer to their goal. Moscow was used to hearing the Romanov name. Sixteen years of effort had at last borne belated fruit in spite of the fact that many had concluded the Romanov star had faded once and for all when Filaret was taken prisoner.

A few days after the courier's departure for Poland the Romanov faction enjoyed a further success. Mikhail's partisans recalled Godunov's election campaign and decided to imitate it. They began by putting their own ranks in order. Trubetskoi and other national leaders carefully scrutinized activity in the Kremlin. The Romanov interests wanted to avoid attracting attention; its members called a meeting in the residence belonging to the Trinity-St. Sergius monastery on Bogoiavlenie in the trading section of Kitaigorod. The Trinity cellarer, Avraamii Palitsyn, was present: "many gentry, lesser boyars, merchants from numerous towns, and atamans and cossacks" appeared at the Trinity residence. The precise names of the chief instigators of this February meeting are not known but they should obviously be sought among those who reaped the greatest rewards as soon as Mikhail was crowned. These were Princes Ivan Cherkasskii and Afanasii Lobanov, Konstantin Mikhalkov, and Vladimir Vishniakov.

This Romanov conclave possessed no more validity than had Godunov's original convocation; neither boyars, prominent national commanders, nor churchmen attended it. The upper church hierarchy had no desire to mar its relationship with the national government, which disposed of the real power. Trinity Abbot Dionisii had been a close friend of Trubetskoi's during the entire siege of Moscow but the monastery refused to let the friendship jeopardize its future. The Trinity leaders were anxious to be on the right side of all the candidates so that they would stand to gain no matter how the election came out. As a result, Abbot Dionisii remained aloof from this delicate matter, but his aide Avraamii received Mikhail's partisans at the monastery residence.

Representatives from the gentry, cossacks, and towns who met on Bogoiavlenie voted to elect Mikhail and drew up a protocol defining his right to the throne. Unlike Godunov's statement, the formulation in support of Mikhail lacked profundity and literary skill. Its framers had had no practice in writing, or fantasizing, and they were short of time. They said no more than that Mikhail was descended from the noble royal family "since he can claim to be the son of Fedor Nikitich, lineal nephew of Queen Anastasiia Romanovna, lawful wife of the worthy Great Sovereign, Ivan Vasilevich."[9] Conference participants decided to show their resolution to boyars and clergy and to designate from among their numbers individuals who would be attending electoral assembly sessions.

The morning of February 7, 1613 that body resumed its deliberations in the Kremlin. Witnesses are unanimous in asserting that it was cossack delegates who undertook to advance Romanov's cause. Feudal landlords feared criticism from the government; their caution made them anxious not to be the first to speak. The cossacks had nothing to lose. They stood on the lowest rung in the hierarchy of assembly members, but they were supported by the majority of the Moscow garrison; thus those in power had to hearken to their views. Muscovites vividly recalled that at the assembly they said: "All cossacks will have it that Mikhail shall be tsar." With passage of time the true story turned into a legend: a humble ataman from the "glorious Don" handed the assembly a note concerning Mikhail. A tradition has survived to the effect that a gentry serving man from Galich came before the assembly and supposedly read a note "about the royal kinship; how pious Tsar Fedor Ioannovich, when departing this world, entrusted his sceptre and crown to his cousin and boyar, Fedor Nikitich." This hoary contrivance devised by the Romanov family concerning Tsar Fedor's last wishes was in the Romanov interest but it apparently played no part in the assembly's formulation. Palitsyn and other conference participants were afraid to harm their cause by telling an outright lie the national authorities could expose on the spot.

Avraamii, who took part in the assembly session, communicates fully believable information about how a certain Smirnov Sudovshchikov, an elected merchant representing Kaluga and the northern towns, came before the assembly, but the cellarer could not resist the temptation to adorn his tale with a miracle. He stated that Sudovshchikov's submission backing Mikhail's election was word for word identical with the communications submitted by gentry and cossacks: "This was the doing of Sole Omnipotent God." Of course there was nothing supernatural about the fact that the communications corresponded word for word. Mikhail's champions at the Bogoiavlenie conclave had devised a general formula, which they circulated in many copies. Those representing different ranks thus could read one and the same document to the assembly.

The moves Romanov's partisans were noisily making produced no impression on the nationalist leaders. Many expressed doubt, again alluding to Mikhail's youth and his absence from the capital. Regent Trubetskoi and the boyars suggested deferring resolution of the issue until the candidate returned to Moscow, but the assembly rank and file and the people were annoyed at the incessant delays, and Romanov's supporters sought to play upon their frustration. Palitsyn and other conference participants proposed that the assembly should move its discussions outside the palace and find out what the people thought of Mikhail as a candidate. Trubetskoi lost his head and was unable to check the Romanov faction. The disunity among the national leaders led to their defeat. Boyar Vasilii Petrovich Morozov ostentatiously went over to Mikhail's camp, apparently motivated less by sympathy for the Romanov cause than by his enmity towards Trubetskoi, his traditional rival. Feodorit, archbishop of Riazan, and Iosif, abbot of Novospasskii monastery, immediately followed his example. For years the Romanov family had been making large contributions to this Moscow monastery.

Accompanied by Avraamii and two other clerics, Morozov proceeded from the palace to the Place of Execution, where he made a speech to soldiers and people gathered there. At the end of his presentation he asked whether Mikhail was fit to be tsar. The crowd responded with loud confusing cries. Witnesses interpreted the noise as a sign of general approval but this popular referendum had little effect on the government. Pressed by Trubetskoi and other commanders, the assembly voted to postpone an electoral decision for two weeks and in the meantime to bring Mstislavskii, president of the boyar council, and his associates back to Moscow.

Romanov's champions and opponents had both deluded themselves into believing the senior boyars would assist each side to foil the plots of the other. Leaders of the electoral assembly calculated that no decision in favor of Mikhail would be final, and so they categorically rejected a proposal to summon the candidate to the capital immediately. Attitudes towards Romanov were still so obscure that the assembly sent the chosen representatives to their towns with a mandate discreetly to ascertain whether the provinces would support his possible election.

On February 21, the day stipulated, the electoral assembly took up its tasks again. A multitude of the chosen representatives of the realm, including gentry, clergy, townsmen, and even crown peasants, gathered in Moscow. The great Kremlin palace was bulging. It was hard to find accommodation for delegates in the palace rooms. Some elected groups, like provincial priests, town dwellers, and peasants, could not be housed. The official record states that those assembled were carried away and unanimously proclaimed Mikhail Romanov tsar. Informed foreigners tell a very different story. From Moscow Swedish agents reported that the cossacks campaigning for Romanov had to besiege Trubetskoi and Pozharskii in their abodes in order to secure the election of the candidate of their choice. Novgorod authorities also asserted that cossack banditry influenced the election. Boyars, gentry, and prominent townsmen could not agree. Information released to Poland corresponded exactly with the Swedish and Novgorod versions. Lew Sapieha, chancellor of Lithiania, taunted the captive Filaret: "The Don cossacks all by themselves have set your son on the Muscovite throne."

Foreign versions and official Muscovite pronouncements are equally lacking in credibility. The testimony of Steward Ivan Chepchugov and two other courtiers whom the Swedes captured in 1614 makes it possible to recreate the actual circumstances surrounding the election of 1613. The three were direct participants in the assembly deliberations. The prisoners were interrogated separately, one after another, and their accounts dovetailed in every respect. These former elected representatives began their story at the time when the assembly decided to summon to Moscow the noblest boyars and men holding conciliar office who had heretofore been absent. After the boyars returned, the body at once turned to discussing how best to discharge its responsibilities: "Are we to elect a sovereign from among our people or is it to be a foreign ruler?" Trubetskoi had calculated correctly. As had been the case before, Mstislavskii and his associates would not hear of giving the crown to Mishka Romanov, whom they considered ignoble. Speeches made by one of Ivan the Terrible's numerous wives concerning the candidate's origins merely provoked irritation. By restoring preeminence to the boyar council the assembly returned to a stage it had long ago passed. The boyars once more began plotting to invite a foreign prince. The people's patience was at an end. As soon as word about the speeches the boyars were making spread throughout Moscow, cossacks and commons noisily charged into the Kremlin and upbraided the boyars: "You won't choose a Russian lord as sovereign because you want to rule yourselves and keep the country's revenues exclusively for your own use. You did it before. You will again submit our realm to a foreigner!" The cossacks proved the most recalcitrant: "We fought the siege of Moscow and liberated it. Now we must needs endure penury and perish utterly. We wish to swear allegiance at once to a tsar so that we will know whom we serve and who is to reward us for our service."[10]

Assembly leaders closed ranks so as somehow to resist the popular thrust from below. Trubetskoi and Mstislavskii both spoke against Mikhail in the same terms. Angered that his nephew should be preferred over him, Boyar Ivan Romanov came out squarely in support of Mstislavskii. The boyars designated him to parley with the people. Romanov mentioned "certain difficulties" to the crowd, alluded to the candidate's youth and, since Mikhail was not present, begged them to postpone deciding the question until the young man had arrived in order to enable everyone "better to reflect on this matter." His speeches produced no effect on the people. The crowd refused to disperse, grew noisy, and demanded boyars and assembly representatives take an oath to Mikhail Romanov on the spot.

After living through the tragic Time of Troubles people more and more often recalled the old lawful tsars. The darkness and cruelty that had existed in Ivan the Terrible's time appeared to have been forgotten. Men remembered the glory and majesty of the tsars' power, wonderful successes in war, and the capture of Kazan. Many naively believed that only a relative of the extinct dynasty, no matter how remote, could restore the greatness of the realm. Mikhail Romanov's partisans based their whole electoral campaign on this mistaken assumption. The ephemeral popularity the defunct dynasty enjoyed elevated an undistinguished individual to the throne, confounding the calculations and forecasts made by nationalist leaders. Their illusions about monarchy had deceived the Russian people cruelly.

The action taken by the cossacks and the armed people decided the outcome of the election and ended the splits and interminable dissension that had plagued the assembly. This intrusion by the lower orders at last enabled Romanov's partisans to seize the initiative and have the assembly representatives vote to elect Mikhail. Chancellery officials ran to draw up a binding document. Members of the council and the assembly immediately ratified it and vowed faithfully to serve Mikhail, his wife (about whom not a word had been said), and his possible offspring. They swore they would never hand the throne over to Lithuanian and Swedish kings or princes, or Russian boyars, or to Marina and her son.

The Russian realm had experienced unparalleled difficulties and needed an experienced leader to cope with enemies active on all sides and to pacify the country. Mikhail, who was only sixteen, bore not the slightest resemblance to such a figure, but his election was an accomplished fact. It was time to escort the candidate to the capital. The mission was important and the assembly selected a delegation worthy of the occasion. Mstislavskii managed to have Fedor Sheremetev head it. He had been the member of the Council of Seven most severely compromised by his cooperation with Gosiewski. Boyar Prince Vladimir Bakhteiarov from the national militia, Associate Boyar Fedor Golovin from those who had endured the siege, national commanders Prince Aleksei Lvov and Isak Pogozhii, as well as other assembly representatives, were assigned to assist Sheremetev.

When the assembly sent the boyars off, ostensibly on a pilgrimage, its leaders had not troubled to ascertain where Elder Marfa Romanovna, her son, and her relatives had gone. As late as January, 1613 assembly leaders had considered it virtually inconceivable that Mikhail might possibly be elected. More than a week after the triumphal proclamation no one in Moscow could say exactly where the sovereign was. Fedor Sheremetev and the assembly delegates were simply told to "go to Yaroslavl or wherever he, the sovereign, will be." On the way Sheremetev explained that Marfa Romanovna, her son, and two nephews, Boris and Mikhail Saltykov, had gone on a pilgrimage to the Ipatevskii monastery at Kostroma. On March 14, 1613 the representatives of the national assembly met Mikhail in the monastery and proclaimed him sovereign. The boyars were accompanied by Archbishop Feodorit, Avraamii Palitsyn, and other clerics, who bestowed the tsar's staff upon Romanov.

It took the tsar-designate a month and a half to reach Moscow. It was not just the thaw that retarded his progress. Romanov's entourage was waiting for an answer to the question agitating everyone: "will the country acknowledge Mikhail?" News from Kazan occasioned great alarm in Kostroma. The loss of Novgorod and Smolensk had made Kazan increasingly important as the second city after Moscow. In spring, 1613 the people of Kazan had gathered a force and sent it to the capital at the behest of the national government. The Kazan commanders heard about the tsar's election in Arzamas. Emissaries from the national assembly wanted the soldiers to swear an oath to Mikhail at once but Secretary Shulgin, who was in charge of the men of Kazan, was opposed. He had been administering Kazan ever since he had persuaded the people to murder Bogdan Belskii and Morozov had departed for Moscow. Shulgin declared: "Until I receive advice from Kazan I will refuse to kiss the cross."[11] The secretary and his closest coadjutors decided to return home as quickly as possible. This action by what was termed the "Kazan realm" threatened Romanov's position. The authorities thus undertook to head Shulgin off on the road. They initiated a pursuit and arrested the secretary in Sviiazhsk. Subsequently he was banished and died of starvation in Siberia.

As the tsar's train slowly wended its way towards Moscow, a new government started forming in Marfa Romanovna's suite. Boris Mikhailovich and Mikhail Mikhailovich Saltykov, relatives of Mikhail Romanov's mother, were among the first to enter it. They had all been living together like a family in Ipatevskii monastery. Concerned with the problem of how to maintain the royal family and court in devastated Moscow, Mikhail's kinsmen created a Great Revenue chancellery at their headquarters and put Boris Saltykov in charge of it. Mikhail Saltykov became a cupbearer. Konstantin Mikhailov, a man close to the Romanov family, was made a chamberlain. These new officials were extremely impatient. Three days after the proclamation was made in Kostroma they had Mikhail insist that Trubetskoi and the boyars send him the sovereign's seal immediately. This encouraged the former council of seven members. Boyar Fedor Sheremetev stayed close to the autocrat. Sheremetev's brother-in-law, Prince Ivan Cherkasskii,

who was Mikhail's cousin, quickly followed him to the tsar's headquarters. Sheremetev, Cherkasskii, and the Saltykov brothers moved
rapidly to undo the influence of Trubetskoi, the nationalist regent. They
addressed rescripts the tsar sent to Moscow not to him but to Mstislavskii. Composing a routine charter, a scribe in the national assembly
intended to write, as was customary, "We, your slaves, Dmitrii Trubetskoi and Dmitrii Pozharskii," but suddenly thinking better of it, struck
out the names of the nationalist leaders.[12] After April 10, 1613 form
letters from Moscow emanated under the name of "your slaves Fedor
Mstislavskii and his associates." The boyar council finally had regained its prerogatives.

During the siege Elder Marfa had known hunger. Before she returned to the Kremlin she asked the boyars over and over again whether
supplies would be available in the palace when the tsar's party arrived
and, if not, where did they expect to find them. Moscow replied that
the royal storehouses now contained ample supplies. Such an answer
failed to satisfy even Mikhail. Chancellery officials listed what they
had. It turned out that the Provisions chancelleries held so few supplies
that they would not last until the sovereign arrived, and "no chancellery
has any ready money."

A practical woman, Marfa was concerned she might not find a habi-
tation in the ruined Kremlin consonant with her rank. Originally she
had planned to move into wooden chambers that had belonged to Vasilii Shuiskii's widow and assign her son the gold canopied palace of
Queen Irina Godunova. The boyars informed her they had given orders
to have Tsar Ivan the Terrible's rooms and the Palace of Facets prepared for Mikhail while Marfa would occupy chambers in the Voznesenskii nunnery in which Marfa Nagaia, Ivan the Terrible's widow,
had resided. The structures which attracted Mikhail's mother had been
totally destroyed. Rooms and suites were without roofs and for some
time lacked benches, doors, or windows. Everything would have to be
rebuilt, but there was no money in the treasury, few carpenters in the
capital, and no quick way to get suitable wood.

Ever since Mikhail had begun to have some understanding of the
world he had become intensely fearful of the fractious people. Two
years under siege had imbued him with hatred for the Thief's commanders and the cossacks serving in the national militia. The nobles
in the tsar's headquarters sedulously fostered his prejudices. Atamans
and cossacks who had come to Kostroma from Moscow felt ill at ease.

By the time Mikhail halted at the Trinity-St. Sergius monastery en route to Moscow many cossacks had deserted him. Almost all the capital's nobles and a host of gentry and other ranks greeted the sovereign at Trinity. Speaking before them, Mikhail wept and inveighed against current cossack rapine. Someone had put the words into Romanov's mouth. The members of the former boyar government had arranged for his appearance. Mstislavskii and his associates were waiting for the first suitable opportunity to remove as many cossacks as possible from Moscow and to substitute compliant fusiliers. In March, 1613, 2,300 cossacks were transferred to Kaluga. Several cossack bands departed for Pskov.

Shortly before the tsar's procession reached Moscow "slaves Mitka Trubetskoi and Mitka Pozharskii" asked the tsar on what day and in what place he bade them and the whole militia army meet him and "behold his tsaric eyes." Mikhail directed his answer to the whole boyar council, not specifically to them. The rivalry between the senior boyars and the national government played into the new autocrat's hands, making it difficult for the assembly to impose restrictions on his power.

On April 14, 1613 the assembly ordered an enabling charter concerning Mikhail's election drawn up. Secretaries modeled it on Godunov's document. Caring nothing for truth, they excerpted entire pages, putting Boris' words to his assembly in Mikhail's mouth and having nun Marfa Romanovna repeat speeches that nun Aleksandra (Godunova) had uttered. The popular election of Boris on New Virgin field was reenacted, this time before Ipatevskii monastery. Emphasizing that Romanov had a right to the throne, the secretaries claimed that before he died Tsar Fedor had entrusted the crown to his cousin Fedor Romanov. This ancient falsehood had now become official doctrine.

It took several weeks to prepare the document. Securing signatures to it took considerably longer. Unlike Godunov, Mikhail was not interested in collecting signatures from all assembly members. The chosen representatives from the towns designated one signatory: a member of the gentry, a man from the town quarter, or, more rarely, a fusilier, to sign for the representatives of his town or district. The tsar's councillors did not invite Kuzma Minin, whom the entire Muscovite realm had elected, Moscow merchants and town quarter elders, or atamans and cossacks from the militia to sign the charter.

Nationalist boyars vainly sought to win recognition of their seniority at Mikhail's coronation. Regent Trubetskoi tried to file a precedence suit against the powerful Ivan Romanov but was quickly rebuffed. The tsar honored his uncle Ivan by having him carry the Cap of Monomakh before him. Trubetskoi had to be content with a more modest role; he bore the sceptre. Pozharskii also took part in the coronation ceremony. He was entrusted with the golden apple. Prince Mstislavskii again proved to be the hero of the day. As the noblest boyar, he poured gold coins over the young tsar.

Dull as he was, Mikhail Romanov understood he would never have won the crown if Pozharskii's army had not rid Moscow of the enemy. Assembly members and the people insisted on recognition for the services the chosen national commander had rendered. Bowing to general sentiment, the tsar made Steward Pozharskii a boyar on the day of his coronation, but he had already awarded boyar rank to Prince Ivan Borisovich Cherkasskii before he bestowed it on Pozharskii. The sequence in which the awards were made was highly symbolic. Prince Pozharskii had led the March uprising in Moscow, whereas Prince Cherkasskii had assisted the interventionists in putting it down. Later Cherkasskii had fought against the advance guard of the militia and had been captured.

The people of Moscow owed more to Kuzma Minin than to anyone else for their liberation. Acting on a motion passed by the entire realm, the militia council had rewarded him with a large estate consisting of some 2,200 acres for taking Moscow, but the new group surrounding Tsar Mikhail had no use for Kuzma. Minin was not assigned ceremonial duties to perform at the coronation. Awarding him the rank of conciliar courtier was prudently delayed for one day. The government granted Minin an income of 200 rubles a year from the whole realm, a substantial allocation; the boyars were being generous after having refused Kuzma a service-tenure estate. Incidentally, gentry received their principal revenues from their estates. Minin's services to the treasury went unrecognized. Not he but Trakhaniotov was made treasurer and placed in charge of the treasury.

Many thought dim-witted Mikhail could not last long on the throne and that he would suffer the fate which had overtaken Fedor Godunov and Shuiskii. However, the intense social crisis was abating; the last echoes of civil war were still to be heard only in remote corners of the country. The lethal danger menacing Russia had united patriotic forces. The people's energy had saved the realm.

Uncoordinated bands of foreigners and Cherkassians continued to appear in the area around Moscow and even in the far north and on the upper coastline. They remembered when Russia was torn with internal factionalism and they could act with impunity. Now it was the interventionists' turn to apprehend danger from every quarter. People wanted nothing more to do with them and combined to eliminate these bands. This war, waged by unsung heroes, brought further benefits. Few of the enemy who penetrated far into the country ever returned alive. The remarkable exploit of Ivan Susanin, a Kostroma peasant, became famous solely because it took place on one of the Romanov hereditary estates. The official version portrays Susanin's achievement in an unbelievable way. The indentured peasant sacrificed his life for his native region, not for the tsar. He did not, as legend has it, lead an enemy detachment into an impenetrable forest and destroy it. The foreigners needed a guide, but Susanin preferred to die rather than to aid the aggressors. He was tortured to death in a village, refusing to give the foe the information he needed.

War continued to consume all available forces in the ravaged land. Sigismund III had not abandoned his plans to conquer Russia. His armies repeatedly crossed the Russian frontier. They burned Kozelsk, Bolkhov, and Peremyshl and appeared before Kaluga. To prevent the enemy from entering Moscow the Russian leaders sent nationalist commanders Dmitrii Cherkasskii and Mikhail Buturlin west with substantial forces. They drove the enemy from Kaluga, liberated Viazma, Dorogobuzh, and Belaia, and besieged Smolensk, where the command concentrated 12,000 men. Half of them were cossacks: 2,340 came from Moscow and 2,250 had left Zarutskii's camp. The struggle finally to expel the aggressors from Russia and liberate Smolensk could not succeed unless the Russian command committed all its troops to the western frontier. This did not happen.

Minin and Pozharskii had managed to avoid fighting the Rzeczpospolita and Sweden simultaneously. Their diplomacy had been crowned with brilliant success. By removing them from leadership, the government implicitly rejected the foreign policy they had devised. While hostilities were at their height before Smolensk the authorities dispatched Prince Dmitrii Trubetskoi and 5,000 men to attack the Swedes in Novgorod.

Senior boyars had been striving to remove the former regent from the capital. The last thousand cossacks who had besieged the Kremlin left Moscow with him. Petty intrigue had prevailed over military considerations. The militia forces were divided and sent in different directions. Minin and Pozharskii, the militia's experienced leaders, had no part in these activities. The tsar and his circle had awarded them conciliar rank only in order to limit the enormous influence they enjoyed in the country, which had brought them to the fore at the moment of greatest crisis. Naming Trubetskoi commander-in-chief of the northern army and sending him to Novgorod had disastrous consequences. As he always did, the inept boyar acted ineffectively and indecisively and failed to keep his army supplied. The campaign was an utter disaster. Hope was succeeded by despair.

Chapter Twenty-Two

THE END OF THE WAR

In this time of severe travail Russia was in need as never before of able commanders and statesmen. The liberation movement produced many such people. Minin and Pozharskii stood at their apex. Pozharskii's military skills were truly remarkable. However, the nobles, who had almost destroyed the Russian realm, could never forgive him either his talents or his humble origin.

Indefatigable Gavrila Pushkin, who had served several tsars and zealously abetted Gosiewski, was the first to employ precedence to block Pozharskii's career. Pushkin was a minor functionary in the boyar council. For this reason the tsar specifically assigned him the task of publishing the edict that made Pozharskii a boyar. The stubborn Pushkin refused to carry out the tsar's behest. Sure his position was unassailable, Prince Dmitrii did not appreciate the danger and failed to lodge a countercomplaint against Gavrila. Six months passed; by then Pozharskii had realized he would not receive further commands unless he compelled the boyars to acknowledge his pedigree.

The elevation of Mikhail Romanov advanced a goodly number of inconsequential people who could boast of nothing save kinship with the sovereign and his mother. The Saltykov brothers became Mikhail's favorites. King Sigismund earlier had praised them for loyal service and had awarded them estates. Boris Saltykov joined the liberation movement later than many others and had not taken an outstanding part in the struggle with the invaders, but by the time of the coronation his dubious past was no longer mentioned. Informed persons said that in Moscow the boyar council would take no action unless Saltykov knew and approved. It was not Saltykov but the tsar's uncle, Ivan Romanov, who dictated policy, not because of his rank but because he was a relative of the elderly nun Marfa, Mikhail's mother. Mikhail first made Boris cupbearer, then boyar. He commissioned Pozharskii to present the new boyar to the court and the people. The illustrious commander could not keep Saltykov out of council but he tried to curb his undue influence by bringing a precedence suit against him.

To prove his preeminence Boris had the impudence to cite the services of his uncle, Mikhail Glebovich Saltykov, whom every Russian considered an arch traitor. Boris' actions understandably met with no criticism from the boyars but Pozharskii was incensed and refused to fulfill the behest of the lad sitting on the throne. Alleging illness, he retired to his residence. Romanov did not dare provoke the commander, but that evening he was seated at dinner with Mstislavskii, Odoevskii, and Fedor Golovin. They insisted Pozharskii must be severely punished. They sent a courtier, Perferii Sekirin, who had served with Pozharskii in Yaroslavl and carried out his instructions, to fetch him. Sekirin brought the commander to Boris Saltykov's residence. Utterly betrayed, Pozharskii was obliged to bow down before his foe and listen on his knees to what the other had to say. After giving Prince Dmitrii a tongue-lashing, Saltykov forgave and dismissed him. In those days a worse humiliation could not be imagined. The insult to Prince Dmitrii was particularly degrading. The services the liberator of Moscow had rendered were simply effaced. His defeat in the precedence suit in effect deprived Pozharskii of the right to hold higher army offices. At a time the country was facing new trials Prince Dmitrii had been dismissed ignominiously from the direction of military matters. Punishment by precedence was a horror for men who regarded family honor as the most important thing in life. On occasion a defeated boyar would become a monk, forsaking secular life entirely. Another might renounce his oath and go over to the enemy. But Prince Dmitrii stood the test. Although he was as sensitive to precedence cavils as other impoverished aristocrats, he refused to become bitter or betray his principles. He endured everything, but the vile draught of insult long poisoned his soul.

Those who had been under siege in the Kremlin were delighted at the humiliation inflicted on the man who had led the people against them. Like other boyars, the Romanov dynasty was terrified by ongoing popular risings. The causes of peasant war had not been completely eliminated. Flames of conflict continued to smoulder near and far in such places as Vologda, Astrakhan, and Riazan.

After withdrawing from Riazan, Zarutskii wintered in Mikhailov. The Tiny Thief, Ivan Dmitrievich, was at his side. Zarutskii's council of elders eagerly fanned popular hopes that the Heir shortly would be elected; boyar slaves and rural peasants poured into Mikhailov from everywhere. Zarutskii's men plundered gentry estates and slew their owners. Soon some 3,000 men had gathered under Zarutskii's banner. They needed food. Cossack foraging was steadily becoming harder for the population to bear.

The tsar's election put an end to any illusions that the Tiny Thief might be invited to Moscow. First petty gentry and later atamans quietly began abandoning his camp. Prince Odoevskii and some gentry units soon came after Zarutskii. The commander knew the enemy with whom he had to deal was formidable and he embarked on the campaign only after serious reflection. Odoevskii encountered the cossacks in the steppe before Voronezh and battled them uninterruptedly for two days. The prince grandly informed Moscow that he had defeated Zarutskii completely and seized his cannon, banners, and transport. He was exaggerating. An official chronicle reported that Odoevskii had not prevailed over Zarutskii at the battle of Voronezh.[1] Nevertheless, the ataman's luck finally had deserted him. The cossacks despised the Polish woman who was their chief's concubine. They no longer fought with their previous enthusiasm for the Tiny Thief the country had rejected. When Zarutskii ordered his men to withdraw to the Don, the bulk of his army abandoned him along the way. Cossacks went back to Moscow and turned themselves in. Apparently by no means all of these, but only some senior cossacks who had seen service in the liberation movement, entered crown service. In need of soldiers, the government at once sent them to Smolensk.

Since the Don cossacks would no longer support him, Zarutskii had to proceed to Astrakhan. The people there, long hostile to Moscow, refused to acknowledge Mikhail Romanov as tsar. It was stated they had taken the initiative to summon Ivan Dmitrievich, the Tiny Thief. Volga cossacks and the Astrakhan commons welcomed him. Rootless sojourners streamed into the town from everywhere. Zarutskii dispatched couriers to the area north of Moscow and to Beloozero. Rebels there were preparing to force their way into the lower Volga region. By spring, 1614 several thousand men were under arms in Astrakhan. Zarutskii intended to lead them on a campaign against Samara and Kazan.

To secure their rear Tsaritsa Marina and Zarutskii negotiated with the shah of Persia. Marina hoped she might find refuge in his country; Shah Abbas played an unusual role in the proceedings. The eastern despot would have liked to induct her into his harem. Not troubling to conceal his curiosity, the shah asked the couriers whether Marina were young and pretty and whether her hand was "hot." Even in her best days Marina had been no beauty and her forays through cossack enclaves and wild days and nights had taken their toll. She had grown ugly and old. The shah's couriers could not determine her age and avoided answering questions as to whether she was pretty. Marina tendered them her hand, which they noticed was very hot. She was feverishly excited during her last months. She felt her end was near.

Zarutskii's and Marina's relations with Persia disturbed Prince Khvorostinin, governor of Astrakhan. Supported by the more prosperous people of the town he planned to take Zarutskii by surprise and capture him and his concubine. The ataman outwitted the conspirators. He killed the governor, many emirs, and prominent men of the town quarter. Cossacks sacked the archbishop's residence and threw the prelate into prison. Then serving men came out against him and, with the help of the local garrison, gentry occupied a redoubt. Zarutskii was besieged in the stone fortress. He had no more than 800 cossacks and fusiliers left. Forces loyal to the government came from the Terek to the aid of the Astrakhan gentry. The ataman despaired of holding out in Astrakhan and fled to the Yaik region. Treason broke out in the former nationalist regent's inner circle. Not wishing to die for a foreign woman, after a few clashes the cossacks handed Marina and Zarutskii over to the authorities. The Romanov family had always dealt ruthlessly with its enemies. Ivan Dmitrievich, the Tiny Thief, was hanged and the same fate overtook his fictitious father, Deacon Matiushka, who had assumed the name of False Dmitrii III. Zarutskii was impaled on a stake. Marina Mniszech could not endure the shame and died in confinement in Tula. The authorities hanged Fedka Andronov along with the Tiny Thief. He was the only one who had to pay with his life for the council of seven's treason.

After putting down the uprising in the Volga region the boyars started to deal more harshly with the cossacks. Whenever they could, they would conduct an inquiry, driving runaway slaves and peasants out of the camps and returning them to their former masters. Fearing opposition, the government proclaimed in advance that it intended to decide issues "in good faith" when cossacks presented petitions indicating where each wished to go. The allusion to good faith deceived nobody. The freedom offered the cossacks was worse than servitude. The boyar decree noted: "Boyar slaves who left [fled from—ed.] their masters and were among the cossacks while the boyars stood before Moscow prior to the time the sovereign was chosen, and those cossacks who wish to be slaves as they were before to their original boyars; to such boyar slaves has been granted freedom to return as slaves to their old masters or to new ones, as they choose."[2]

The selfish policy of the ruling boyars, who were trying to force their slaves and peasants to return to them from the cossack units, aroused ferment among the cossacks throughout the country. They refused to be reconciled to the fact that they, the men who had liberated Moscow, would again have to live in poverty while the traitorous boyars were reinstated as their masters. Proceeding to Novgorod with an army, the prominent ataman Kozlov, a hero of the national movement, requisitioned provisions and other goods from patrimonial estates belonging to Mstislavskii and Marfa Romanovna. When he met the abbot of the Kirillo-Belozersk monastery on the highway the ataman ordered his sableskin coat torn off.

Cossack atamans and the local populace helped commanders to subdue enemy units that had been perpetrating outrages in Vologda, Kargopol, and the Dvina land. But fighting still continued and in the countryside the situation was growing more and more unstable. There were no gentry landlords in the Vologda region. The majority of the population consisted of taxpaying crown peasants. The Romanov group, ignoring tradition, awarded Vologda lands to courtiers. The peasants refused to be indentured to service-tenure landlords. They beat to death or expelled the landlords who had been foisted upon them. Cossacks frequently joined the people in these sanguinary actions.

Trubetskoi's defeat before Novgorod infused new vigor into the free cossack movement. Abandoning the retreating army, cossack units refused to proceed to Moscow, where inquiries awaited them. They had not volunteered to take up arms and fight the Swedes only again to be restored to servitude. Cossack units were constantly growing in the north and on the upper coastline. Peasants, slaves and fusiliers swelled their ranks. An entire army formed under the aegis of Ataman Mikhail Balovnia.

The government tried to dampen the flames of cossack revolt and soon achieved some success. In January, 1615 Balovnia initiated talks with Commander Volynskii about a return to crown service. The cossacks sent Ataman Titov to Moscow to express their penitence and then went there themselves. Some joined militia units at Moscow and others took up arms against the Swedes and Cherkassians. They agreed to go and fight the enemy at Smolensk if all of them were registered as cossacks and received a salary in cash. A cossack conclave enacted that if the sovereign should order an inquiries into those who had been boyar slaves or peasants but now were cossacks and put them to death for this reason, they would depart for the towns or go off to the Don.

The cossacks received a nasty surprise in Moscow. On July 23, 1615 the tsar lured Balovnia and other cossack leaders into the city and arrested them. At that moment Commander Lykov fell upon the cossack enclaves, which were not anticipating such perfidy. Left without leaders, the cossacks were unable to fight back, and they fled from Moscow. Lykov chased them and forced them to surrender before Maloiaroslavets. Some 3,250 cossacks were returned to Moscow, where they were subjected to inquiry. The boyars cared little for the service cossacks had rendered. Many atamans and cossacks who had served in the national militia were imprisoned. The boyars who had been in the Kremlin with the Poles remembered past insults and took savage vengeance on the cossacks. Balovnia and other leaders were hanged. Many cossacks were reinscribed on the tax rolls or reduced to slavery.

War had become intolerable to the ruined, exhausted land. Alarming news came to Moscow from the frontiers. Trubetskoi before Novgorod and Cherkasskii before Smolensk both urgently appealed for help. Casualties and hunger were decimating Trubetskoi's forces, which were positioned about thirteen miles from Novgorod. In July, 1614 the commander sounded a general retreat. During the withdrawal panic broke out in the ranks. Soldiers sought refuge in forests and swamps. The former nationalist regent had not expected attacks from the rear. He swerved from the road into a wood and wandered around in a wilderness for a long time until he finally made it on foot to Torzhok.[3]

Commander Prince Dmitrii Cherkasskii enjoyed some initial success before Smolensk. His armies built stout redoubts along the old boundary and blockaded the Smolensk garrison. Famine broke out in the besieged town; the surrender of the fortress seemed imminent, but the Russians were not strong enough to bring the war at Smolensk to an end. Without consulting Cherkasskii the advance guard withdrew from the redoubts to the main camp before Smolensk. Foreign forces made their way into the fortress and moved up wagons to deliver supplies. Captains sent to construct a new redoubt on the boundary were attacked fiercely and lost more than 2,000 men.

An unfavorable situation had developed on the southern steppe frontier. In 1613, 20,000 Nogais had forced their way across the Oka river and got as far as the suburbs of Moscow. During the next two years they often invaded Russia along the border from Alatyr to Briansk. Inhabitants of the southern region complained that the Tatars burned down villages, destroyed their settlements, and "there is no way we can live with them."

The Swedes took advantage of these new setbacks Russian armies had suffered in order to expand the scope of their intervention. King Gustav Adolphus decided to take Pskov. He wanted to achieve what the Polish king Stefan Batory had failed to accomplish at the end of the Livonian war. In 1615 the Swedish king's army laid siege to Pskov. If the city fell, the entire Russian defense system in the northwest would collapse. The Swedes were confident they could succeed in bringing Russia to her knees, but their hopes proved unfounded. For nearly three months the people of Pskov courageously repelled the attacks launched by the king's army and finally forced it to withdraw.

For approximately four years Lord Lisowski had managed to remain with his unit in the Pskov suburbs where, during this time, he had played havoc with local populations. In the spring of 1615 Lisowski and his men appeared before Pskov, ostensibly to come to terms. He stripped the environs bare and left Pskov for Smolensk with wagon-loads of provisions. When Lisowski and his men arrived at Smolensk they occupied Karachev. The boyars in Moscow were in despair; they remembered his murderous forays. They had long been seeking someone to whom they might entrust the task of destroying so formidable a foe. None of the commanders showed the slightest desire to tangle with Lisowski. At last Pozharskii's name came up. More than two years of incessant struggle had gone by, but during all this time humbly-born Prince Dmitrii had received no military assignments. The leader of the liberation movement had been humiliated, but no one could rob him of the glory he had won. The chief problem was that scarcely any troops were left in Moscow and without a substantial army there was no question of defeating the impetuous and elusive Lisowski. The appointment did not promise easy victories but Pozharskii accepted it without hesitation.

Secretaries drew up a roster, according to which the complement of Pozharskii's army was to reach 7,000 men. This seemed impressive on paper, but in reality such an army still had to be collected. Detachments and units were scattered among various towns; landlords were resting on their estates. Pozharkii could find no more than 1,000 gentry, fusiliers, and cossacks in Moscow. The capital gentry displayed no enthusiasm for joining Prince Dmitrii's unit. The Shakhovskoi princes tried to avoid going with him on the excuse that their previous service had exhausted them. Not until the tsar ordered Prince Semen Shakhovskoi banished did the rest of the Shakhovskoi family submit.

On June 29, 1615 Pozharskii left Moscow at the head of a modest force. Arriving in Borovsk, he immediately sent out recruiters all over the region with instructions to round up serving men. Cossacks from Balovnia's army drove Prince Dmitrii out of Belev, but many of these had served in the national militia. Pozharskii impressed them into his unit and administered an oath to them. From Bolkhov the commander sent cossack representatives to remote towns, demanding they furnish men. Some 2,000 Tatars who arrived proved to be of little use. After their first encounter with the Poles they took to their heels and fled.

August, 1615 found Lisowski and his men at Karachev. The minute he learned Pozharskii had come up, he set off at top speed for Orel. Prince Dmitrii reached Orel right behind him. On August 30 Captain Ivan Pushkin and some cavalry detachments charged into the Polish camp. There was great commotion. Lisowski and his men, who were pitching tents, barely managed to snatch up their arms and beat back the attackers. At that moment Pozharskii arrived. The battle in a field before Orel lasted several hours. Prince Dmitrii stubbornly attacked Lisowski three times. The Russians took a number of prisoners, several banners, and some drums, but gradually their enthusiasm began to slacken. Lisowski and his men counterattacked and knocked a detachment led by Islenev out of position. The Tatars panicked and fled and the rest of the soldiers followed them. Pozharskii held his ground. All he had left was two gentry units, forty fusiliers, and a few hundred other soldiers, but the Russians struck back so fiercely that Lisowski was forced to abandon the initiative. Prince Dmitrii employed the respite to strengthen his position by lining up the wagons surrounding his forces in several rows. Captain Ivan Pushkin and Grigorii Gorikhvostov stood by the commander, but Grigorii was soon wounded. Some gentry suggested to Pozharskii that he should withdraw to Bolkhov but he replied: "It is better for all of us to perish where we are than to yield the battlefield to the enemy." Pozharskii had no more than 600 men. Lisowski had much larger forces, but the Poles did not know how many men the Russians actually had. The battle was exhausting; its outcome was inconclusive. At dusk Lisowski and his men withdrew a mile or so and disposed themselves for the night. At dawn the next day Islenev and other fugitives returned to the fires burning in the Russian camp.

Pozharskii called a council of war and took a decision to make an example of anyone who failed to carry out his orders.

Pozharskii's and Lisowski's armies faced one another for three days before Orel. Prince Dmitrii was waiting for reinforcements in order to renew the battle. In Moscow he had taken into his unit an old acquaintance, Captain Jacob Shaw, and eleven of his countrymen. Once in Yaroslavl the council had turned down Shaw's request to enter nationalist service, but the enterprising Scotchman persevered and finally achieved his aim. Tsar Mikhail took him into his service. Shaw proved extremely useful to Pozharskii. He sent men to the enemy camp who quickly discovered common ground with the Englishmen and Scotchmen in Lisowski's service. As soon as Shaw produced results, Pozharskii sent the mercenaries a letter under his signature. The commander promised the foreigners substantial rewards, "such as you cannot imagine," and vowed to observe any agreement he made with the Scotchman: "I have pledged my soul in full support of Captain Jacob Shaw." The Englishmen saw the Russian side had the advantage and came over in crowds from Lisowski's camp.

The days when Russian rebels had flocked to Lisowski's standard were long gone. His army was swiftly melting away, while Pozharskii's forces were growing stronger. Despairing of defeating the Russians, Lisowski left Orel for Kromy, suddenly turned north to Bolkhov, and sped to Kaluga. The knights rode day and night, giving their horses little rest. Lisowski hoped the Russians, having concentrated their forces at Orel, had left Kaluga unprotected. After covering 100 miles Lisowski and his men occupied Peremyshl and posed a direct threat to Kaluga, but they did not manage to outwit Pozharskii. The commander rushed captains and cavalry to Kaluga while remaining himself in Likhven to threaten Lisowski's flank. Reinforcements were on their way to Prince Dmitrii. The authorities held a levy in the Kazan area and collected as many as 7,000 Tatars, Cheremis, and Chuvash, "some baptized, some not." Each three residences furnished one soldier. Their weapons were primitive, consisting of pikes, axes, and spears. Many had nothing but bows and arrows. Prince Dmitrii took these reinforcements and advanced on Peremyshl. Lisowski had no intention of waiting for him. He burned the town and went off to Viazma. The threat to Moscow from Kaluga was eliminated.

After the exhausting campaign Prince Pozharskii was growing weary and had an attack of epilepsy. He assigned his brother, Lopata Pozharskii, the task of pursuing the enemy. Prince Lopata followed

Lisowski closely, but he was forced to abandon pursuit because "the people of Kazan all fled back home." The Cheremis force of 7,000 men dissolved before giving battle. The commander informed Moscow that "the soldiers have left service; those who remain are no good." Tsar Mikhail was angered. He ordered Lopata arrested and imprisoned. Driven out of Kaluga, Lisowski and his forces went to Rzhev. He had lost as much as half his army in his struggle with Pozharskii. All that remained of his 2,000-man detachment was 1,000 Lithuanians and Cherkassians, and 150 Russian cossacks. Lisowski had no foreigners left.

Boyar Fedor Sheremetev and his men were in Rzhev. The commander could have attacked Lisowski's tattered army but he preferred to stay in the fortress. Sheremetev's cowardly behavior encouraged Lisowski. Leaving Rzhev, he and his men moved east to Uglich without interference. They kept going, following isolated country tracks, past Yaroslavl, Suzdal, Murom, Riazan, and Tula, destroying everything they found along their way. The commanders were too slack to stop them. Prince Kurakin fought Lisowski after the latter had closed the circle and come out by Aleksin and Kaluga from the east but failed to check him.

The military problems forced Tsar Mikhail to remember the heroes of the liberation movement. The Moscow commons once again expressed alarm and concern. In order to keep the capital calm the authorities were obliged to solicit the services of men popular among the people. In spring, 1615 Romanov repaired to the Trinity-St. Sergius monastery, entrusting the capital to a boyar commission headed by the former council of seven member, Prince Ivan Vasilevich Golitsyn. Kuzma Minin was the most junior of his four assistants.

The war made new demands of the treasury. In 1616 elected representatives from the towns and taxpaying communes met in Moscow. The financial system was in disarray and the authorities could not obtain money from the people unless they received support from the national council. The selectmen agreed to assess an exceptional tax of a fifth of everyone's income and to create a special financial body, which was headed by the man in whom the people reposed the greatest trust. This was Prince Dmitrii Pozharskii, assisted by Semen Golovin, a secretary of the national militia, and three monks.

The country had never forgotten that it was Kuzma Minin who had conducted Pozharskii's financial levies. His tireless will and energy had enabled the army to acquire the resources it needed in order to undertake the Moscow campaign. He would have been Pozharskii's logical assistant, but Kuzma was absent from Moscow during the time the money was being collected. The Tatars and Cheremis in the Volga region rebelled during the winter of 1614-1615. Regional commanders put down the revolt, but late in 1615 the Moscow authorities sent Prince Romodanovskii and Kuzma Minin to Kazan to investigate the causes of popular discontent. Minin listened to complaints and determined that a local official, Sava Aristov, had burdened the people with exceptional fines, which he called sales, and imposts. He had Aristov tortured, although the man was of gentry origin.

The assignment in Kazan was the last service rendered by the man whom the entire country had elected. Minin had not been young when he had first appealed to the people of Nizhnii Novgorod to defend the motherland. He alone had been responsible for organizing the army. The Moscow campaign had exacted untold physical and moral sacrifices from him. When Moscow was liberated, Kuzma could consider his mission in life had been accomplished. He lived less than four years after the victory. The Kazan assignment hastened his demise. On the way back to Moscow in 1616 he was taken ill and died en route. So ended the life of this ordinary man from the town quarter, a mighty Russian patriot. Pozharskii was much younger than his colleague. He was destined to live another quarter of a century. His life was fraught with difficulties, trouble, and illness. He took part in all the major events of his time, but still remains an enigmatic figure.

The wars with the Rzeczpospolita and Sweden kept dragging on, bringing ruin and destruction to Russia. Pozharskii understood better than anyone it was impossible to fight on all fronts at once; he insisted on concluding immediate peace with Sweden. He held numerous meetings with an Englishman, John Merrick, who had assumed the task of diplomatic intermediary in the negotiations between Moscow and Stockholm. At the end of 1616 the national assembly in Moscow approved the terms of a treaty Russian diplomats had devised with Pozharskii's help. Eternal peace between the two countries was signed in the village of Stolbovo early in 1617. Russia lost control of the mouths of the Neva and Narova rivers, the Izhorsk land, and Karelia, but secured the return of what had been called the "Novgorod realm," including Great Novgorod, Staraia Rusa, and Ladoga.

Peace with Sweden came not a moment too soon. King Sigismund was again collecting forces throughout the Rzeczpospolita to crush the fractious Muscovites. He placed Chodkiewicz in command of the army. The 22-year-old Wladyslaw went with him. The young aspirant to the Muscovite throne set out for Russia determined to win it. The Muscovite commanders abandoned their positions before Smolensk and retired towards Moscow. The hetman did not press into Russia and had told his forces to prepare a winter camp, but as soon as he heard the tsar's commanders had cowardly fled from Viazma he at once ordered his men to occupy the town.

Lord Alexander Lisowski died shortly before the new Moscow campaign got under way and his detachment took no part in Wladyslaw's invasion. The hetman ordered Lisowski's men to storm across the Russian frontier from the southwest, where they again menaced Kaluga. Faced with this danger, the people of Kaluga sent to Moscow men chosen from all ranks, who insistently asked Tsar Mikhail to send Pozharskii to defend their town. The boyars complied with their request and on October 18, 1617 Prince Dmitrii was on his way to Kaluga, accompanied by two groups of Moscow gentry and three fusilier units. In Kaluga the command had had time to collect no more than some 800 lesser boyars and fusiliers. Pozharskii essentially was faced with the task of forming an army from scratch.

As it always had, the Russian command kept strong forces stationed on the frontier with the Tatars. When autumn came the threat of invasion by the Crimeans decreased. Pozharskii decided to bring up more than 1,000 gentry from the southern army. Fortresses along the steppe frontier were told to send to Kaluga 1,000 garrison fusiliers, cossacks and Zaporozhians in battle readiness.

As he had before, Pozharskii relied chiefly on the cossacks. Shortly prior to his departure for Moscow, Ivan Timofeev, nicknamed Sapozhok, a cossack captain, had asked him to send a competent commander to the Ugra area, where some 2,000 cossacks had gathered to forage for food. Prince Dmitrii enthusiastically agreed. His task was to bring the Ugra cossacks into nationalist service, give and receive mutual guarantees, and see to it they were supplied after they were assigned to camps on gentry estates in Kozelsk, Belev, and other districts. The treasury furnished Pozharskii 5,000 rubles. This money enabled him to pay salaries to approximately 1,000 cossacks. Pozharskii's success surpassed all expectations. One unit after another arrived in Kaluga. More than 2,000 cossacks ultimately joined Prince Dmitrii.

The Kaluga campaign showed how enormously popular Prince Dmitrii was. He attracted soldiers like a magnet. People seemed to be recalling the exciting days when the national militia was in the process of formation. Cossacks marched under Pozharskii's banner because they trusted him. They knew the illustrious national commander would never let them down, make them slaves to their former masters, or hang their leaders, and that he would do everything in his power to provide them with food and stipends.

Pozharskii's efforts were remarkably effective. He helped to keep the cossacks from wavering. After Wladyslaw invaded, unstable elements among them had begun to go over to the aggressor, but now cossack attitudes changed. Late in 1617 many cossacks were getting ready to leave Wladyslaw's army "in the sovereign's name for Zarutskii's cossacks at Kaluga." The following year several prominent atamans with their hosts, including Taras Chernyi, leader of the cossack army, and Ataman Yakovlev, abandoned the king's camp.

The Time of Troubles had taught the Russian people much. They now understood the importance of an armed popular militia. Arriving in Kaluga, Pozharskii called all citizens capable of bearing arms to the colors. Townsmen, their children and relatives, prisoners, neighbors, and sojourners were assigned to gates, towers, and walls in anticipation of enemy attack. More than 1,000 inhabitants of Kaluga, men from the town quarter and posting stations, and taxpaying peasants on monastery lands, were given arms, including rifles and other weapons, and took their place as defenders of the town. Pozharskii's preparations were most timely. Hetman Chodkiewicz considered Kaluga the main bastion protecting Moscow. If he could acquire the town the Poles would find themselves on the closest approaches to the Russian capital. The hetman decided to use more than just Lisowski's men against Kaluga; he accordingly dispatched Commander Opalinski and heavily-armed hussar cavalry.

Pozharskii had brought only a small detachment with him. Reinforcements coming from distant towns were slow and dilatory in arriving; thus it was not surprising that the first encounters with the enemy went badly for the Russians. On December 13, 1617 Opalinski's cavalry ambushed the Kaluga army and utterly routed it. One hundred men were killed and more than fifty wounded. The Poles captured Prince Dmitrii's young nephew. Ten days later the enemy tried to storm Kaluga. Opalinski devised a stratagem to keep down his losses. In the middle of the night his soldiers cautiously approached the inner defense line and suddenly charged down upon the sleeping town. The attack caught Pozharskii unawares, but although he could not prevent the enemy from advancing beyond the foreposts, the commander then counterattacked with all his forces. The foreigners turned and fled after suffering losses.[4] Unable to take Kaluga, Opalinski set up winter camp in the village of Tovarkov, ten miles away. Russians made sorties, kept the camp in a state of constant turmoil, took prisoners, and pressed Opalinski hard. The hussars also caused much harm to the people of Kaluga. Fortune favored first one side, then the other.

The Poles frequently tried to block the road that connected Kaluga with Moscow. Pozharskii cleverly foiled their attempts. Once he was told a band of knights had appeared on the Moscow highway; he immediately attacked and dispersed them. Enemy foragers active around Serpukhov and Obolensk caused great damage to the Russians. Pozharskii resolved to isolate them and had a redoubt built at Gorki. Opalinski tried to drive the Russians out of Gorki but failed to do so.

Although the boyars had excluded Pozharskii from the roster of major commanders, they often asked him to take charge of the main forces of the Russian army while naming noble commanders like Prince Boris Lykov, Pozharkii's longtime foe, to the supreme command. Mozhaisk had become the place where the bulk of the Russian forces were concentrated. Late in 1617 Wladyslaw tried to storm it but soon had to withdraw to Viazma. Early in summer, 1618 Hetman Chodkiewicz held a council of war in Viazma and unveiled his plan for the new Russian campaign. The hetman urged Wladyslaw to stay away from the ruined Smolensk highway and move to the area around Kaluga, which contained abundant supplies. The Polish command, anxious to avoid the main Russian forces massed in Mozhaisk and Volokolamsk, intended to break the Russian defense line at Kaluga, where there were fewer troops. Chodkiewicz was well informed about the humiliations Pozharskii had suffered. He first proposed to approach the distinguished commander and win him to the side of Lawful Tsar Wladyslaw. The Lithuanian hetman had crossed swords with Pozharskii on the battlefield but he had never been able to take his opponent's measure. To be true to the motherland was Pozharskii's guiding principle in life.

Meantime inconsequential people pestered the commander in Kaluga incessantly. Despite his exceptional services to the country, the traditional nobility and the newly-created lords constantly harassed him with precedence suits. A certain Ivan Koltovskii refused to accept appointment as junior commander at Kaluga. On June 10, 1618 Prince Dmitrii informed Moscow he had suffered an attack and lay near death. Tsar Mikhail told Steward Yurii Tatishchev to go to Kaluga, comfort Pozharskii, and help him regain his health. Tatishchev categorically

refused to visit the sick man. Times were tense; the tsar had such stubborn courtiers beaten with a knout and handed over to Prince Dmitrii.

Hetman Chodkiewicz was not allowed to attack Kaluga. The war
council in Viazma rejected his plan, although it was an excellent one.
Sigismund III's emissaries insisted that Wladyslaw should march
directly to Moscow. Kaluga was now less important than it had been.
Opalinski struck his camp in Tovarkov and went to Mozhaisk to link
up with Chodkiewicz. Freed from their dangerous neighbor, the people
of Kaluga heaved a sigh of relief. Wladyslaw's move on Moscow began inauspiciously. His armies attempted to overrun Borisov, a small
town near Mozhaisk, but the defenders of the tiny fortress courageously beat back two attacks. Then Chodkiewicz brought his troops
right up to Mozhaisk, set out batteries, and bombarded the town. So
many men were stationed in Mozhaisk that losses were inevitable. Supplies would not last long and famine threatened.

In order to rescue Lykov's army, which was encircled before
Mozhaisk, it was decided to summon Dmitrii Cherkasskii's regiments
and Pozharskii's Kaluga units. Cherkasskii moved from Volokolamsk
to Ruza and then sent a unit led by Prince Vasilii Cherkasskii to
Borovsk to assist Pozharskii. Several cossack units Pozharskii had
dispatched from Kaluga were present in Borovsk. They were told to
dig in near Pafnutii monastery and wait for the main force to arrive.
Prince Vasilii Cherkasskii was unwilling to take orders from Pozharskii or share the fruits of victory with him. A rash, impatient man, he
started persuading the atamans to attack the enemy at once, without
further delay. The Lithuanians were four and a half miles away from
the Borovsk monastery; without pausing to reflect, the cossacks joined
Cherkasskii and fought a battle, but the results were inconclusive. Each
commander followed his own inclinations. Beaten back by the foreigners, the soldiers grew confused and fled. Things would have gone very
badly indeed if two cavalry detachments of Smolensk gentry had not
rushed in to help. One hundred and fifty soldiers from Kaluga and sixty
men from Smolensk were left dead on the battlefield. Vasilii Cherkasskii, who was responsible for the defeat, returned ingloriously to Ruza.

The high command hoped for better things from the army led by
Prince Dmitrii Mamstriukovich Cherkasskii. The tsar ordered him to
proceed to Mozhaisk at once and dig in near the Luzhets monastery
close to town to ensure free access to the besieged camp. Cherkasskii
followed instructions, but as soon as his troops attempted to erect a
fortified redoubt before the monastery Chodkiewicz moved out

powerful forces against them. Unable to resist their onset, Cherkasskii barely managed to get back to Mozhaisk. He abandoned his baggage to the enemy.

Cherkasskii's defeat adversely affected the military situation. Supplies in Mozhaisk were running short. Cherkasskii's men had no provisions, nor could they obtain any. The intense battles around Mozhaisk continued unabated. The king's artillery intensified its bombardment. Units sustained losses; Prince Cherkasskii was nearly killed by cannon fire and was taken to Moscow more dead than alive. The boyars in the capital finally were forced to realize they had to rescue the army at Mozhaisk. Cherkasskii had failed. Now everything depended upon Pozharskii.

Prince Dmitrii moved to Borovsk from Kaluga. The problems at Borovsk had had an effect; the army was no longer confident and it was difficult to replenish the ranks. But Pozharskii firmly clung to the plan he had devised. His soldiers erected a redoubt near Pafnutii monastery and they were in solid control of the Mozhaisk road. Pozharskii's cavalry units attacked Chodkiewicz's siege camp incessantly. Staying away from major enemy detachments, they assailed his transport, harried his patrols, and took prisoners.

The boyars had to forget about settling old scores. They immediately dispatched any reinforcements that had arrived in Moscow to Pozharskii in Borovsk. The first to appear was an Astrakhan fusilier unit and Emir Karmash with some Tatars. Next, Associate Boyar Prince Grigorii Volkonskii arrived. This was the first instance when the boyars allowed a pedigreed nobleman of conciliar rank to serve under Pozharskii, but the situation was critical and there was no time to make choices. A picked force of more than 670 gentry from Moscow, Yaroslavl, and Kostroma accompanied Volkonskii to Borovsk. After receiving these reinforcements Prince Dmitrii proceeded to carry out his operation. He had to break the circle surrounding Lykov's and Cherkasskii's forces, immobilize the enemy, and prevent him from destroying the Russian army as it withdrew. This maneuvre required military skill and iron will. Confronting Chodkiewicz directly once more, Pozharskii acted coolly and resolutely.

The order to abandon the camp at Mozhaisk was unwelcome to many. People with timorous natures feared they might not survive if they retired. Commander Konstantin Ivashkin, who had heretofore been sitting impassively in the citadel of Borovsk, fled the town with his soldiers to Pozharskii's camp. The foreigners could have occupied the empty fortress but they were unable to do so because Pozharskii had anticipated them. Astrakhan fusiliers had appeared around the fortress somewhat earlier than the king's soldiers. Avoiding battle, the fusiliers ran up into the fortress and slammed the gate shut in the foe's face. Pozharskii himself and his regiments soon entered the Borovsk citadel. He straightway dispatched cavalry units to the outskirts of Mozhaisk. Although it was midsummer, the weather suddenly changed. Heavy rains fell and there were fierce thunderstorms almost every day. The bad weather proved advantageous for Pozharskii. One black rainy night Lykov's forces quitted the camp and quickly made their way to join Pozharskii. Commander Fedor Volynskii and an infantry detachment were all that was left under siege in Mozhaisk. Lykov successfully reached Borovsk on August 6, 1618. Prince Dmitrii admitted the retreating army and drew up behind it, ready to fight a rearguard action. Imminent catastrophe had been averted.

King Sigismund carefully followed his army's progress and looked everywhere for reinforcements. In 1617 Crown Hetman Zolkiewski had reached an agreement with Petr Sagadaichnyi and his senior council. A thousand Ukrainian cossacks were placed on the royal service register. A year later Sagadaichnyi participated in Wladyslaw's Moscow campaign.

While the main royal army was advancing from the west, Sagadaichnyi burned down Livny and Elets and started marching on the capital from the south. The Moscow command tried to stop the Zaporozhians on the Oka river. At this dangerous juncture Pozharskii's name was once more on everyone's lips. Prince Dmitrii was ordered to attack Sagadaichnyi at the ford across the Oka and check his advance on Moscow. Illness continued to plague Pozharskii but he hoped to overcome his malady. The distinguished commander's presence made the soldiers devoted and happy, but Pozharskii could not manage to bring the campaign to a conclusion. Fresh assaults on Serpukhov occurred and everyone expected the sick man might die at any time. The tsar ordered Pozharskii to come to the capital and entrusted the army to his assistant, Prince Grigorii Volkonskii, who was charged with occupying the fords across the Oka and barring Sagadaichnyi's route to Moscow. Volkonskii failed to achieve this goal and withdrew from the Oka to Kolomna. As soon as the troops were deprived of an authoritative leader disputes between cossacks and gentry at once broke out.

In times of war cossacks had to bear the heaviest burdens. Members of the gentry derived income from their estates but landless cossacks had to make do on modest salaries paid in cash. They received five rubles a year, which defrayed no more than part of their expenses: one horse cost five or ten rubles. During the Serpukhov campaign, the cossacks in Pozharskii's army sent a petition to Moscow "about our want and poverty, and about our salaries and maintenance." Since they had no money, the cossacks took fodder for their horses from the people. Volkonskii tried to stop the thieving and ordered them punished. Disturbances broke out in the ranks. The cossacks said: "Here for a year you've been promising us salaries while we, naked and barefoot, are dying. And what are we dying for? You will take our straw and hay, while we are beaten with a knout!" A rumor went round in the cossack camps that Boyar Lykov was on his way to Serpukhov to deal with disobedient cossacks.

Volkonskii lacked authority and proved incapable of coping with cossack unrest. Atamans deserted him and continued to fight on their own. They went to Vladimir, where they defeated a large Zaporozhian detachment; afterwards they stayed in camps situated in the Yaroslavl district. In Tsar Vasilii's day this district had belonged to Mstislavskii. When Zarutskii was head of the original national government he had divided it up in order to maintain his cossacks, but Mikhail Romanov gave the land back to his president of the boyar council. The cossacks had not forgiven Mstislavskii for his treason. They had not besieged him for eighteen months in the Kremlin to see his power and wealth restored to him. Pozharskii's units contained many cossacks who had formerly served under Zarutskii. After taking the Yaropolcheskii area the cossacks showed what they thought of those they termed "wicked boyars."

The cossack army soon exceeded 2,500 or 3,000 men. The war council tried to maintain strict discipline. Drinking wine was forbidden under pain of death, but the order was not enforced. Cossacks were taking supplies from the holdings of Mstislavskii and other boyars and gentry as well, with the sole exception of Dmitrii Pozharskii's estates. When Commander Lykov sent couriers to the cossacks they told them: "In Viazniki the cossack assembly has enacted that no one shall set foot on Boyar Prince Dmitrii Mikhailovich Pozharskii's patrimonies, or his villages, or his hamlets, or set fire to, kill, or rob his peasants." The cossack conclave's decree proved that Pozharskii continued to enjoy remarkable popularity among the unfortunate. The statute pertaining to Prince Dmitrii's patrimonies was rigorously adhered to. Pozharskii's peasants freely journeyed to cossack encampments, sold supplies, and bought all sorts of goods.

Cossacks were not the bandits official documents claim they were. Their petitions to the tsar provide a clear picture of what they wanted and demanded. They were willing to go back into service but they refused to give up the freedom they had paid for in blood. The cossack army contained many fugitive slaves and indentured peasants. Its assembly sternly insisted the tsar must not constrain any of them to revert to his former status. Veterans of the national liberation movement wrote that they had received no reward for freeing Moscow. Now they were suffering and nobody cared. They were "naked, barefoot, and in lack of everything." They asked for higher salaries and permission to keep the supplies they had removed from Mstislavskii's domain.

The cossacks built a strong redoubt in Viazniki. Their demands were supported by units stationed in Moscow. Early in November some 3,000 cossacks broke through the wall of Wooden Town across the Yauza river, left Moscow, and took the Vladimir highway for Viazniki. The tsar sent Boyar Trubetskoi in pursuit. The former national commander found it difficult to persuade them to return. The entire complement of the boyar council had to come out to negotiate with the cossacks in their camps. Tsar and boyars frequently sent couriers to Viazniki. No matter what they said, the cossacks replied that they were prepared to serve only if the authorities met their demands and they were again allowed to fight under Pozharskii. The illustrious commander had reason to be proud that the people believed so strongly in him.

Once more the war had exposed how shaky the edifice of the Romanov monarchy actually was. The elected national representatives had no idea what sort of man they had placed over the realm, but for five years the people had been in a position to observe him. The savage reprisals he had taken against cossacks and rebels had not endeared him to the populace. Mikhail had proved incapable of giving the country an effective government. The people saw his entourage filled with the same treacherous boyars, whose abilities to handle difficult situations again had signally failed to pass the test. As soon as Boyar Lykov withdrew from Mozhaisk, serving men and the people of Moscow demanded an explanation from the senior boyars. An armed crowd stormed into the Kremlin, led by Zhezdrinskii from Nizhnii Novgorod, Turgenev from Yaroslavl, and Tukhachevskii from Smolensk. The people loudly charged into the palace, where Mstislavskii and his associates were in session, and threatened to do them in. The confrontation almost came to blows. Patriots were ready to strike down Wladyslaw's covert supporters with their own hands.

Moscow's ruling circles were alarmed. Wladyslaw's secret partisans had good reason to hide away grant deeds the prince had given them. They tried to sow panic everywhere. At the time a strange natural phenomenon attracted attention. A comet paused above Moscow. Holding their hands aloft, people of little confidence exclaimed: "The prince will take Moscow. This dark-red comet portends unprecedented misfortune and bloodshed."

On September 20, 1618 the king's army approached the capital from Volokolamsk. Former Moscow Elder Gosiewski and Hetman Chodkiewicz were once more at the city's gate and this time Tsar Wladyslaw was with them. They were sure their supporters would cooperate. The people watched suspiciously each move the boyars made. Everyone remembered the recent disaster. In areas of new construction there were huge gaping holes and old burned-out buildings, which served as reminders how the interventionists had behaved in Moscow. Patriots' fears intensified when Sagadaichnyi's troops came up to the city from the south. As the garrison looked on, the Zaporozhians conducted their forces past Donskoi monastery to Wladyslaw's camp. The Russian command concentrated a large force in the Transriver district. Regiments entered the field and formed up in battle array to prevent the two enemy armies from linking up. At the decisive moment the boyars wavered and did not dare attack the enemy. Soldiers dejectedly walked back along the streets of the capital to the fortress. The confusion and disorder existing among the ranks of the senior boyars once more had threatened to cause great misfortune.

Early in September, 1618 the national council held sessions in Moscow. Assembly members decided to summon the city's entire population to defend the fortress. The tsar and his suite were forcibly reminded that the armed people had been essential to the liberation of Moscow. Now they were demanding arms once more to protect the capital from the enemy. The Military Affairs chancellery disposed merchants and townsmen along walls and gates with the soldiers. The walls of White Town and the Transriver district were guarded by 6,500 men; taxpaying men from the town quarter constituted the largest group. Some 2,000 citizens had muskets while 2,500 more patrolled with spears. Several days before the epochal encounter with the Poles, Tsar Mikhail had invited Pozharskii to a banquet in his palace and gave him a gold pitcher and a sable coat. He employed the occasion to enumerate Prince Dmitrii's services: he had resisted the foreigners, built a redoubt, slain many of the enemy, often sent prisoners he had taken to the ruler, been concerned with the sovereign's and the nation's problems and pondered them, and had assisted Lykov while he was proceeding from Mozhaisk to Moscow.

Just before the decisive engagement two French sappers who had been serving in Wladyslaw's army defected to the Russians. They gave information about the preparations for the attack and where it would fall. The boyars suspected Chodkiewicz had sent the sappers and refused to believe them. Out of caution they sent reinforcements to the west gate. In this instance they were well advised. After midnight on September 30, 1618 the king's forces moved up to storm the Russian capital. Advancing under cover of darkness to Earthen Town, soldiers smashed in the gate of the wooden redoubt and charged inside. Picking their way along the streets of Earthen Town, troops reached the Arbat and Tver gates of White Town. Lord Nowodworski and his sappers were ready to set a charge and blow up the Arbat gate, but the Muscovites greeted the invaders with a hail of bullets. Wounded in the arm, Nowodworski was unable to execute the hetman's order.

Shots aroused the sleeping capital. Snatching up weapons, the people ran to the site of the nocturnal conflict. From his residence Prince Dmitrii, accompanied by a large armed retinue, reached Arbat gate before any of the others. The arrival of the popular commander inspired the soldiers. Once again, as in his greatest years, Prince Dmitrii "fought in battles and attacks, not sparing his person."[5] As soon as the night haze lifted the Russians opened the gate and fell upon the foe. Nowodworski had to beat a hasty retreat. The unit trying to penetrate White Town from Tver gate had no better luck. The ladders the soldiers mounted were too short. The men realized this after they had clambered up but could not reach the edge of the walls from the highest rung.

Since he had sustained heavy losses, Chodkiewicz decided not to order another attack. He had failed to pierce even the outer line of stone walls and behind it loomed the impregnable Kremlin with cannon pointing in every direction. After this failure before Moscow, Chodkiewicz withdrew towards the Trinity monastery. Wladyslaw demanded the monks take an oath to him. He was answered with cannon fire. The king's army retreated beyond Trinity to the village of Rogachevo, the site of the hetman's former camp. Bands of mercenaries fanned out to plunder the river towns, but they met with no success anywhere. Commanders from Yaroslavl defeated the foreigners at Nerekhta and Poshekhone.

Sagadaichnyi left Moscow for Kaluga but could not take the fortress. An assembly of cossack elders had allowed King Sigismund to use the Zaporozhian army in the war with Russia, but ordinary cossacks were intensely dissatisfied with a conflict that seemed pointless to them. Wladyslaw soon became convinced the Zaporozhians were fickle. Colonel Zhdan Konshin took his force of 600 men over into Russian service. A year later, on behalf of the entire cossack host Sagadachnyi asked the patriarch of the Orthodox church in Constantinople to be forgiven for having participated in the Moscow campaign, and told the Muscovite government that the Ukrainian cossacks were genuinely anxious to serve Russia.

Wladyslaw's army remained in Rogachevo, where it had to endure a harsh winter in hostile country. His army lacked an effective communication system. Chodkiewicz had not managed to take a single one of the Russian redoubts to his rear. Wladyslaw was literally forced to give up the war because the Polish assembly had refused to finance his campaign beyond the end of the year, which was rapidly approaching. Voices in the Rzeczpospolita were constantly raised, insisting that peace with Russia should be concluded at once. The Turks were menacing Poland's southern frontiers; fighting in Livonia had slackened, but the two-year truce that had been signed meant neither war nor peace. The enemy attack once more had aroused Russia's patriots, who demanded decisive action against the invaders. Regiments were hastily formed in Nizhnii Novgorod and Yaroslavl. But the Romanov faction was not the group to lead a popular crusade.

The senior boyars could not get over their fear of Lord Gosiewski. When Fedor Sheremetev and Prince Mezetskii came to negotiate with the Poles they had to listen again to arrogant speeches. Gosiewski and other envoys never stopped boasting about their presumed might and they sought to instil fear into the boyars. They promised they would give Russia a peace in which "not a single young man will survive either in Moscow or in the other towns." Wladyslaw and his army were advancing on the Transriver district. The country would be utterly ruined and devastated. There would be nothing left but earth and water. Gosiewski did not hesitate to expostulate with the boyars who had recently groveled before him. He hinted to Sheremetev that another Dmitrii might soon appear in Muscovy. In Wladyslaw's camp people were openly saying it was another child that had been hanged in Moscow; the real Ivan Dmitrievich had gone into hiding in Lithuania.

The council of seven's treachery had cost the country dear. Many sons of the fatherland had died to liberate Moscow. But the new dynasty had restored power to the same boyars, who still had no idea of how to protect the national interest. The goal of Polish-Lithuanian diplomacy was to isolate and appropriate western Belorussia. The boyar council made concessions that were to cause Russia no end of trouble. On December 1, 1618 Sheremetev signed a fourteen-year truce at Dulino. Its conditions were onerous. Lithuania obtained the whole of the Smolensk and Chernigov regions. In addition to the towns the foreigners had occupied, Sigismund acquired border fortresses that had resisted the attacks of his mercenaries. The boyars agreed to surrender the fortresses as they stood, including cannon and military equipment, rural peasants, and town quarters. The king acquired some thirty towns. The new frontier now ran close to Viazma, Rzhev, and Kaluga. Sigismund had made another war inevitable.

Enormous effort had been expended in the attempt to unify the Great Russian nation. The truce confounded the goals of this movement. The king's diplomats had played adroitly upon the weaknesses of the Romanov dynasty. Filaret Romanov was still a prisoner in Poland. When Sigismund set out to conquer Muscovy the former tsar, Vasilii Shuiskii, and his brother had only just died. The Romanov faction recalled what had happened to them and felt concern about Filaret. This group heedlessly subordinated the national interest to personal concerns. To every new demand Lew Sapieha put forward, energetic Marfa and her son replied that all conditions would be accepted provided Filaret was released.

The peace was cruel and humiliating, but the Russian people accepted it with a sigh of relief. For fifteen years Russia had been devastated by civil war and foreign intervention. Innumerable burned-out edifices and ruins covered the land from the southern steppe to the Arctic Ocean. Towns and villages were depopulated. Ravens fluttered above the ashes. But the gloom was over. The Russian people had defended their native realm and now could return to peaceful work. Their efforts alone would restore Russia's prosperity and power.

NOTES

EDITOR'S INTRODUCTION

1. A popular study, *Minin i Pozharskii* (Moscow, 1981), in the series "Lives of Celebrated Men" founded in 1933 by Maksim Gorkii, and a scientific monograph, *Sotsialno-politicheskaia borba v russkom gosudarstve v nachale XVII veka* (Leningrad, 1985).

2. R.G. Skrynnikov, *Boris Godunov*. Ed. and trans. by Hugh F.Graham (Gulf Breeze Fla., Academic International Press, 1982), pp. 126-154.

3. S.F. Platonov, *The Time of Troubles* (Trans. by John T. Alexander), 2nd. ed., Lawrence, Kan., 1985. The first edition of this translation appeared in 1970. In a supplement "For Further Reading" (reproduced as pp. 183-191 in the second edition) Professor Alexander has provided an exhaustive bibliography of materials in English pertaining broadly to the late sixteenth and early seventeenth centuries. In his 1985 "Bibliographical Update" (pp. 192-204 of the second edition) Professor Alexander demonstrates the truth of his contention that, "since 1970, research published in English on late medieval and early modern Muscovy has literally exploded," although not all the materials he cites deal specifically with the period from 1604 to 1617 that forms the subject of Professor Skrynnikov's present book.

AUTHOR'S INTRODUCTION

1. V.N. Tatishchev, *Istoriia rossiiskaia,* Vol.7 (Leningrad, 1968), p. 367.

2. M.M. Shcherbatov, *Istoriia rossiiskaia*, Vol.7, Pt.2 (Moscow, 1791), p. 147.

3. N.M. Karamzin, *Istoriia gosudarstva rossiiskogo*, Vol. 12 (St. Petersburg, 1843), p. 15.

4. S.M. Soloviev, *Istoriia Rossii s drevneishikh vremen*, Bk. 4, Vols.7-8 (Moscow, 1960), p. 391.

5. N.I. Kostomarov, "Smutnoe vremia Moskovskogo gosudarstva v nachale XVII v.," in *Istoricheskie monografii i issledovaniia*, Bk. 2 (1904), pp. 280, 637-638.

6. M.V. Nechkina, *Vasilii Osipovich Kliuchevskii* (Moscow, 1974), p. 517.

7. V.O. Kliuchevskii, *Sochineniia*, Vol. 3 (Moscow, 1957), p. 48.

8. *Ibid.*, p. 60.

9. *Ibid.*, p. 51.

10. S.F. Platonov, *Ocherki po istorii Smuty v Moskovskom gosudarstve XVI-XVII vv.* (Moscow, 1937), pp. 475-476.

11. *Ibid.*, pp. 291, 412, 430.

12. M.N. Pokrovskii, *Russkaia istoriia v samom szhatom ocherke*, Pt. 1, Moscow, 1920.

13. N.N. Firsov, Krestianskaia revoliutsiia na Rusi v XVII v., Moscow and Leningrad, 1927 [M.-L.]; S.G.Tominskii, *Krestianskoe dvizhenie v feodalno-krepostnoi Rossii*, Moscow, 1932.

14. S.M. Dubrovskii, "Krestianskie voiny v Rossii XVII-XVIII vv.," in *Krestianskie voiny*, Moscow, 1925.

15. B.D. Grekov, *Krestiane na Rusi*, Bk.2, Moscow, 1954.

16. I.I. Smirnov, *Vosstanie Bolotnikova*, Moscow, 1951. [He followed this with *Kratkii ocherk istorii vosstaniia Bolotnikova*, Moscow, 1953. See also A.I.Kopane and

A.G.Mankov, eds., *Vosstanie I. Bolotnikova. Dokumenty i materialy*, Moscow, 1959— ed.].

17. *Smuta* [disorder, troubles] is a term known to Russian historical thought in the seventeenth century. It was interpreted narrowly in bourgeois-court literature as synonymous with anarchy and revolt of the lower orders against society. Pokrovskii imbued the word with new meaning by viewing the Time of Troubles as primarily a string of risings by the popular masses. However, Smirnov indefensibly rejected this concept of the Troubles by declaring the term "bourgeois." This led Smirnov to abandon the concept that the events of the early seventeenth century constituted a single set of social, political, and military upheavals.

18. L.B. Gelkin, *Iaroslavskii krai i razgrom polskoi interventsii v Moskovskom gosudarstve v nachale XVII v.*, Yaroslavl, 1939; P.G. Liubomirov, *Ocherk istorii Nizhegorodskogo opolcheniia 1611-1613 gg.*, Moscow, 1939 [reprinted, The Hague, 1969—ed.].

19. I.S. Shepelev, *Osvoboditelnaia i klassovaia borba v Russkom gosudarstve v 1608-1610 gg.*, Piatigorsk, 1957. A book by N.P.Dolinin, *Podmoskovskie polki ("kazatskie tabory") v natsionalno-osvoboditelnom dvizhenii 1611-1612 gg.* (Kharkov, 1958), has much in common with Shepelev's work.

20. "O krestianskoi voine v Russkom gosudarstve v nachale XVII v. (obzor diskussii)," *Voprosy istorii*, 5 (1961), pp. 102-120.

21. A.A. Zimin, "Voprosy istorii krestianskoi voiny v Rossii v nachale XVII v.," *Voprosy istorii*, 3 (1958), p. 99.

22. D.P. Makovskii, *Pervaia krestianskaia voina v Rossii*, Smolensk, 1967.

23. V.I. Koretskii, *Formirovanie krepostnogo prava i pervaia krestianskaia voina v Rossii*, Moscow, 1975.

24. V.D.Nazarov, "O nekotorykh osobennostiakh krestianskoi voiny nachala XVII v.," in *Feodalnaia Rossiia vo vsemirno-istoricheskom protsesse* (Moscow, 1972), pp. 120, 126.

25. L.V. Cherepnin, "Krestianskie voiny v Rossii perioda feodalizma," in L.V.Cherepnin, ed., *Voprosy metodologii istoricheskogo issledovaniia* (Moscow, 1981), pp. 166-167.

26. V.I. Kutanov, *Krestianskaia voina v Rossii XVII-XVIII vv.* (Moscow, 1976), p. 49.

27. B.N. Floria, *Russko-polskie otnosheniia i baltiiskii vopros v kontse XVI-nachale XVII v.*, Moscow, 1973; id., *Russko-polskie otnosheniia i politicheskoe razvitie vostochnoi Evropy vo vtoroi polovine XVI-nachale XVII v.*, Moscow, 1978; V.D. Nazarov and B.N. Floria, "Krestianskoe vosstanie pod predvoditelstvom I.I. Bolotnikova i Rech Pospolitaia," in *Krestianskie voiny v Rossii XVII-XVII vv. Problemy, poiski, resheniia*, Moscow, 1974.

28. L.V. Cherepnin, *Zemskie sobory russkogo gosudarstva v XVI-XVII vv.*, Moscow, 1978.

29. [Better known as *Synodicals*, these were lists of individuals slain during the oprichnina years that Ivan the Terrible caused to have drawn up at the end of his life so that prayers for the souls of the deceased might be uttered in churches. Professor Skrynnikov has improved upon the pioneering work Academician S.B. Veselovskii did on the Synodicals and now they serve as a vital source for the oprichnina phase of Ivan's reign. See R.G. Skrynnikov, *Ivan the Terrible*. Ed. and trans. by Hugh F.

Graham (Gulf Breeze Fla., Academic International Press, 1981, pp. 108-111—ed.].

CHAPTER 1

1. Stanislaw Niemojewski, *Pamietnik*, ed. by A. Hirschberg. The Russian translation Professor Skrynnikov uses is "Zapiski," in A.A. Titov, *Rukopisi sliavianskie i russkie, prinadlezhashchie I. A. Vakhromeevu*, No. 6 (Moscow, 1907), p. 115.

2. *Russkaia istoricheskaia biblioteka* (RIB) 13, 2nd. ed., (SPb., 1909), Col. 734.

3. *Akty, sobrannye i izdannye v bibliotekakh i arkhivakh rossiiskoi Imperii arkheograficheskoi ekspeditsiei*, Vol. 2 (1836), p. 385 (AAE).

4. A. Dmitrievskii, *Arsenii, arkhiepiskop Elassonskii. Istoricheskie memuary* (Kiev, 1899), p. 102.

5. *Sobranie gosudarstevnnykh gramot i dogovorov*, 2 (1819), p. 208 (SGGD).

6. RIB, 1 (1872), col. 109; *Starina i novizna*, 14 (1911), p. 540 (SN).

7. Jacques Margeret, "Zapiski," in N.G. Ustrialov, ed., *Skazaniia sovremennikov o Dmitrie samozvantse*, 3rd. ed., Pt. 1 (SPb., 1859), p. 87 [Readers can find this French source in a recent, accessible edition: Chester S.L. Dunning, ed. and trans., *The Russian Empire and the Grand Duchy of Moscow*, Pittsburgh, Penn., 1983—ed.]; Nie-mojewski, *Zapiski*, p. 114.

8. *Polnoe sobranie russkikh letopisei* (PSRL), 14 (1965), p. 67; SN, p. 253; "Pinezhskii letopisets," in *Rukopisnye nasledie Drevnei Rusi* (Leningrad, 1972), p. 83.

9. AAE, 2, p. 94.

10. PSRL, 14, p. 67.

11. Smirnov, *Bolotnikov. Prilozheniia*, p. 552.

12. RIB, 1, cols. 400-402.

13. SGGD, 2, p. 234.

14. Paul Pierling, S.J., *Dmitrii Samozvanets* (Moscow, 1912), p. 318.

15. SGGD, 2, p. 262.

CHAPTER 2

1. SGGD, 2, p. 260.

2. Stanislaw Zolkiewski, *Poczatek i progres wojny moskiewskiej* (Waclaw Sobieski, ed.), Kraków, 1920; Jarema Maciszewski, ed., Warsaw, 1966). [These are recent editions of the original, which Professor Skrynnikov quotes from a translation: *Zapiski getmana Zholkevskogo o Moskovskoi voine* (SPb., 1871), p.11. Readers can find this Polish source in an accessible edition: Jedrzej Giertych, trans., *Expedition to Moscow. A Memoir by Hetman Stanislaw Zolkiewski* (with a preface by Sir Robert Bruce Lockhart), London, 1959—ed.]; P. Petreius, *Istoriia o velikom kniazhestve Moskovskom* (Moscow, 1867), p. 373.

3. Y. A. Limonov, ed., *Relatsiia Petra Petreia o Rossii nachala XVII v.* (Moscow, 1976), pp. 99-100.

4. Zolkiewski, p. 10.

5. A. Morozov, ed. and trans., *Isaak Massa. Kratkoe izvestie o Moskovii v nachale XVII v.*, Moscow, 1937 [Professor Skrynnikov uses a Russian translation. Readers can find this Dutch source in a recent, accessible edition: G.Edward Orchard, trans., *A Short History of the Beginnings and Origins of These Present Wars in Moscow under the Reigns of Various Sovereigns down to the Year 1610, by Isaac Massa*, Toronto, 1982—ed.].

6. *Pamiatniki starinnogo russkogo iazyka i slovesnosti XV-XVII stoletii*, 1 (SPb., 1907), pp. 5-6, 11.
7. Pierling, p. 304.
8. SGGD, 2, p. 243.

CHAPTER 3

1. K. Bussow, *Moskovskaia khronika 1583-1613 gg.* (Moscow and Leningrad, 1961), p. 110.
2. AAE, 2, p. 175.
3. *Pamiatniki russkogo prava*, 4 (1956), p. 376.
4. *Ibid.*, pp. 540-541.
5. Niemojewski, p. 65.
6. *Akty iuridicheskie, ili sobrannye form starinnogo deloproizvodstva* (SPb.,1838), p. 389.
7. Pierling, p. 266.
8. SGGD, 2, p. 298.
9. Bussow, p. 132.
10. SGGD, 2, p. 298.
11. Niemojewski, p. 75.
12. Massa, p.137; Bussow, p. 118.
13. Niemojewski, pp. 95-97; Ustrialov, *Skazaniia*, 4, pp. 190-191.

CHAPTER 4

1. O.A. Derzhavina, ed., "Piskarevskii letopisets," *Materialy po istorii SSSR (XV-XVII vv.)*, 2 (1955), p. 123.
2. Bussow, pp. 133-134.
3. SGGD, 2, pp. 299-300.
4. Niemojewski, p. 102.
5. Massa, p. 130.
6. Margeret, p. 100.
7. RIB, 13, cols. 1314-1315.
8. A.M. Gnevushev, *Akty vremeni pravleniia tsaria Vasiliia Shuiskogo* (Moscow, 1915), p. 3.
9. W. Dyamentowski, "Pamietnik," in A. Hirschberg, ed., *Polska a Moskwa w pierwszej polowie wieku XVII*, Lwow, 1901.
10. *Sbornik Imperatorskogo russkogo istoricheskogo obshchestva*, 137 (1912), p. 375 (SIRIO).
11. AAE, 2, pp. 138-147.
12. Massa, pp. 299-300.
13. Smirnov, p. 489.

CHAPTER 5

1. Koretskii, *Formirovanie krepostnogo prava*, pp. 347-351.
2. Bussow, p. 144.
3. Zolkiewski, *Prilozheniia*, p. 192.
4. S. Maltsev, "Barkulabovskaia letopis," *Arkheograficheskii ezhegodnik za 1960*

god (Moscow, 1962), p. 317.

5. Shepelev, *Osvoboditelnaia i klassovaia borba*, p. 42

CHAPTER 6

1. Soloviev, *Istoriia Rossii*, 4, p. 530.

2. PSRL, 14, p. 87.

3. A. Hirschberg, *Marina Mniszchowna*, Lwow, 1906; Russian translation (quoted here) by A.A. Titov (Moscow, 1908), p. 147.

4. Zolkiewski, p. 15.

CHAPTER 7

1. RIB, 1, col. 167.

2. "Dnevnik Martyna Stadnitskogo, Pt. 2," *Russkii arkhiv*, 6 (1906), p. 189.

3. Bussow, p. 163.

4. RIB, 1, cols. 163-164.

5. *Ibid.*, col. 524.

6. SIRIO, 142 (1913), p. 69.

7. PSRL, 14, pp. 92-93.

8. *Skazaniia Massy i Gerkmana o Smutnom vremeni v Rossii* (SPb., 1874), pp. 313-314.

9. V.S. Ikonnikov, *Kniaz M.V. Skopin* (SPb., 1875), pp. 229-230.

10. Zolkiewski, pp. 59-61; S.A. Belokurov, *Razriadnye zapisi za smutnoe vremia* (Moscow, 1907), pp. 54-55; RIB, 1, col. 623; Samuel Maskiewicz: see "Pamietnik Samuela Maskiewicza" in Wladyslaw Czaplinski, ed., *Pamietniki Samuela i Boguslawa Maskiewiczow*, Wroclaw, 1961. [Skrynnikov cites this work from Ustrialov, *Skazaniia*, Pt. 2 (SPb., 1859), pp. 40-42—ed.].

11. PSRL, 14, p. 99.

CHAPTER 8

1. PSRL, 14, p. 99; A.N. Popov, *Obzor khronografov russkoi redaktsii*, Vol. 2 (Moscow, 1869), p. 346.

2. Bussow, p. 174.

3. PSRL, 34, p. 255.

4. SGGD, 2, pp. 388-389; Belokurov, p. 19.

5. S.F. Platonov, *Ocherki po istorii Smuty v Moskovskom gosudarstve XVI-XVII vv.* (Moscow, 1937), p. 426.

6. SGGD, 2, p. 389.

7. RIB, 1, col. 203.

8. D.V.Tsvetaev, *K istorii Smutnogo vremeni*, Vol. 1 (Moscow, 1916), pp. 12-15; Zolkiewski, pp. 78-79.

9. SIRIO, 142, p. 93.

10. *Ibid.*, p. 108.

11. *Akty istoricheskie, sobrannye i izdannye arkheograficheskoi komissiei*, 2 (1841), p. 355 (AI).

12. Zolkiewski, p. 89; PSRL, 14, p. 102.

13. RIB, 1, cols. 680-683.

14. Maskiewicz, in *Skazaniia*, 2, p. 47.
15. M. Marchocki, *Historia wojny moskiewskiej*, Poznan, 1841.
16. Soloviev, 4, pp. 601, 606.

CHAPTER 9

1. AI, 2, p. 422.
2. *Ibid.*, pp. 438-440.
3. Soloviev, 4, p. 611.
4. *Akty zapadnoi Rossii*, 4 (1852), pp. 327, 347.
5. Maskiewicz, p. 47.
6. *Ibid.*, p. 46.
7. Soloviev, 4, p. 617.
8. *Ibid.*, p. 627.
9. RIB, 1, col. 691.
10. AAE, 2, p. 301.
11. Bussow, p. 170.
12. *Sbornik kniazia Khilkova*, 12 (1879), p. 126.
13. Bussow, p. 178; AI, 2, p. 364.
14. Zolkiewski, p. 113.
15. Bussow, p. 29, Note 12.
16. AI, 2, pp. 358-359.
17. Zolkiewski, pp. 114-115.
18. RIB, 13, col. 210.

CHAPTER 10

1. AAE, 2, p. 308.
2. Maskiewicz, p. 49; *Rukopis, Zholkevskogo, izd. Pavlom Mukhanovym* (Moscow, 1835), pp. 304-305.
3. Dmitrievskii, *Arsenii*, p. 146.
4. M.N.Tikhomirov, *Rossia v XVI stoletii* (Moscow, 1962), p. 79.
5. Maskiewicz, p. 61.
6. Bussow, p. 187.
7. Dmitrievskii, p. 147.
8. Maskiewicz, p. 62.
9. PSRL, 14, p. 109.
10. Bussow, p. 187.

CHAPTER 11

1. Belokurov, p. 166; Maskiewicz, p. 66; Marchocki, p. 118.
2. AAE, 2, p. 312.
3. PSRL, 14, pp. 109-112.
4. G.V.Forsten, *Baltiiskii vopros v XVI i XVII stoletiiakh* (1544-1648), Vol. 2, (SPb., 1894), p. 87.
5. AAE, 2, p. 317.
6. I. Videkind, *Istoriia shvedsko-moskovskoi voiny*. Manuscript in Arkhiv LOII, F. 276, op. 1, No. 140, p. 169. [This is Johan Widekindi (1618?-1678),*Then fordom*

stormachtigste, hogborne furstes och herres Gustaff Adolphs, den Andres och stores...,
Stockholm, 1691—ed.].

7. *Ibid.*, p. 168.
8. *Novgorodskie letopisi* (SPb., 1879), p. 352.
9. Videkind, p. 203.
10. *Ibid.*, p. 302.
11. Forsten, *Baltiiskii vopros*, p. 148.

CHAPTER 12

1. D. Ch. A. Veltman, "O sokhrannosti utvarei tsarskogo china, ili regalii, vo vremia bytnosti polskikh i litovskikh voisk v Moskve v 1610-1612 godakh," *Chteniia Imperatorskogo obshchestva istorii i drevnostei rossiiskikh pri Moskovskom universitete* 5 (1848), p. 63 [ChIOIDR].
2. RIB, 13, col. 550.
3. *Rukopis...Mukhanovym*, p. 183.
4. I.E. Zabelin, *Minin i Pozharskii*, 3rd. ed. (Moscow, 1896), Prilozheniia, p. 264.
5. *Ibid.*, p. 265.
6. AAE, 2, p. 326.
7. L.M. Sukhotin, ed., "Zemelnye pozhalovaniia v Moskovskom gosudarstve pri tsare Vladislave. 1610-1611 gg," ChIOIDR, Bk. 4 (239), No. 8 (1911), p. xiii, Note 2.
8. Videkind, p. 168.
9. AAE, 2, p. 243.
10. PSRL, 14, p. 112.
11. ChIOIDR (see Note 7 above), pp. 3-4.
12. AAE, 2, p. 240.

CHAPTER 13

1. A. Hirschberg, *Maryna Mniszchowna*, pp. 308-309.
2. RIB, 2 (1874), col. 326.
3. Dmitrievskii, p. 157.
4. RIB, 1, cols. 283-284.

CHAPTER 14

1. PSRL, 4, pp. 323, 325.
2. *Pskovskie letopisi* 1 (M.-L., 1940), pp. 136-137.
3. Videkind, p. 165.
4. *Ibid.*, p. 109.
5. *Pskovskie letopisi*, 2 (M.-L.), 1955, p. 276.
6. RIB, 1, col. 287.
7. Zabelin, *Minin i Pozharskii*, p. 282.

CHAPTER 15

1. AAE, 2, p. 246.
2. *Ibid.*, p. 243.

3. *Pamiatniki istorii Nizhnegorodskogo dvizheniia v epokhu Smuty*, Vol. 11 (Nizhnii Novgorod, 1912), p. 428.
1. *Ibid.*, p. 129.
5. *Ibid.*, pp. 446-448.
6. *Vremennik Moskovskogo obshchestva istorii i drevnostei rossiiskikh*, 17 (1853), p. 145.
7. SGGD, 2, p. 281.
8. GPB., OR., Pogodin sobranie, No. 1501, 1.48 ob.
9. AAE, 2, p. 250.
10. *Ibid.*

CHAPTER 16
1. GPB., OR., Pogodin sobranie, No. 1501, 1.50 ob.
2. SGGD, 2, p. 596.
3. *Pamiatniki nizhegorodskogo dvizheniia*, p. 165.
4. "Smutnoe vremia Moskovskogo gosudarstva 1604-1613 gg. Akty vremeni mezhdutsarstva," ChIOIDR, 4 (255), (1915), No. 3, pp. 54-56.
5. AAE, 2, p. 256.
6. *Ibid.*
7. *Pamiatniki nizhegorodskogo dvizheniia*, pp. 252-253.
8. Liubomirov, *Ocherki...nizhegorodskogo opolcheniia*, p. 145.
9. *Pamiatniki nizhegorodskogo dvizheniia*, p. 254.
10. SGGD, 2, p. 598.
11. AAE, 2, p. 279.
12. *Dopolneniia k aktam istoricheskim*, 1 (1846), p. 288.

CHAPTER 17
1. RIB, 1, col. 295.
2. RIB, 2, cols. 223-229.

CHAPTER 18
1. *Pamiatniki nizhegorodskogo dvizheniia*, p. 171.
2. *Pskovskie letopisi*, 2, p. 277.
3. O.A. Derzhavina and E.V. Kolosovaia, eds., *Skazaniia Avraamiia Palitsyna* (M.-L., 1955), p. 220-222.
4. PSRL, 14, p. 118.
5. "*Piskarevskii letopisets*," p. 138.
PSRL, 14, p. 121.

CHAPTER 19
1. RIB, 1, col. 337.
2. *Skazaniia Avraamiia Palitsyna*, p. 222.
3. RIB, 1, col. 320.
4. PSRL, 14, p. 125.
5. *Rukopis...Mukhanovym*, p. 321.

6. PSRL, 14, pp. 125-126.

CHAPTER 20

1. *Pamiatniki nizhegorodskogo dvizheniia*, p. 124.
2. RIB, 1, col. 330.
3. *Skazaniia Avraamiia Palitsyna*, p. 226.
4. AAE, 2, p. 369.
5. *Ibid.*, p. 373.
6. RIB, 1, col. 326.
7. *Ibid.*, p. 337.
8. *Ibid.*, p. 314.
9. Dmitrievskii, pp. 159-160.
10. RIB, 1, col. 348; *Pamiatniki nizhegorodskogo dvizheniia*, p. 493.
11. "Akty podmoskovnykh opolchenii i zemskogo sobora 1611-1613 gg.," ChIOIDR, 4 (239), No. 5 (1911), p. 97.
12. "Piskarevskii letopisets," p. 139.
13. RIB, 1, col. 352.

CHAPTER 21

1. D.V.Tsvetaev, *Tsar Vasilii Shuiskii...*,Vol. 1 (Moscow, 1910), p. 90.
2. A. Hirschberg, *Polska a Moskwa* (Titov translation), p. 363.
3. RIB, 1, col. 354.
4. PSRL, 14, p. 127.
5. *Dopolneniia*, 1, pp. 291-294.
6. PSRL, 14, p. 129.
7. *Piskarevskii letopisets*, p. 140.
8. "Dokladnaia vypiska 121 (1613 goda) o votchinakh i pomestiakh," ChIOIDR, 1 (172), (1895), p. 16.
9. *Skazaniia Avraamiia Palitsyna*, p. 232.
10. Arsenios' papers pertaining to Sweden are found in *Sbornik obshchestva liubitilei drevnosti*, 7, Novgorod, 1911.
11. PSRL, 14, p. 130.
12. *Dvortsovye razriady*, 1 (Moscow, 1850), p. 1083, Note 1.

CHAPTER 22

1. *Dvortsovye razriady*, 1, p. 94; PSRL, 14, p. 130.
2. AI, 2, p. 90.
3. A. Popov, *Izbornik sliavianskikh i russkikh sochinenii i statei, vnesennykh v khronografy russkoi redaktsii* (Moscow, 1869), p. 360; PSRL, 14, p. 135.
4. PSRL, 14, p. 142.
5. *Pamiatniki nizhegorodskogo dvizheniia*, p. 325.

Notes are presented as Professor Skrynnikov has given them; certain supplementary material is by the editor.

INDEX

Abbas, shah of Persia, 285
Alatyr, town, 182, 191, 289
Aleksandrovskaia Sloboda, town, 80
Aleksin, town, 120,
Aleksin, 292
Aliabev, Andrei, courtier, 189
Amos, archpriest, 149
Andronov, Fedor (Fedka) 154-155, 170-171, 250, 252, 254, 263-264, 286
Ankudinov, Mina, 186
Arctic Ocean, 305
Aristov, Sava, 293
Arkhangelsk, 198
Arsenios of Elassoniki, archbishop, 10, 125, 130, 251, 253-254
Arzamas, town, 67, 182, 191, 195, 278
Astrakhan, town, 15, 24, 51, 67, 69, 112, 159, 160, 198, 284-285
Babel, Tower of, 87
Bakhteiarov, A.I., 51
Bakhteiarov, V.I., commander, 161, 170, 277
Balakhna, town, 67, 71, 186, 192, 197, 200, 263, 269
Balovnia, Mikhail, ataman, 287, 288
Baltic sea, 78
Bashkiria, 49
Basmanov, Petr, commander, 5-7, 16, 19, 29, 30-31, 37-39
Batory, Stefan, king of Poland, 153, 289
Begichev, Ivan, 228
Begichev, Kazarin, 181
Bekbulatovich, Simeon, 29-30
Belaia, 282
Belev, 290, 294
Beloozero, town, 22, 57, 60, 61, 62, 63, 78, 203, 213, 234, 285, 305
Belskii, Bogdan, boyar, 3, 5-7, 122, 130, 205, 278
Bezhetsk, 206
Bezobrazov, Ivan, courtier, 17-18, 29, 106, 250, 252, 254, 263-264
Bezzubtsev, Yurii, ataman, 52, 60, 68, 82

Birkin, Ivan, steward, 122, 168, 196, 204-205, 270
Bludov, Berkut, 248
Boborykin, Fedor, 271
Bolkhov, town, 60-61, 64, 282, 290-291
Bolotnikov, Ivan, ataman, 52-60, 68-70, 110, 112, 176
Bolshie Luzhniki, 240-241
Boltin, Zhdan, 190
Boriatynskii, Fedor, 269-270
Borisov, 297
Borisovgorod, 51
Borovsk, town, 77, 290, 297-298
Borsza, Stanislaw, 29
Botvinia, captain, 57
Briansk, 61, 289
Briantsev, Fedor, 18
Bronnitsa, 152
Brooks: Pochainyi, 185; Skhodnia, 70
Buczynski, Jan, secretary, 14, 28, 33, 46
Buczynski, Stanislaw, 46
Budzillo, J., Polish colonel, 238, 252, 254-256, 261
Bussow, Konrad, 29, 135
Buturlin, E.V., 51
Buturlin, I.M., 130-131,
Buturlin, Mikhail, commander, 264, 269-270, 282
Buturlin, Vasilii, nationalist commander, 74, 87, 117-118, 145-149, 152, 163, 199, 212, 248, 254, 268, 270,
Cap of Godunov, 221
Cap of Monomakh, 10, 29, 47, 162, 281
Caspian sea, 185
Cathedrals: Archangel, 9, 46, 48, 221, 251-252; Annunciation, 221; Assumption, 2; Dormition 2, 4, 9, 33, 36, 43, 57, 96, 98, 111, 252, 260, 270; Spaso-Preobrazhenskii, 185
Caucasus, northern, 28
Ceylon, 221
Chancelleries: foreign affairs, 6, 11; fusilier, 92, 106-107, 155; great revenue, 278; military affairs, 162, 165, 167, 174, 208, 229, 248, 302;

monastery, 202, 214; provision, 279; service-tenure, 162, 174, 202; treasury, 220, 250
Charonda, 106
Cheglokov, Kornilii, courtier, 106, 143, 227
Chepchugov, Ivan, steward, 106, 234, 275
Cherkashenin, Mishka, 119
Cherkasskii, Dmitrii Mamstriukovich, prince, 213, 265, 297-298
Cherkasskii, Dmitrii Mikhailovich, prince, 201, 205-206, 208, 213, 231, 248, 265, 269-270, 282, 288
Cherkasskii, Ivan, prince, 45, 49, 204, 210, 272, 278-279
Cherkasskii, Ivan B., prince, 271, 281
Cherkasskii, Vasilii, prince, 95, 102, 297
Chernigov, town, 12, 15, 26, 58, 65
Chernyi, Taras, 207, 295
Chertenskii, Smaga, 24
Chertov, Vasilii, 119
Chmelewski, Polish captain, 207, 230, 243
Chodkiewicz, Jan Karol, hetman of Lithuania, 169-173, 179, 199, 206, 213, 218, 220, 222, 230, 235-242, 244, 249-250, 258-259, 261, 293, 295-298, 302-304
Churches: All-saints, 255; Egorevskii, 239; Nikolskii, 62; Ilin, 38; Prophet Elijah, 240; St. Clement, 239, 241-242; St. Nikita, 139, 242; St. Peter, 139; Universal Salvation, 211; Vasilii the Blessed, 2, 135; Vvedenskii, 130, 133
Coinage office, Yaroslavl, 203
Constantinople, 304
Constanza of Austria, 17
Council of Seven, 93-95, 97-98, 100-101, 104, 107-108, 111, 116-119, 124, 126, 142-143, 153-154, 157, 160, 190, 204, 208-211, 239, 253-254, 263, 265, 268, 277
Council of the Entire Realm, 158, 161, 174, 194, 207

Cracow, Polish city, 13, 17, 22
Cyprus, 4
Czechoslovakia, 79
Danilov, Mikhail, 199
De la Gardie, Jacob, Swedish general, 85-88, 143-152, 178, 211-212, 214, 216, 266
Dimitrovka, 249
Dionisii, abbot of Trinity monastery, 247, 270, 273
Dmitriev, Mikhail, commander, 231-232, 236, 248
Dmitrii II, also known as Bogdan the Jew, False Dmitrii II, Mitka, Thief, Thief of Starodub, Thief of Tushino, 60-71, 73-75 80-82, 84, 89, 90-92, 94, 96-100, 102, 109-112, 114-115, 119, 122, 137, 158, 161, 178, 189-181, 225, 268-269
Dmitrii III, also known as Deacon Matiushka, False Dmitrii III, Matvei, Mishka, Sidorka, Thief, Thief of Pskov, 177-178, 180-182, 194-195, 197, 201-203, 207-208, 213, 223-228, 264, 286
Dmitrii Ivanovich of Uglich, third son of Ivan IV, 17, 45, 47, 57
Dolgorukii, Vladimir, boyar, 204, 248, 270
Domoracki, M., 18
Dorogobuzh, 191, 282
Dorogomilov, posting-station, 236
Dosmagmet, Azov commandant, 27
Dovodchikov, Ivan, 229
Durov, Ratmin, 18,
Efanov, Ivan, 248
Efrem, metropolitan of Kazan, 233
Elagin, Ivan, 192-193
Elena, holy fool, 29
Elets, fortress, 28, 32, 51-53, 299
England, 208
Epanchin, Ivan, 262
Europe, 27, 76, 106, 144, 207, 222
Evdokimov, Gerasim, 122
Facets, palace of, 33, 156, 279
Fedor Ivanovich, tsar, 24, 45, 94, 265, 268, 273

Fedor, court archpriest, 33
Fedor, village priest, 62
Fedorovskoe, village, 218-219, 261-262
Feodorit, archbishop of Riazan, 270,
    274, 278
Feodosii, abbot of Pechorskii monas-
    tery, 190
Fiery Furnace, 134
Filaret, *also known as* Fedor Nikitich
    Romanov, metropolitan of Rostov,
    patriarch, 44-49, 70, 83-84, 91-93,
    96, 99, 104, 124, 210, 233, 272-
    273, 275, 280, 305
Filosofov, Ivan, 260, 263-264
Finland, 12
Fletcher, Giles, 127
Furs, captain, 57
Gagarin, Roman, 73, 198
Gaiutin, Vasilii, 149
Galich, town, 16, 75, 98, 273
Gdov, fortress, 146, 226
Gedimin, 15
Georgia, 20
Germany, 79
Godunov, Boris, tsar, 4, 8, 10, 15, 20,
    25-26, 31, 37, 39, 44, 47, 57, 79,
    94, 106, 155, 166, 221, 230, 268,
    271, 280
Godunov, Fedor, tsar, 1, 5, 36, 53, 57,
    91, 281
Godunov, Ivan, 112
Godunova, Irina (nun Aleksandra), 279-
    280
Godunova, Kseniia, daughter of Boris
    Godunov, 19-22, 57
Golenishchev, Afinogen, 149
Golitsyn, Andrei, prince, 101, 103, 108-
    111, 124, 135, 184
Golitsyn, Ivan Andreevich, prince, 160,
    270
Golitsyn, Ivan Vasilevich, prince, 5,
    124, 160, 254, 265, 292
Golitsyn, Vasilii, prince, 31, 38, 73-74,
    90-91, 93, 96, 99, 104, 109-110,
    124, 190, 210, 265, 272
Golovin, Dmitrii, 248
Golovin, Fedor, 277, 284

Golovin, Semen, 204, 270, 292
Golovin, V.P., 154
Gordian knot, 202
Gorikhvostov, Grigorii, 290
Gorki, fort, 296
Gosiewski, Alexander, Polish colonel,
    17-18, 31, 40, 100-102, 107-109,
    111, 116, 119, 123-126, 128-135,
    137, 141, 145, 153-156, 160, 168,
    170-171, 173, 220-222, 239, 250-
    251, 253, 277, 283, 302, 304
Gostun, castle, 258
Grajewski, Polish officer, 241
Gramotin, Ivan, 106
Great Assembly Council, 266
Gregory of Austria, 215
Griaznoi, Timofei, courtier, 73, 264
Gustav Adolphus, king of Sweden, 152-
    153, 211, 289
Gustav, Swedish prince, 20
Herberstein, Sigismund, 250
Hermogen, metropolitan of Kazan,
    patriarch, 28, 44, 49, 55, 73, 91-93,
    96, 98, 101-103, 108-111, 118-119,
    122, 125-126, 130, 156-157, 164,
    171, 183-184, 210, 232, 251
Holland, 208
Horn, Ewert, Swedish general, 86-88,
    212-213
Hungary, 27, 52
Ignatii, patriarch, 4, 6, 9, 28, 41, 171,
    260
Ilarion, priest, 109-110
Iosif, abbot of Novospasskii monastery,
    274
Iov, patriarch, 4, 57
Isaiia, abbot of Savvin-Storozhevskii
    monastery, 233
Isidor, metropolitan of Novgorod, 47,
    145, 150-151, 233
Islenev, captain, 290
Ivan IV, the Terrible, tsar, 1, 5-6, 9, 14,
    16, 27, 29-30, 69, 192, 268, 273
Ivan Kalita, grand prince, 155, 250
Ivan-Avgust, heir, pretender, 69-70
Ivangorod, town, 144-146, 153, 177-178,
    180

Ivashka, partisan, 220
Ivashkin, Konstantin, 298
Izhorsk, fort, 145
Izmailov, Artemii, commander, 44, 117, 123-124, 134, 136-138, 161, 174, 181, 195, 197, 203, 236, 270
Izmailov, Ivan, 248
Izmailov, Vasilii, 174
Janibeg, Crimean khan, 77
Janikowski, Tushino leader, 113
Johann, Danish count, 20
John III, king of Sweden, 77, 153
Kadyshev, 128
Kalachnik, Fedor, merchant, 1, 7
Kaliazin, 77
Kaluga, town, 52-53, 56-58, 60, 81-83, 89, 95, 98-99, 102, 110, 113-115, 117-118, 121-122, 124-125, 136, 140, 158, 162, 165, 177-178, 182, 223, 274, 280, 282, 291-292, 294, 298, 303, 305
Kantemir-murza, 89
Karachev, 60, 289-290
Karamyshev, Sergei, ataman, 166-167
Karela, cossack ataman, 8
Karelia, 293
Kargopol, 59, 287
Karl IX, king of Sweden, 76-77, 86, 88, 143-147, 151-153, 169, 178, 211, 217
Karl Philip, Swedish prince, 211, 216-217, 266
Kashin, 201, 206
Kashinets, Grigorii, 60
Kashira, 90
Kasimov, 113, 201
Katyrev, M.P., boyar, 15
Kazan, town, 29, 59, 121-122, 124, 130, 139, 160, 182-183, 189, 193, 196, 204-205, 276, 278, 285, 292-293
Khariton, priest, 109-111, 116
Khodynka, 64, 74
Kholui, 269
Khovanskii, Ivan, prince, 180, 226, 231-233

Khripunov, renegade, 29
Khvalibog, 46
Khvorostinin, Ivan A., prince, 16, 45
Khvorostinin, Ivan D., prince, 156, 286
Khvostov, Nikita, 179
Kineshma, 197, 202
Kirill, elder, 254
Klushino, battleground, 86-87, 89, 99, 143, 145, 150, 212, 222
Kola, peninsula, 144, 212
Kolomenskoe, village, 1, 54-56, 98, 240
Kolomna, town, 53-54, 72, 74, 77, 90, 120, 123-124, 132, 164, 182, 232, 299
Koltovskii, Ivan, 296
Koltovskoi, Ivan, 130-131
Kon, Fedor, 1, 79
Konshin, Zhdan, 304
Konstantinov, Mishka, 242
Kopore, fortress, 144, 146, 153
Korela, fortress, 76, 143-144, 146, 150-151
Koshelev, Petr, 113
Koshurin, Ivan, 100
Kostia, medic, 1
Kostroma, town, 67, 75-76, 100, 108, 121, 138, 158, 174, 182, 195-198, 201, 269, 277-279
Kotly, village, 46, 56
Kozelsk, town, 100, 218, 282, 294
Kozlov, Ivan, captain, 100, 248, 287
Krasnoe, 55
Kremlin, administrative center of Moscow, *passim*; gate, Spasskii, 257
Kremlin, Nizhnii Novgorod, 185
Kremlin, Novgorod, 150, 152, 211
Kremlin, Yaroslavl, 198-199
Kriuk-Kolychev, Ivan, boyar, 74
Kromy, town, 4-5, 31, 52-53, 291
Kulishki, village, 127, 131-133, 249, 255
Kurakin, Andrei, boyar, 123-124, 199, 204, 270, 292
Kurmysh, town, 191-193, 195
Kursk, 61
Ladoga, town, 143-147, 212, 293
Landekh, lower, 268-269

Landekh, upper, 269
Leonid (False Otrepev), 16
Liapunov, Prokofii, nationalist leader, 53, 55, 85, 89, 91, 105, 120-124, 130, 134, 136, 138, 140-141, 143-147, 157-161, 163-169, 174, 181, 183, 191, 194, 203, 205-207, 209-210, 227, 245, 263, 271
Liapunov, Fedor, 90
Liapunov, Zakhar, 91-93, 100, 117
Likhven, 291
Lisowski, Alexander, Polish irregular, 65, 75, 119, 178-179, 224, 226-227, 289-292, 294
Lithuania, 2, 13, 15, 29, 50, 52, 57, 67, 69, 79, 113, 125, 144, 169, 171, 233, 259, 262, 271, 305
Livny, 51, 299
Livonia, 57, 77-78, 144, 153, 169, 179, 213, 304
Lobanov, Afanasii, 272
London, 20, 127
Lopata Pozharskii, Dmitrii, prince, 196, 199, 201, 206, 213, 232, 236, 240, 291-292
Luzhniki, 141, 243
Lvov, Aleksei, prince, 106, 268, 277
Lykov, Boris, prince, 5-6, 89, 93, 129, 156, 288, 296, 299-301, 303
Lytkin, Yaroslavl merchant, 200
Maloiaroslavets, 288
Mansurov, Petr, 206
Marchocki, M., 168
Margeret, Jacques, mercenary captain, 19, 37-38, 43, 49, 129, 170, 207-208
Markov, Neliub, 262
Massa, Isaac, 19
Maximilian, Austrian archduke, 215
Merrick, John, 293
Meshchera, 269-270
Meshcherskii, Fedor, prince, 74, 106, 264
Mezetskii, D.I., prince, 99, 260, 304
Mezhakov, Filat, 238
Miechowiecki, M., Lord, 60, 63, 80-81

Mikhailov, 284-285
Mikhailov, Konstantin, 278
Mikhalkov, 272
Mikhnev, Ignatii, 270
Mikulin, Danila, 248
Miliutin, Grigorii, 30
Minin, Kuzma, leader of liberation movement, 186-192, 195-196, 199-203, 205, 207-208, 210-212, 214, 223-224, 227-228, 230-236, 243, 245-249, 251, 257, 262-267, 270, 280-283, 292-293
Mitka of Astrakhan, 24
Mlotski, Lord, 82
Mnishkov, cook, 46
Mniszech, Jerzy, father of Marina, 15, 19, 22-23, 36, 41, 46, 65-67, 110
Mniszech, Marina, wife of pretenders, 19, 21, 28, 32-35, 66-67, 75, 80-82, 112, 114-115, 163-164, 180, 182, 194, 224-225, 227-228, 264, 277, 285-286
Mogilev, town, 62-63, 65
Molchanov, Mikhail, courtier, 16, 19, 50, 52, 70, 73-74, 83, 106
Monasteries: Abramiev, 139; Andronov, 137, 172; Antonev-Krasnokholmskii, 206; Antoniev-Siiskii, 44; Barsanophius, 57; Danilov, 92; Donskoi, 237, 239-240, 244, 302; Ipatevskii, 277-278, 280; Kaliazin, 100; Kirillo-Belozersk, 28, 30, 156, 213, 287; Joseph of Volokolamsk, 28; Miracles, 3, 16, 41, 44, 93, 183; New Virgin, 103, 140-142, 172, 237, 239; Luzhets, 297; Nikolskii, 98-99, 137, 165; Pafnutii, 297-298; Pechorskii, 185; Pskovo-Pecherskii, 179; Salvation, 198; Simonov, 97, 137, 175; Solovetskii, 162, 202; Spaso-Efimev, 232; Trinity-St Sergius, 28, 57, 68, 72, 75-77, 84, 134, 166-167, 187, 219, 223-224, 231, 233-234, 246, 254, 272, 280, 292, 303; Vozdvizhesnkii, 267
Monk, Swedish general, 212

Morozov, Vasilii, commander, 195-196, 204-205, 231, 270, 274, 278

Mosalskii, Dmitrii, 62

Mosalskii, Vasilii, prince, 5, 62, 122

Mosalskii, Vasilii Litvinov, commander, 134, 138, 141, 161, 174

Moscow: capital, and focus of liberation movement, *passim*; gates: Arbat, 170, 234, 236, 303; Chertole, 132, 137, 234, 237; Frolov, 9, 38, 128; Ilin, 130; Nikitskii, 137, 170, 232; Pokrov, 138, 231, 257; Serpukhov, 92, 94, 239, 240-241, 244; Trekhsviatyi, 141; Tver, 131-132, 141, 174, 181, 231, 237, 303; Vodianyi, 110, 128, 131, 238; Yauza, 131, 137-138, 141, 174; areas: Arbat, 19, 62, 127, 140, 170, 235, 237, 257, 267; Bogoiavlenie, 272-273; Bolshaia Ordynka, 239, 241-242, 244; Cannon court, 127, 130, 248; Chertole, 19, 127, 132-133, 236-237; Crimean court, 237, 239-240, 243; Currency court, 155; Dmitrovka, 127; Earthen Town, 127-129, 133, 240, 303; Kitaigorod, 103, 116, 126-132, 135, 138-139, 141, 171-173, 220, 223, 249, 250, 254-257, 272; Lubianka, 128, 130, 132; Ostozhenka, 240; Petrovka, 174; Piatitska, 239; Poklonnyi hill, 237; Prechistoe znamenie, 62; Sparrow Hills, 244; Sretenka, 130, 132-133; Stone Town, 237, 240; Traders' court, 154; Treasury court, 154; Truba, 130, 138, 174, 181, 248; White Town, 103, 116, 126-129, 131-133, 135, 137, 141-142, 236, 256, 302-303; Wooden Town 116, 133, 239, 240, 246, 301; streets: Greater Bronnyi, 127, Lesser Bronnyi, 127, Tver, 131

Moseev, Rodion, 183-184

Mozhaisk, town, 86, 88, 117, 170, 219, 296-299, 301, 303

Mstislavskii, Fedor, boyar, prince, 15,

42, 44, 49, 54, 56, 91-94, 96, 98-103, 106-109, 128-129, 132-133, 140, 153, 157, 169-171, 247, 251, 254-256, 260, 265-266, 268, 270-271, 275-277, 279-281, 284, 287, 300-301

Mugreevo, village, 130, 189-191

Murom, town, 122, 124, 134, 141, 158, 268, 292

Muscovy, 14-15, 66, 159, 186-187, 208-209

Myt, 269

Nagaia, Marfa (Nun Mariia), 8-9, 17-18, 40, 42, 46-47, 49, 51, 279

Nagoi, Afanasii, 16

Nagoi, Andrei, 59-60

Nagoi, Mikhail, master of horse, 15, 42, 170-171

Nalivaiko, Andrei, ataman, 120, 206, 213, 231, 236

Narva, town, 12, 45, 153, 178

Naumov, Ivan, 201

Nefed, son of Minin, 186

Nekhoroshevo, 220

Nerekhta, 303

New Virgin field, 96-97, 280

Nikitnikov, Yaroslavl merchant, 200, 203

Nikolai, jeweler, 222

Nizhnii Novgorod, town, 59, 79, 92, 119, 122, 124, 134, 158, 164, 182-196, 199-201, 204-205, 269, 293, 301, 304

Novgorod (the Great), city, 7, 44, 53, 59, 74, 76, 100, 142-153, 159, 176-180, 211-217, 266, 278, 282-283, 287-288, 293

Novgorod-Seversk, town, 12, 26, 65

Novokreshchenov, Lavrentii, 248

Nowodworski, B., 303

Nunneries, Georgiev, 249, Resurrection, 9, Voznesenskii, 279

Obolensk, 296

Obolenskii, Fedor, 216-217

Obrezek, cossack, 229

Odoev, 246

Odoevskii, Ivan, prince, 145, 148-149,

150-152, 212, 270, 284-285
Odoevskii, Nikita, prince, 204
Opalinski, L., Polish commander, 295-297
Oprichnina, 5, 14, 16, 30
Orel, town, 52-53, 61, 63-64, 68, 290-291
Oreshek, 143-144, 147, 150, 212
Orlov, Grigorii, 239
Orlov, Vasilii, 149
Osipov, Timofei, 37
Oskol, 51
Otrepev, Grigorii, Grisha, Grishka, also known as Deceiver, Defrocked One, Destroyer, Dmitrii, False Dmitrii I, Thief, 1-42, 44-47, 49-55, 57, 59-60, 62-67, 77, 81, 91, 107, 155, 209, 221, 233
Pafnutii, metropolitan of Krutitsa, 233
Pagalevskii, Ivan, 207
Pakhra, 110
Palchowski, Pawel, 78
Palitsyn, Avraamii, Trinity cellarer, 100, 231, 242-243, 246, 272-274, 278
Pashkov, Istoma, commander, 51-54, 56, 58
Pavlov, 189
Pereiaslavl, town, 67, 124, 141, 158, 170, 201, 233
Peremyshl, town, 228, 282, 291
Peresvetov, Ivan, 27
Persia, 160, 215, 286
Peshkov, Aleksei, 91
Petr, heir, also known as Ileika of Murom, pretender, 24, 37, 47, 56-58, 69
Petreius, Peter, 17
Place of Execution, 39, 42-43, 45, 48, 73, 92, 257, 274
Pleshcheev, Fedor, commander, 110, 132, 137, 176, 248
Pleshcheev, Ivan, boyar, 123, 132, 165, 225, 227, 245, 248
Pleshcheev, Lev, 106
Pleshcheev, Matvei, boyar, 165, 197-198, 248

Pleshcheev, Nikifor, 248
Pogorelyi, 259, 261
Pogozhii, Fedor, 117, 138, 203
Pogozhii, Isak, commander, 174, 181, 203, 270, 277
Poland (Rzeczpospolita), 10, 12-14, 17, 21-23, 27-28, 34, 40, 59, 63-64, 67, 77-79, 83, 94, 103-104, 107, 145, 153, 169, 171, 210, 213-215, 255, 258, 265, 272, 282, 293, 304-305
Popov, Gerasim, 180
Porkhov, 226
Poshekhone, 201, 303
Potemkin, Yurii, 166, 206
Pozharskii, Dmitrii Mikhailovich, prince, leader of liberation movement, 72, 89-90, 105, 117, 120-121, 130, 132-134, 164, 168-169, 189-205, 207-211, 213-217, 223-224, 227-228, 231-240, 242-243, 245-249, 251, 253-257, 260-271, 275, 279-284, 289-303
Pozharskii, Roman, 201, 212
Presna, 64
Pronsk, 120-121
Pronskii, Petr, 204
Propoisk, 63
Prosovetskii, Andrei, ataman, 119, 122-124, 134, 136-137, 165, 170, 175, 193, 195-196, 201
Prosovetskii, Ivan, 195
Prozorovskii, Semen, 206
Pskov, town, 49, 53, 67, 79, 119, 121, 130, 148, 152-153, 177-182, 194-195, 212, 220, 223, 225-227, 280, 289
Pushkin, Gavrila, courtier, 88, 93, 283
Pushkin, Ivan, commander, 72, 135, 143-144, 290
Putivl, town, 3, 5, 14, 29, 50-53, 55-59, 61, 77
Razdory, 24
Red Porch, 24, 38-39
Red Square, 3, 38, 42, 44-45, 49, 57, 92, 127
Repnin, Aleksandr, commander, 71, 134, 138, 161, 189

Repnin, Andrei, 174
Reshma, 197
Riazan, town, 4, 26, 53, 72-73, 79, 93, 100, 105, 116-125, 132, 136, 138, 194, 223, 264, 268-270, 284, 292
Riazhsk, 27
Rivers: Dneiper, 80; Don, 24, 285; Kazanka, 121; Kostroma, 197; Kotorosl, 198; Moscow, 16-19, 56, 70, 116, 127, 131, 133, 137, 238-239, 240; Narova, 293; Neglinnyi, 138, 141, 248, 256; Neva, 145, 293; Oka, 53, 77, 89, 184-185, 288, 299; Pakhra, 52; Prona, 120; Terek, 24; Ugra, 53, 140; Ugresha, 137; Upa, 58; Volga, 24, 121, 160, 184-185, 194, 196-198, 201; Volkhov, 142, 145, 148-150; Vuoksa, 143; Vysksa, 8; Yachenka, 114; Yauza, 128, 137, 139, 170, 172, 177, 220, 234, 235, 243, 301
Rodnia, 218
Rogachevo, village, 173, 218, 303-304
Roman, cossack, 229
Romanov, Ivan Nikitich, boyar, 5, 42, 44, 93, 101-102, 129, 153, 210, 256, 271, 276, 280-281, 283
Romanov, Mikhail, tsar, 45, 93, 99, 210, 256, 265, 267, 271-281, 283, 285, 291-292, 294, 296, 300-302
Romanovna, Anastasiia, 273
Romanovna, Marfa, nun, mother of Mikhail, 277, 279-280, 283, 287, 305
Rome, 78
Romodanovskii, Grigorii, commander, 141, 169, 264, 293
Rostov, town, 44, 67, 91, 98, 124, 138, 158, 170, 195, 201, 233
Rukin, Aleshka, 60
Rurik, 15
Russia, 2, 8, 12, 15, 27, 29, 34, 51, 61, 64-65, 76-80, 83-84, 86, 89, 94, 97-98, 103-105, 107-108, 115, 118, 120, 122, 125, 144-145, 147, 153, 160-161, 163, 182, 184-185, 207-208, 221, 237, 251, 255, 258-260, 262, 264, 267, 281-283, 289, 293-294, 304-305
Ruza, village, 219, 260-261, 297
Ruzynski, Roman, Tushino leader, 63-66, 68-72, 75, 77, 80-82, 84
Rylsk, 61,
Rzhev, 218, 292, 305
Rzhevskii, Grigorii, 106
Rzhevskii, Ivan, associate boyar, 106, 108, 167
Saburov, Mikhail, commander, 15, 51
Sagadaichnyi, Petr, ataman, 299, 303-304
Saltykov, Boris Mikhailovich, boyar, 204, 210, 271, 277-278, 283
Saltykov, Ivan Mikhailovich, boyar, 86, 89, 106-107, 142
Saltykov, Ivan Nikitich, associate boyar, 92, 264
Saltykov, Mikhail Glebovich, boyar, 5, 70, 81, 83-84, 96, 98, 100, 102-103, 106, 109, 111, 124-125, 128-131, 143, 154, 170-171, 189, 209, 270, 284
Saltykov, Mikhail Mikhailovich, 277-278
Samara, 285
Sambor, Polish town, 21-22, 52, 59, 98, Sapieha, Jan Piotr, Polish irregular, 65, 68, 72, 75-77, 80, 82, 84, 89, 94, 98-99, 112, 114, 121, 123, 136, 140-141, 169, 170, 172, 195, 256
Sapieha, Lew, chancellor of Lithuania, 78, 104, 275, 305
Sapozhek, 269
Savva, archpriest, 204
Sebezh, 206
Sekirin, Perferii, 217, 284
Sergii of Radonezh, 254
Serpukhov, town, 52-53, 56, 77, 82, 89, 109-110, 112, 124, 132, 223, 296, 299, 300
Shakhovskoi, Grigorii, prince, 50, 56, 58, 70, 114, 165, 245, 248
Shakhovskoi, Petr, 5
Shakhovskoi, Semen, 290
Shalda, fusilier, 229
Shapkin, Semen, 8

Sharov, Timofei, 149
Shaw, Jacob, 291
Shchelkalov, Vasilii, 5
Shein, Mikhail, 124
Sheputskii, posting-station, 233
Sheremetev, Fedor, boyar, 5, 92-93, 96, 129, 155-156, 160, 277-279, 292, 304-305
Sheremetev, Ivan, commander, 160, 165, 168, 174, 197-198, 210, 245, 248, 270
Sheremetev, Petr, boyar, 45, 49, 130, 176
Sheremetev, Vasilii, steward, 174, 270
Shirai, ataman, 206, 236
Shishkin, envoy, 217
Shklova, 62
Shuiskii, Dmitrii, prince, 38, 56, 64, 85-89, 259
Shuiskii, Ivan, prince (Ivan Levin), 53, 56, 75, 92, 259
Shuiskii, Vasilii (monk Varlaam), tsar. 1-2, 5-7, 15, 33-34, 38, 40-42, 44-51, 53-61, 64-65, 67, 70-77, 80, 83-85, 89-94, 97, 99, 101, 107, 113, 142-143, 154-155, 158, 161, 166, 176-178, 258-259, 266, 268-269, 281, 305
Shulgin, Nikanor, 205, 278
Siberia, 16, 185, 198, 278
Sigismund III Vasa, king of Poland, 12-14, 17-18, 23, 27, 31-32, 41, 63, 65-66, 77-80, 82, 84, 91, 95, 97, 100, 103-104, 106, 109, 111, 113, 119, 124-125, 139-140, 144-146, 152, 154, 157, 163, 167, 169, 171, 179, 189, 210-211, 217, 229, 236, 249-250, 255-256, 258-262, 264, 268, 270, 282-283, 293, 299, 303, 305
Simon, monk, 219
Sitskii, Andrei, 248
Skopin-Shuiskii, Mikhail, commander, 5, 52-54, 56, 64, 74, 76, 80, 84-85, 145
Skuratov, Maliuta, 16
Skuratova-Shuiskaia, Elena, 85
Smirnoi-Otrepev, 216

Smolensk, town, 56, 59, 76, 78-80, 82-84, 86, 89, 91, 99-101, 103-104, 108-109, 113, 117-118, 124-125, 139-140, 144, 147, 153-155, 163, 169, 191-192, 196, 206, 218, 222, 229-230, 236, 251, 260, 262, 272, 278, 282, 285, 288-289, 294, 297, 301
Smyvalov, Mikhalko, 44
Sokovnin, Prokofii, 248
Sol-Vychegodsk, 207
Sophiia Side (Novgorod), 150
Spain, 27
St. George's Day, 25, 50, 159
St. Nicholas' Day, 34, 36
Stadnicki, Marcin, 67
Stadnicki, Stanislaw, 13
Staraia Rusa, town, 142, 206, 293
Staritsa, 57, 218,
Starodub, town, 59-61, 68-69, 209
Stepan, cossack, 229
Stockholm, 145, 211, 216, 293
Stolbovo, 293
Struys, Jacob, mercenary commander, 133, 218, 220, 222, 237, 250, 252-256, 263
Sudovshchikov, Smirnov, 274
Sukin, Vasilii, 224
Suleshev, Yurii, 270,
Sumbulov, Grigorii, 73, 120-121
Sumskii, fort, 212
Susanin, Ivan, 282
Sutupov, Bogdan, 70
Suzdal, town, 67, 98, 108, 123, 170, 194-196, 201-202, 232-233, 269, 292
Sviiazhsk, town, 15, 189, 278
Sweden, 12, 76-77, 144-147, 151-153, 163, 211-216, 282, 293
Taininskoe, 9
Talmud, 115
Tarusa, 77
Tashlykov, Stepan, 263
Tatars, Azov, 27, 51
Tatars, Crimean, 19, 27-28, 31, 51-52, 68, 77, 89, 294
Tatars, Nogai, 288-289
Tatars of Romanov, 206

Tatev, Boris, boyar, 5-6
Tatishchev, Mikhail, associate boyar, 18, 30-31, 39, 74
Tatishchev, Stepan, 214-216
Tatishchev, Yurii, 296
Teliatevskii, Andrei, 15, 58
Terentii, archpriest, 2
Tikhvin, 212-213
Time of Troubles, 59, 84, 97, 106, 118, 157-158, 185-186, 189, 198, 268-269, 276, 295
Timofeev, Ivan ("Sapozhok"), 294
Tiny Thief (Heir Ivan Dmitrievich), 115, 163-164, 180, 182, 194-195, 208, 224-225, 264, 284-286
Tiszkiewicz, Lord, 61, 81
Titov, ataman, 287
Tiufiakin, Vasilii, 246
Tiumen, 15
Tolstoi, Silvestr, 166
Tolstoi, Vasilii, 201
Toropets, 142, 206
Torzhok, town, 76, 202, 213, 288
Totma, 106
Tovarkov, 296-297
Trading Side, (Novgorod), 150, 152
Trakhaniotov, N.V., 281
Trans-Onega district, 212
Transriver district, 92, 94, 127, 131-133, 237-244, 247, 249, 302, 304
Trepets, Kudekusha, 176
Tretiak, Yurlov, 37
Troekurov, Ivan, prince, 204, 210, 271
Troitskoe, 54
Trubetskoi, Andrei, 93
Trubetskoi, Dmitrii, nationalist leader, 52, 70, 91-92, 136, 138, 161, 174, 181-182, 192-193, 195, 207, 224-225, 227, 230, 234-236, 238-240, 242, 247-248, 255, 260-261, 265, 267-272, 274-276, 279-283, 288, 301
Trubetskoi, Yurii, 115, 170
Tsarev Zaimishche, 86
Tukhachevskii, Smolensk agitator, 301
Tula, town, 3, 8, 52, 58-61, 69, 89, 112, 119-121, 124, 223, 286, 292
Turenin, Vasilii, commander, 231, 234, 240, 248
Turgenev, Petr, 7
Turgenev, Yaroslavl agitator, 301
Turks, Ottoman empire, 27, 32, 52, 304
Tushino, pretender's encampment, 64-74, 76-77, 80-84, 86, 89-92, 94-96, 98, 100, 102, 113, 115, 145, 154, 161, 165, 178, 180, 185, 198, 206, 224, 245, 261, 268-269, 270
Tver, town, 76, 98, 201, 223
Uglich, town, 17, 45-48, 138, 174, 178, 203, 206, 292
Ukraine, 52, 57, 61-62, 78
Uraz-Mohamed, 113-114
Urusov, Petr, 113-114
Ustiug, 15, 20
Vaga district, 106, 230, 258, 270-271
Vagankovo, 261
Valiazhskii, Lord, 61
Valuev, Grigorii, commander, 86, 89, 94-96, 103, 106
Vasilii III, 250
Vasilsursk, 192
Vatican (Holy See), 10, 27, 33, 46, 115
Veliaminov, Leontii, 206, 212
Veliaminov, Miron, commander, 174, 181, 203
Veliaminov, Nikita, commander, 179-180, 264
Venev, 51, 53
Viatka, 30
Viazemskii, Semen, 71-72
Viazma, town, 89, 117, 191, 196, 218, 259, 282, 291, 294, 296-297, 305
Viazniki, 300-301
Vienna, 20, 215
Vishentsa, 219
Vishniakov, Vladimir, 272
Vitivtov, Timofei, 202
Vladimir, town, 67, 98, 122-124, 134, 158, 195-197, 201, 300
Vladimirka, 184
Vlasev, Afanasii, 21-22, 37
Vnukov, Kruchina, 233

Volkonskii, Fedor, commander, 138, 203, 270
Volkonskii, Grigorii, 298-300
Vologda, town, 67, 75, 121, 123, 158, 194, 206, 245, 263, 284, 287
Volokolamsk, town, 84, 91, 206, 218-219, 222, 259, 261-262, 296-297, 302
Volynskii, Fedor, 287, 299
Volynskii, Ivan, 138
Voronezh, 112, 285
Vorotynskii, Ivan, commander, 5, 51-52, 54, 58, 92-93, 101, 109-111, 129, 153, 256
Vyborg, 144, 216
Vysotskii, 72
Warsaw, 13, 258
White sea, 212
Wisniowiecki, Adam, Polish prince, 36, 64, 81
Wladyslaw, heir, son of King Sigismund III, 18, 29, 41, 83-84, 89, 93-99, 102-110, 113, 115, 117, 119, 122, 126, 142, 151, 170-171, 177, 179, 250, 255-256, 258, 260, 293, 295-297, 302-304
Yakovlev, ataman, 295
Yam, fortress, 144, 146, 153
Yanov, Vasilii, 44
Yaropolk, 191
Yaroslavl, town, 16, 65, 67, 71, 75-76, 100, 122-123, 138, 158, 170, 182, 185, 195-196, 198-207, 209-211, 213-216, 220, 223-224, 227-233, 238, 245, 265, 267-268, 277, 284,

291-292, 298, 301, 303-304
Yurevets, 197
Yurevets Polskii, 123
Zabore, 56
Zaborovskii, ataman, 236
Zamiatin Otrepev, 16
Zamoyski, Jan, 12
Zaraisk, town, 90, 105, 117, 120-121, 130
Zarutskii, Ivan, cossack leader, 60, 68-71, 82, 86, 95-96, 112, 114, 119, 121, 124, 136, 138, 140-142, 157, 161, 163-165, 168, 172, 175, 180-184, 191-193, 195, 197, 201, 206-207, 222-225, 227-232, 234, 264, 268, 270, 284-286, 300
Zasekin, Ivan, prince, 110, 165, 245, 248
Zavarzin, Sidorka, 168, 209
Zavidov, Kirill, metropolitan of Rostov, 44, 210, 233, 270
Zborowski, Polish officer, 220
Zebrzydowski, Mikolaj, 13
Zertynski, Lord, 63
Zhezdrinskii, Dmitrii, 193, 301
Zhvalov, Senka, 229
Zolkiewski, Adam, 222
Zolkiewski, Stanislaw, Polish hetman, 17, 65, 71, 78, 86, 88-89, 94-96, 98-104, 106-108, 114, 125, 142, 169, 299
Zvenigorod, 233
Zvenigorodskii, Fedor, 106
Zvenigorodskii, Vasilii, 189
Zybin, Ivan 248

Boris Godunov

Marina Mniszech

False Dmitrii I

Tsar Mikhail Fedorovich Romanov

Nizhnii Novgorod

Adam Olearius, *Vermehrte Newe Beschreibung der Muscowitischen und Persischen
Reyse*, 1656

Map 1   False Dmitrii's Route to Moscow in 1604 ➭
                          Routes of the Cossacks in 1604 ⟶

Map 2   Bolotnikov's March in 1606 ⟶
          False Dmitrii II's Operations in 1608 ⟶

Map 3   Muscovite Counterattack in 1609 ➡
          Zolkiewski's March in 1610 ➡

Map 4   Liapunov's Route in 1612 ✦
The Forces of Zarutskii and Trubetskoi in 1612 ➤
Swedish Invasion ➤

Map 5 Area under Polish control, 1612-1613
Chodkiewicz's March in 1612
Minin and Pozharskii in 1612
Area under Swedish control, 1613
Annexed by Sweden, 1617

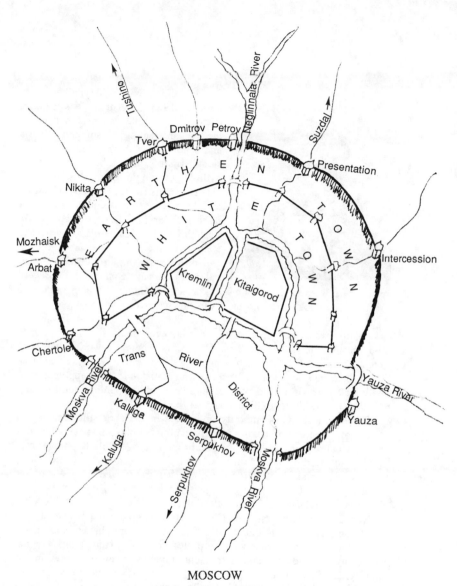

MOSCOW

Adapted from a plan of the city attributed to Fedor Borisovich Godunov (1589-1605) as printed in K.V. Bazilevich et al, *Atlas istorii SSR* (Moscow, 1950), Vol. 1.

 Ruslan Grigorevich Skrynnikov was born in 1931 in Kutais. His parents, natives of a small cossack village in the Kuban region of southern Russia and schoolmates there, attended professional schools, his father becoming an hydrological engineer and his mother a chemistry instructor. Lovers of music and literature, the parents named their three children after characters in Pushkin's tales—Liudmila, Ruslan and Ratmir. In the 1930s the family moved to North Russia to help build an electrical plant on the Svir river. The construction crew erected for themselves a large building in Leningrad where Professor Skrynnikov met his future wife and where he lives today.

Returning to Leningrad from the Urals after World War II, he was drawn to physics and mathematics but, to everyone's surprise, began to study history at Leningrad State University where he worked with the noted historians D.S. Likhachev and B.A. Romanov. With their help he found his greatest interest, success and satisfaction in applying new analytical methods to old sources in search of new information of significance for the history of his country.

The foremost living authority on Russia in the sixteenth century and author of three major studies and numerous monographs detailing this era, he has brought Old Russia to life in a series of scholarly-popular biographies of leading personalities of that time—Ivan the Terrible, Boris Godunov, Yermak. Professor Skrynnikov has transferred the focus of his scholarly interests to the period generally referred to as the Time of Troubles, of which this book is a reflection.

Now Research Professor of History at Leningrad State University, he is a frequent consultant and technical adviser to films, ballets and operas set in Old Russia. Twice visiting professor at the Hungarian National University in Budapest and a frequent traveller to historic sites in his country, he finds time for his violin, film and stamp interests, and for the theater and concerts with his family, including a son who is a second-year student in mathematics and computer science at Leningrad State University and a daughter now finishing secondary education.

ACADEMIC INTERNATIONAL PRESS

THE RUSSIAN SERIES

1 S.F. Platonov *History of Russia* Out of Print
2 *The Nicky-Sunny Letters, Correspondence of Nicholas and Alexandra, 1914-1917*
3 Ken Shen Weigh *Russo-Chinese Diplomacy, 1689-1924* Out of Print
4 Gaston Cahen *Relations of Russia with China . . . 1689-1730* Out of Print
5 M.N. Pokrovsky *Brief History of Russia* 2 Volumes Out of Print
6 M.N. Pokrovsky *History of Russia from Earliest Times . . .* Out of Print
7 Robert J. Kerner *Bohemia in the Eighteenth Century*
8 *Memoirs of Prince Adam Czartoryski and His Correspondence with Alexander I* 2 vols.
9 S.F. Platonov *Moscow and the West*
10 S.F. Platonov *Boris Godunov*
11 Boris Nikolajewsky *Aseff the Spy*
12 Francis Dvornik *Les Legendes de Constantin et de Méthode vues de Byzance*
13 Francis Dvornik *Les Slaves, Byzance et Rome au XIe Siecle*
14 A. Leroy-Beaulieu *Un Homme d'Etat Russe (Nicolas Miliutine) . . .*
15 Nicholas Berdyaev *Leontiev* (In English)
16 V.O. Kliuchevskii *Istoriia soslovii v Rossii*
17 *Tehran Yalta Potsdam. The Soviet Protocols*
18 *The Chronicle of Novgorod*
19 Paul N. Miliukov *Outlines of Russian Culture* Vol. III (2 vols.)
20 P.A. Zaionchkovsky *The Abolition of Serfdom in Russia*
21 V.V. Vinogradov *Russkii iazyk. Grammaticheskoe uchenie o slove*
22 P.A. Zaionchkovsky *The Russian Autocracy under Alexander III*
23 A.E. Presniakov *Emperor Nicholas I of Russia. The Apogee of Autocracy*
24 V.I. Semevskii *Krestianskii vopros v Rossii v XVIII i pervoi polovine XIX veka* Out of Print
25 S.S. Oldenburg *Last Tsar! Nicholas II, His Reign and His Russia* 4 volumes
26 Carl von Clausewitz *The Campaign of 1812 in Russia*
27 M.K. Liubavskii *Obrazovanie osnovnoi gosudarstvennoi territorii velikorusskoi narodnosti. Zaselenie i obedinenie tsentra*
28 S.F. Platonov *Ivan the Terrible* Paper
29 Paul N. Miliukov *Iz istorii russkoi intelligentsii. Sbornik Statei i etiudov*
30 A.E. Presniakov *The Tsardom of Muscovy* Paper
31 M. Gorky, J. Stalin et al., *History of the Civil War in Russia* 2 vols. Out of Print
32 R.G. Skrynnikov *Ivan the Terrible*
33 P.A. Zaionchkovsky *The Russian Autocracy in Crisis, 1878-1882*
34 Joseph T. Fuhrmann *Tsar Alexis. His Reign and His Russia*
35 R.G. Skrynnikov *Boris Godunov*
43 Nicholas Zernov *Three Russian Prophets: Khomiakov, Dostoevsky, Soloviev* Out of Print
44 Paul N. Miliukov *The Russian Revolution* 3 vols.
45 Anton I. Denikin *The White Army* Out of Print
55 M.V. Rodzianko *The Reign of Rasputin—An Empire's Collapse. Memoirs* Out of Print
56 *The Memoirs of Alexander Iswolsky*

THE CENTRAL AND EAST EUROPEAN SERIES

1 Louis Eisenmann *Le Compromis Austro-Hongrois de 1867*
3 Francis Dvornik *The Making of Central and Eastern Europe* 2nd edition
4 Feodor F. Zigel *Lectures on Slavonic Law*
10 Doros Alastos *Venizelos—Patriot, Statesman, Revolutionary*
20 Paul Teleki *The Evolution of Hungary and its Place in European History*

FORUM ASIATICA

1 M.I. Sladkovsky *China and Japan—Past and Present*

THE ACADEMIC INTERNATIONAL REFERENCE SERIES

The Modern Encyclopedia of Russian and Soviet History 50 vols. 1976-
The Modern Encyclopedia of Russian and Soviet Literatures 50 vols. 1977-
Soviet Armed Forces Review Annual 1977-
USSR Facts & Figures Annual 1977-
Military-Naval Encyclopedia of Russia and the Soviet Union 50 vols. 1978-
China Facts & Figures Annual 1978-
Encyclopedia USA. The Encyclopedia of the United States of America Past & Present 50 vols. 1983-
The International Military Encyclopedia 50 vols.
Sports Encyclopedia North America 50 vols. 1985-

SPECIAL WORKS

S.M. Soloviev *History of Russia* 50 vols.
SAFRA Papers 1985-